Sport, Culture & Society, Vol. 9
Nick T. Pappas
The Dark Side of Sports

DEDICATION

This book is dedicated to athletes who strive for excellence and promote it both on and off the field of competition.

ABOUT THE SERIES – SPORT, CULTURE & SOCIETY

The Sport, Culture and Society series deals with issues intersecting sport, physical activity and cultural concerns. The focus of the book series is interdisciplinary, ground-breaking work that draws on different disciplines and theoretical approaches, such as sociology, philosophy, cultural anthropology, history, cultural studies, feminist studies, postmodernism, or critical theory. The Sport, Culture and Society series seeks to reflect both, the variety of research concerns from a multi-disciplinary perspective and discussions of current topics in sport and physical activity and their relationship to culture.

The editors:

Karin Volkwein-Caplan (USA), Keith Gilbert (UK), and Jasmin Tahmaseb McConatha (USA)

For further information about the book series or the submission of proposals please contact:

Karin Volkwein-Caplan, West Chester University, Department of Kinesiology, West Chester, PA 19383, USA, e-mail: kvolkwein@wcupa.edu

Keith Gilbert, University of the West of England, Hartpury College, Hartpury House, Gloucester, Gloustershire, GL19 3BE, UK, e-mail: keith.gilbert@hartpury.ac.uk

Jasmin Tahmaseb McConatha, West Chester University, Department of Kinesiology, West Chester, PA 19383, USA, e-mail: jtahmasebmcconatha@wcupa.edu

Sport, Culture & Society, Vol. 9

Nick T. Pappas

The Dark Side of Sports

Exposing the Sexual Culture of
Collegiate and Professional Athletes

Meyer & Meyer Sport

British Library Cataloguing in Publication Data
A catalogue record for this book is available from the British Library

Nick T. Pappas
The Dark Side of Sports
Maidenhead: Meyer & Meyer Sport (UK) Ltd., 2012
(Sport, Culture & Society; Vol. 9)
ISBN 978-1-84126-338-0

© 2012 by Meyer & Meyer Sport (UK) Ltd.
Auckland, Beirut, Budapest, Cairo, Cape Town, Dubai, Indianapolis,
Kindberg, Maidenhead, Sydney, Olten, Singapore, Tehran, Toronto
Member of the World
Sports Publishers' Association (WSPA)
www.w-s-p-a.org
Printed by: Beltz Druckpartner GmbH & Co. KG
ISBN 978-1-84126-338-0
E-Mail: info@m-m-sports.com
www.m-m-sports.com

Contents

Introduction: An Insider Perspective

Pick up a newspaper, sports magazine, or turn on the television or Internet, and it is not uncommon to find athletes appearing in the news headlines because of their involvement in aggression and violence. While some of this negative behavior takes place within sports competition, not all athlete aggression is restricted to sports opponents. The past two decades have witnessed increasing documentation of athlete aggression outside the sports arena that has been directed against both males as well as females in a variety of settings.[1] At the same time, athletes have also appeared in the media for their participation in an array of sexually deviant and/or aggressive practices.[2] Incidences involving golf superstar Tiger Woods' infidelity, The Minnesota Vikings' Sex Boat Scandal, and Duke University lacrosse players' alleged gang rape all generated national interest because the cliché "sex sells" is particularly true when it involves elite-level athletes. Although such situations raise numerous questions about the extent of these and other sexual behaviors, research investigating the sexual culture of elite-level athletes remains very limited in scope aside from incidences involving reported sexual assaults. In addition, journalistic reporting of athletes' sexual deviancy often reveals little beyond "tip of the iceberg" events the media are fortunate to report. Over the years, a host of deviant sexual practices have remained hidden within impenetrable and diverse athlete cultures that are slow to reveal their secrets to outsiders, including researchers, who are often unaware that such behaviors even exist.

My unique position as an insider, however, has enabled me to gather cutting-edge research that has superseded this glimpse to reveal both shocking and disturbing information highlighting athletes' clandestine sexual practices. While athletes' physical and/or sexual assaults surfacing in the news often coincides with negative publicity and outcomes for the victim and the offender(s), an array of concealed sexual behaviors never receive media attention. This is problematic because seemingly harmless sexual behaviors that are often overlooked when they are not illegal can, in fact, negatively impact lives as well as become stepping stones to more pronounced forms of sexually deviant and/or aggressive practices that are against the law. The fact that certain types of sexual deviancy have thrived without attention for nearly 50 years and have seldom been disclosed in print – much less with a population of elite-level athletes – means the book that you are about to read will shine a large spotlight on collegiate and professional athletes' unique sexual culture.

I became aware of athlete sexual deviancy during my career as a collegiate and professional hockey player and coach. Formal data collection for this research began in the summer of 2001 when I conducted in depth interviews for my doctoral dissertation on 23 collegiate and professional hockey players' out-of-sport aggression.[3] Because the sexual deviancy I uncovered did not always lead to unlawful aggression, I withheld these significant findings for future use. In order to show these practices were widespread within other sports cultures, I interviewed an additional 119 collegiate and/or professional athletes from other athlete cultures including major leaguers, National, and/or Olympic Team members. Wrestlers, hockey, baseball, basketball, and football players comprise the study's main participants; however, various participants revealed awareness throughout this study that male athletes representing virtually every collegiate sport also engaged in a variety of sexually deviant and/or aggressive behavior. Using in-depth interviews with this large and diverse sample also enabled me to gather frequencies related to certain behaviors, processes describing how they occur, motivation for participating, and detrimental outcomes related to a host of negative sexual practices occurring at all levels of athletic competition. While participants often observed such practices among high school athletes, this research will highlight collegiate and professional athletes' involvement in sexually deviant and/or aggressive behaviors that occurred during careers spanning the early 1960s-2010. The findings in this book and the fact that we live in a world where athletes are held in high regard establish that longstanding sexual deviancy and aggression must be exposed because what people do not know can hurt them and countless others.

Out-of-sport athlete aggression, as defined in this study, is illegal behavior that involves physical and/or sexual assaults. Sexual aggression includes sexual assault (i.e., nonconsensual petting, oral/anal sex, sexual intercourse, and penetration with objects through the use of force, argument, pressure, drugs, or alcohol) and/or rape (i.e., nonconsensual penile-vaginal penetration through the use or threat of force).[4] Athlete sexual deviancy and/or sexually deviant behaviors include an array of perverted and seedy sexual practices that are demeaning and harmful. While deviancy is defined as an abnormality differing from accepted standards, certain sexual behaviors routinely occurring suggest such practices may be considered normal within various athlete cultures.[5] However, because "normal" in this sense does not make negative practices acceptable, deviancy may not be the most appropriate term; but for lack of a better word it will suffice.

HOW I BECAME AN INSIDER

Like many youngsters, I had aspirations of becoming a professional athlete from an early age growing up in the Chicago/Northern Indiana area. After a successful high school hockey career which included a season of junior hockey my senior year, I played the following season on both Canadian Junior A (tier II) and Junior B hockey teams in Quebec and Ontario. The next year, I attended

Division I Bowling Green State University and made the hockey team as a freshman "walk-on." My freshman class at BGSU showcased their talent by winning the 1984 Division I National Championship as seniors. I played one year of varsity hockey at BGSU before I was cut, so I spent my sophomore season playing on the university's club hockey team. The following year I transferred to Penn State University because it enabled me to play immediately on a high-level non-varsity collegiate hockey team that regularly competed against Division I, II, and III varsity teams. During three seasons at PSU, my team won a National Championship and placed runner-up twice while I earned the Most Valuable Player Award and a Bachelor's degree in Elementary Education my senior year. It was an honor to be inducted into the Penn State Hockey Hall of Fame and the Andrean High School Sports Hall of Fame in 2004.

After college, I followed my childhood dream by playing five years of minor professional hockey. My first three seasons were spent playing on three minor league championship teams, and I was the team captain during my third season. I gained invaluable experience during my second and third championship seasons when I was coached by John Tortorella, who later went on to coach the NHL's Tampa Bay Lightning when they won the Stanley Cup in 2004. My final two seasons of professional hockey were spent in Europe playing first in Skovde, Sweden and then in Copenhagen, Denmark as a player-coach. In the end, I was very satisfied with my professional career because I felt I had played to my full potential.

After retiring as a professional athlete, I spent the next three years working first as a high school teacher and hockey coach and then as an adolescent counselor in group homes for troubled teenagers. I left this position to become an assistant coach for the Ohio University Men's Ice Hockey Team while I attended graduate school. In three years, I helped lead the Bobcats to back-to-back League, Playoff, and National Championships. During this time, I also interned as a high school and substance abuse counselor en route to earning my master's degree in school, college, and community mental health counseling.

I worked the next two years as a school counselor before returning to complete a doctorate degree in Human Development and Family Science with a minor in Sociology of Sport from The Ohio State University. As a doctoral student, I taught counseling classes to college seniors and was the head coach of the OSU Women's Club Hockey Team for four years. Upon finishing my degree, I coached a season of professional hockey as an assistant for the Johnstown Chiefs of the East Coast Hockey League, which was the AA affiliate for the NHL's Calgary Flames, in addition to teaching undergraduate and graduate-level classes as an adjunct professor. Overall, I have 25 years of consecutive coaching experience as an ice hockey camp instructor, and I have been part of six championship teams during my elite-level hockey career – two as a collegiate coach, three as a minor professional athlete, and one as a collegiate athlete. My present work with athletes includes personal/athletic life coaching and providing presentations on athlete-related issues including out-of-sport deviancy and aggression in order to promote personal and team excellence.

I have presented my athletic, academic, and occupational background because research for this book began during my junior, collegiate, and professional hockey career, and it continued as a coach, teacher, counselor, graduate student, professor, and researcher. The past 30 plus years have provided me with unique experiences and insight into the sexual culture of collegiate and professional athletes. I have found that elite-level athletes and coaches often receive a thorough education to the hidden, darker practices occurring within their own sports culture as well as other athlete cultures that they happen to come into contact with. My insider perspective as a player and coach in combination with over 13 years of formal study and research involving out-of-sport athlete deviancy and aggression that has included interviews with over 142 athletes has thoroughly prepared me to examine this unique and controversial material. While some readers without elite-level athletic experience may question – or dispute – certain findings within these pages, I believe the majority of collegiate and/or professional athletes and coaches, who are not living in denial or a protected, secluded bubble, will support this work and acknowledge its value as a beneficial component for risk management.

PUTTING IT ALL TOGETHER

Detailed interviews conducted in person and by phone were used to gather information for this book at several different time periods. Preliminary academic research initially began in 1999 when I conducted five interviews for a graduate class project which would later become a published study on collegiate/ professional hockey players' out-of-sport aggression.[6] This work set the stage for the first major wave of interviews which occurred in the summer/fall of 2001 during my doctoral dissertation involving 23 collegiate and/or professional hockey players' out of sport physical and sexual aggression. The interview questions built upon the previous study and included questions about athletes' sexual deviancy. Approximately 85% of the participants in this book were interviewed in the second wave of data collection which began in the fall of 2005 and ended about the same time in 2010. The study's questionnaire originated from my doctoral dissertation although I added additional questions that focused specifically on certain types and frequencies of sexually deviant practices which sometimes emerged as the study progressed.[7] Percentages related to various motives detailed within the chapters sometimes total more than 100% because participants often identified multiple influences for certain behaviors.

Player interviews lasted between 50 minutes and $3^1/_2$ hours with most averaging about $1^1/_2$ hours in duration. Athletes were referred to the study by numerous sources which included other athletes, coaches and managers, team staff and/or affiliates, previous participants, and numerous friends and acquaintances. Moreover, participants provided information from multiple perspectives which means the athletes described what they knew and/or observed among teammates or other athletes as well as what they personally engaged in and experienced. Essentially, the player narratives act as a window through which readers can peer into the hidden culture of elite-level athletes so they can observe the prevalence, processes, underlying causes and motivation, and the effects of a host of detailed sexual practices found within this sample of athletes.

Participants ranged in age from 20 to 58 at the time of their interview and averaged 35 years old; the most common ages (mode) were 31 and 35. The overall sample contained 142 collegiate and/or professional athletes; however, 27 athletes from each of the five sports totaling 135 participants were used to calculate the percentages that appeared in the different chapters (and keep the numbers even). Additional data from seven participants that were not used in the percentages included six hockey players from my dissertation data and one collegiate football. Similar numbers of players in their 20s (approximately one third of the participants), 30s (just over one third), and 40s (approximately one third) in addition to 1-2 athletes per sport in their 50s (4%) enabled me to examine, compare, and contrast athletes' experiences from different sports and eras. This means over two thirds of the participants competed and/or coached at the collegiate and/or professional level during 2000-2010 and/or 1990-1999, approximately 50% had similar athletic experiences during careers in the 1980s, 20% in the 1970s, and about 3% during the 1960s. Various participants had playing careers that overlapped two or even three different decades of time and when this included coaching experience, it could reach as high as five decades. Athlete sexual deviancy as well as aggression was discovered during every decade of competition from the early 1960s-2010.

Sixty-two percent of the participants had professional playing experience at the minor and/or major league level, and from this group approximately 40% had major league experience. In addition, over 90% of the participants competed at the collegiate level and approximately one third had elite-level coaching experience at the junior (i.e., hockey-related), collegiate, and/or minor/major league levels. This athletic experience was often quite recent because at the time of their interview, approximately 40% of the participants were currently competing or coaching at the collegiate or professional level. Following their interviews, most coaches continued in their careers with some receiving promotions to head coach or to the major leagues, while other participants who worked with elite-level teams in various capacities made their way into collegiate or professional coaching.

The 32 participants with major league experience were easily the most difficult to find and interview for the study. Many had trust issues from observing that athletes, including themselves, were often misquoted or even burned by journalists during their career. Consequently, big leaguers were often reluctant to participate and discuss their exclusive, hidden culture because they feared their names would be linked to what they had said. Despite such challenges, every sport in this study contained 7-9 confirmed major leaguers that combined for an average of 65 years of major league experience in *each* of the different sports. Consequently, there are high profile athletes and coaches representing every sport in this study. This includes numerous athletes who won championships at the collegiate, minor, and major league levels in addition to major league All-Stars, Hall of Fame Inductees, and National and/or Olympic Team Members. While wrestling contained no professionals because professional wrestling was considered entertainment and not a sport, the sample contained five National and/or Olympic Team Members including four International Medalists, 12 All Americans, two NCAA champions, and nine current collegiate coaches. In the end, the participants' extensive playing and/or coaching experiences at elite-levels were essential to my gathering the array of negative, clandestine behaviors that have thrived for decades with little or no attention.

KEEPING EXPLANATIONS SIMPLE BUT NOT SIMPLISTIC

One of my goals and challenges during this project was to convey my unique findings in such as way that the information remained clear and in a reader-friendly format so that different interest groups could benefit from the material. This means the athletes' descriptions of the different practices were in their own words whenever possible, and this occurred in combination with my insights and other supplemented material to provide information and explanations using understandable language and ideas. I opted against using complicated theoretical perspectives that attempt to explain, but often confuse the understanding of a phenomenon in addition to severely limiting the readability of the material.

I discovered through years of research that athletes' sexual deviancy and aggression are learned within a variety of social environments and particularly bonded male peer groups such as athletic teams. Like all other social behaviors, humans learn deviant and aggressive acts by watching influential people (e.g., parents, peers, and athletes, etc.) model certain behaviors that are perceived as useful or rewarding.[8] Learning also occurs by observing the consequences of another's behavior, forming ideas about which behaviors are appropriate, trying out or practicing various behaviors, and continuing to use those behaviors if they bring positive or fulfilling results.[9] People may learn how to perform certain behaviors but would never do them if they resulted in disastrous consequences for the model and any observer who enacted the behaviors.[10] Failing to punish deviant and/or aggressive behavior through deterring consequences further encourages the likelihood that someone will continue to engage in negative practices.[11] Sexual deviancy and aggression, therefore, are not inevitable or biologically based, but social behavior that is learned, shaped by its consequences, and continued if it is reinforced or rewarded in some way.[12]

In addition, sports cultures serve as primary learning centers where athletes become apprentices to the different practices revealed within these chapters. This is because all-male athletic environments are among the few remaining strongholds where young men have the luxury of conducting themselves in ways that enable them to avoid the harsh censorship and scrutiny they would otherwise experience outside the world of sports. In short, sports act as a refuge where athletes can celebrate – with few repercussions – the attributes of masculinity which promote athletic success through the use of physical strength, dominance, and aggression.[13] At the same time, this uninhibited world of male superiority encourages an array of bizarre and repulsive behaviors that highlight a darker side of sports which is as common and unique as the athletes themselves.[14] The fuel for such behavior centers upon the fact that athletes are rewarded within many sports cultures for demonstrating bravado and the ability to entertain, or ridicule someone or something, whenever a group gets together.[15] This promotes constant seeking for the next target and/or exploitive behavior, which is certain to produce a humorous story, while simultaneously encouraging athletic environments to become breeding grounds for the outrageous.[16] Indeed, there is no shortage of observant, comedic athletes as well as teammates who are more than willing to create entertainment by engaging in a host of bizarre and/or squalid behavior. Such stories live on indefinitely since they are often communicated from one generation of athletes to the next even though certain behaviors can be harmful, demeaning, and have the potential to create an array of problems and consequences for everyone involved. In the end, sports environments house close-knit teams that encourage the unusual because outrageous behaviors provide desirable entertainment while producing unique identities and status that reward those who actively engage in such activities.[17]

PLAN OF THE BOOK

The chapters that follow expose an array of sexually deviant and/or aggressive practices that build in intensity and set the stage for more harmful behaviors later on. Chapter 1 reveals various practices occurring within all-male environments such as exhibitionism, deviant masturbation, and bodily discharges that sometimes make their way into the outside world. Such information is important because if athletes target close teammates with deviant acts, how will this influence the way they treat casual female sexual partners with whom they are not bonded? Chapter 2 discusses athletes' pornography use that can be rampant and act as a "how to" guide for sexual deviancy/aggression, and its negative impact on relationships, personal well-being, and other behaviors, including addiction, is undeniable. Chapter 3 describes athletes' involvement with females in the sex industry which can cause negative repercussions for these women as well as the athletes' families, finances, athletic careers, and personal well-being. Chapter 4 examines the routine practice of picking up women although for some athletes, this can include using a darker version verbal "game," which involves deception, manipulation, coercion, and sexual pressure. Such practices raise questions regarding how far some athletes are willing to go in order to experience and/or force casual sex. Chapter 5 highlights the unending supply of female fans that make themselves sexually available in unimaginable ways even though this unwittingly encourages and enables some athletes' sexually deviant and/or aggressive practices to thrive more easily. Chapter 6 exposes rampant infidelity along with the practice of juggling numerous female sexual partners. This often involves an array of consequences and the majority of players on teams regardless of whether they are in committed relationships or not. Chapter 7 highlights athletes' ultra competitive nature which carries into their social and sexual behavior targeting women through different sexual contests and competitions. Certain collegiate and professional athletes take great pride in tallying their sexual conquests which can be both shocking as well as disturbing and include different consequences. Chapter 8 reveals the different ways in which collegiate athletes, coaches, and other supporters promote sex in the recruiting process in order to insure that high-level high school athletes choose their particular university. Chapter 9 exposes a variety of widespread and related practices that involve live pornography through athletes' participation in voyeurism, recording sexual encounters with and without consent, male-female exhibitionism, and attempting to join in teammates' sexual encounters with and without permission. Because the latter events involve sexual assault and/or rape, this provides an easy transition to chapter 10 which continues to showcase an array of athletes individual and group sexual assaults along with the processes, motives, and outcomes related to these incidences. Throughout this book, the reader will also find "Athletes Corner: Points to Ponder" following each chapter. These points offer practical and thought-provoking information that challenge athletes to examine their own attitudes and behaviors toward issues highlighted in the chapter and then make changes that will improve themselves, their teams, and the athlete culture as a whole.

Chapter 1
Athletes' Exhibitionism, Deviant Masturbation, and Bodily Discharges

Hearing words like male exhibitionism, deviant masturbation and bodily discharges stirs up thoughts of sinister older men with mental health issues who appear in dark alleys wearing long overcoats. Now ask yourself if such reactions would be the same if these behaviors occurred among a highly regarded group of young men who also happened to be elite-level athletes? People may laugh with disbelief or question the source, but it is true: Male athletic environments offer a unique and protective safe haven where young men are relatively free to speak and act in whatever way they please. This enables profanity-filled stories highlighting sexual exploits, bravado, deviancy, and/or aggression to flourish because virtually no one monitors athletes but themselves while they remain within sheltered strongholds including locker rooms.[1] Moreover, the same holds true when it comes to behavior because some athletes choose to differentiate themselves by engaging in bizarre and often repulsive behaviors which reward them with special identities and status while simultaneously revealing a darker, hidden side of sports.[2] Athletes' desire for entertainment, bragging rights, and one-upmanship often motivate an array of outrageous behaviors which raise both questions and eye-brows even when they remain confined to all-male athletic environments. At the same time, a variety of deviant practices can and do make their way into the public domain, which dramatically increases the potential risks and negative impact for everyone involved. It will become apparent that all-male sports environments encourage bizarre and outrageous behaviors even though some are harmful, demeaning, and have the potential to create all kinds of problems and consequences.

SEXUAL ANTICS OR HOMOEROTICISM?

Athletes spend tremendous amounts of time training, socializing, and living together which results in deep histories and friendships within certain teams. This is particularly true at the collegiate level where players can spend four or five years together on a team. As a result of their bonding, many athletes feel very safe and comfortable with their teammates, and this is reflected in players' language as well as their behaviors.[3] Since the locker room is the predominant safe haven where athletes spend extensive time together, it is logical to assume that some uninhibited displays and clowning will involve sexual behaviors in this secluded environment. For example, a wrestler and a collegiate baseball and hockey player described a variety of sexual antics and nudity among collegiate teammates in this way:

> I mean in a shower you did all kinds of stupid things, you know, put hot water in your mouth and hold your dick and put it on like you spit it out, as if you're peeing on him, stupid stuff like that...I mean, you know, when there were a bunch of guys sitting there talking in a room about the girl they laid and some guy's grabbing himself and wanting to expose himself and show him that he's got a hard on, that's about extent of [it] you know, [and] everybody saying you know, "Get the hell out of here, what are you doing?" yea we had a couple of guys that just wanted to show off I think at times.

> I remember there was one sick guy [laughs] on the fucking baseball team...he wasn't circumcised and in the shower...as a practical joke... he was always messing with [it], he'd fill up his fucking...dick...the extra skin with water and walk over to him and fucking spray him, which is probably one of the most disgusting things I've ever seen [laughs] in my life. And he'd do it on a regular occasion, but other than that man, nothing crazy.

> ...in the showers, people are always...making a comment about somebody else's penis or toweling some guy in the ass, or dropping the soap – all just in play...you see that. We had a guy my freshman year who always came in and made a comment about...somebody else's piece (penis) everyday. He'd just walk in, staring, look around. He'd be the first guy in and last guy [out], and...it was just him being weird or whatever. Nothing ever sexual or homosexual about it...

While most sexual antics were described as nothing more than demented practical jokes promoting humor, homoeroticism is another possible interpretation of certain behaviors. Homoeroticism, defined as sexual attraction or desire toward members of the same sex, is thought to occur whenever bonding activities involve genital contact and exposure through events such as group masturbation, sexualized initiations, and same-sex group nudity.[4] Moreover, the description of the athlete's constant fixation on his teammates' genitals in the third narrative seemed to suggest this possibility. However, researchers, who observed an array of ritualized sexual behaviors including naked male-to-male contact and even genital touching among rugby players, noted that these acts should not be construed as actual homosexual behavior but rather an extension of their masculine competition from the match.[5] Whether sexual antics reflect humorous entertainment or homoeroticism is irrelevant in light of the fact that these behaviors did not always stop at the locker room's door as another collegiate hockey player discussed in this way:

> Just a lot of nudity…I mean I lived with eight [hockey] guys. There was always naked dudes walking around the house and other times at parties guys would get naked, just with other guys around, just to be stupid. Actually on bus rides a lot of guys – if someone was sleeping, a guy would get a hard on and walk over and stick it in his ear, something like that, you know, just to screw with him. There was a lot of that stuff, mostly just nudity. Sometimes…for some reason we would "gear down" [a teammate] and take pictures of him and there was nothing he could do about it…just take all his clothes off and he'd be fighting and kicking and just…take pictures of him. He'd be fighting for his clothes and fighting for the door [laughing], all that stuff…[it] took about four of us usually…we used to get [one teammate] when he was taking naps [laughing]… and we'd go all around his room, just jump on him…just start taking all his clothes off, and put him in a room and just start taking pictures of him. We'd get some good action photos of him…trying to fight [laughter].

After detailing a "gear down" attack on an unsuspecting teammate, this athlete discussed the motive by saying, "Boredom I'd say, just nothing to do… it seemed like the right thing to do at the time [laughing]…it'd be like picking a mine field." Obviously, these attacks were somewhat demeaning because the victim was helpless to defend himself against four athletes, and they were photographed. Because no one wants embarrassing pictures appearing unexpectedly in places including The Internet, this is perhaps another reason victims fought so hard during these attacks. Furthermore, the appearance of nude photographs is no laughing matter since it has resulted in severe consequences for athletes, and this was noted when two University of Nebraska wrestlers were dismissed from their team after allegedly posing naked for an Internet pornography site.[6] However, premeditated attacks on teammates undoubtedly alleviated boredom and proved to be extremely humorous entertainment that was later shared with others. It will be evident that the desire to entertain teammates through humorous story-telling is a powerful catalyst for engaging in these and other deviant behaviors.

NAKED INHIBITIONS AND EXHIBITIONISM

Not all nudity happens within the confines of the team locker room or at athletes' residence because accounts of public exposure also appear in this study. Moreover, nudity spilling into the public sector can result in legal charges involving indecent exposure in addition to other consequences. Indecent exposure laws in most states make it a crime to purposefully display one's genitals or socially deemed "private parts" in public causing alarm or offense often for the purpose of sexual excitement and satisfaction or social rebellion.[7] While indecent exposure is a legal term for public nudity, it is used interchangeably with exhibitionism, which is a specific mental health disorder and paraphilia describing uncommon sexual expression.[8] Exhibitionism occurs when someone intentionally exposes their genitals to an unwilling observer typically for the purpose of sexual gratification, and this can involve masturbation in the moment or at a later time.[9] Often, exhibitionists are males targeting young adults, adolescents, or children of the opposite sex, and the age of onset for exhibitionism begins in the middle teen years and the mid-20s.[10] In this study, exhibitionism will also include consensual sexual activities performed for others and public nudity without sexual intent, which could include open urination or defecation and behaviors like streaking (i.e., running naked in public).

More than one third of all males arrested for sexual offenses are arrested for exhibitionism, and 40-60% of college and community samples of women have reported being victims of exhibitionism.[11] According to two studies involving college men, 2-4% had participated in exhibitionism while 7% expressed the desire to do so.[12] My observations of exhibitionist behaviors outside the locker room area are limited to one event when as a freshman, I was taking pictures of my collegiate teammates outside the dormitory when a number of them decided to expose themselves in a variety of ways to be humorous. Nearly 20% of the participants representing every sport in this study revealed their awareness and/or participation in some type of male exhibitionism often in combination with other behaviors. For example, a minor league baseball player and a collegiate football player described their awareness and/or participation in exhibitionism in this way:

> ...you know [laughing] one night, teammates were in their apartment drinking and one of the guys got a little bit crazy and took...I think he was a sophomore at the time, drove him across campus, and they stripped naked in the car, and kicked him out of the car, and he had to make his way back naked, which again I think the guy got a rush out of it cause then they just started running around campus naked on occasion, just because he wanted to.

> ...it seemed like in the off season whenever you were bored it always leads to mischievous things you know. One night we were sitting, it was a tradition that kind of faded...but three years prior to us doing it, there was a tradition that starts from the apartment and [you] streak down

to the middle of the campus and take a picture in front of the student store...that's where everybody had hung out during class time and so one night we were bored and said, "Alright, we're going to streak down" which is about a mile and a half in front of all the apartments and the dorms so we just...got in our baseball caps and our tennis shoes and five of us...ran down you know one night and had cops chasing us and streaked down and back, took a picture, and just something to do.

Boredom, alcohol consumption, tradition, and the desire to be "crazy" fueled these collegiate athletes' decision to "streak" through campus which produced an adrenaline "rush" as well as the desire to repeat this event. While "streaking" is generally considered harmless and humorous, it can still produce legal and team problems when athletes are caught.

Not all athletes who engage in public nudity are college age or have the desire to run away following their public exposure. For example, MLB player, Rick Bosetti, was refused service at one upscale restaurant during his career which perhaps stripped him of his dignity; this prompted Bosetti on his next visit to reveal his displeasure and social rebellion by disrobing in the men's room and walking naked through the dining room and out the door.[13] Some athletes display even greater boldness by refusing to leave the scene of their exhibitionism as one minor league hockey player discussed in this manner:

...just a couple of years ago...in a pick-up league...some of them were just guys [who never played pro hockey] but...I'd say two thirds of them guys [played professionally] – They came into town...we had a tournament here...and they rented...a private dining room, and they all got sat down and...two waitresses came in and took their orders...when they left, everybody stripped down naked...and they were all sitting there naked and here come the waitress back with their food. I guess it was funny, the way they described it...

The stereotype of the dirty old man engaging in exhibitionism in parks with sneakers and a raincoat is untrue since most offenders are in their 20s and 30s with over half being married or formerly married.[14] Surprisingly, these older athletes matching this profile disregarded logic and reasoning by exposing themselves as a large group even though their exhibitionism was probably not sexually driven. Moreover, the previous participant discussed the motives for this by saying, "It's just...you get 15 guys together, everybody tries to out-do everybody else...just doing something more bizarre [chuckles]." It is evident that some bizarre behaviors, including exhibitionism, happen because athletes' competitive nature creates a desire to "outdo" their teammates. Furthermore, the desire to engage in outrageous acts does not simply end because the men were older and retired from professional competition. Because one third of the group did not play professionally, it is possible that these players felt peer pressure to conform to the group's antics and expectations. It is also evident that athletes' passion for telling captivating stories at any age occurs because it enhances someone's reputation whenever these stories are retold, and this subsequently raises the bar for other athletes to engage in even more bizarre behaviors. Although outrageous stories circulate to create both entertainment and one-upmanship, engaging in exhibitionism is probably not the best decision since this is disturbing and abusive to many victims and has the potential for legal ramifications that can negatively influence the men's personal reputations, families, and careers.

While athletes' exhibitionism in the previous narratives does not appear to be fueled by their desire for sexual gratification or arousal, this is not always the case. Indeed, some athletes have taken their exhibitionism to extremes by carrying it into social settings on campus, and in the process, intentionally crossed paths with females. For example, a wrestler and a minor league hockey player noted their awareness of exhibitionism during their collegiate careers in this way:

> ...he was well endowed anyway so he didn't have a problem with just flipping his dick out and walking around the house and kind of flaunting it. We would have parties and he would pull it out of his pants and walk around and talk to girls and wait until one of them would notice and you know that was his way of meeting girls and he actually met quite a few who thought that was an endearment that they needed to seek further and so I think for him...it was, "I got a big dick and I'm going to show everybody" so that's kind of like...how he worked.

> ...there was one incident...[a hockey] player...I remember there was a party and he was chasing some girls across campus with his pants down and...this guy was hung like a horse you know – so we were at a party and all these girls [you'd have] thought it was like the first time they had ever seen a dick you know, and that was just funny and...everyone knew that [happened] but...everybody kept quiet about that.

Exhibitionists have been portrayed as narcissists deriving pleasure from seeing themselves nude, providing a service or kindness by exposing themselves, and wishing to be envied for possession of a penis.[15] Although one study revealed that all of the exhibitionists in the sample preferred targeting adult women, 79% exposed themselves occasionally to females 15 years of age or younger.[16] Another noteworthy finding revealed exhibitionists are not always passive, inhibited individuals because 20% had a history of violence-related offenses that included rape and sexual assault as exhibitionism was used to entrap, demean, and incite fear through power and control tactics.[17] Therefore, exhibitionism is not always a humorous, harmless behavior because its association with sexual violence for some offenders is undeniable.

Still, many athletes find exhibitionism entertaining although there is nothing humorous when law enforcement officials identify an offender since this can create serious problems and consequences for coaches, teams, and players. These notions were highlighted in the book, *When All the Laughter Died in Sorrow*, which detailed Lance Rentzel's exhibitionism that targeted female children in Minnesota and Dallas during his NFL career.[18] Although child molestation or pedophilia and exhibitionism are often confused and sometimes overlap because children are victimized, the pedophile seeks bodily contact while the exhibitionist wishes to be seen and sometimes, but not in the Rentzel case, masturbating.[19] Therapy helped Rentzel to realize the pressure he felt to please his family and prove his masculinity repeatedly through football and sexual conquests with women.[20] Exhibitionism during times of stress was seen as another way for Rentzel to prove his masculinity.[21] However, Rentzel's exhibitionism resulted in extreme criticism and negative publicity for him and his family, the demise of his marriage to a leading actress, sitting out a portion of the season while his team played in the 1970 Super Bowl, and the possibility of serving 12-15 years in prison since indecent exposure involving children under 16 years of age in Texas is a potential felony.[22] In the end, Rentzel received probation and was court ordered to undergo therapy; however, he was not the only major league athlete charged with exhibitionism.[23] During his Hall of Fame NHL career, Dino Ciccarelli also pleaded guilty to a misdemeanor charge of indecent exposure in 1988 and received probation after a neighbor reported that she had repeatedly seen him exposing himself.[24] More recently, former University of Southern California and current Cincinnati Bengals defensive end, Frostee Rucker, lost his first football scholarship at Colorado State University in the spring of 2002 following accusations of his involvement in two sexual assaults and an indecent exposure incident.[25] Rucker pleaded guilty to a reduced misdemeanor harassment charge and received a one-year deferred sentence.[26] While exhibitionism is alarming and can lead to legal ramifications, perhaps this is a symptom of deeper issues as some athletes go beyond public displays of nudity by engaging in behaviors that are much more sexually explicit and perverse.

EXAMINING MASTURBATION AMONG ELITE-LEVEL ATHLETES

Masturbation, or self stimulation of the genitals for the purpose of sexual pleasure, has evolved from a condemned practice that was thought to be abnormal and mentally and physically debilitating by physicians and authorities alike to one that has gained acceptance as normal behavior among significant percentages of people of all ages.[27] Dr. Alfred Kinsey and colleagues reported that 92% of the men surveyed masturbated by age 20 (most began between ages 13 and 15) while many of the 58% of females who reported masturbating began in early adulthood.[28] Masturbation is thought to provide a release from sexual tension and the opportunity to explore sexual functioning although many adolescents overlook these positives by responding only to the negative messages that can produce guilt following these practices.[29] However, guilt is not a universal response for all adolescents or young men because some males athletes have turned private masturbation practices into open displays that can include group events sometimes referred to as "circle jerks."[30] While sexualized initiations and rites of passage are not new to certain athlete cultures, the fact that approximately one third of the participants in this study, who competed in careers that spanned the 1970s through 2010, were able to discuss a variety of sexualized behaviors occurring within all-male team settings, not linked to initiations, suggests that such practices abound within certain athletic teams.[31]

My personal encounter with sexualized practices occurring apart from team initiations happened when I was 18-years-old and playing Junior A hockey in Quebec, Canada. Junior hockey or simply "juniors" is considered elite-level hockey because it is among the highest caliber of amateur competition available for players ages 15-20 and less than 5% of all youngsters registered with the Canadian Minor Hockey Association achieve the Junior A or B levels of competition.[32] Juniors can act as a stepping-stone to collegiate and/or professional hockey in much the same way that collegiate football and basketball act as the training ground for players to advance to the professional level in these sports.

A group masturbation event occurred when my junior team was on the bus returning from a game and about half of the team were congregating and making quite a bit of noise. I went to investigate what I thought was gambling and realized that two players were masturbating in what seemed to be some type of competition since the cheering encouraged the players to continue. Many junior hockey players live far from their parents and friends, which means that teams act as surrogate families. Team friendships, therefore, become extremely important because few, if any, male friendships develop outside of some teams. Because many players feel bonded as well as uninhibited around each other, open displays of masturbation occurring within certain junior teams were not uncommon as a collegiate hockey player discussed in this way:

> ...you know the hockey players are usually more open about sexual activity than any other group, sports teams that I've played on...but I

think guys you know talk about masturbation all the time – they don't care...some guys are, you know willing to just sit there and be playing with their dong right in front of you...anybody, they don't really care...I knew guys that used to...jerk off at the same time...in their hotel room and stuff like that...guys are watching a porno in there and three guys jerking off...I didn't hear about that stuff until I'd say I was in high school playing juniors and not too often.

The previous participant experienced the hockey world as one of the most sexually liberal cultures along with lacrosse, although lacrosse players were not interviewed for the study. While masturbation occurred among certain teammates openly as well as sporadically in groups, two minor league hockey players discussed a higher prevalence of these practices in this way:

...I remember in juniors was the first time I ever saw someone spank off (masturbate) right in front of you...a guy on the team bus sitting there with a *Playboy*. I looked over at him and I was like, "Holy hell!" He goes, "Look the other way...you're killing my buzz (erection) here," [laughing] and he's spanking it off [laughing] – Yeah, I remember that kid, I don't know whatever happened to him – probably not much...there was things like that I mean, yeah, [in] college – college, a lot of guys...

All through juniors there was porn on the bus, [and] there were guys sitting around beating off to it. You know, circle jerks, to see who could get off first [laughs], all that stuff, but for the most part it's harmless. Nobody's doing it that doesn't want to do it...[in] juniors it happened a lot. These guys always used to bring their dicks out on the bus, play around with it, get hard first, get off first, and that kind of thing. At the time I could see that an outside observer, someone who's not involved with hockey, how they could be taken back by it – like, "What the hell are you guys doing? Are you all gay?" [laughs]. I'll have to admit, when I was around it, I didn't really think much of it. I didn't personally do it, I didn't care to do it, but I thought it was funny...I'd just have to laugh and go back to sleep or whatever I was doing. It didn't screw me up mentally. I just thought they were goofy guys [laughs] getting stupid. Whatever innate sexual tendencies were there, I don't know either...

The previous participants described open displays of both individual and group masturbation as frequent events during road trips among both American and Canadian junior hockey players as well as among collegiate athletes. Interestingly, the final participant mentioned homoeroticism as a potential motive based on the frequency and nature of these practices which could be construed by outsiders as having homosexual undertones. Despite their actions, players who masturbated openly were not considered homosexuals by their teammates. Furthermore, the fact that each of the previous participants mentioned masturbation occurring in the presence of pornography, which was readily available in one form or another, highlights another potential danger associated with these practices. Dr. Alex Kwee and his colleagues found through clinical experience that the vast majority of college men who struggled with compulsive masturbation also used pornography to accompany these behaviors.[33] This tendency was further highlighted in another study that showed pornography played a significant role in fueling the addictions of 90% of the male sex addicts who were surveyed.[34] Because the world is full of distorted sexuality norms and easy access to pornography, many individuals, including athletes, face the challenge of differentiating between normal, appropriate masturbation practices and those escalating into unhealthy excess and compulsivity that are addictive and not easily overcome.[35] Interestingly, one of the previous participants further elaborated on these experiences as well as other underlying motives fueling masturbation practices in this way:

> Well circle jerks – I only saw two or three of those [laughs] but the porn and beat off sessions – that was a pretty regular occurrence...it was more like if you want to sit around and beat off, then go ahead, if you don't want to that's cool too...I was at parties where I saw some of that stuff going on, but I wasn't forced to do it. You know circle jerks and that...in most cases it's light-hearted [laughs]. Guys were doing it because it was funny. Whatever makes them feel like a part of the team...that's the way I looked at it. You know, that shit feels good – can't be that bad...I've thought about [motives for] that – some of it is camaraderie. I think that for some guys, too, actually it may be kind of hot for them. They're not gay, but it's still like a sexual thing to be sitting around with your guys talking about your girlfriends and what they do to them...I mean, they're not getting off on the guy next to you because you can see his rod (penis) or anything. It's just more or less like just sitting around watching porn all night. It's just a sexual atmosphere and they're all charged up and the next thing you know – they snap one off (masturbate) [laughs]. I had a little bit harder time figuring that one out than I do some of the issues behind violence. I'm not as in tune with that stuff as much...I have my opinions and ideas about what makes certain guys do it or whatever. I think that you can't be shy. I think that you have to be a relatively open person – a real extrovert to be able to do that kind of stuff – and I'm not on that end of the continuum.

The above participant differentiated group masturbation or "circle jerks" from a teammate individually masturbating while watching pornography in the presence of others. Moreover, group masturbation was described as a pleasurable, "light-hearted" activity occurring sometimes at parties "because it was funny," and entertaining to peers. Themes of "camaraderie" and "feeling like a part of the team" also highlighted players' desire for group acceptance by participating in masturbation; this also suggests high levels of closeness and bonding among teammates. Although the players who masturbated were not labeled as homosexuals once again, they would become sexually aroused from the combination of viewing pornography, discussing their own heterosexual activities with women, and perhaps the homoeroticism of this event as well. Because some players felt extremely connected and at ease with others on their team, masturbation in the presence of teammates was not considered an unusual event. However, high levels of team bonding, which result in events including group masturbation, have the potential to desensitize males to these and other sexual practices so that in time, this may lead to more perverse sexualized behaviors.

MASTURBATION AMONG COLLEGIATE ATHLETES

College is a time of increasing sexual experiences for many students who are free from parental authority.[36] One study of college undergraduates revealed that 64% of females and 98% of the males masturbated in the past with the men masturbating on an average of 36 times in the past three months; the higher frequencies occurred among males who believed their peers masturbated frequently and found it pleasurable.[37] Indeed, masturbation is considered normal developmental behavior that can be influenced by its perceived pleasure and acceptance within one's peer group. Moreover, a wrestler discussed camaraderie as a catalyst for certain sexual antics among his collegiate teammates by saying, "We were a pretty close group and so it wasn't nothing new to get a magazine and get an erection and see who had the biggest dick and you know compare them...just, that's what you did." Similarly, a collegiate basketball player revealed, "You're so close, you know to each other, so much... you know smacking somebody on their behind...or you know you be bored at the study table and nobody's looking and you might have an erection and pull it out and everybody start laughing – something like that." Participants from every sport revealed various homoerotic antics although basketball players were the only athletes in this study that did not engage in open or group masturbation for reasons that will be discussed later. In contrast, narratives from a wrestler, a minor league baseball player, and a collegiate hockey player revealed group masturbation among certain collegiate teammates in this way:

> I know of a situation one time where [laughs]...two guys were at a hotel and they rented one [a porn] from the TV and one of them said to the other, "Okay let's put a pillow between the two of us so it's not

homosexual" you know something like that. I mean...it was just out in the open as far as that, but...they were masturbating, and...so it wouldn't be homosexual, they put a pillow between them...[it] didn't go on often, it was these two guys were just out there...

Yea [laughing] there was guys that would talk about, you know, they're sitting there you know watching the movie and some guy's you know masturbating underneath his you know blanket or whatever... and the funny part to me is that it didn't seem to phase them. That guy that said that he was doing it, it was just, "You know, okay whatever, you know what else are you going to do when you're watching a porn?" There was never any – to my knowledge – there was never any homosexual activity on any of the teams that I've been on but you know masturbating in bathrooms and masturbating in front of other guys – that was not a rare occurrence...these guys were you know four guys living in their own apartment and they just told stories when they came to practice...it happened for sure [but] it was pretty much the same guys over and over again to be honest with you...

I mean, I wouldn't find it uncommon if I was walking down the bus to see someone masturbating right there...[and] jerking-off. And, I'm not sure what type of mentality we had, hard to say...that wasn't common with a lot of other teams and a lot of guys would be surprised to hear that...one player put it from [another university] that there are a lot of a homosexual undertones with your team. And I was like..."Well no one's gay so what the hell, we don't care having a good time...we think it's funny when we're on the bus for eight hours"...

Together these participants clearly reinforced the notion that masturbation practices were not intended to promote homosexuality with teammates or even an inclination toward this particular orientation. Instead, participants routinely described masturbation as common and occurring in conjunction with pornography within certain close-knit teams for the purpose of alleviating boredom while providing entertainment. The third participant noted that although onlookers viewed certain practices as having "homosexual undertones," masturbation was readily accepted as normal because teammates found this behavior extremely humorous. Because the prevalence and acceptance of pornography appears to be very influential in promoting masturbation within certain teams, and not all athletes have strong interests in pornography, this may be one feasible explanation for why open displays of masturbation do not occur within all teams.

MASTURBATION AMONG PROFESSIONAL ATHLETES

Open masturbation was not limited to amateur athletes because two baseball minor leaguers and a hockey minor leaguer revealed masturbation practices among professional athletes in this way:

> ...in the pros...with the Latin guys...I mean I don't know if they did it all the time or not, but I heard two stories about it, just them – I wouldn't even say stories – just like the next day when you came into the clubhouse they were like, "Oh yeah," [I] went over and see them sitting on the couch going at it [masturbating] watching the porn...

> Some of the guys on the team...two or three I think, went to one of these little sex shops and bought...some anal beads and some other stuff and...you know as a joke...the kid sticks them up his butt and starts, you know that [masturbation] type of thing...you know you have some guys who are very open, you know, walk around naked all over and you have other guys who cover up. But when it comes to homosexual [acts] or as guys are together – other than that instance – that was a one-time deal. I can't think of anything else...that was [in] pro.

> ...the most unusual thing I've seen in 15 years of pro hockey was a guy jerk off and shooting his load...on the team bus, where there's nothing but guys...we were parked in the parking lot and he was watching some girl in the parking lot and he just started jerking off and...blew his load...I've never seen any homosexuality...things or nothing too goofy. I've never seen...no sick shit between guys...fortunately [chuckles]. I think too many guys would take offense to it and stop it before something ever would happen. I've never even actually heard of anything...just with guys.

Each of the above participants noted open displays of masturbation occurring individually as well as among groups of athletes during their minor league careers. Surprisingly, the third participant thought this situation, along with other sexually deviant group behaviors subsequently revealed, was not considered abnormal because an athlete's reference group determines what is normal from what is not. Homosexuality was clearly unacceptable when teams labeled it as such. Because it appears that certain levels of camaraderie need to exist for open or group masturbation to occur, this may explain why approximately 5% of participants with minor league experience in baseball and hockey exclusively reported these practices compared to nearly 20% of participants representing virtually every sport who noted these behaviors among collegiate athletes. Stronger team bonding appears to be more common at the collegiate level compared to many professional teams because collegiate athletes often play together longer while spending large amounts of time socializing and living together. In contrast, major league baseball players noted that teammates often did not socialize together in larger groups outside of the locker room because many were married, it drew too much attention, and their friendships were diversified. This did not hold true for many minor leaguers who bond and socialize together in larger groups as a result of the time spent traveling together and living in close proximity. However, team bonding in professional sports and particularly at the minor league level is affected by the significant turnover of players within teams from one year to the next as athletes retire, join new teams and leagues, or get traded. Interestingly, a wrestler noted the importance male bonding as a catalyst for sexually deviant practices by saying, "I don't know if it's just athletes. I think anytime you're in a group of guys, you'll do stupid things. I don't know if it's just because we're athletes. I don't think that. I just think being with people you're more comfortable with you're gonna do more things." This participant's belief that peer bonding as opposed to athletic participation was responsible for sexual deviancy and/ or aggression among athletes and non-athletes alike was, in fact, supported by an abundance of research findings.[38] This may also help to explain other fundamental differences when comparing an array of sexual practices involving professional and collegiate players.

MASTURBATION AS A BASKETBALL TABOO

The majority of all-male sexual practices discussed throughout this chapter appeared within the sports of hockey, football, baseball, and wrestling but not in basketball. This phenomenon was examined and a collegiate basketball player offered one explanation by saying, "Oh no...we didn't do anything like that...like a group masturbation, uh ah [making a negative sound]...that would get you more [chuckles] more ostracized than anything." This participant revealed group masturbation as a taboo and although homoerotic behaviors were previously mentioned among collegiate basketball players, they did not include open or group masturbation. Furthermore, two minor league basketball players provided additional insights into why open masturbation practices were forbidden acts:

> I've never even heard of anything like that from any athletes, I've heard of stuff like that with, you know, just some college guys that would have like some weird video situations going on...I heard one situation where guys would circle jerk around a pizza or something like that and watch porns and stuff like that and...some of the more strange sexual experiences, I heard a lot of wild things like that from like the lacrosse team...I've never seen anything like that or heard anything like that with basketball players no, because anything like that would be looked

at as heavily gay, and not too many guys are willing – at least that I've met through my career – that would be willing to potentially close the thought processes of being possibly gay.

That's a foreign language for my culture as a basketball player when I hear about porn and group masturbation I'm like, "Really?" cause I can't fathom that. I can't even imagine a group of basketball players sitting around when I was playing and a group masturbation occurring. Now porn thrown in with five guys and three women, you've got a different dynamic and there will be sex acts performed, but it won't be group masturbation – guys will try their best to make sure they're not touching each other – that's what's going to happen in our world. When you talked about homosexuality [acts], I know for sure a basketball player wouldn't admit to it – anything pertaining to homosexuality a basketball player is going to shut off – and…I want to say it's because…especially now, it's so dominated by African American males and that's not a subject we're talking about – whether it's happening or not – we're not going there. So…I would almost bet that you're going to get a lot of, "It just wouldn't happen," almost a denial…

Although the previous African American athletes clearly reinforced the notion that open or group masturbation was unacceptable and "looked at as heavily gay," the first participant was aware of college students and members of the lacrosse team engaging in these practices. Similarly, the second participant mentioned that any discussion of group masturbation was "denied" – even if it was occurring – because African Americans racially dominated basketball and these behaviors were considered homosexual acts. Therefore, any behaviors that could label African American basketball players as homosexuals were conversationally off limits. Researchers provided additional insights when they discovered that self-identifying heterosexual men who engaged in sex with other men do so with secrecy, and this was particularly true for African American men who are less likely to disclose their gay identity because the black community is less accepting of homosexuality compared to the white community.[39] It also appears that masturbation practices are more rooted in culture than athletics because researchers found that although 67% of Caucasian and Latino-American men and 61% Asian-American men had masturbated within the past year, only 40% of African-American men reported engaging in these behaviors – perhaps because of its perceived stigma.[40] At the same time, this participant implied that group sex with multiple partners from both sexes was completely acceptable and even expected. Indeed, various sports teams and cultures and even racial groups within a team make it very clear about the kinds of sexual behaviors that are acceptable as well as those that can get someone shunned.

Homophobia, defined as the irrational fear of homosexuals or the possibility of homosexuality in oneself, is a strong, prevalent influence dictating athletes acceptable and unacceptable behaviors.[41] Moreover, homophobia has prompted some gay athletes to openly express disgust for homosexuality out of fear that they would be discovered or stigmatized by their teammates.[42] And yet, homosexual behaviors are not uncommon among both non-athletes and athletes. Comparisons from several large-scale studies revealed that while 3-5% of men in the general population described themselves as homosexual, the Kinsey data revealed that 37% of all males had at least one homosexual experience resulting in orgasm in adulthood.[43] One study involving intercollegiate athletes from three major sports at several large state universities revealed 6% of the athletes were homosexual while 25% had a homosexual experience (i.e., engaging in two or more incidences involving oral-genital or anal-genital sex in the past two years).[44] More recent research on university team-sport athletes revealed that less than 4% have engaged in same-sex sex.[45] Interestingly, a February 27th, 2006 *Sports Illustrated* magazine poll of 1,401 professional team-sport athletes that showed the majority (and 80% of National Hockey League players) would welcome a gay teammate suggests homophobia may be declining. Based on such statistics and behaviors, it was not surprising when an experienced NHL player revealed an obvious explanation for some of the all-male sexual practices:

> You know I would say that as I think about it, the society that we live in today when it comes to sex...there's a greater number of hockey players – and I know a lot of athletes – but from the hockey aspect... there are more hockey players that are – I'll call them switch hitters that...you know don't mind being with girls, but then also are attracted to guys and you know live a different lifestyle that's more of a closet type of lifestyle when it comes to...being gay or being attracted to other guys...I mean I sensed it a little when I was playing early in my career and then as I got older and played longer, you hear things, you see things...and then as I retired and coached you can feel that...I mean if somebody would ask me, "Is there a strong population of guys that are both?" I don't want to say a large number, but I think it's bigger than people think it would be. I would probably have to say...league-wide... there's no doubt in my mind that...it's probably one every two teams... that is bi- or homosexual...you know it's a small number, but I think it's a lot more than what people would ever think.

The previous participant noted a silent minority of bisexual and homosexual players compete within National Hockey League teams, and it would be logical to assume that similar percentages exist among collegiate and professional athletes in other sports as well. Athletes such as former NFL running back David Kopay and offensive guard Roy Simmons, MLB players Glenn Burke (deceased) and Billy Bean, and former NBA player John Amaechi revealed their homosexuality although for some, this resulted in being shunned from the sports world.[46] In the end, it is understandable why most athletes choose to conceal their homosexual orientation because this enables them to avoid discrimination and potential banishment from a culture that continues to condemn alternative lifestyles. It also provides another explanation for some athletes' participation in open and group masturbation within various sports cultures.

MASTURBATION AS A DEVIANT PRACTICE

While masturbation is generally considered a benign behavior, there are exceptions to this particularly when masturbation involves blatantly open displays, compulsivity and mental fixation, or when it combines with other demeaning practices. One collegiate hockey coach observed his team's attachment to pornography that often occurred in conjunction with discussions of personal masturbation practices in this way:

> ...we don't let them watch it [pornography] on the bus, but...they certainly clamor for it – I know when we're at hotels...on the road, they'll rent the soft porn stuff that's on the hotel [channels]...they pay for it because...they can't charge it to us...but I still know what's going on because you hear them talking about it – "Hey, did you guys watch? you know, this went on last night" – I've never seen them do anything with group masturbation or anything like that, but they talk so openly about the fact that they themselves masturbate and things like that – and...I think you know that 99% of all men masturbate, [and] the other 1% are liars – the point is don't talk about it like it's no big deal...even if you did it – Why do you brag about it?...they'll make comments about, "Oh yea...I've shot my load on her picture before"...I don't need to know that, I don't need to hear about it...realizing these guys are doing it, but they talk about it openly...

This participant was obviously troubled by his team's fixation with pornography as well as their open discussions flaunting masturbation while revealing seedy personal practices (i.e., "I've shot my load on her picture"); however, males are more likely to fantasize during masturbation, report their sexual fantasies, and reveal becoming sexually aroused from their fantasies compared to females.[47] At the same time, masturbation is still considered a solitary sex act that remains somewhat stigmatized, is not as openly discussed as other sexual activities, and is linked with guilt and various myths.[48] Nevertheless, it is apparent that certain groups of athletes have succeeded in making private behaviors extremely public; however, the greater problem involves engaging in compulsive and/or decadent masturbation practices in an effort to one-up teammates. For example, one minor league baseball player revealed, "We had guys that probably jerked off everyday for sure – absolutely everyday." Like previous narratives that raised questions suggestive of compulsive masturbation among certain athletes, this participant noted similar patterns occurring among his collegiate teammates. Sexual compulsivity or addiction is defined by the use of masturbation or sex to cope with unpleasant or uncontrollable emotions including anxiety or depression.[49] Addiction is also associated with compulsivity, dependency, repetition, and continuation of behaviors in spite of significant harmful consequences, and because the compulsive person lacks adaptive coping skills to regulate unpleasant emotional states, sexual stimulation is used instead.[50] It is apparent that one's mindset and motives for engaging in masturbation are important factors influencing the development of sexual behaviors that become out of control.

Besides the potential for engaging in compulsive masturbation, one collegiate baseball player revealed other inappropriate practices by saying, "Oh man, [one] knucklehead actually fucking masturbated and spewed in the guy's glove and put it in the freshman's locker...he did it like a couple of times to different guys, you know, till guys really start paying attention and looking." Whether this athlete was seeking attention and notoriety for his actions or perhaps developing a sexual fetish is not known for certain, but in either case, teammates found his practices both entertaining and "disgusting." Fetishism refers to sexual behaviors in which a person obtains sexual excitement primarily from contact with inanimate objects or certain body parts.[51] While it is possible, though unlikely, that this athlete was developing a fetish with baseball gloves, clothing such as underwear or bras as well as people's feet have been noted as common fetishes that produce sexual arousal for some people.[52]

In addition, other types of deviant masturbation practices were revealed by a wrestler and a minor league hockey player in this way:

> [Laughing] I had a couple teammates that were big into that and I had one teammate who was into it to the point that he didn't care if you would be sitting there watching him, he would beat off [masturbate] and do stuff like that just because he needed to, and so it didn't matter what it was, it's just what he did [laughing]...he was the main one but... then when we were on road trips if you fell asleep, he would try to masturbate and shoot it on you just because you fell asleep and that's kind of what he did [laughing] – that was his thing...and so I think for him, it wasn't so much homosexual-heterosexual it was, "I got a big dick and I'm going to show everybody"...

...I remember this...kid in college [hockey], it was like before every game, he would make himself get a hard-on. It was the weirdest thing... this kid was a freshman at the time...he was sitting over there and we'd be in our normal ritual time, like thinking about the game, getting dressed, you know quiet, and he'd go, "Hey!" Just to get us to look over. And he'd say, "Check this out!" And we'd be like, "What the hell is that kid [doing]?"...and this would be like every game. It would be to the point where you'd forget about it because you'd be in your game mode and he'd do this thing. And it was every game...

Both of the above participants appeared to be describing paraphilias or uncommon types of sexual expression, which involved collegiate athletes' inappropriate masturbation patterns as well as exhibitionism.[53] Although exhibitionism usually involves exposing one's genitals (with or without masturbation) to an unsuspecting stranger of the opposite sex, it is apparent that teammates can be targeted as well.[54] However, the first participant's statement, "I got a big dick and I'm going to show everybody" describing his teammate's attitude that prompted him to regularly ejaculate on unsuspecting teammates during road trips was unquestionably humiliating. Moreover, these events along with this wrestler's inclination to expose his genitals to females seemed to suggest exhibitionism as an authentic disorder. While the second participant also noted exhibitionism when a teammate consistently called attention to his masturbation and erection during preparation for games, it appeared that this player was using masturbation and exhibitionism as a way to cope with his pre-game tension and stress. This can be likened to former NFL player Lance Rentzel.[55] Because most athletes find these practices both entertaining and humorous, offending athletes are rewarded for their deviant practices making them more likely to continue.

Deviant masturbation practices were not relegated to collegiate athletes because a minor league hockey player noted these practices during his professional career:

It was a road trip. I can't remember where it was to but the radio announcer...was in his seat, sleeping...well, they used to put the luggage up top [in the bus] – some of the guys would get up there and sleep. Well, one guy got up there and started masturbating and ejaculated [laughs] all over the guy below him that was sleeping, the radio announcer [laughing] and...that's the only time I've seen anything like that. And you know...I don't think it was done out of harm, and...I don't know if the guy really even knew what it was...nobody claimed who did it, so he never knew what happened or who did it...

Unlike the previous collegiate athlete who openly ejaculated on sleeping teammates, no one on this participant's team confessed to this event perhaps because the perpetrator realized it was a perverse and demeaning act. Furthermore, admitting to this behavior could negatively influence a professional athlete's reputation, career, and his consideration as a team leader and role model. Still, this does not change every professional athlete's behavior because although deviant masturbation practices were not found among major leaguers in my sample, they still occur. For example, in his book, *Boys Will Be Boys: The Glory Days and Party Nights of the Dallas Cowboys Dynasty*, author Jeff Pearlman documented former NFL lineman Charles Haley's frequent displays of open masturbation occurring within the locker room, the trainer's room, and even during positional team meetings with two different NFL teams.[56] Moreover, Haley became infamous for stroking his phallus near an unsuspecting teammate's face while making lewd sexual remarks, and his graphic conversations targeting players' wives while he masturbated sometimes resulted in ejaculation during team meetings.[57] In the end, these and other athletes avoided negative consequences for engaging in a variety of inappropriate sexual practices only because their behaviors were confined to all-male athletic environments that did not discourage deviant behavior through consequences.

Competitions Involving Masturbation

Few will disagree that elite-level athletes are extremely competitive, and this trait is arguably one of the most important separating those who compete at the collegiate and professional levels from those who observe these events. Therefore, it was no surprise when researchers, who examined competitiveness in college men and included collegiate club or varsity athletes, found that athletic participation was highly linked with scores of competitiveness, win orientation, and goal orientation.[58] Based on the findings from my research, it is also apparent that some athletes' competitive drive continues away from the playing field and emerges into certain sexual activities, which for some athletes can resemble a type of competition. While competitive sexual events have involved both females and males alike, this discussion will focus on masturbation competitions within all-male groups. In all, about 7% of the participants were aware of masturbation competitions at the high school or collegiate level that occurred apart from team initiations, and nearly 80% of these events involved only collegiate athletes in wrestling, hockey, baseball, or football. For example, one wrestler reported his awareness by saying, "Yea I have heard of them...just of wrestlers talking about their friends and trying to outdo each other and under those circumstances, how far they could shoot their load." While attempting to "outdo each other" involved ejaculating the farthest, a minor league football player revealed other competitions by saying, "Two guys that were on my [football] team that occasionally had races... [in] college...to see who could get off [and ejaculate] first." In addition, two wrestlers and a collegiate hockey player noted more elaborate speed-based masturbation contests in this way:

> Yea we had two guys who...would race each other to see how fast they could (ejaculate), they would put their times up each week, you know, on the outside of their door, it was in the dorms...these two stole the show...they would do it once a week...I don't know about their whole career, the one guy ended up failing out, but the first year for sure.

> I mean...we had a couple of individuals that they would...have a contest, "Oh I can get off three times in 20 minutes or whatever." One individual, he was more of our team clown, he would do it, but just as a joke...like he'd bet how many times I can do it, but...I don't remember it much as a team, but I remember one individual that he was just proud of that fact [laughs] and...there were, you know, times where he would go into a room and he would brag on it, and he was just different in that sense, but it was more of a joke amongst everybody else..

> ...we used to have a game where you'd sit on the bus and everybody would masturbate just for the hell of it, why not?...you'd just be there, really a lot of times we'd prefer that we should pass the hat and whatever team ejaculates last going up the row of seats – loses...yeah, that scenario was done – not that often – twice a season, passing it up the rows that would just be Jerk-Off Derby, more or less [laughs] – see who can get done the quickest...I didn't go to prep school...but a lot of guys... their initiation as a rookie is everybody gets in a room, masturbates on a cracker, or a piece of bread and the last guy to go has to eat it. So, that...I've heard of...we never pushed it that far [for losing]...

Each of the above athletes described different types of speed-based masturbation competitions involving collegiate teammates as well as the participant himself in the third narrative. It is evident that certain athletes prided themselves on their ability to devise creative, yet deviant masturbation practices, which provided humor and entertainment while increasing notoriety and status for those involved. While the third participant noted that the losers in the masturbation races in which he was involved were not forced to eat their own semen – unlike rookie players during prep school initiations, one minor league baseball player described a similar experience among his collegiate teammates in this way:

...the one year we had the cookie with the circle jerk and they all had to jerk off and the last guy to throw their load out there had to eat the cookie so it kind of got – that was a little crazy, that was my second year that that happened...the guy actually ate the cookie, I mean he had to, he had to, you got 20 guys around you forcing you to do it, what are you going to do? He had to you know...that was more for the rookie initiations.

The above participant revealed a very demeaning event during his collegiate team's initiation like two other athletes who reported similar initiations on their junior hockey teams. While the above event could have produced serious consequences for the athletes, their program, and coaches, it was never reported. Collegiate athletic teams have come under close scrutiny since the University of Vermont cancelled its 1999-2000 hockey season and Montreal's McGill University cancelled the 2005-06 football season following reports of sexualized initiations.[59] Although it appears that team initiations have been reduced, lessened in severity, and in some cases stopped altogether, they continue to flourish within certain athlete cultures. In this study, about 80% of the participants observed, experienced, and/or participated in initiating athletes on their collegiate and/or professional teams. From this group, approximately 45% revealed initiations involving nudity or other sexualized practices within their teams. Together, these narratives reinforced the fact that elite-level athletes thrive on competition, and it is evident that some athletes have carried their competitive drive into perverse sexual events involving masturbation contests that were particularly demeaning during team initiations.

PUSHING THE LIMITS INTO THE BIZARRE

As athletes become more comfortable and bonded with each other, heightened levels of team camaraderie encourage some athletes to push the limits into more shocking and sexualized behaviors. This happens because the more outrageous the event, the more entertainment and status-producing stories emerge for those making victims of practical jokes look foolish. Several narratives from a minor leaguer and a collegiate hockey player described some of the more extreme sexual behaviors that happened during their junior and collegiate careers in this way:

...a funny situation once where one of my buddies in juniors was passed out on a couch and...his mouth was drooling...[and] wide open because he was breathing heavy. Guys were walking over and almost sticking their dicks just outside of his mouth and taking pictures of it so it looked like he was blowing them. It was funny as hell to see the pictures because it looked so real...that's the only incidence that I had with somebody passed out...and of course he had no idea those pictures were even taken. He walks into the dressing room and they're plastered all over the board, so it was actually like he was blowing these guys. It was so funny...[but] he was like, "You mother fucker." It was light-hearted, but it was like, "You bastards, I can't believe you did that to me, don't let these get out to anybody" tearing them off the wall, putting them in his pockets. It was...just kind of like a ha ha kind of thing. Those pictures never really got out or circulated or anything like that...

...we had this thing, it's called a frappe, where a girl's passed out [laughs] [you'd] get, I guess a semi-erection and you smacked their penis off her arm or forehead or whatever and...it's like smack, smack, and you'd call it a frappe beat. That's happened a couple times but... we were all there when a group of lacrosse guys had did it, so...[we] just thought it was funny that [if] you passed out and it's your fault, tough, you got a frappe. And I'd see guys...teabag them...it wasn't anything criminal...it's when you take your testicles and you rest them on a guy's eyes, or a girl's, who passed out, and take a photo of it, something like that...oh, male and female, probably at least a dozen [happened]...I like it cause it's special, funny as hell, I want to see it everyday you know [laughs] cause they're funny, I get a kick out of them. [I] never performed one. As far as I know I've never had one performed on me either, but you never know, somebody might have done it and forgot to get it [the photos] developed.

We had one guy, they call him The Dagger...what he would do is get a full-blown erection and you'd be asleep and he'd tap you on the shoulder and you'd turn and you'd get hit in the eye with his hard-on. And we called it Dagger Vision and everybody thought it was funny as hell. But, stuff like that, I mean there weren't even women involved or around, and we didn't find it to be uncommon, it was humorous and [in] our showers...guys would be playing grab-ass and doing whatever, having fun, we thought it was funny, we had to entertain ourselves somehow...a lot of us knew one another from when we were very young...and then we all ended back at [college together]...so, I don't know if that...was part of it, [or] made it, I guess more of a relaxed environment for us together. I don't know.

It is evident that the level of bonding and comfort was very high among these teammates because players' extensive history together appeared to normalize sexual practices that could be considered extremely humiliating as well as homosexual acts. Frequently, athletes, who are infamous for their outrageous and entertaining conduct, simultaneously gain admiration and status because they are viewed as unique, impulsive, and out-of-control – all of which are traits carrying higher prestige in the athlete culture. While the first participant noted junior players creating very demeaning homemade pornography when a teammate "passed out," the second participant noted collegiate lacrosse players teaching hockey players their specialized practice called a "frappe" which was subsequently adopted, and like tea bagging, targeted "passed out" collegiate athletes and females. In all, collegiate lacrosse players were mentioned several times in this chapter by different participants for their participation in a variety of sexual practices even though they were not interviewed for this study. Furthermore, because athletes are constantly learning from each other, it is vital that peers convey positive messages so that negative behavior, including sexual deviancy and aggression, is not perpetuated. Indeed, sexual aggression, which involves any sexual activity performed against someone's will through the use of force, argument, pressure, drugs or alcohol, or authority, is apparent in certain behaviors in the previous narratives.[60] It is also interesting to note that each of these outrageous behaviors targeted teammates who were considered close and bonded peers. Consequently, if teammates have little regard for the way they treat each other, how will this influence the way they treat casual female sexual partners with whom they are not bonded? In the end, athletes themselves always have the final say regarding the type of behaviors that are deemed acceptable from those that are not within the various teams. Unfortunately, sexually deviant practices lacking censorship can create upsetting and harmful circumstances as well as major problems for both athletes and those who are victimized.

PLAYING WITH BODILY DISCHARGES

Not all of athletes' bizarre behaviors involved their genitalia or masturbation urges because some participants recalled outrageous antics involving bodily discharges of flatulence, urination, and excrement. Moreover, some behaviors involving bodily substances are considered bizarre fetishes when they involve sexual arousal in combination with specific bodily discharges.[61] For example, urophiliacs are sexually aroused by urine or the act of urination (often called "golden showers" during sex) while coprophiliacs are sexually aroused by excrement.[62] Coprophiliacs also may play with, masturbate with, or even eat feces, and certain brothels around the world cater to these patrons by allowing them to watch prostitutes defecate from under a glass.[63] My first encounter with fetishes occurred during my collegiate career, when a collegiate wrestler, tennis player, and I were socializing with three female athletes and during the evening, my tennis friend who was into "golden showers" urinated on his partner during sex. While living in the athlete dormitory my freshman year, one athlete found pleasure in using toilet paper and then plastering the feces-ridden paper all over the inside of the stalls to the point that the cleaning staff refused to remove it; this became a major health concern as the weather got warmer. As a professional player, I knew a collegiate athlete who became a collegiate coach that was infamous for defecating in holes during golf outings. Although it is highly unlikely that these behaviors were motivated by sexual arousal, one study discovered 6% of men and 3% of women in the survey believed the practice of urinating on a partner was very normal or alright while 3% of men and 1% of women thought being defecated upon was very normal or alright.[64] However, because it cannot be known for certain if the athletes described in my study engaged with bodily discharges to be outrageously entertaining, to promote sexual arousal, or both, I will simply describe the events in most cases. For example, a wrestler and a collegiate football player discussed their awareness as well as personal experiences involving unusual behaviors in this way:

> I knew a wrestler who...he had a thing with being pee'd on and he was mad at his girlfriend because she wouldn't pee on him and he eventually got her to...one of my current teammates was taking a shower with a girl once and thought it would be funny while her back was turned to piss on her leg, so he did that to her.

> ...for awhile there we would sit around and light farts, we was lighting farts like it was going out of style...and doing stuff [like] sitting around playing spades and fart and then light it and...yea, the one guy he got up pretty quick and he said it [the flame] went up into him [laughing] but I remember him wiping his ass like a dog across the carpet [still laughing].

In addition, other participants revealed athletes pushing the limits through their fixation and fascination with feces and defecating in inappropriate places. For example, one collegiate baseball player recalled, "There was a couple of disgusting guys, man, they would do shit like [laughs] I remember one guy basically took a dump in one of the freshman's gloves and stuck it in his locker [laughing] I guess that's pretty memorable now that I think about it [laughs]." While these behaviors were disgusting, demeaning, and entertaining at the same time, other athletes' use of human excrement was even more bizarre as a minor league hockey player and wrestler observed in this way:

> ...there was a guy I played with in junior...that kept a jar above his locker...it wasn't a contest, it was more or less a personal contest. It was filled with a big turd about that long in a big pickle jar full of piss and turds...[he] just keep adding to it. It sat above the stall. I'd look at it every day and think, "What the hell is he doing with that thing?" It was like, "Yep, when we win the whatever [championship]...at the end of

the year, I'm just going to open it up and spray it all over the room" kind of thing. It wasn't so much a contest as it was just gross. I'm not sure what that was about. He was one of those guys that would go to parties and he would shit in the upper part of the toilet where the water actually sits in the tank – not down in the bowl. It's called an "Upper Decker"... you know it sits in there and festers...nobody can figure out where the smell is coming from [laughs] and it just stinks up your apartment. He'd used to strategically place these little turds around the house like in the heating vents...like somewhere down in the grand piano somewhere. Anywhere you wouldn't think to look for that crap. You know, if it gets in the heating vent, of course, the heat activates it, and stinks up the whole house. You don't know where it's coming from because he'd take the vent cover off and actually stick it way down as far as he could with his hand. He'd just place it way down there with his hand. I mean, you'd never think of looking in a place like that for a piece of shit...it was those kind of things.

...there's a story about a wrestler, he might have even been there when I was there, if not, it was the year before I came there, where he [and] another light weight...was walking back with some of the other teammates that...I know. Two of the [wrestling] guys that were part of the story...were bigger guys but there was a guy that started [a fight with them]...I don't know how it started, somebody was talking smack, and they ended up squaring off in the street. The little guy shit in his pants, reached back and at least shit a little bit out, stuck his hand into his pants, smeared a little bit on his finger, and then put it on his potential [adversary] – you know the guy that's going to fight him – on his face. Absolutely...that's the most deviant or one of those stories if you had to come up with...that was like unbelievable – how off you can be. And that guy ended up transferring to another college but, you know, I have a friend that wrestled at [XXX University with him] and he came through with quite a few more of those deviant stories.

The first participant described a teammate who regularly used human excrement and defecation in antics that earned him unique attention and recognition with his peers. Whether these behaviors related to the early stages of coprophilia is not known for certain, although it is certainly possible given the time and effort this athlete exerted collecting and playing with human feces. In contrast, the second participant described an event where one of his teammates decided to literally "get shitty" with an adversary he was preparing to fight because he defecated and then wiped his own excrement on him. This situation undoubtedly caused shock and outrage in his opponent as well as in his own teammates who were on hand for support and protection if it was needed. Moreover, this participant attempted to explain his teammate's behavior as well as how the culture of wrestling may, in fact, promote these and other outrageous behaviors:

> ...he was one of those guys that...wanted to sensationalize himself with being twisted, over the edge. I mean wrestlers as a whole are different, a different breed, I don't know...if you know many or your experience interviewing them has told you that or not, but you know there are a lot more twisted people in wrestling...than your average sport...

While wrestling was thought to attract more than its share of deviant athletes who thrived on constructing "twisted" personas and reputations, this participant also observed that not every collegiate program, including his own, consisted of an abundance of wrestlers with deviant goals and aspirations. At the same time, it is all too apparent that when deviancy and aggression are rewarded, negative behaviors are likely to increase because status-producing stories "take on a life of their own once they're told" within a sports culture while simultaneously providing perpetrators with great renown. This notion was highlighted by a minor league hockey player who described the competitive extremes within certain athlete cultures at the professional level:

> ...something that I wasn't involved with...but my brother was involved... actually the bar put it on, it was a gross-out contest. And all of the [minor league] hockey players were involved in it. Whoever wins gets free drinks for the rest of the night. Well, my brother was in there one night and a guy ate his own shit. Shit on a plate and ate it...and some other guy did something crazy and won [also], I don't know what he...ate, his snot or something like that. I can't remember what he did...[but] this guy just dropped an ear [human excrement] on a plate and just took a knife and fork and went right at it...[just] some of the bizarre things that I've heard about...

The following narrative is arguably one of the more disturbing examples that epitomized one-upmanship involving deviant behaviors within all-male groups because it poignantly shows the level of extremes that some athletes will go to in order to outdo a teammate or competitor. Because elite-level athletes thrive on demonstrating their competitive prowess, it is naïve to assume that these urges will cease once they leave the field of competition because they do not.

Not every event involving bodily discharges turned out to be humor-filled and harmless because some have resulted in consequences. For example, former NFL lineman Charles Haley cut a hole in the roof of a teammate's BMW convertible and urinated in it shortly before he engaged in an outrageous event that involved wiping his rear end in a team positional meeting after returning from the restroom and throwing feces-soiled toilet paper at his defensive line coach John Marshall.[65] Although the latter situation resulted in Haley being traded quickly despite his contribution to the San Francisco 49ers defense, Haley's actions could have easily resulted in much more serious consequences had they occurred anywhere outside of the athletic arena.[66] Furthermore, a minor league baseball player and a wrestler reported other events involving bodily discharges that carried much more severe ramifications:

...there was one instance where we had a couple of guys on our [minor league baseball] team...high draft picks...[who were] thrown off the team for doing stupid stuff, and I believe it was...two guys got thrown off the team for shitting on pizza boxes and leaving them in the room when we were on the road [laughing] – that was a classic one, actually these two guys got in trouble a couple of times and...the reason they got released because they trashed the rooms and they shit on the pizza boxes and you know when we're leaving town...that got obviously back to the coaches and who was in those rooms...

...we were all pretty drunk and we went up to a bar and it was on a Sunday night towards the end of the year, so there weren't a lot of people out and we were out and we were dancing and drinking more and my roommate and I left...our coach told us, you know, he told us specifically, "Keep an eye on this guy [a wrestling teammate] cause I don't want him getting thrown in jail," and it was almost closing time and we left...he was still there and there was some girls there and they had a birthday cake, and she had a birthday party, and they were singing happy birthday, and he just walked up...and he said, "Hey, it's your birthday, happy birthday" and he pissed on her cake you know, so he got thrown in jail and our coach calls us the next morning just ripping our ass because it was our job to keep him out of jail and we blew it...that's just the way he was, he didn't care, it was if it popped in his head, he would do it, so that's the kind of individuals I hung out with.

While the professional baseball players' defecation in their hotel room appeared to be the "final straw" event which led to their team dismissal, the second participant insightfully observed a definite lack of impulse control within his teammate – as well as in other wrestlers on his team – which is certain to impact the outcome of different events. Whenever people, including athletes, act irrationally before considering all consequences, it is logical to experience problems of all kinds as these athletes discovered. Furthermore, it is interesting to speculate what the two professional athletes were thinking following their dismissal which potentially ended their professional athletic careers permanently. The same can be said for the wrestler following his arrest. One can only wonder that if each athlete had that day to do over again, would they reconsider their behaviors and opt against them? I would bet on it since I cannot fathom that there would not be regret given the time, passion, and effort required in building an elite-level career. In the end, it is sad and often traumatic when athletic careers end under the best of circumstances, and these events are certain to produce a lifetime of wondering "what if?" for those involved.

ATHLETES' CORNER: POINTS TO PONDER

1. Participating in obscene, demeaning, or aggressive behaviors may provide temporary attention, belonging, and status within certain teams; however, personal, team, and family reputations highlighting excellence that took years to build can suffer permanent damage in the blink of an eye. Know that negative practices that are reported as well as those remaining temporarily hidden from public view have resulted in consequences, injury, and harm affecting victims as well as offenders long after athletic careers end.

2. Teammates exercise strong influence by rewarding members who behave in certain ways while simultaneously punishing those who do not conform to expectations through ridicule, criticism, or exclusion. Negative peers provide a clear signal that it is time to find positive ones. Also know that friends are only as powerful as you allow them to be so avoiding any group encouraging negative practices is acting with intelligence and foresight.

3. Remember that athletes are considered role models in many societies, which means they are constantly being observed regardless of whether they want this kind of attention and responsibility or not. This means that ALL athletes must begin acting as if others were looking up to them both in and out of sport since this is already occurring at all times. Therefore, make excellence your daily goal both on and off the field of competition measuring your thoughts, words, and actions by the highest standards that you know.

Chapter 2
Pornography: Gateway to Deviancy

My introduction to pornography within the hockey culture began when I played tier II Junior A in Quebec, Canada, and my particular team began frequenting a certain bar that showed very graphic, hard-core pornographic movies to its patrons. Additional exposure occurred during my first year of professional hockey when a teammate and I would occasionally watch late-night, soft-core pornography on satellite television. I also recall one pornographic movie was played on a team bus trip during my final year of pro hockey in Europe. Aside from these experiences, I do not remember any of my teammates using pornography during my collegiate and professional career, although this probably occured without my knowledge. As a coach, I would sometimes see porn magazines on bus trips among the collegiate and professional players, and I recall a porn movie being played once on a team bus during a collegiate road trip although I did not endorse this. While my observations were limited, my findings will show that pornography is a significant source of entertainment for many elite-level athletes that flourishes in a variety of forms.

Webster's New World Collegiate Dictionary defines pornography as "writing, pictures, etc. intended to arouse sexual desire," and this can take the form of books, magazines, photographs, videos/DVD's, Internet websites, the telephone, and live shows featuring erotic dancers.[1] Pornography has grown to become big business with an estimated revenue of $13 billion in the United States in 2009, nearly $100 billion worldwide, and the $4.3 billion from the U.S. total that was spent on DVD sales and rentals alone was more than the annual revenue accrued by either the National Football League (NFL), the National Basketball Association (NBA), or Major League Baseball (MLB).[2] Moreover, a national study revealed that nearly one third of Americans (41% of the men, 16% of the women) engaged in at least one of the following activities in the past year: viewed an x-rated movie, video, book, or magazine, called a "pay-by-the minute" phone sex number, or attended a strip club.[3]

College men reportedly spent an average of six hours per month looking at sexually explicit material while college women spent two hours although this occurred before widespread Internet use.[4] In contrast, one Internet traffic measuring service, comScore, discovered that 70% of 18–24 year-old men visit pornography sites during a typical month which was about 40% more than the average user; these young men also accounted for about 25% of all online pornography visits.[5] Usage among men in their 20s and 30s was nearly as high with about 66% of all men between the ages of 18 and 34 viewing Internet pornography each month.[6] With pornography usage occurring with regularity among the general population, it would be naïve to believe that athletes are immune from its far-reaching influence. Furthermore, previous narratives already revealed athletes' use of pornography occurred in conjunction with open-masturbation practices although the frequency of this pornography use was not disclosed. Indeed, pornography is a substantial presence among collegiate, minor, and major league athletes representing every sport in this study, and athletes' pornography use is alarming given its prevalence and the research citing an array of potentially negative effects that result from its use.

EXAMINING COLLEGIATE ATHLETES' PORNOGRAPHY USE

Based on the frequency of pornography use within the general population, it was not surprising to discover that 95% of the athletes representing every level and sport in this study were exposed to a variety of pornography within their teams. What is startling is the fact that over 55% of the participants revealed a higher prevalence of pornography use which took the form of magazines, The Internet, and videos/DVDs. Recall that although college men's use of pornography averaged an hour and a half weekly or six hours per month *before* the advent of Internet pornography, the affordability, accessibility, and anonymity of Internet pornography readily encourages more frequent use because it is so easy to acquire.[7] Furthermore, the frequency of pornography use is an important piece of information, which is sometimes missing from studies, because this can impact viewers in very different ways particularly when pornography is used with the regularity numerous athletes revealed during their collegiate careers.[8] For example, a variety of wrestlers noted, "Quite a bit," "Yea, guys did like to have porn on their laptops," "Oh everybody had dirty magazines," and "I had a couple of teammates that were big into that." Likewise, a minor league baseball player revealed, "All the time, yea, there was always some sort of pornography on the computer or on TV...I don't think there's a guy on the team that didn't look at pornography." A minor league hockey player similarly observed, "There was certainly porn presence...there were 12 guys in that [college] house and three floors, every floor had TV and porno tapes laying around everywhere." In addition, a minor league football player noted, "I'd say it's something that's fairly common you know amongst friends...I know in college you know we had a subscription to a *Penthouse* and *Playboy* that we split among four football players the cost." And an NFL player expressively noted pornography usage during his college career by saying, "Everywhere, everywhere, there was porn everywhere...in your locker...on the trips...in guys' rooms, it was everywhere."

While certain participants revealed easy access to pornography and a higher prevalence of use during collegiate careers that spanned the 1970s through 2010, others quantified their team and/or personal pornography use. For example, a current minor league basketball player estimated that while "98%" of his collegiate teammates used pornography with heavy use occurring "everyday," he used pornography about "three times a week." Likewise, a current minor league football player recalled, "College, I'm going to have to say 100% everybody," and he revealed his own pornography use by saying, "Oh man I was bad with it, everyday I was always watching some kind of porn or showing some kind of pictures around." A wrestler revealed his collegiate team's pornography use was "probably everyday" while a collegiate hockey player noted his pornography use by saying, "I usually watch porno once a day, once every couple of days while I'm in college." Other participants including another collegiate hockey player and a minor league baseball player elaborated in this way:

> I was always one of the guys that...hung out with the guys I played hockey with, so I'd say probably three or four times a week I was involved in that [pornography]. There was probably some guys that would do that six, seven days a week with other people...it was a fairly common occurrence.

> College for sure, college, you know in my house I had four baseball players and one guy that didn't play baseball and...there was probably 15 of them [videos] in our house – yea...probably [used them] five or six days a week I'm sure...[and] oh yea, magazines would be passed around...on the bus, most guys had them on their computers, yea that was different, [but] we couldn't pop it in on the bus [video] and fire it up.

The above participants noted collegiate athletes, including themselves, used pornography anywhere from 3-7 days per week because magazine subscriptions, videos/DVDs, and computers made pornography readily available particularly when players pooled their resources to purchase materials. In addition, a minor league basketball player commented on players' use of technology to access pornography based on his experiences as a recent player and current collegiate coach:

> Everybody had some form of porn almost, as far as magazines not so much, but with The Internet being widely available, you'd find a lot... there were a lot of sexually explicit porn sites that guys would kind of pass around amongst each other and, you know, laugh at and check out, things like that, but I would say there's a lot more Internet porn type stuff, you know, websites and as far as videos and things like that, a lot of guys had some access to that type of stuff...

Cyber-porn, which is explicit sexual material available through The Internet, is a relatively new form of pornography that athletes, like many others, have discovered, and men constitute 86% of the cyber-porn users.[9] Although there were approximately 900 pornography websites in 1997, Websense, a provider of Internet management software, revealed that the number of pornography websites in their database had increased seventeen-fold from 88,000 in 2000 to nearly 1.6 million in April 2004.[10] Technological advances in combination with soaring profits suggest there is no reason to believe the cyber-porn trend will reverse itself anytime soon despite the potential for negative repercussions.

EXAMINING PROFESSIONAL ATHLETES' PORNOGRAPHY USE

Intuitively, there are two opposing schools of thought when speculating about professional athletes' use of pornography. One is that professionals use pornography less often than collegiate athletes because they are older, more mature, and have outgrown such practices. The second, which my study supported, is that professionals use pornography as frequently or more often than collegiate athletes because they have more money and time to spend on such pursuits. While pornography usage always involves individual interests and preferences, its presence was undeniable among numerous professionals in this study. For example, a minor league baseball player revealed, "Oh, it was everywhere, all the time, it was in guys' rooms, wherever you went it was there...strip clubs...videos...magazines...laptops, they'd stick them in their laptops...usually [viewed individually] or a couple of them circle around, yeah." While this participant found pornography equally prevalent during his collegiate and professional baseball career, a minor league football player discussed his experiences with pornography by saying, "Oh shit that's everyday, I know guys live with that even when I was here and I played...with the [minor league team] shit we used to – that used to be part of our morning routine." Daily pornography usage occurred as readily during this participant's professional playing career as it did among the professionals he currently coached in the new millennium. Current minor league players from football and basketball similarly estimated that "60-70%" and "100%" of their professional teammates used pornography on a regular basis, which could mean "every day" for athletes from both sports. At the same time, an NHL player observed as a current professional coach that certain minor league organizations were trying to clean up their locker rooms literally by banning pornographic magazines even though players' pornographic collections were much more extensive than when he competed a decade earlier. Moreover, other minor leaguers from basketball and hockey elaborated on their experiences with pornography in this way:

That's all you talk about [laughs], that's all you talk about I mean you know women are a big subject...who looks good or this and that...the big magazines are now is *FHM*, you know *XXX, XXL magazine, Maxim*, you know there's a lot of, you know, people just look at magazines and...look at the chicks you know what I'm saying, that's an always thing...I think in, more professional, people do that under the cover, but in this last team that I was with, a lot of people had magazines and talked about this...but in like in any other professional team...it wasn't like full blown [openness] or anything like that...

...At the minor pro level...I would say that 75% of the players watch it like on a regular basis and...the [AAA] level I would say less...[but] I would say junior, [AA level], and stuff like that I would say pornography and strippers are probably number one [form of] entertainment...I would say at the lower [A] levels – all the time – I mean too much time on their hands is what it is, there's got to be something that they can do, I mean it's a great life, you don't have anything to do all day, but that's where they're running into trouble...

Both of the above participants revealed a high prevalence of pornography usage during minor league careers that spanned the late 1980s through the mid-2000s although this came with notable differences. The first participant was among a number of professionals who observed that pornography was both prevalent and more discreet within certain professional teams perhaps because no one wanted their private behaviors revealed in such a way that they could tarnish personal reputations. It is also likely that some professionals are embarrassed by their pornography use particularly when it could be considered excessive. In contrast, the second participant revealed that pornography usage was not discreet since it was the "number one" source of entertainment among most players during his professional career that was explained by sheer boredom because most players failed to occupy their down time with meaningful activities. Unfortunately, boredom sometimes encourages athletes' quest for excitement, and when this combines with substance abuse, negative peer influences, and the belief in athlete privilege, it can produce a recipe for disaster that has resulted in all kinds of criminal involvement among athletes including drug dealing, robbery, assaults, and sexual deviancy and aggression.[11]

Higher pornography usage was not relegated to only minor leaguers because it was also discovered among major leaguers. Big league salaries make pornography easily affordable and because teams travel by planes rather than on buses, players often have more free time to spend on such pursuits. In addition, certain major league organizations are accepting of pornography to the point that they provided free materials to the athletes. For example, one

MLB player noted, "A lot of the major league clubhouse bathrooms have girly magazines everywhere" while another revealed, "Oh in the clubhouse...they would be there, they would be all over I guess, every clubhouse...just the major leagues [not in the minor leagues]." The majority of MLB players in this study noted a high prevalence of pornography magazines in major league clubhouses wherever they played. While pornographic videos were less common in these settings, they appeared periodically in the "players only area" though "not every clubhouse had that." One MLB player noted that he and other players with stronger spiritual affiliations were successful in convincing clubhouse attendants to place the pornography magazines in a specific area so that they were available – just not everywhere you looked.

Other participants including an NFL player revealed their awareness of pornography by saying, "Magazines very little, the actual porn videos, uh quite a bit, I think that a good 70-80% of the guys that I know of had some sort of videos...but it's about the same [in college and the NFL]." While certain participants noted both a higher and similar prevalence of pornography during their collegiate and NFL careers, others found pornography more prevalent in the pros because "in college you aien't got the money." Moreover, an NFL player recalled rampant pornography usage among major leaguers by saying, "It was big, it was real big...to have a 25-30 DVD/video porno collection was about average – again unless you're like a devout Christian or something that was about average." And sometimes pornography arrived in unique and unexpected ways as this NFL player recalled by saying, "When I played professional football I mean I was just an average guy, but...the naked, the nude photos...the underwear, and the mail, I used to get that stuff you know believe it or not...I mean that was real."

Like the previous athletes, one participant with recent and diverse playing experiences at the collegiate, minor league, and NBA level revealed pornography usage within the basketball culture by saying, "Oh wow that was very prevalent on every level, the guys did that from high school to majors." Similarly, an NHL player observed pornography usage during his major league career by saying, "[Watching] the videos as a group very rarely, roommates and stuff turning on a porno flick...was common, the magazines and stuff was probably a lot more consistency in that than there was actually [with] the pornos and [video] stuff as a group." Overall, participants provided ample evidence that a high prevalence of pornography exists among minor and major league athletes during professional playing and/or coaching careers that spanned the early 1970s through 2010. While players' use of pornography occurred in a variety of settings including team road trips, players' age in combination with the era in which they competed determined the type of pornography that was most prevalent in their experiences.

PORNOGRAPHY'S IMPACT ON MALES, FEMALES, AND RELATIONSHIPS

Opponents of pornography attempt to emphasize its harm by highlighting its potential for influencing men's violence and rape.[12] And yet, there are other more subtle ways that pornography impacts its users. For example, the 2004 *Elle*-MSNBC.com survey of 15,246 Americans revealed that 13% of men admitted that viewing pornography online caused them to worry that they might not be able to satisfy their partner's needs, 10% felt they needed to do more to keep their partner sexually interested, 8% felt porn caused them to feel poorly about their own bodies, and 15% admitted their online habit made them feel sleazy.[13] While such findings show the use of pornography is not benign as many males would like to believe, its negative influence expands beyond this to include depreciating attitudes and behaviors toward females and relationships which also can be very pronounced. For example, men who viewed pornography had lower opinions of women as well as more negative attitudes toward intimate relationships than men who do not view pornography.[14] Certain athletes in this study including a collegiate hockey player supported such notions and elaborated in this way:

> ...I guess in pornos you see those types of behaviors where you see guys, I guess you could say disrespecting women, and I think some people may argue with that, but I would say a porno is definitely that, you know, treating women as sexual objects, kind a just moving onto other women, things like that. I think subliminally that may affect you that you think that's alright to act like that, or you do act like that, or you see something that happens and, you know, it makes it alright for you to try that sort of thing.

This athlete's beliefs were supported by findings from a 2004 *Pornified/Harris* poll involving 2,555 U. S. adults that was conducted exclusively for Pamela Paul's book, *Pornified: How Pornography is Damaging Our Lives, Our Relationships, and Our Families.*[15] Results from this poll revealed that pornography does, in fact, impact real women because nearly 50% of Americans, including more women (58%) than men (37%), thought pornography was demeaning to females; 51% of Americans also believed that pornography raised expectations of how women should look while 48% thought it changed men's expectations of how women should behave.[16]

Along with its negative impact on women, research has also challenged various misconceptions concerning pornography's clandestine effects on intimate relationships. After repeated exposure to pornographic films, one study revealed that both male and female research subjects became less satisfied with their partners' physical appearance, levels of affection, and sexual performance.[17] More recent findings from the 2004 *Elle*-MSNBC.com survey supported these discoveries by revealing that as a result of viewing online pornography, 10% of men admitted to becoming more critical of their partner's body, 10% of men said that he or his partner had become bored with their sexual practices, and 17% noted that viewing pornography made sex less arousing for them.[18] Indeed, such findings highlight both the harmful effects on relationships as well as the difficulty in trying to compete with pornographic images of highly paid professionals who sell their physical attributes along with their sexual prowess. Prolonged use of pornography also produced greater acceptance of extramarital sex (i.e., cheating), a strengthened belief in male and female promiscuity, male dominance, female servitude, doubts regarding the value of marriage, and a decreased desire to have children.[19]

The 2004 *Elle*-MSNBC.com survey also supported certain findings by revealing that while nearly 60% of women believed their partner was using The Internet for sex, 30% of the men admitted that they go online with the desire to cheat on their wives or girlfriends through the use of pornography, online dating, or sexual chat rooms.[20] Certainly online dating that results in physical intimacies constitutes cheating while the use of pornography and sexual chat rooms involve definite gray areas for many individuals. Although indeed controversial, many consider pornography to be a form of cheating because of the time, money, sexual energy, and focus spent on sexual entertainment and companionship that involves someone or something other than their partner.[21] Such issues were further examined as well as substantiated in the 2004 Pornified/Harris poll because 54% of conservatives compared to 30% of liberals thought pornography harmed intimate male-female relationships while 39% conservatives and 15% of liberals saw pornography as cheating.[22] Together, these findings provide a better understanding of how pornography can negatively impact the stability of intimate and monogamous relationships.

One of the less obvious but equally harmful effects of compulsive pornography use is that it can cause adherents to become numb to the pleasures of traditional sex.[23] This means that frequent users learn to prefer the company of pornographic images over face-to-face sexual intimacies, and this can lead to sexual insecurities, disinterest, and major sexual dysfunctions that destroy relationships and are difficult to overcome.[24] I know this type of situation was devastating to one female acquaintance because her husband had developed an addiction to pornography during his professional athletic career unbeknownst to her. Ultimately, this resulted in his sexual dysfunction as well as a quick demise of their new marriage. It is apparent that this phenomenon occurs because heavy users become so accustomed to experiencing sexual arousal through pornography that in time, they can lose their ability to become aroused through actual partners.[25] At the same time, compulsive users also require more intense pornographic images, which can involve an array of darker fetishes, child pornography, sadomasochism, group sex, and bestiality, in order to become sexually aroused because the images that once satisfied them, lose their impact.[26] Findings from the 2004 *Elle*-MSNBC. com-survey supported this by revealing that nearly 25% of the men admitted that they were afraid that they were "over-stimulating" themselves with online sex which could result in becoming sexually desensitized as well as dysfunctional.[27]

On the other extreme, individuals may try to pressure partners into engaging in typical pornographic behaviors that are learned and often rejected by females partners; this can include ejaculating on a woman's face or body and coercing them into engaging in group or anal sex.[28] Moreover, certain participants in this study including a minor league hockey player supported these notions in this way:

> ...I get a tendency actually to mimic some of the people who are in those movies and some of the things they are doing. They even got names for some [sexual acts]...there is a name for everything...everyone knows who all the [porn] stars were...and all that. I mean to what degree it motivated you to...actually go ahead and do something? I don't know, but...I am sure it influenced some bizarre happenings during lovemaking, but I personally don't think it promoted violence or anything like that, but it certainly promoted new positions and new experiences.

This participant noted his own tendency to imitate the sexually deviant, but not aggressive, behaviors that he observed in porn films which means pornography acted as a salient teacher for him. Social learning principles reveal that behaviors are learned directly from observing influential models (e.g., parents, peers, athletes, or porn stars) provided the behaviors are rewarded and perceived as useful to the observer.[29] However, because pornographic themes stress male performance, hurried non-sensual interactions, conquest over pleasure, little or no emotional intimacy, and women as submissive sexual objects deriving all their pleasure from male domination, such unhealthy, unrealistic images make for poor sex education particularly among those raised with little education about sexuality or where sex was treated as a "taboo."[30]

Furthermore, researchers discovered pornography emerged as the second most important source of sexual information – second only to peers, although subjects who reported learning more information from pornography also held attitudes more supportive of violence against women.[31] In the end, it is evident that pornography can act as a teaching tool, although the greatest concern involves the type of learning that is being conveyed and whether pornography influences the actual use of sexual aggression with women.

PORNOGRAPHY AS A SEXUAL ADDICTION

Psychotherapy insights conclude that a variety of sexual practices including the use of pornography can become compulsive and addictive in the same way that drugs and gambling produce out-of-control behaviors enslaving those who use them.[32] The phenomenon of sexual addiction gained national attention among elite-level athletes in 1988 when Hall of Fame baseball player Wade Boggs asserted that he was a sex addict after his former mistress, Margo Adams, filed a multimillion-dollar palimony lawsuit which was later settled out of court.[33] Therapists often agree that addiction exists when sexual behaviors negatively impact the user's work, family, relationships, finances, health, and well-being despite recurrent attempts to stop the activity.[34] In this way, sexual addiction is commonly defined through compelling, consuming, and out-of-control behavior that is met with denial to the seriousness of sexual activities which continue in spite of their harmful consequences.[35] Approximately 4% of the participants in this study inferred or revealed their own potential sexual addictions in one form or another while other athletes noted possible addictions in the making among teammates during their careers.

Using a sample of 100 men with paraphilias and paraphilia-related disorders (i.e., engaging in uncommon types of sexual expression), Dr. Martin Kafka noted the influence of pornography as he focused on creating a universal definition for hypersexuality (i.e., defined as an excessive, insatiable sex drive).[36] On average, the subjects reported spending one to two hours each day engaged in sexual fantasies and sexual release behaviors in the previous six months which related to their eccentric sexual activities that began between the ages of 19 and 21.[37] The most common unconventional behaviors included compulsive masturbation (67% of the men), long-term promiscuity (56%), and dependence on pornography (41%) while the most common paraphilias were exhibitionism (35% of men with paraphilias), voyeurism (27%), and pedophilia (25%).[38]

Despite abundant and compelling clinical evidence, neither sexual compulsivity nor sexual dependence, which form the basis for sexual addiction, are found in the current *Diagnostic and Statistical Manual of Mental Disorders (DSM-IV-TR)* although compulsive sexual behaviors are vaguely described under the category of Sexual Disorder Not Otherwise Specified.[39] This may be attributed to the lack of expert agreement in adequately defining sexual compulsivity and dependency since this type of addiction does not involve a substance such as alcohol or physical withdrawal symptoms.[40] Nevertheless, treatment, support groups, and recovery regimens such as 12-step programs, closely resemble established procedures that successfully assist alcoholics as well as drug and gambling addicts to recovery and normal functioning lives.[41] The best estimates of sexual addiction place the prevalence at 3-6% in the general population, and one study of 932 sex addicts revealed that for 90% of men and 77% of women, pornography played a significant role in their addiction.[42] Various participants in this study including an NFL player and a minor league baseball player discussed pornography as an addictive influence in this way:

...you know pornography's a huge problem in our society today, and I mean you've got pornography addictions just like you have got drug and alcohol addictions...it's kind of accepted [by] men, you know we tend to think of pornography as somehow you know a part of masculinity, which is one of one of the great lies of today...it's a cultural problem, it's not a sports problem...you know we've got over a million pornography sites on The Internet so to say, "Can a coach do something?" I don't think [so], I think it starts with mom and dad, I think it starts with the leaders, I think they can be of help, yes...[but] to blame it on sports, no, I think it's much broader and much deeper than that.

Addiction has to do with sexual deviancy...but that's just the behavior that is frowned upon as opposed to the addiction, I mean we have about eight different addictions and people don't have a real appreciation for what that really means to a person who is addicted to something whether it's tobacco, nicotine, or sex, drugs, food, alcohol, gambling oh yes...too much emphasis on the self, too much interest on the dollar and greed... and there's a lot of criticism about athletes making all this money and being so out of control...again it goes back to the family, how are they prepared to make a transition from poverty to prosperity?...[and] I just want to emphasize that pornography has a lot to do with what we see in sports, what we see in families, what we see in school, and how we see people dress seductively, particularly the teenagers, I think we need to get rid of the cliché, "Sex sells" – sex provokes, sex is very destructive because we just need to educate our people about sex education, I know we don't allow that to be taught in school because it's taboo, yet we as a country... we just spend so much money on pornography, it's just so interesting to see the confusion around sex and how it is portrayed and how it's treated and in a very destructive and unhealthy way, I think that if we come to grips with that, we could start addressing the issues regarding aggressive sexual behaviors in sports as well as in families, schools, and you know in jobs...I think we have to look at it in a different way and be honest with ourselves because it's not going to go away, it's just going to get worse and worse, but you know this country is so hung up on economics, making money, and that's the problem...too much money is made on sex.

The second participant, as an addictions specialist, believed that sexual addiction was responsible for a variety of sexually deviant and aggressive behaviors, and pornography happened to be one of the major underlying causes of sexual addiction. Furthermore, this participant believed that until sexual addiction was properly addressed rather than focusing on an individual's sexually deviant behaviors reported in the media, the problem would not be uprooted at its core and, in time, would only grow worse. Addictions by their very nature are subtle and insidious to the point that those becoming addicted are not even aware of the extent of their problem because peer groups normalize deviant behavior so that it is not identified or confronted while denial shields compulsive users from recognizing their excessive behavior.[43] This enables the line between the so-called recreational user and the more compulsive pornography consumer to become blurred and easily overlooked. In this way, various sexual behaviors become the drug of choice that provides relief from pain or stress, and like an alcoholic, a sex addict's behavior often continues to escalate to include more twisted fetishes in an effort to sustain the "high" in spite of serious negative consequences.[44] Interestingly, an NFL player discussed pornography's sinister and addictive influence in his life in this way:

Oh that was more in the pros, I mean we would literally...be in a position where when we made a road trip, you know before we would get on the plane, we had guys that would stop at the gift shops at the airport and buy, you know, a *Penthouse* or that would read them on the way out and then have them for the way back I guess as well...[but] I mean today you're talking about between The Internet, between cable TV, and things like that, you know, it's much more accessible...you know as far as and even when I engaged in that, you know, it wasn't a matter of being around my buddies, it was..."I'm at home tonight and you know one happens to come on, and on it goes"...there's a computer I have at home that I have to stay off of because you know, you know I've had different sites...it had no firewalls...[and] I got to stay off of it because, you know, if I get on that computer, I'll find myself heading to the porn...

This participant described his and his teammates' use of pornography during his professional career as well as his current struggle to avoid pornography's addictive influence in his life. Today, because pornography is all too accessible and affordable, it becomes a real challenge for those trying to avoid its constant presence because pornography comes looking for users through The Internet.[45] While researchers discovered most of the online sexuality involved exploration or recreational use without negative consequences, subjects who spent 11 hours or more in weekly online sexual pursuits (some reported spending more than 50 hours) showed signs of psychological distress and admitted that their behavior interfered with some area(s) of their lives.[46] Results from the 2004 *Elle*-MSNBC.com survey revealed that problems can develop with even less time dedicated to online sexual pursuits because 45% of men, who viewed Internet pornography for five or more hours per week, admitted they were masturbating too much, 35% found real sex with a women less arousing, 20% admitted that real sex did not compare to cybersex anymore, and 37% said pornography took time away from their work and the time previously devoted to family.[47] Furthermore, researchers noted that if 8% of the previous study's compulsive cyberporn users were generalized to the 184 million U.S. adults who use The Internet today, a startling 15 million people, not counting teenagers, could be at risk for cyberporn sexual addiction.[48] Indeed, there is ample support for Dr. Jennifer Schneider's belief that The Internet is the crack cocaine of sexual addiction.[49] Finally, because pornography can entice sex addicts to take their behaviors offline by hiring prostitutes, attending strip and swingers clubs, exposing themselves in public, and sexually assaulting women and children, this means there is the potential for public harm to accompany the personal and family devastation such addictions produce.[50]

No one begins using drugs, alcohol, or pornography recreationally with the intention of becoming addicted although certain sexual behaviors can grow in time to become full-fledged addictions particularly when they are strongly reinforced through the physical and psychological "highs" accompanying these activities. Unfortunately, addicts usually must hit "rock bottom" before they are willing to seek treatment and recovery, and this means acknowledging that the pain they are experiencing and causing outweighs their euphoria.[51] Such addictions provide more formidable challenges that are intensified when peer groups within sports cultures participate in addictive behaviors together.

MALE BONDING THROUGH PORNOGRAPHY

Athletes develop solid friendships with teammates and strong bonds through discussions about women both in and out of the locker room (although these conversations frequently depict women as sexual objects who only exist for men's pleasure).[52] With women and sex as constant topics of discussion, it was no surprise to discover males bonding through the use of pornography. Such bonding rituals are not new since they were first observed among ordinary groups of men, who would get together to watch the 12-minute, 35-millimeter stag films that featured prostitutes having sex with men recruited from bars, who disguised themselves with fake mustaches and masks.[53] The technical incompetence of these early pornographic films made them a humorous, social bonding event rather than an occasion for solitary masturbation that video/DVDs would later allow.[54] *The Hite Report on Men and Male Sexuality* also revealed pornography acted as a male bonding event which enabled men to lust over pornographic pictures as a form of entertainment.[55] Similar bonding events in this study were encouraged within certain athletic teams as one minor league football player recalled by saying, "In college...if we were winning, on Friday the day before our game in our meeting...someone would bring in a new one [pornographic movie] every week, yea." While collegiate coaches used pornography to bond and motivate their athletes in the late 1990s, a minor league hockey player in this study along with findings from Laura Robinson's book, *Crossing the Line: Violence and Sexual Assault in Canada's National Sport,* revealed comparable events among Canadian youth hockey teams.[56] In the latter, pornography magazines were also used as incentives since the more victories the team had, the more pornography was distributed to the players.[57] As a result, collegiate and adolescent athletes receive poor messages from influential role models condoning the use of pornography, which ultimately promote false, degrading images of females, who as sexual objects, desire to be raped and penetrated in an array of sexually deviant ways.[58] Other participants including a minor league basketball player recalled bonding through pornography:

> Sometimes...guys might have some porn with them or look at some porn websites on the road, you know from their personal computers sometimes, and when that would happen, a lot of times that would be something for the guys as a collective group – you know a lot of times guys would share – you know three, four, five guys around you know looking at some website...

This participant found bonding through pornography much more common among collegiate teammates compared to minor leaguers who often lacked community on his teams, although other minor leaguers from football and baseball discussed contrasting experiences in this way:

> ...a guy played with the [XXX NFL team], got rings with the [NFL team], he was at it just like watching game tape [laughing] and the guy would walk in, you know, six o'clock in the morning and that was what we watched first, we'd watch pornos before we'd go out there on the field [laughing] cause that was like, you know, building team camaraderie I guess, we all watched pornos together.

...one guy who's a high profile guy right now [laughing]...his room was the porn room in spring training and I guess when everybody was done, we couldn't have alcohol in our rooms with the [particular MLB team/ organization]...I mean we get it and we would end up with some, but we would have lookouts just to make sure nobody came around because we weren't supposed to have it, and we would go to this guy's room, and he was the porn guy, and we would drink some beers down there and watch his porn movies and...really the only time that I know that the group of guys got together to watch these porn movies and drink beer...I mean we'd go, we'd laugh, we'd drink, and then we got out of there.

The previous participants described pornography as a bonding mechanism among their professional teammates, and this camaraderie was perhaps enhanced even more in the second narrative because players knew they were risking consequences for their actions particularly when it involved alcohol consumption during spring training. While pornography promoted athlete bonding, this could include non-athletes as a minor league football player noted by saying, "I will say this, in college that existed with both athletes and non-athletes, I guess that was the one thing that brought us all closer together [laughing]." For college males living in the dormitory, pornography became a shared activity and common topic of conversation that enabled non-athletes and athletes to bond with one another since their focus of attention centered on objectifying females who were engaged in sex.

In addition, some athletes take their desire to enhance camaraderie to more unusual levels, and this was apparent when one collegiate hockey player noted his collegiate team compensating for not being allowed to watch pornography on their team bus, for example:

We weren't really allowed to do it on the bus [but] we'd have...a game we'd play when we come back on road trips usually late on Saturday night after the bars are closing, three in the morning or so and coach would let us go and buy beer, but we'd have to keep it underneath the bus, so we'd have it for when we'd get back. And...it wasn't uncommon if we'd go and buy...10 cases of beer...and what we would do is have a 30-pack race. And we'd put...a porno or...a scene of a porno on and we had to finish the 30-pack [30 beers]...before the [the male porn star] guy would ejaculate on the porno...certain scenes were quick and you kind of had to go [drink] fast. It was fun and...we had maybe 18, 19 guys there, [so] you don't have the whole compliment of 30 [players]... and you'd have your group there, laughing your ass off while you're doing it...it had to be scenes where it was just one [porn actor] guy too or it would be an unfair advantage for the team [laughs]...if there were two [porn actor] guys on there. And most of the time we had seen the movie before so we would know when he [the porn actor] was going to go [ejaculate]. We'd put the ticker on too, so we'd know from the timer how much time we had...

The previous participant noted that approximately two thirds of his team would show up late night to participate in a competitive drinking event that involved pornography, team bonding, camaraderie, and perhaps some peer pressure as well. Furthermore, it is apparent that these activities were normalized within this team's culture because the players knew exactly how much time they had to finish their "30 pack" since they were all too familiar with the pornography scenes and its accompanying binge drinking. While male bonding through pornography can be potentially harmful to the male viewers, researchers also discovered that pornography influenced groups of high school male athletes and college fraternity members to engage in increasingly deviant, decadent, and sexually aggressive behaviors with females.[59] In this way, pornography served as a "how to" guide that was linked to a variety of sexually deviant group behaviors including group sexual assaults targeting high school and college females.[60] Interestingly, certain participants in this study including two collegiate hockey players discussed these notions in this way:

I've never really thought about it before, but I'm sure now that you bring it up, that you do see things like that happening, so I think it would be an influence [on sexual deviancy]. You know, it's never been like, "Hey let's do this because we saw it in a porno," but I'm sure it facilitates it because you do see other things like that happening maybe in a surreal world, but a porno, it does make it more acceptable to you. I think it would have an influence on you.

I don't want to be a porn star you know, but...when you see something on a porn, maybe I'm going to try that tomorrow or tonight when I bring a girl home. I think a lot of ideas come, where we get these ideas, comes from that. They're not natural, some of the things we tried to do. Like the two-on-ones, the three-on-ones, whatever. You see it in porn movies and everyone wants to be a porn star so, I think it has a big influence [on sexual deviancy]...I think it's the stuff you've heard about, stuff you've seen – the porno stuff, or guys' older brothers have done and told them about it. It's kind of like [the] legends you hear. You hear things that go on and you're always trying to try it out for yourself – because that's what everyone tells you about.

Both participants as heavy pornography users were convinced that this material influenced deviant sexual behaviors because constantly watching demeaning acts made them "more acceptable" in addition to providing "a lot of ideas" for personal and/or group experimentation with women. Furthermore, these players' insights were supported by an array of researchers who discovered clear evidence that sexual assaults were related to the use of violent and degrading pornography and membership in a peer support group which sexually objectified women.[61] Research involving 71 self-reported date rapists revealed that when compared to a group of non-aggressive college males, offenders were part of a highly erotic peer group which began in middle and high school.[62] Indeed, pornography as a source of male bonding has a clandestine, insidious side that can be harmful to both males, who may become sexually violent, and females who are victimized. Finally, pornography's influence on group sexual deviancy and aggression extends beyond peer group bonding to include individual sexual aggression as well.

PORNOGRAPHY AS A SOURCE OF SEXUAL AGGRESSION

Pornography is classified as hard-core whenever explicit images of genitals are shown whereas soft-core illustrations stop short of revealing genitals.[63] Hard- and soft-core pornography are further separated into additional categories that may include: (1) erotica which consists of respectful, affectionate, and pleasurable portrayals of mutual sexual interactions; (2) degrading pornography which objectifies, degrades, and humiliates its subjects; (3) and violent pornography which involves aggression and brutality in the form of rape, beatings, and murder.[64] Sexual themes involving high levels of violence (i.e., choking, punching, kicking, bondage, torture, and weapons) generally account for less than 10% of sexually explicit videos and magazines, although one comprehensive review of porn magazines found almost 25% contained a paraphilia act of which sadomasochism (i.e., sexual domination and submission practices) was by far the most common type.[65] Similar themes ranging from verbal aggression to torture and mutilation appeared in 27% of pornographic videos while Internet newsgroups (Usenet) revealed almost 50% of the sex scenes displayed high or extreme sexual violence that targeted mostly women.[66] Moreover, such findings make the question of whether pornography influences the use of sexual aggression against women an important one that was addressed by a minor league baseball player in this way:

> I think one of the underlying factors to aggressive sexual behavior is pornography. This country here spends approximately $6-$60 billion a year on pornography, not necessarily hard-core, but soft-core pornography as well, for example it's used in selling clothes, it's used in selling home appliances, it's used to sell cars, and promoting alcohol. Now since we have The Internet, it's just out of control, but then you

have to look at the other part of it, you know, is it addiction for a lot of people? Or is it entertainment? Or recreation? Or if it's become obsessive and compulsive, we know that those are signs of addiction. And if it's used as a way to exploit people to buy a product, or to participate in a market where it is money involved, that has to be factored into it, but it has to be something [addressed]...within the home. I think that if an athlete has a solid foundation, it is unlikely that he will participate in devious sexual activities when he is not at home, or away, I think the probability of that to happen is very, very low, but pornography has a lot to do with it [aggression], and we just spend too much money on pornography as a country.

While pornography and sexual aggression were clearly linked in this participant's view, pornography supporters are quick to deny claims that porn is harmful to women by pointing to a few studies that failed to support a direct cause and effect relationship between viewing pornography and male initiated violence against women.[67] However, these advocates overlook the fact that an even larger body of research provides considerable evidence that men who view pornography are more dangerous than men who do not.[68] Various studies revealed that after watching violent sexually explicit films, many of the male subjects were less sympathetic toward female rape victims, believed females were more responsible for being assaulted, displayed increased hostility toward women in the lab, and indicated a greater likelihood that they would commit rape themselves if they were certain they would not get caught.[69] Moreover, a collegiate hockey player from this study supported these findings in this way:

...just about every guy I know watches porn, you know big, big stack at my house...[and] I know guys who want to try...every guy wants to try what they saw in a porn...[and] I think if they're abusive and they're people who...have these cravings for any kind of violence, and they sort of watch this sort of thing, they're going to want to try it, you know with a girl.

The previous participant believed that aggressive men, including athletes, were more likely to use sexual force after watching violent pornography particularly because certain viewers like to imitate what they see. Research supports these views by revealing that men, who were at high risk for committing sexual aggression and reported very high use of pornography, were much more likely to have engaged in sexual aggression (approximately four times higher) compared to men who used pornography less frequently.[70] While heavy pornography use may be a symptom of a compulsion or addiction, it could also be the catalyst and "tipping point" that in some cases changes an individual's unexpressed desire into actual behavior.[71] This is not surprising given the research efforts during the late 1960s and early 1970s that led a majority of researchers and the surgeon general to conclude that excessive television violence increases the likelihood that at least some of the viewers will behave more violently.[72] The media's influence on violence became strikingly evident when a civil lawsuit was brought against NBC alleging that a gang rape portrayal in a television movie, *Born Innocent,* resulted in some juveniles committing a "copycat" rape against their female victim.[73] Because ethical constraints prevent researchers from creating experimental conditions that might increase serious aggression through exposing subjects to large doses of violent pornography to determine if some men commit rape, experimentation to study the direct effects of pornography can only be performed in a very limited manner.[74]

In addition, research findings suggest that television shows or PG-rated films promoting rape in a positive manner could be much more detrimental than X-rated movies that do not show sexual violence since the amount of sexual explicitness may be less important than the message conveyed by the sexual aggression.[75] The classic movie, *Gone with the Wind,* provides one such illustration promoting sexual aggression inadvertently because after Rhett Butler became sexually forceful with Scarlet O'Hara, she is later shown smiling and feeling content.[76] And in 1978, the daytime soap opera *General Hospital* became the model for disgraceful characterization of rape because Luke and Laura's initial sexual involvement occurred when he raped her.[77] Furthermore, the show used this event and the couple's ensuing relationship to expand the audience to include younger fans while it promoted a poor message to impressionable viewers.[78] Thus, positive rape portrayals depicted through movies, television, and pornography desensitize men to the seriousness of this crime while increasing men's acceptance of rape myths which include beliefs that women secretly desire to be raped even though they resist, drunk women and prostitutes cannot be raped, women are responsible for being raped, and only a stranger with a weapon can commit rape.[79] In the end, it is more than apparent that pornography can influence certain men to engage in sexually aggressive behavior with women, and because many elite-level sports demand their athletes develop an ultra aggressive nature in order to promote success, certain athletes are at-risk for participating in sexual aggression particularly when they frequently use degrading, violent pornography and begin to accept the harmful messages it contains.

PORNOGRAPHY, THE INTERNET, AND CHILDREN

Athletes' frequent use of pornography, which can encourage sexual aggression, is certainly alarming, and even more disturbing is the fact that athletes and coaches have been implicated for their use of child pornography and sexual predatory behaviors targeting children. The sale, production, and distribution of sexually explicit material involving children under the age of 18 are illegal in the United States under numerous federal and state laws, and therefore, it is excluded from First Amendment protection of freedom of speech.[80] Most American consumers and especially commercial producers of pornography are careful to avoid any association with child pornography because severe legal consequences for a first time offense can carry up to 10 years imprisonment and a $100,000 fine; participating parents and/or guardians can be sentenced 20 years to life in prison.[81] Despite such constraints, The Internet has caused a surge in child pornography making it a $20 billion per year industry worldwide, and it is estimated that over 100,000 pornographic websites contain at least some illegal material involving children.[82]

Although participants in this study were not specifically asked about athletes' use of child pornography, athletes and coaches have experienced legal ramifications for their association with it. For example, John David Burnes, a 20 year-old member of the 2008 Canadian Olympic Archery Team and aspiring medical student, was arrested and charged with possession and making available child pornography in February of 2009 along with 31 others who were part of an Ontario-wide child pornography sweep.[83] The overall investigation rescued two victims – a 4-year-old boy and a 12-year-old girl – from homes where sexual acts involving children and even infants were being made, recorded, and distributed.[84]

In a similar fashion, Harrison Zolnierczyk and fellow Canadian junior hockey teammate, Bradley Harding, were charged with the production, distribution, and accessing of child pornography after they secretly videotaped a sex act with Harding's 17-year-old girlfriend in the fall of 2006 and subsequently downloaded it onto an Internet website.[85] The video was allegedly played in the team's dressing room which prompted one player to notify the victim.[86] The Alberni Valley owners and coaching staff released Harding, a utility forward, when the child porn charges arose while Zolnierczyk, who was later named most valuable player, was allowed to remain on the roster.[87] The next season, 20-year-old Zolnierczyk received a hockey scholarship to the prestigious Ivy League Brown University, and not surprisingly, Brown's coaches and university officials were aware of Zolnierczyk's charges and still allowed him to play in 16 games during the 2007-08 season.[88] It was only when the story broke after Zolnierczyk failed to appear in court that he was dismissed from the team for the season, but was allowed to remain enrolled in the university.[89] In the summer of 2008, Zolnierczyk and Harding both pleaded guilty to two counts of electric voyeurism and were sentenced in a Vancouver Island courtroom to a conditional discharge and three years' probation; Harding was ordered to undergo court-directed counseling and perform 150 hours of community service.[90] Canadian prosecutor, Gordon Baines, noted the charges in this case for the production, distribution, and accessing of child porn carried a minimum sentence of 90 days in jail and a maximum sentence of 18 months prison time while voyeurism charges carried a minimum sentence of discharge without criminal record and a maximum sentence of six months jail time.[91] However, because the athletes' original charges involving child pornography were dramatically reduced, the overall consequences for this crime amounted to nothing more than a slap on the wrist compared to the pain, betrayal, and humiliation the underage female victim experienced. It is evident that the Canadian legal system as well as the coaches, team, and university officials in this case are guilty of sending a very poor message to athletes and countless others regarding the seriousness of sexual offenses by allowing Zolnierczyk to continue his career with little interruption while administering few deterring consequences to both athletes in the process.

Likewise, coaches have also been implicated for their use of child pornography although the punishment for these crimes in the United States can be much more severe. For example, 40-year-old Brian Hindson, the former Kokomo High School swim coach and chief executive of Central Indiana Aquatics, admitted to using hidden cameras to videotape girls in their locker room.[92] Hindson secretly videotaped his female high school athletes while they undressed over a 10-year period, and these images along with other files containing minors engaging in sexually explicit behaviors were found on a computer he sold as well as in his home.[93] This resulted in Hindson being sentenced in October of 2008 to more than 33 years in federal prison on 16 counts of child pornography.[94]

Dr. William L. Marshall compared rapists, incest and non-incest child molesters, and non-offenders in their use of hardcore pornography and found that most groups of sexual offenders used pornography more than non-offenders and offenders often reported using pornography to instigate their crimes.[95] Another study revealed that as adults, child molesters used more pornography than adult rapists, and they were more likely to include pornography in their sexual offending by viewing photographs before engaging in contact with their victims.[96] Additional compelling evidence that possessing child pornography involved more than simply viewing images was highlighted in a 2009 study of 155 convicted child pornography sex offenders who participated in a specific treatment program at a medium-security federal prison.[97] At the time of their sentencing, 74% of the subjects had no documented victims while 26% with known histories of engaging in child sexual abuse produced a total of 75 victims (1.88 victims per offender).[98] Following completion of the program, 85% of the group admitted to engaging in at least one hands-on sex offense and the overall number of victims had increased to a total of 1,777 (13.56 victims per offender).[99] This dramatic increase of 2,369% challenged the assertion that child pornography offenders "only look at pictures" while simultaneously revealing that many offenders conceal and/or minimize the full extent of their sex crimes against children.[100]

In addition, it is extremely disturbing that athletes and coaches have been discovered using The Internet to engage in online sexual predatory behaviors targeting underage females, and some have been severely punished for their poor judgment. For example, former collegiate baseball star and Chicago State University assistant coach, Brandon Candiano, was sentenced in May of 2006 to 82 months in prison for using a computer chat room to solicit sex from what he thought were two underage girls.[101] Prosecutors showed that the 24-year-old Candiano tried to lure the seemingly unsupervised females into meeting him for sex during a 48-minute exchange of emails.[102] More recently, 25-year-old Matthew Hensley, a former varsity and junior varsity girls assistant basketball coach, was one of 14 Indiana men (24 in all), who was apprehended as part of an extensive Internet-predator undercover operation, for attempting to induce, entice, and coerce sex from federal agents posing as 13-year-old girls on The Internet.[103] Hensley was convicted in January of 2008 for using multiple Internet identities in an attempt to have sex with underage girls online, and this resulted in a conviction of slightly more than the 10-year minimum prison sentence.[104] That same month, Howard University's head soccer coach, Joseph Okoh age 40, was also arrested and charged with using the Internet to solicit sex from someone he thought was a 13-year-old female; Okoh was found guilty in November of 2008 by a jury who recommended a 14-year prison sentence after he drove to have a sexual encounter with what he believed was an underage female who turned out to be police officers.[105]

Coaches have also preyed upon young male athletes they have coached in a variety of sports and at all levels.[106] One notable case involved former NHL hockey player, Sheldon Kennedy, who was sexually abused from age 14-19 along with other players by his Canadian junior coach Graham James; James pleaded guilty in 1997 to over 350 counts and was sentenced to only three and a half years in a Canadian prison.[107] Upon his release from prison, James continued his youth hockey coaching career in Europe for awhile because he was banned for life from coaching in Canada.[108] Similar allegations involving the sexual abuse of young boys, who were not athletes, surfaced in November of 2011 when former Penn State University football coach, Jerry Sandusky, was charged with 40 counts of sexually abusing young boys over a period of 15 years; Sandusky met the alleged victims through a charitable organization for disadvantaged children that he founded called the Second Mile.[109] In the end, it is an unfortunate reality that some athletes and coaches use their influence as role models and teachers to become sexual predators who target male and female children in a variety of ways until they are exposed and stopped.

EXPLAINING LOWER PORNOGRAPHY CONSUMPTION

Despite the higher prevalence of pornography cited among a majority of participants, pornography consumption was not a common activity among all collegiate and professional athletes. Some athletes noted religious convictions kept them from using pornography while others cited a lack of interest or money or involvement in an intimate relationship. Other participants including a collegiate wrestler/football player noted teammates in both sports were extremely homophobic, and since no one wanted to be considered "degenerate," this made pornography a taboo. One minor league basketball player elaborated by saying, "Male basketball players just aren't going to sit up there in the room and watch porn – by themselves, yes – with a group of guys, no – that's seen as gay, that's homosexual, no, we're not doing that, there has to be some women involved." It is evident that although homophobia prevented certain teammates from bonding through the use of pornography, this was not the case for others who previously revealed pornography was a large part of their camaraderie. One collegiate basketball player recalled a different activity that occupied many basketball teammates' as well as football players' time by saying, "[Pornographic] magazines and videos weren't something that was just prevalent [and] around, not very often...we gambled all the time, that's all we did." While athletes who gambled appeared to be substituting pornography for another vice that is arguably just as addictive, it is apparent within the previous disclosures that group norms had the final say in dictating the different behaviors that promoted group acceptance or ridicule and rejection.

In addition, some participants revealed that pictures and films depicting naked females were not satisfying, and this caused many to seek the company of live women in one way or another. For example, a wrestler noted, "I don't think there was too much of the porn stuff going on...because like I said, I mean you know you got the real thing on campus." As a result, certain athletes spent their time and energy trying to meet and pick-up women at bars or parties where "there would be tons of girls." Ultimately, having sex was the goal rather than simply watching as another wrestler noted by saying, "I would actually think that athletes are less prone to pornography [laughs] because to put it lightly, they probably have sex more often [laughs] than non-athletes." These notions were particularly emphasized among certain major leaguers including one NBA player revealed:

> I think [porn] it'd be more prevalent like in high school, in college some, but once you become a professional athlete and you see and do some of the things that you do, those magazines don't do it anymore, that's just for hooks and for people that don't actually get any action I guess, when you're a professional athlete, you don't have to worry about magazines that's for sure.

The previous participant found pornography was unnecessary because high female availability at the major league level enabled athletes to experience what others only imagined through pornography. A different NBA player revealed yet another alternative to viewing pornographic material by saying, "No I would say we never had to watch videos and whatever in the pros cause…we'd always just go to a strip bar, so you could see it live, why watch it on tape." As a result, collegiate and professional athletes with access and resources often preferred the company of live women and exotic dancers over pornographic images, and some athletes' fondness for female strip clubs promoted additional opportunities for male bonding and an array of potential problems that will be discussed.

ATHLETES' CORNER: POINTS TO PONDER

1. Despite its widespread prevalence, pornography is not the harmless activity many believe. As a teaching instrument, pornography conveys an array of negative messages impacting women, children, relationships, and individual behavior in detrimental ways. Pornography has been linked to sexual abuse and aggression because certain users try to imitate what they see. This has resulted in harm for victims while sexual predators have suffered harsh legal consequences which have impacted their athletic careers and lives.

2. Certain athletes use pornography to bond with one another even though this pursuit has created peer groups that encourage participation in sexually deviant and aggressive behaviors. Pornography is not in business to promote healthy attitudes and behaviors because its images and information degrade, demean, and harm more often than not. Know that choosing to walk with a herd that engages in unhealthy behavior increases the likelihood of stepping in its residual "dung" sooner or later. Avoid the company of deviant peers who have the potential to take you down because they will.

3. Addiction happens over time through repetitive behaviors that eventually take over someone's will without announcement. Group consensus enables harmful behaviors to appear normal, and this allows addictive behaviors to grow and dominate a person's life. Know that harmful behaviors can easily become out of control, which means addictions must be confronted or they will escalate and produce devastation that impacts multiple areas of life. Personal excellence requires a disciplined mindset that takes no vacations because negative influences are forever trying to infiltrate the mind and gain a stronghold on thinking processes which in time impact behavior.

Chapter 3
Athletes and Women in the Sex Industry

ATHLETES AND STRIP CLUBS

In addition to pornography, another aspect of the highly profitable sex industry is exotic dancing. In 1967, 7,000 strippers worked in the United States and by 1998, this number increased to approximately 250,000 employed in some 2,500 clubs.[1] Today, there are about 3,600 strip or gentlemen's clubs nationwide, and the estimated $14 billion per year Americans spend in such establishments is a figure that supersedes Hollywood estimates of annual movie ticket sales by over $5 billion.[2] Because dancers can earn $600 a day or more, there is no shortage of competition among the estimated 2,500 dancers in cities like Las Vegas, Nevada although this number can increase considerably during big conventions and the busy season.[3]

Strip clubs provide individuals, including athletes, with the opportunity to observe naked females dancing in sexually provocative ways which can occur through personal lap dances upon special request. During lap dances, the "no touching" rule explicitly posted in clubs is often totally ignored as the women dance on patrons' laps, rub their breasts in the men's faces, and even kiss some on the mouth.[4] This occurs because dancers are all too aware that additional tips and dances are often contingent on the physical contact they provide to clients. The popularity of strip clubs was further highlighted by the fact that almost 95% of the participants in this study were able to discuss their own and/or their teammates' strip club experiences during their collegiate or professional careers.

My experience with strip clubs occurred during my junior hockey career in Quebec, Canada when teammates began regularly attending the establishment in our particular town since underage players were granted entry without any problem. Some players began attending on a bi-weekly basis and because the women were constantly rotated within a strip-club circuit, there were always new faces and bodies to observe. Since this was my first and only experience attending a strip club, it was eye-opening for me as an 18-year-old who had only heard stories about such establishments. While the "no touching" rule was strictly enforced at this particular club as one of my teammates discovered, this is very different from the blatant sexual contact that can occur between a customer and a female stripper during such off-stage dances at clubs today. Years later as a collegiate coach, I was aware of my players' strip club attendance in cities outside the university, and this also occurred on one occasion with other coaches during a team road trip. In addition, my work as an instructor at summer hockey camps for 25 years put me in contact with numerous collegiate and professional athletes and coaches who would discuss their attendance at the town's local strip club which was both accessible and affordable. In the end, my experiences are consistent with the numerous athletes representing every sport and level of competition in this study who support the industry of strippers and strip clubs even though this can result in its own unique set of problems.

COLLEGIATE ATHLETES' STRIP CLUB ATTENDANCE

Academic responsibilities, being underage, strict team rules, fear of consequences, and the lack of money and/or access to clubs influenced collegiate athletes' strip club attendance during collegiate careers spanning the early 1970s through 2010 much more than professional athletes. And yet, these obstacles did not deter all collegiate athletes' attendance because an NFL and a current minor league football player who both played in college during the new millennium estimated that about 30% of their teammates attended strip clubs. Another minor league football player elaborated by saying, "I mean I think it's just exactly the same as the general population...some guys [go] more often than others, some guys are going you know every week, some guys will go once a year, some guys will go twice a year." While this player, like others, noted a range of attendance among athletes and non-athletes alike, some participants, including a collegiate football player, noted higher rates of athlete attendance in the 2000s by saying, "Oh god, there was guys there every weekend, at least some guy there every frickin weekend." Another minor league football player revealing an even higher attendance noted, "Oh I'd say quite a bit...hitting the strip club at least once a week [in college]."

Like the football players, wrestlers discussed a range of strip club attendance which could also be frequent as one participant recalled, "I'd say every weekend you know we'd go check them out...there were at the time maybe four or five, so we'd try a new place just to see what the girls looked like...more out of curiosity than anything else." Because the dancers were more focused on making money than socializing solely with wrestlers, boredom prompted these athletes to move onto more desirable venues. Another wrestler revealed, "We went quite a bit just because they had a good special at $10 all you can drink, the whole night. A lot of guys just hit it up for that reason...out-of-season... some guys went two to three times a week." Unlike the previous athletes, these wrestlers were content with drinking to excess while watching the dancers, and therefore, were not affected by any lack of social interaction with the women.

Similar to the previous athletes, a minor league basketball player revealed his experiences by saying, "That was probably more our thing...we went to a couple of strip clubs...and get all fired up and I'd say once every couple of weeks." Another minor leaguer recalled, "It really depended on the guy, there were some guys who really liked to go to the strip clubs, and then there were some who never went...I would say maybe out of 12 [basketball] guys, maybe you would get like three or four in college who would go maybe once or twice a month." Despite an age difference of over 25 years as these players competed collegiately during the early 1970s and the late 1990s, it is evident that little has changed over the past 30-40 years regarding some collegiate athletes' strip club attendance since both reported similar bi-monthly attendance.

Various participants also noted how strip club attendance often related to special circumstances that one minor league basketball player recalled by saying, "In college every chance they get, but they don't get too many chances...it'd be a special occasion...you know if it's someone's birthday party or something like that." Moreover, other participants including a minor league baseball player and a collegiate football player further elaborated on other types of circumstances that encouraged collegiate athletes' strip club attendance:

There wasn't a strip club in our town in college so you had to go about 50 miles to the nearest strip club so it wasn't that prevalent in college, you had guys who would do it for sure, you know on a weekend here, weekend there out of season, [but] summer ball is where a lot of that happens, so you know within my college years, it was during summer baseball where, you know, you're living let's say in a junior college dormitory playing ball in a town that's away from your parents, away from your college coach, you're playing with a bunch of guys that you really don't know all that well, you get to know them over the course of the summer and, you know, there happens to be...a strip club, a Deja Vu, or whatever within a couple miles...then you know that would be a fairly frequent thing cause you don't have class...you have your games but usually not an authority figure there, you're kind of expected to be, you know, learning to become an adult – supposedly.

...the football players will frequent the strip clubs – especially during the bowl games...because when you go down to a bowl game they give you spending money right? And...it's usually a couple hundred bucks, and then they provide you at the bowl game with free transportation usually back and forth to wherever you want to go, and so that's just like, "Okay we got this time, we don't have to be up for awhile tomorrow morning," and guys they just go and shit, I've been to plenty of them I mean, but...it's definitely because like they provide you with money – like play money almost – and guys go out and fucking you know live it up at the strip clubs. It's like almost at a bowl game, like one of the first couple of nights, it's almost designated that the whole team will go to a strip club or most of the guys, or a big group will go, but the whole team's probably a little exaggerated, but there's definitely at least a group of 20 going.

One minor league football player recounted how he and his college teammates took special care to avoid any problems that could occur inside the strip clubs because no one wanted to spoil a tradition that was found as readily among collegiate players who played in the mid-1980s as it was among those who competed in 2010.

PROFESSIONAL ATHLETES' ATTENDANCE

Some minor leaguers mentioned low salaries, no nearby clubs, and/or low-level strip clubs stifled their attendance; however, this was in contrast to one minor league baseball player who revealed, "We had two separate groups in the pros, we had just the normal beer drinking guys that went out to the bars looking to pick-up chicks and we had guys who...went to strip clubs, strip clubs were huge...some of the guys on the team [went] three and four times [per week]." While the previous athletes were known for their specific club preferences, an NHL player noted a high rate of club attendance came with a practical motive, "A lot of [minor league] guys like to go to strip clubs, and then there's some guys just on a daily basis almost go, and I know some guys, a couple of guys on our team date strippers." This participant was one of a number of athletes from different sports who noted players dating strippers, and this prompted frequent club visits from numerous teammates, and in some cases coaches, who gathered together for informal "team meetings." Longtime Dallas Cowboys safety, Ray Horton, even noted that position meetings were sometimes held at strip clubs during his NFL career.[5] It is apparent that some coaches, including those I have worked with or played for, saw no problem with their players' attending strip clubs even though such outings can involve heavy alcohol consumption, late nights, and all kinds of trouble. Furthermore, frequenting strip clubs with players could definitely impact a coach's credibility with some players and particularly if a coach attempted to impose stricter discipline at some point in the season.

In addition, a minor league football player recalled his experiences by saying, "Oh shit, we hit them all the time, and...[in] professional oh shit...about eight, nine times a week I mean that can happen, you never know, I mean everybody go to strip clubs, everybody got their favorite...especially if you're in a nice city." It is apparent that some athletes frequented strip clubs in the afternoons and the evenings when their schedules permitted, and a minor league basketball player supported this by saying, "A lot, a lot...basketball guys up here lived there it would seem." Interestingly, a minor league baseball player revealing the highest rate of attendance explained why his teammates seemed to live at the strip club:

> It'd happen – I wouldn't say rarely...[because] when we played minor leagues...actually they put us up in a hotel right next to a strip club, which is pretty wild when you think about that. They kind a knew what they were doing there...in the morning, they had [food]...when it opened up, and then like guys were there at night, for lunch, it was convenient you know...the fact that they could just walk over there and get something to eat plus there was...more to it than that...

Like the minor league players, major leaguers also discussed their strip club experiences including one MLB player who revealed, "I was never a strip club guy [but] I did play with guys throughout minor and major leagues who loved the strip bars and were you know going to them you know two, three, four nights a week to see the girls and hang out and have a party." Although this participant found attendance was more common in his minor league career because players were younger and shared more travel time together, most MLB players thought otherwise because of the expense and accompanying perks. For example, one MLB player explained, "I think it was almost advertised, you know we'll come and pick you up in a limo, we'll take you to a private room," and this prompted "a quarter of the guys" to attend "fairly regularly" while "a few more would do it occasionally." Another MLB player noted, "They're treated VIP – which I think the ego plays a part of it where you walk into there and basically you know here's your section, here's whatever you want and...I think athletes feed on that stuff."

Similar to MLB players, an NHL player noted, "A lot in pros...I think both [in minor and majors]" while another revealed, "I would probably say 30% of the guys consistently [go], there's probably a 30% group that would go the majority of the time when they had an opportunity – especially on the road, now I would probably say that number bumps up to be half of the league frequents them, you know, when they're on the road." Another NHL player explained the allure of strip clubs on road trips in this way:

> I think it was kind of like a ritual in certain cities...I remember being a rookie and...everyone said, "Ok we're meeting at eight o'clock, everyone's going to be there," and the guys I guess went to the famous strip joints I never heard of until I got in the NHL, and that kind of died out as my career went on, it wasn't a big deal to go out."

This was in contrast to an NBA player who revealed, "Oh every city we went to…yea, you know [in] the pros, guys couldn't wait to get into the next city, you know…'I'll meet you back down in the lobby in 15 minutes, you know call a cab, let's head to, you know, some of the more famous and renown strip clubs.'" In addition, two major leaguers from the NBA and NFL elaborated on athletes' attachment to strip clubs in this way:

Oh it was huge that – not so much in college again, because you have to watch, you know, where you go and a lot of people know who you are, so you try to stay away from it in college, and as a professional, I mean it happens daily, nightly, it's just a place to go to hang out where… money's exchanged, there's women there, and there's drinking, and the fact that it's nude women I mean it goes on, yes it happens I mean everybody in the pros does it, they hang out there, that's a primary location.

See cause half your college career you're not 21…so it's not really big in college, but in the pros I mean it's a way of life for a lot of guys – a way of life, I mean that's how they spend their afternoons, they'll go get a couple of drinks, tip someone, and then go home to your wife, you know what I mean that's kind of like a norm. For example, we went on road trips you know that's what we would do, I mean we would find out where the top strip club was whatever, or where a strip club in the hood was, and we'd get in our track shoes and go down to the hood, tip someone, you know have a drink, and then be back in the hotel by curfew, I mean that was the norm, you know that was the norm in the pros…shit, I know guys that would go every damn day, I know guys that would go five days a week you know, and then I know guys like, you know, that would go once a week just for entertainment purposes, but guys go five days a week, I mean they'd go to where they'd know everybody by name you know what I mean, check into the VIP sections and stuff like that, getting drinks without paying for them at this point in time, yea I know guys like that no doubt.

Professionals in all sports noted a higher prevalence of strip club attendance compared to collegiate athletes because they had more time and money to afford this pastime, which was particularly evident during road trips. It is possible that road trips encouraged attendance because players were less recognizable and shared greater camaraderie with teammates while they were away from their wives and families. In addition, strip clubs provided major leaguers with a pampered atmosphere that was preferable to spending time in a hotel room. Major leaguers noting a lower prevalence of attendance cited the desire to avoid tarnishing their personal, family, or team's reputation while chartered flights and more serious pre-game preparation curtailed other players' attendance. In the end, it is apparent that numerous athletes spend large amounts of time in strip clubs during minor and major league careers spanning the mid-1970s through 2010 although this does not occur without its share of problems.

WHEN STRIP CLUB VISITS GO AWRY

Like pornography usage, the practice of hiring strippers and/or attending strip clubs has the potential to create its own unique set of problems that negatively influence the lives and careers of athletes and coaches at all levels. This was evident when various collegiate coaches including men's golf coach Brad Neher at the University of Colorado as well as Duke University lacrosse coach Mike Pressler lost their jobs in 2006 because of players' unsanctioned strip club visits or other stripper-related controversies.[6] New York University's golf coach Jay Donovan noted he was forced to resign in fall of 2006 after he accompanied his players to a strip club while they were competing in Florida, because the visit was inconsistent with the athletic department's highest standards of good judgment.[7]

At the professional level, NFL cornerback Adam "Packman" Jones of the Tennessee Titans and NBA swingman Stephen Jackson of the Golden State Warriors had involvement in late-night brawls/shooting incidences at strip clubs, and this was a major factor for Jones' season-long suspension from the NFL in 2007.[8] The combination of alcohol and egos create a fertile setting for an array of potential problems to occur in these emotionally charged environments, and various participants in this study commented on the problems that could result from attending strip clubs. For example, a minor league baseball player noted that because visiting strip clubs often required travel, "you really don't want to be drinking and driving...[since] the odds of you getting busted in a college town, in a college area, is so much bigger." Furthermore, while some coaches condone strip clubs, this was not always the case as a collegiate basketball player recalled by saying, "There was some strip clubs but the thing was, we wouldn't go to those because again, we were too high profile and everyone knew everyone of us in town there, so you didn't want any of that getting back to the coach... we would have been punished, you know physically or something." Indeed, a coach's demeanor can impact players' behaviors provided the discipline is strong and consistent. In addition, a collegiate baseball player revealed, "Especially because you're kind of like a profile guy and I think if you were off campus, you were more likely to get in trouble...you know out at the strip clubs." While this participant suggested that athletes' popularity could create jealousy and result in conflict with other male patrons, one minor league baseball player detailed a distressing strip club experience:

...I do know that in my minor league career, there was one guy's birthday one time and probably 8-10 of us probably went to a strip bar, and to me it's places like that...[which] get people that either hang out there for the wrong reasons, whatever the wrong reason might be, [but] there's trouble going to happen there so and sure enough... trouble happened that time so I just never went to them...the guy that's birthday it was reached out and touched one of the dancers, and at the time I was up top talking to a bouncer I think and he left me and ran down there and sat him down and he [the player] insisted on, it was his birthday he wanted to touch it or touch her, and they ended up kicking him out and he kind of flipped a little bit and when he [went] out the door, he pushed a − it was a double swing glass door and it came off the hinge, and they called the cops and next thing you know all of our guys that are with us are spread out running, trying to keep away from the cops cause they know they'd be in trouble cause there was a curfew in the minor leagues, and they were all breaking curfew and ended up I think six out of the eight ended up getting an escort home, the police and the manager was called, and that was all of us down in like a conference room and talked to us...you know there was fines for missing curfew...I know a couple of guys got released later and not far after that, that was a bad time to do it for those guys, for all of us actually, but more so for them guys cause they were borderline ball players and it was right before the draft and once the draft came out and they drafted players, pretty soon two or three of them were gone. Minor league professional relations don't like troublesome guys and I was embarrassed for the way that I was involved with it, not that I did anything wrong, actually I was back before curfew, but you know I was in an embarrassing situation and having to be associated with a bad thing like that, but you know it didn't hurt my career, I kept going on and I learned from it.

What began as a seemingly innocent birthday celebration quickly turned into a negative chain of events that caused an array of problems. Because this participant's baseball organization had little tolerance for minor leaguers getting into embarrassing trouble, they sent a strong message that he would later use to teach valuable lessons to his players as a current collegiate coach.

THE HIDDEN COSTS OF STRIP CLUBS

Like pornography, strip clubs have a darker side that can be just as addictive, if not more so, because they involve live, naked women as one minor league basketball player observed:

On the pro level that's probably a form of natural entertainment for a lot of people so I think on the pro level that happens, can happen you know three times a week...and I think that it becomes addictive...I've seen it become addictive for guys, who like I said, they're in a strip club three times a week and...even more.

No one begins attending strip clubs with the intention of becoming addicted to them, and yet this participant observed its occurrence firsthand among teammates during his professional career. Previous player narratives revealed that numerous athletes could be on a similar path to addiction because their strip club attendance was often two or three times per day. Moreover, one consequence of addiction is the toll that it takes on a person's finances, and this was evident to one minor league baseball player who observed certain teammates' problematic spending by saying, "Some of the younger guys that's what they would blow their fucking pay on, you know they'd go to [the] strip, the strip club you know." A minor league football player also noted, "Professionally...pretty much the last two years, the guys in our team man, that's where they go, that's where they spend their money." Similar notions pointing to addiction were supported by various investigators who found that some patrons would spend their whole paycheck in a single night at a strip club, and one dancer actually returned the $800 she earned one evening from doing lap dances for a regular customer when she found out the money was taken from his children's college fund.[9] During his 17-year major league baseball career, Jose Canseco also noted that professional athletes were relentless in their pursuit of exotic dancers, and some would spend more than $10,000 a night on lap dances, private rooms, and alcohol.[10] Indeed, strip club addictions have hidden costs and consequences that cause athletes and non-athletes alike to take valuable time and resources away from their female partners and/or children on a regular basis. And because untreated addictions often escalate in intensity, these problems become more and more apparent and pronounced as time goes on and resources continue to disappear.

DAMAGING REPUTATIONS AND RELATIONSHIPS

Some athletes live with an attitude that they are going to live it up by partying as much as possible during their elite-level careers. A current professional hockey coach noted certain players rationalizing such behaviors by saying, "Hey, I'm only in this world once, and I'm going to do it my way and that's how I'm going to do it." Moreover, athletes' life in the fast lane, which involved frequent strip clubbing, occurred among numerous athletes at all levels including those who competed for their National and/or Olympic team. For example, one wrestler noted, "Not a whole lot cause in [college], there wasn't any back there then...

[afterwards] that was pretty prevalent yea, especially on away trips, road trips, guys would just be off and go to strip clubs" while another revealed, "Whatever city we were in or whatever country we were in, you definitely found out...where the bars were and where the strip clubs were." It is apparent that these high profile wrestlers, like numerous major leaguers, were not overly concerned with the possibility that frequent strip club attendance in whatever city, or country, they happened to be competing in could negatively impact their athletic careers by tarnishing their individual, team, or even country's reputation. This notion was highlighted by one minor league hockey player, who despite an extremely successful playing career that included competing for his country's national team and winning numerous championships at the junior and professional level, realized that the reason he was repeatedly denied the opportunity to scout or coach professionally was because his off-ice behavior tarnished his character and credibility to the point that colleagues who could have hired him, chose not to. Consequently, some athletes come to realize and regret, though often too late, that participating in certain behaviors, including frequent strip clubbing, can negatively impact personal and team reputations as well as their well-being because some establishments put athletes in contact with a host of negative influences including alcohol, drugs, violence, and extramarital sex, which do nothing to enhance athletic careers or reputations.[11] Various athletes including an NFL and a MLB player elaborated on these notions in this way:

> ...in all my time with the [XXX NFL team], I can remember going to one and the majority of the time playing eight ball and it was actually because on Thursday nights we would go out as a group and we decided to go to some place in [the city]...and I think guys, as much as anything else, I mean guys were more reluctant at least to go to some of those places because you don't want that necessarily – I don't know how it gets reported – I'm surprised guys do that now, they're stupid enough to put themselves in positions that get the negative publicity with reporters and people watching everywhere.

> ...the last thing you want...is to be seen out in public at a place like this when you're married with children...when you're single, you have carte blanche to do whatever you want, you're married and you have kids, you know as I said you have to really watch it because when you're a professional athlete, you're a public figure and people will talk and...if you don't really have much self-worth for yourself, you don't mind that the word gets around that you hang around at a strip club...that's your choice, but I don't know of too many guys that feel that way.

One of the more blatant negative effects that strip club visits have is on relationships with family members and especially partners because the excessive time spent away from home is spent in the company of attractive, naked women. In time, this can take its toll on athlete marriages and lead to affairs as well as divorce because strip clubs bring out "the worst" behaviors in men and women including greed and lust according to Nicole Berti, author of *A Face in the Crowd: My Life as an NFL Wife.*[12] This was evident when Joumana Kidd, the estranged wife of NBA star Jason Kidd of the New Jersey Nets, filed a counterclaim for divorce in 2007 and blamed her husband's extramarital affairs with strip club dancers from five different states were responsible for helping to end their 10-year marriage.[13] Former Dallas Cowboys' cornerback Clayton Holmes's marriage similarly ended in divorce after his wife found him in a strip club while he was high on drugs and in the company of a woman who was performing a multitude of sexual acts on him.[14]

While not all athletes' sexual encounters or extramarital affairs with strippers end in divorce, these situations can create family conflict whenever a wife discovers her husband's indiscriminant behavior and subsequently confronts it.[15] In his book, *Public Heroes, Private Felons,* author Jeff Benedict revealed that this was the case with former Minnesota Vikings star quarterback, Warren Moon, whose physically violent dispute with his wife allegedly occurred after one of Moon's repeated infidelities with various females, including exotic dancers, was discovered.[16] In the end, some athletes come to the realization that their decision to discard wives and children in favor of short-lived excesses with exotic dancers was regretful because sometimes it caused permanent relational damage.[17]

WHEN ENTERTAINMENT TURNS INTO ABUSE

Although numerous collegiate athletes enjoy their visits to strip clubs, some prefer to hire exotic dancers and bring them into personal residences during larger gatherings or special events. This enables males with no access or limited resources to enjoy the company of naked females in a cost-effective way and in the privacy of someone's nearby home. Two collegiate football players discussed these practices in this way:

> ...they'd like order the strippers to come to their house...that's like a special occasion type of deal like if somebody's having like a twenty-first birthday or...it's like the end of the season or something that probably only happened maybe like a couple of times during the year.

> ...in college it was kind of expensive, usually...what we did is part of the fraternity, the pledges, would throw a party for the brothers and at that time there would be a stripper, we'd hire a stripper to come to our house

and that was usually the way it would happen...usually once or twice a year, you know, it was kind of like the big group thing at the house.

These types of situations can pose risks that can include different types of abuse for both the athletes and especially the dancer who is a vulnerable target among a group of males who are often intoxicated. A minor league baseball player recalled one such experience in which intoxication did not factor into the event; for example:

> We had a skit show that we had to do and it was like all of the first year players in spring training had to do a skit in front of the other players and...the coaches and everybody was there – one guy did juggling and told a joke, that's how simple as it could be, but a bunch of guys got together and they got a stripper and they brought her in and did *The Jerry Springer Show* and this was the nastiest girl I'd ever seen in my life, I mean she looked like she was just beat up, and I think that they were doing it just to make fun of her and it was a good laugh...because they knew she was pretty nasty, I don't know where they got her [from] during that.

While the previous situation could be considered emotionally abusive and in poor taste, a minor league hockey player discussed his observation of an even more serious physical assault on a female stripper:

> Okay last week, we went to bachelor party with old friends, past [college] hockey teams, and set-up a night with a couple of strippers for the bachelor. We got them for like two hours. For the first hour, everything was fine. People continued to drink and have a good time and one of the former ice hockey players tried to get a little side action with one of the girls. Took her into the bathroom and she was dancing on the toilet. He was touching her and a couple of us were watching. He just proceeded to bite down on her nipple. Just bit at it and it cut her. It cut her on the top and the bottom of her nipple. And she proceeded to scream at him and punch at him back, and it became a little bit of an issue. She ran out, grabbed her clothes, and said that he didn't know how to treat women. She called that one out and said that she wasn't going to do the rest of the show. So, that's exactly what happened... they were doing a dyke show. That's what they were building on. They were built as two girls; they had these long suckers, these lollipop suckers. They were putting them in each other and really had the crowd going. It was pretty exciting and this guy proceeded to get a little side action and give her a little extra money. And obviously she was a stripper and she was going to do it for him, but she wasn't expecting for him to

bite down like that...there was a laceration. There was blood on both sides, the top and bottom of her areola, I guess you could say. She said that she was going to have to take this up with us later because her insurance might not cover [a] hepatitis shot and all the necessary stuff she'd have to go through. The morning she woke up she never thought that this was going to happen tonight. She was very upset and she did have to go to the emergency room...it was a bachelor party and ruined the whole evening because she bolted. Other people had to go too [as] we got them from a friend and we had to make sure she was okay. It was just a big melee, it sucked.

This player continued to elaborate on the situation while discussing a variety of reactions to the event in this way:

...when that guy bit into the breast of the stripper, it was really sick. It was a violent act, and she definitely was hurting. Everybody else there basically had, at least one time in their life, played hockey. They were athletes...[and] they were upset with him. They were appalled. They apologized. They were embarrassed. Right now that kid is the buffoon. He's an absolute idiot for doing that. It was wrong...first of all, it ruined an hour of stripping [laughs] – and that's wrong – completely wrong. And second of all, this girl was injured...she's bleeding, it's just nasty...I felt bad for her. It was a sobering experience. Everybody was like, "Holy shit! This guy just..." It was nasty. You just don't do that to anybody. Whatever, she's a stripper; she's there for fun, but you can't beat her up or anything...his eyes were closed and he just bit her. I watched it happen. It was really disgusting. It was violent...and I never want that to happen again. But everybody recognized it as being wrong...so afterwards, she got dressed. We had two rooms rented and she went to the other room. It was just myself, another guy, and the two strippers. They were both very livid – talking about getting hepatitis shots, how they had to go to...how one emergency room was faster than the other...they didn't want to go to downtown [city], they wanted to go to [a nearby state]. It was just sick. She was showing us. She actually took her top up, and it was continually bleeding on her shirt. She was like, "Look at my fucking tit, like it's just blood. What kind of sick-o would do something like that?" Some other people came in and witnessed it and it was just sick. I can't believe he was even invited to the party.

Despite the obvious sexual objectification of these women, this player along with the other athletes recognized their friend's assault was both wrong and violent. This is an excellent example of how a peer group can provide punishment for behaviors they considered wrong because it was apparent that the offender was instantly unpopular, verbally reprimanded, and ostracized by the others. Furthermore, this incident made the woman question why someone would act violently against her in an unprovoked manner. This player was posed the very same question, and he attempted to explain the aggressor's motive for biting the woman in this way:

> ...I couldn't even tell you what motivated him to do it. It definitely wasn't the male ego thing. Maybe he was just so drunk or it was his fetish I don't know...I don't know – tough to tell. I think he had some drinks in him. Maybe he was living out a little bit of a fantasy or something like that...I couldn't see how he wasn't trying to hurt her – I mean he bit her pretty hard, especially to cut the skin like that. To break the skin – I don't know what his motive was but he just bit down all in one motion and chomped down on her breast. It was pretty sick.

Women in the male entertainment industry are often marginalized and viewed as sexual objects, and therefore can be subjected to abusive conduct.[18] This also explained why another minor league hockey player recalled that two female strippers' hired performance included a large male body guard who was there to protect them.

WHEN STRIPPERS TARGET ATHLETES

While the previous narratives described athletes' participation in emotionally and physically abusive behavior that targeted exotic dancers, sometimes athletes can be on the receiving end of abusive situations as one minor league hockey player discussed in this way:

> I was about 15. First time it ever kicked it off for me – you know in [XXX] you're allowed to get into nudie bars when you're like 16. Legally you're not, but they'll let you in. My first experience with group sex was with two feature strippers that were dancing. They were movie caliber women. They were porn stars. I mean, I was all young and innocent and they happened to pinpoint me out in there one night. They took me upstairs and both of them did it. I was like, shit, what am I going to do. I was just a little kid basically [laughs]. I mean, they were 23 at the time I thought these are older women, this is pretty sweet [laughs]. That was the first time and from there on out...for many years that was...almost like the trying to get back [to] your first high with drugs. You're just trying to get back to it again every time [laughs]. So you start messing with two girls, then three girls and it's not enough, you have to have four or five around you. I mean, that kind of thing. And that's what started it for me, and

it wasn't even my doing. It was just a lucky situation…well, I shouldn't say lucky, but for a lot of guys it sounds like a lucky situation. You know, [when] you're approached by two beautiful women.

This player was asked to elaborate on how his experience had been initiated, and he responded:

They were flirting with me all week because I was in there all week drinking. Because they were that good-looking, I had been there all week with a buddy and we'd hang out after and talk to them. They'd hang out longer than usual. They started out…in the beginning…taking pictures with me downstairs and stuff like that. And pretty soon they were taking off all of their clothes and taking pictures with me. And then they got to the point where they were like, "What are you doing tomorrow during the day, before we start dancing again?" "Oh…I can't do nothing, you know I've got a girlfriend." "Well, just come back in tomorrow night and we'll be here." So I did. And one night I went back in there and that was it. Both of them took me upstairs. Because what happened was both of them wanted to take me out, but neither of them wanted to piss the other off, so it got to the point where [they thought], "We'll just both do him then." That was kind of how that one took off and that was the first one… and then it was just a down hill slide from there [laughs]…

This player implied that because he was not able to find subsequent sexual experiences that compared to the memory of this early experience, it drove him to pursue more and more group sexual encounters almost as an obsession. Since every new sexual experience fell short of his expectations, this athlete felt as if he were chasing the memory of his early experience in the same way drug users chase the high they originally experienced the first time they used drugs. Although the word "lucky" was tentatively used to describe his early sexual experience which was in fact sexual abuse, it also provoked an addictive pattern of behavior that was perhaps in need of intervention. Indeed, sex with older females is not the delightful male rite of passage once believed, but rather sexual abuse that victimizes anywhere from 9%-25% of males and is related to the sexual risk-taking behaviors previously noted as well as earlier onset of sexual intercourse, more frequent sexual intercourse, and less frequent use of contraceptives.[19] Even more dangerous is the fact that men experiencing childhood sexual abuse were also more likely to commit a sexual assault as an adult compared to men who were not abused as children.[20] Overall, men commit at least 90% of child sexual abuse and although girls are sexually abused three times as often as boys, boys are more likely to be seriously harmed or killed during such assaults.[21] Even though childhood sexual abuse information was not collected from the participants in my study, one has to wonder how many of the athletes participating in sexually deviant and/or aggressive behavior experienced sexual victimization themselves as children. In short, these findings shed interesting information on the ramifications of childhood sexual abuse as an unwitting catalyst for male athlete participation in sexual deviancy and aggression.

Minors are not the only targets of female strippers because a former topless dancer falsely accused former Dallas Cowboys Michael Irvin, Erik Williams, and an unidentified third man of a gang rape in 1996.[22] Similar events gained national attention at the collegiate level in the spring of 2006 when the Duke University lacrosse team hired two female strippers for $400 each, and one of the women falsely accused team members of kidnapping and gang rape.[23] This resulted in a series of events that included the university forcing the resignation of team coach Mike Pressler, cancellation of the lacrosse season, university suspensions for two of the three accused players (one player had already graduated), persecution for the players and their families, and estimated legal fees for each of the accused totaling more than $100,000 per month.[24] Despite poor evidence that a crime had actually been committed, District Attorney Mike Nifong pressed forward in this case seeing it as an opportunity to gain votes during an election year.[25] Ultimately, Nifong's unethical behavior and poor judgment caused him to be removed from the case and his office, stripped of his law license, and sued for malicious prosecution by the accused players who were declared innocent and had all charges dropped.[26]

False accusations involving exotic dancers and athletes appear to be the exception rather than the rule. However, there are instances where an exotic dancer is justified in alerting law enforcement authorities to athletes' criminal activities as one collegiate football player recalled:

...I had a firsthand experience that we had, a situation when I was at [XXX University]...that [involved] a bunch of actually star players and... they were selling marijuana, right? And somehow they're out, and it's pretty big name football players at the school while I was there...they had a stripper come back to their apartment I guess late night after she got off or whatever...and somehow they disrespected her and I don't know, I've never heard the full story...but somehow she, she felt like she was disrespected, so she left and went and got the cops and the cops came back and ended up nailing all these guys...they had a pretty substantial amount of marijuana at their apartment...[and] this one guy actually had to go through some pretty serious legal battles just to stay out of jail...three out of the guys that were involved in that went on to the NFL. Four of the guys actually had to transfer and go to finish up schooling at another place, and then two other guys ended up getting, you know, basically their names stayed out of the paper from being involved in it. One guy took the rap for it..

This female decided to hold these athletes accountable for whatever had transpired by summoning the police to their residence which was filled with a substantial amount of marijuana that the players were distributing. Furthermore, this player was asked if the disrespect involved a sexual assault, and he responded:

...I can't confirm that it was a sexual assault cause, I don't think there was, I don't think in any fashion that [since] nobody got charged on sexual assault, [and] I would imagine she would have. I think they just you know probably they pissed her off in some fashion...I don't know what degree that was, but I don't think it was sexually involved, no.

Working in the male entertainment industry by itself can negatively impact a female's character and credibility during certain legal investigations and court proceedings; however, this had no impact when this woman led police to discover these athletes' drugs.[27] In the end, it is all too apparent that criminal involvement of all kinds before and/or during a career does not prevent many athletes from continuing their careers at the collegiate and/or professional level.[28]

FROM STRIP CLUBS TO SEX CLUBS

Some professional athletes who played abroad as well as those who competed on National teams revealed that overseas strip clubs were a popular attraction for them and their teammates. One minor league basketball player in particular found one of the unexpected attractions was that such clubs were great places to meet English-speaking women who worked as exotic dancers. Another surprise finding appeared when several minor league basketball players described another overseas venue that differed from strip clubs and houses of prostitution and were known as sex clubs. One of the minor leaguers discussed his awareness of sex clubs in this way:

...guys would go just cause there's sex clubs in Europe, so they're a little bit more intense than in strip clubs and...they're actually performing sex acts on the stage which was a lot different than here. It's accepted, I never saw any players actually having sex with any of the performers, but there would be people from the audience that would get involved... [in] intercourse, oral sex, anything that you can imagine would happen on stage.

On-stage sex performances were not limited to overseas establishments because similar practices occurred in rented New York storefronts that were operated by organized crime.[29] In addition, this participant discussed the frequency of him and his teammates' attendance in this way:

> Not very often, I can't even think of a time when the whole team would go – a couple of guys might go and I've walked in one just cause you hear about the bodies and you want to see what's up but again, I wouldn't keep myself in those situations just because I didn't want to be associated with it and have my name set-up in the papers because the papers in Europe are more like our tabloids here – and you just didn't want to be associated with that.

This participant and his teammates were well aware that their attendance at sex clubs could tarnish their individual as well as his team's reputation, and therefore like certain major leaguers who avoided strip clubs for the same reason, these athletes limited their attendance.

WHEN STRIPPERS CROSS THE LINE TO PROSTITUTION

The distinction between female strippers and prostitutes becomes blurred anytime an exotic dancer engages in sex for money. The location where sex takes place is secondary to the behavior since sex can occur at a residence or hotel where a dancer is hired to perform just as easily as sexual acts can happen while women are performing at their club. One female stripper who was interviewed during a study involving five strip clubs discussed exotic dancers who also prostituted themselves in this way:

> "I don't like any of the girls in here and they don't like me. We're all in this for the money, and the more one of us makes, the less there is for the rest. Plus look around at these girls. Most of 'em are nothin' but whores. They come in here, dance naked, give guys hand jobs and blowjobs, and then strut around as if there's nothin' wrong with that. I just don't do that stuff. I'm not that kind of girl. Sure I show my tits, but I come in here, dance, make my money, and go home."[30]

Strippers are in competition for patrons' money and their dislike for one another can stem from the fact that some engage in prostitution which takes money away from those trying to earn it legitimately. Another stripper interviewed from the same study rationalized her prostitution by saying, "This job is just like any other job, or anything in life, for that matter – it's all about sex. Sex sells. The way you move up in corporate America is to sleep your way to the top. In here, if you want to make more money, it's the same. I always say, if you want to get ahead, you've gotta give a little head."[31] Such practices gained national attention in 1999 when Atlanta's highly reputable Gold Club was busted for nearly every crime related to money or sex including prostitution.[32] The story created high-level interest when employees testified that celebrities and professional basketball, baseball, and football players received sexual favors from strippers at the Club.[33] High-profile athletes such as New York Knicks Patrick Ewing and Atlanta Braves Andruw Jones subsequently testified that they had in fact received "special treatment" from strippers at the Gold Club or nearby hotels, and the payment for sex had already been "taken care of."[34]

More recently, author Don Yaeger reported in his book, *It's Not About the Truth: The Untold Story of the Duke Lacrosse Case and the Lives It Shattered,* that some strippers often do anything for money, and this is especially true for those who are considered lower-level dancers commonly referred to "ghetto strippers."[35] Moreover, Crystal Gail Mangum, the stripper who falsely accused the Duke University Lacrosse Team of gang rape, appeared to epitomize these notions because her alleged prostitution, advertised through her stripping, became evident when semen from at least four unidentified men were found in her genital region or underwear during DNA testing, which matched no one on Duke's lacrosse team.[36] Indeed, there appears to be a fine line between some strippers and prostitutes that was discovered in this study at the collegiate, minor, and major league level. For example, a minor league baseball player revealed that he and "8-10" of his teammates had yearly parties with "real dancers" who had sex with the players, which included himself, "either one-on-one or right there out in the open" during his recent professional career. Other participants including a collegiate football player, a minor league hockey player, and a MLB player elaborated on their awareness of this phenomenon at each of these levels of competition in the new millennium:

Oh god, I never heard of anybody like going out like to get a hooker or anything, but I have heard of and I don't know if this is considered prostitution, but they'd like order the strippers to come to their house, you know what I'm saying and sometimes like, you know, they said the one guy took the chick upstairs and gave her like a $100 and she you know – they did the deed – but as far as guys like going out to seek out prostitution I've never heard of anybody doing that, but as far as you know calling someone to your house to do a strip show or to do whatever yea, I've heard of guys doing that yea…

…on a road trip in the [AAA minor leagues], we were in this one town for like three or four days and the guys hired a [stripper and/or] prostitute and she came in and I was there, and it was a girl-on-girl show and then it was supposed to end at that, and it proceeded that this one guy had sex with the hooker...and they were asking for more money and then because I'm a cheap ass, I just left, and I remember guys just asking around, "Who's got more money?" and I'm just like, "I'm out you know, see you later."

...the one thing that did happen a few times is you know you have a team party at the end of the year and someone makes some phone calls, and there'd be a few girls that would come in to do a strip act, or you know and end up and I don't know what all would end up happening, but you know for a little bit extra money, there was stuff going on that goes beyond just stripping, and you know that's the type of thing that you know again, you're sitting there and you're at a team party and you've got to make a decision that, you know, this is crossing the line to what I want to be a part of, and then you have to alienate yourself from your team and say, "I'm not going to be part of the team party" or you have to take part in something that you don't want to take part in.

The second participant revealed that "probably a dozen of us" watched one of his professional teammates engage in sex with a female from a "girl-on-girl" show, while the other dancer who appeared to be embarrassed by her partner's actions remained nearby their bodyguard. This participant subsequently discussed other athletes' reactions to this sexual event in this way:

Guys were just like losing it, like they just thought, "I can't believe this was happening," and a lot of the guys were really drunk, and that was probably the two factors that were just [obvious] and even myself, I'm just like, "I can't believe this guy is doing this you know...what the hell's this guy doing you know?"

This participant could not understand why a very skilled athlete, who was married with a child while competing at the highest level of minor league hockey, would jeopardize his health (i.e., risking sexually transmitted diseases including AIDS), relationship and family (i.e., risking relational and family dissolution), and possibly his career (i.e., similar to what transpired when Ervin "Magic" Johnson contracted HIV and lost his NBA career) by having blatant sex with a prostitute. Perhaps this intoxicated athlete engaged in an observable sexual act as a way of asserting his masculinity since this showed teammates he was still in control of his life and could do whatever he pleased despite being married with a family. Similar events occurred in more private settings during wrestlers, hockey, and football players' bachelor parties, however, some of these athletes, including a prospective groom, also experienced personal consequences which made them feel "real guilty" and "like crap" following their sexual involvement with a stripper/prostitute.

The third participant from the previous narratives noted stripper/prostitutes appearing at his major league team's year end parties and because these practices conflicted with his sense of morals, he chose not to attend team functions that he suspected might include stripper/prostitutes. While this participant believed there were teams throughout the league which did not include strippers at their parties, his assumption that other team parties also included them was supported by another MLB player who revealed virtually the same thing.

Strippers/prostitutes were not relegated to servicing individual major leaguers at year end parties because similar events also occurred at informal gatherings or when players went clubbing. Furthermore, they could include group sexual encounters as two NFL players revealed:

> ...I think that one team that I was with, they used to have these – they call them these "gangster parties" on like Monday evenings where they have some strippers come over to the house and do a show and then if guys wanted to, you know, have a private show or whatever then, they'd do that too and you had to pay whatever money for them to do that for you, and I went to those like one time during my pro career, but I ended up leaving early cause I was uncomfortable with what was going on...well I mean I knew they were stripping, but I think it was going to get more drastic than that and I didn't want to be around for that, so I ended up leaving...it wasn't a great percentage at all, I mean it might be like four or five guys.

> ...the situation with me in the pros what happened was we all went out, a bunch of the veteran guys took the younger guys out, so there was probably eight or nine or ten guys, and [they] decided that because I was the young guy, I got to go first, and so she gave me a blow job. I didn't feel comfortable staying and watching her with you know with seven, eight other guys that were going to come behind me, and so I ended up leaving and going home...she wasn't the only girl there right, so there were two other girls that were messing with other guys there, it just happened that with this one girl I was first, and she went on down the line.

It is interesting to note in the first narrative that the players' choice of the word "gangster" in describing a private party appeared to advertise the fact that something gang-related and/or criminal was perhaps on the agenda. This became readily apparent when this participant made a hasty exit after seeing the type of sexual activities that were unfolding. Furthermore, this participant was asked if his teammates engaged in group sex during these parties and he answered, "Quite possibly, but I'm not sure because I wasn't there and when that stuff was going on, if it did...go on, I was gone." Although this participant was evasive in his last statement, his early departure from the party suggested that these particular "gangster" parties included not only stripping but group sex with paid professionals as well. Interestingly, this narrative suggesting the hidden nature of group sex among major leaguers was not the only one of its kind. Similar information from an NBA player as well as a minor league basketball player with nominal NBA experience revealed that major leaguers often kept their involvement in group sexual encounters discreet as this minor leaguer noted, "They're secretive...some people don't know, some people do know, it just depends on how cool you are with the other players."

In contrast, the second participant noted that while he was certain that this female stripper was paid for having group sex, he also revealed, "I know that girls are available to athletes and they're available to multiple athletes at the same time both at the college level and the pro level. Some of the girls are explicitly getting paid for it, other girls just like being around, you know like getting the attention from men." While this participant estimated that "less than 10%" of his collegiate teammates participated in group sex, he also observed that during his recent pro career "probably something like 20%...a half a dozen to 10 guys on every team were into that." Indeed, there is a fine line between some female strippers and prostitutes; however, this mattered little to certain athletes who paid for individual as well as group sex whenever it was available.

A CLOSER EXAMINATION OF ATHLETES AND PROSTITUTES

Prostitutes participate in what is believed to be the world's oldest profession because there is a demand for sexual services.[37] Surveys of U. S. men from the 1990s revealed that 16%-20% paid for sex at some point during their lifetime, and although fewer men today have their first sexual experiences with prostitutes than in the past, former NBA player Dennis Rodman revealed that his first sexual experience at age 20 occurred when he and his friends paid a prostitute $20 for sex.[38] Although the once-common houses of prostitution are legal only in certain counties in Nevada, approximately 84,000 women work each year as full-time prostitutes in the United States, not counting the women who exchange sex for drugs.[39] These numbers are further supplemented because one study revealed 5% of females engaged in part-time or short-term prostitution, and estimates for the number of teenage prostitutes are as high as 2.4 million.[40]

While some athletes noted the use of prostitutes was frowned upon or unnecessary because of a constant supply of females who were very sexually available, others discussed a variety of reasons for using these services. A brief summary of athletes' rationale for using prostitutes that is expanded upon within the next sections included time and cost-efficient sex, peer pressure, satisfying fantasies and curiosity, easy availability and accessibility, desiring a new and/or group sexual experience, building camaraderie, excessive time and alcohol, boredom, sexual anonymity, an acceptable recreational option, lack of rejection because of players' physical size, heightened sex drive, guilt-free no-obligation sex, paying a female to leave their lives after sex, and avoiding "fatal attraction" scenarios with women who would latch onto them.

My first awareness of my teammates' involvement with a prostitute occurred during my freshman year of college, and I will elaborate upon this situation later. I also worked with a coach who sought out prostitution services on at least one occasion while he traveled. In this study, approximately 55% of participants had awareness of athletes' using prostitutes during collegiate and/ or professional playing and/or coaching careers spanning the 1960s through 2010. Furthermore, approximately 6% of the participants engaged in sexual encounters with female prostitutes during their elite-level careers.

COLLEGIATE ATHLETES, OLYMPIANS, AND PROSTITUTES

Collegiate athletes in this study noted a lower prevalence of using prostitutes when compared to minor and major league athletes as a group, and this was understandable given most collegiate athletes' limited financial means and players noting an abundance of sexually available females on college campuses. And yet, contrary to one NBA player's assertion, "Ain't nobody can afford a prostitute in college for the most part," nearly 20% of participants noted awareness of prostitution use among collegiate athletes representing every sport who competed in collegiate careers spanning the 1970s through 2010. For example, a collegiate basketball player recalled, "That may have happened a couple of times…that's something I never did, but I know a couple guys that did do it…again, just to see if you can and is there something different, the mystique." In contrast, a minor league hockey player revealed, "Only once in college yeah – no twice – the guys had rookie night my junior [and] senior year…I went up and hired a hooker, two hookers to come in and give blow jobs to all the rookies, and… other than that, nothing really in college." In addition, two wrestlers discussed their awareness of teammates using prostitutes in this way:

I think over a two-week period we were on the road over Christmas, yeah... [they] just looked in the phone book...two or three guys would go to a hotel and meet them. Most of the time we were in [XXX] and we went down to [XXX]...everybody's getting their own [hooker]. I never participated in that though...prostitutes snuck in and [when] the coach wasn't there.

...I never have, never felt that I had to, needed to have sex, but yeah, I definitely know a lot of athletes who have definitely been with prostitutes...just one-on-one...most of them, I wouldn't say [at the] college, but I would say more of in a city atmosphere...plus there are escorts you can call up and you know have them come over and pay them a fee and have sex with them... ranging from probably about 60 some dollars to you know $180.

Despite their 30-year age difference, both participants revealed their teammates engaging with prostitutes on road trips in the 1970s and in the mid-2000s. While the first participant noted this occurred unbeknownst to their coach, the second thought athletes' higher "sex drive" and not getting the opportunity "to hook up" motivated these practices.

Not all athletes' encounters with prostitutes were one-on-one as a collegiate baseball player noted by saying, "I only know of one time it happened...two guys went out and got one, when we were over in [XXX]...I think [for] $800... one guy was well off." In addition, a minor league baseball player recalled his collegiate teammates' involvement in an even larger, more expensive group sexual encounter with a prostitute that was detailed in this way:

...with a prostitute probably only once...I wasn't there but, you know, obviously you hear stuff, you know...these guys got together and put their money together and...whatever they wanted, she did, you know it was pretty much an all-night situation, they kept her all night and you know as far as I know, they filled all her holes, you know at one time, at one point so...four guys in that...I think it was up around three or four grand yea... some of the guys on the team had money I mean that was the thing, some of them had money – three or four grand (i.e., $3,000 or $4,000).

It is evident that these athletes intended to get their money's worth of group sex during this male-bonding event even if it was at the physical expense of a hired escort. While financial resources tend to limit most collegiate athletes' use of prostitutes, there are always exceptions.

Like the collegiate athletes, Olympic athletes also hired prostitutes as one wrestler discussed his post-collegiate awareness of these practices in this way:

I mean that happened, it wasn't like a group thing where everybody did it, but there'd always be, you know, let's say if there was a group of 20 of us on tour, there'd probably be three or four or maybe two that would venture that way and...let's say there's 10 trips a year, maybe on five of them, two, three, maybe four guys would find that type of club to go to or least inquire.

With up to 20% of Olympic wrestlers seeking out prostitutes for potential sexual encounters during approximately half of their road trips overseas, it is apparent that not all athletes were concerned with the manner in which they represented themselves and their country while competing at tournaments in foreign countries. Moreover, this participant continued to elaborate on his awareness in this way:

...it was to the point where when we traveled, when we went to Europe, we stayed in one particular hotel in [XXX] and when we got there, it was where most of the athletes stayed even the [XXX] athletes and they would know...when we were coming in and what happened was they would wait in the hotel lobby and it wouldn't necessarily be the women, it would be like their brother you know, or their boyfriend, and they would you know talk to us and basically...you know in not so many words saying, "If you want company, you know I have my sister." I mean literally their sister or their girlfriend, you know [to] call, and they give us a number or whatever, or what room are you in, and they would send the girl up you know, so it was kind of strange like that, but that's how, you know like I said...there'd always be one or two guys, you know, three guys that would at least be interested, now if they followed through with it fine, but they would at least inquire about it and try to negotiate, and then you get into your negotiating the price...for whatever they're looking for.

While the above participant noted male civilians from one particular overseas city prostituting their sister or girlfriend, he also explained the reasoning behind these practices in this way:

Well again, I don't think it's just strictly wrestling, I think it's whatever athletes came through there...so I think it was just a matter of making money and they don't have any in [XXX], there's no jobs, I mean it's not like you can work at the Seven-Eleven or anything like that, so I really think that's just about it, I mean when you got you know a family, a grandma, and grand kids, and brothers and sisters all living in a two bedroom apartment...that's got no heat and you know may have running water, you're pretty much going to do whatever it takes to get some extra money...

PROFESSIONAL ATHLETES AND PROSTITUTES

Over 40% of participants representing every sport revealed awareness and/or personal use of prostitutes at the minor league level, and this could occur in spite of players' involvement in committed relationships. For example, a minor league baseball player revealed, "I would say about, for pro ball, about 5-10% of the time" the players wanted casual sex they hired prostitutes because of "sexual fantasies" and "easy accessibility." Moreover, a minor league football player observed, "I know there's a lot of guys on our teams that would go to the red light district and actually, you know, get prostitutes. I know that happened quite a bit" while another said, "That only occurred in the pros in my experience and that was something that happened every week...I knew four guys that did that on a regular basis." This participant also noted frequent use of prostitutes was appealing because sex was treated as a business transaction with clear expectations and because no strings were attached, a player would not feel obligated or guilty to see the female again since he was only interested in an evening of casual sex. In addition, a minor league basketball player observed his overseas teammates using prostitutes by saying, "Certain nights I know a lot, a lot of players would go and...you got whore houses, prostitute houses whatever they call them over there that guys would take advantage of... [and] I knew of certain situations where a guy, guys would go there a couple times a week." This participant found some of his teammates were proud to the point of being boastful for having VIP cards to frequently used "whore houses" even though they were paying to have sex. While various participants including a current minor league football player recalled laughing at teammates who would "pay for ass" because "we feel they shouldn't have to do that," this did not end such practices. Another minor league basketball player recalled his own experience with prostitutes in this way:

> Just the red light district a little bit, but other than that no...yea I've been in there a few times sure...at the time it was 40 guilders which is about $20-$25...I probably would say in total four times, four to five times... cause I was in Europe and it was there as an available option, more so than a necessity...that's not anywhere else in the states...

This participant noted athletes, including himself, using prostitutes as a "recreational" option and because sex was a certainty at the end of the evening rather than a possibility with an unfamiliar woman that was recently met in a bar. While some players used these services at least several times per month and often on road trips perhaps because they were away from their steady female partners and less likely to be discovered, sometimes teammates assisted in setting up an encounter with a prostitute as one minor league hockey player revealed:

...when I was in [the A level minor leagues], there was one guy on our team what he and his wife had turned into a common law marriage...I remember it was his birthday and the bus driver knew and as most truckers know...what truck stops have hookers or prostitutes or things like that. Our whole bus, filled with hockey players, stopped at this rest stop area. Two guys went out...I guess they went out with the bus driver and found the truck that had the prostitutes in it, knocked on the door, made their deal, came back, took this guy who was a veteran. He went and I guess this girl gave him oral sex. And then we're all on the bus and I guess the coach... there was a reporter from the newspaper, and the coach basically threatened the [guy] like, "If any of this gets printed, you're going to have to answer to me." The reporter was like, "I wouldn't even know what to print. I don't think people would believe me if I printed it." Then the next scene of that was that the two guys that went and made the deal they came back, I guess with this guy on their shoulders. He's got a cigarette and sunglasses on. This is pitch black, I don't know like one o'clock in the morning somewhere in god knows where [southern state]. He's got his shades on and...it was just him [with the prostitute], he got on the bus and we took off.

The above participant observed a surprising situation where his coach used intimidation to insure that the newspaper reporter on the bus would not reveal a sexually deviant event he essentially condoned, which involved one of his player's infidelity and illicit activity with a prostitute.

Similarly, over 55% of participants with major league experience representing every sport noted players' use of prostitutes at the major league level, and this included an NHL player who recalled, "I know that for sure that guys did that yes...[more common in] majors [than in the minors]...probably because they didn't have to work for it." A different NHL player revealed, "I'd say you know maybe 15%" of teammates used these services while another NHL player recalled his teammate's rationalization for using prostitutes by saying, "I mean his philosophy was that...by the time you go out and buy someone drinks and waste your time out there...it's going to be x amount of dollars, and so I want to spend x amount of dollars and go get a prostitute...that's how calculated he was with it...[at the] major league level yea."

In addition, a MLB player revealed, "Yes, it's kind of by word of mouth... and it's not like widespread, but it does happen...oh definitely [more common in] major leagues, you don't have enough money in the minor leagues" while another MLB player recalled, "As far as escorts services, it wasn't a lot, but it was certainly there in the minors and the major leagues." Baseball and hockey major leaguers also noted prostitution services could result from hiring various masseuses who provided "additional" favors beyond a massage for a higher fee. Moreover, an NFL player with recent experience noted players' use of prostitutes by saying, "In the pros, a bunch," and he estimated that "probably 10%, 15%" of his teammates used such services. While certain major leaguers from the NFL and NBA in this study noted a lower prevalence of using prostitutes, participants from these sports also admitted that they would not know for certain whether a teammate was with a hired prostitute or a woman he already knew. This was in contrast to certain players from the Dallas Cowboys' dynasty teams of the 1990s who rented a place they called the "White House" because it provided them with "an oasis" where they could go to privately use prostitutes, drugs, and have casual sex with women.[41] Many teams throughout the league reportedly had similar places, although the Dallas Cowboy's "White House" perhaps received the most attention and scrutiny because of the team's success.[42] While such establishments could easily conceal certain players' illicit behaviors from even their teammates, a minor league basketball player offered another explanation for NBA players' lower use of prostitutes which included an alternative practice that was discussed in this way:

> ...in basketball, a lot of the women that the guys are with are on the payroll. They wouldn't say that they're called hoes or escorts, but they are – they're given a sum of money to be available when guys come into town...yea it is [a form of prostitution] – it is, but they would never say they were prostitutes – they would never think of themselves that way – you know they may only see the guy two or three times a year...the guys pay them already, the dude just do it on their own – the whole thing with [the one NBA star] back in the day when his wife was ready to leave him and a woman came out and said that she was with him and that she wanted all his money. She was mad because he cut her off. So that's why the story came out 10 years after the fact. That's the way basketball players tend to do it...what [one NBA player] said about [his teammate] you know, he said he's seen him pay women, pay them off and keep it quiet...that's true, you don't put that out there – you know you don't talk about that stuff – and I know for a fact that from friends of mine...NBA players ya know [will pay] $5,000 to $10,000 per month to females to be available when they call – you have to be available that night when the team comes to town or they'll fly you out to some place...and you come out to them and keep it quiet – as long as they are taken care of, then they're not going to say anything. And that's how the basketball world keeps all if its extracurricular sexuality stuff quiet.

The above participant subsequently revealed that most wives know about players' indiscretions, yet chose not to address it, as long as cheating remained a concealed behavior. However, such arrangements created problems for certain high profile NBA players who were confronted either by an angry woman when she was financially cut-off or by a teammate criticizing another player's behaviors publicly. Such practices blurred the line defining prostitution while perhaps strengthening the argument for using only authentic prostitutes as one NBA player noted by saying, "I've heard guys say that they would do it because they're paying the girl to go away you know what I mean, that way they're going to go away, they don't have to deal with a lot of the drama of you know them hanging around, calling them, wanting to be around the next day or whatever...[more prevalent] in pros...because again for the financial reasons."

Not all professional athletes' encounters with prostitutes were individual because some involved larger groups as an NBA player and a minor league hockey player revealed in this way:

Just once...yea we had landed in the city you know a couple of guys were you know talking about the last time that they were in this particular city, and you know what had happened, and you know...if they had wanted to do it again, so yea, they called and the girls showed up and about, you know an hour or two later and, you know, that was it, you know I didn't participate, but I knew what was happening, so yea... man it was more than one girl so it was four guys, yea four guys...two girls....that was the only time that I can recall...[in] pro.

...we got into [the city] [after] we left [a previous city]...we went to [XXX], we picked up a hooker on the street and...we tried three times to get her in the hotel and hostess kept catching us. So...our bus was parked on the side street so...we got the keys to the bus and we got this hooker in the back and the guys were lined up at the door, down the street. I was running the door. I'd open the door and, "Twenty bucks and okay, you go back there" [chuckles]. At the end of the night it got to where guys were saying, "Well, I haven't got any money, I'll pay you tomorrow." So, I'd be, "Okayyy"...that was just one time, I've never seen anything like that before. That night it was just unbelievable...and then our coach, he was supposed to help with the meal money, said he was going to dole it out the next day...our coach came down and said, "Guys, I don't have any money. I got rolled [robbed] last night." So there we were, we had a day off in [XXX], no money. I mean the first time I ever been in downtown [XXX], and...I'm dead broke...well, I paid her and I collected it, but we still owed her more money because guys said, "I'll pay you tomorrow, I'll pay you tomorrow." And I had IOU's there for 10 guys [laughs]...

The second participant believed that close bonds within any male group – not only among athletes – encouraged such participation, and this suggests that camaraderie as opposed to a particular affiliation influenced some males' decision to engage in group sex with a prostitute. Similar practices were briefly noted in the book, *Out of Their League,* when former NFL linebacker Dave Meggyesy revealed his teammates gathering for what they called "sets" which involved "mass sex scenes" of group sex with several hired prostitutes during the late 1960s.[43] Separate orgies were held among African American as well as Caucasian teammates and reflected the racial divisions of this era.[44] In the end, minor and major league athletes representing every sport in this study were discovered hiring prostitutes for individual as well as group sexual encounters during careers that spanned the 1960s though 2010.

HARMFUL EFFECTS INVOLVING PROSTITUTION

My first awareness of my teammates' use of a prostitute occurred during my freshman year of college. Following Christmas break I was pleasantly surprised to find myself in the line-up because seven of my teammates, including our co-captains, were suspended for a week of practice and the upcoming weekend series.[45] Apparently, during the holiday tournament in another city, my teammates allegedly became involved with a prostitute and following their group sexual encounter decided not to pay her. This prompted the woman, who obviously felt cheated and taken advantage of, to alert the coaching staff to the situation, which resulted in suspensions for "training violations" that were never publicly disclosed.[46] With the exception of the two star athletes and one other player, the remaining offenders soon found themselves being conveniently "phased out" which essentially involved losing their collegiate careers permanently by the start of the next season.

While such consequences sent a strong message that sexual deviancy was unacceptable, it appeared that the more talented players avoided the eventual outcome that the others could not. Therefore, if coaches and administrators are serious about ending deviant behaviors, they must first address this double standard through administering harsh, consistent consequences for all players who are disciplined. Indeed, any actions to the contrary will only perpetuate athlete privilege and cause a loss of respect for coaches and administrators who are guilty of diminishing team excellence through poor disciplinary practices. Even though this event happened 30 years ago, the players and coaches that I contacted had no interest in anonymously discussing its details. This suggests that some are content to keep the darker side of the sports culture hidden particularly when it involves their personal and/or team's deviant behavior. In the end, I am certain that my teammates who lost their collegiate careers would gladly decline involvement if they could go back in time and change their behavior as well as the consequences they experienced.

Not all athletes are content in just using prostitutes because some desire greater involvement although this carries its own set of consequences. For example, one minor league football player revealed, "I know of from another team that a guy was running a prostitution ring...but pretty much the gist of the story was this guy had a group of girls and...pretty much was their pimp and got arrested for it and I believe went to jail a little while for it and unfortunately...was still back in the [minor league] now."

Like pornography and strip club attendance, sexual involvement with prostitutes has a darker side because it involves potentially addictive practices that were highlighted by a minor league basketball player:

> Well I think that yea, in the pros that happens a lot because...guys don't like commitment, but they love free sex and I think that happens because they can afford to do it, and I think that it becomes addictive which I've seen it become addictive for guys who like I said they're in a strip club three times a week, and you know they're at the sex club twice a week or even more if they have an opportunity...

While sex clubs could refer to establishments involving live on-stage sex acts, this participant was referring to his teammates' potentially addictive use of prostitutes at European brothels which he observed during his overseas career. Similar findings suggesting possible addiction were discovered in a study of U.S. men because 93% of the sample had contact with a prostitute at least once a month.[47] This potentially compulsive behavior was even more surprising when viewed in combination with another study that revealed only one third of the men who used female prostitutes enjoyed the sex and 57% reported that they had tried to stop using prostitutes.[48] Indeed, it is apparent that something beyond sexual enjoyment, which is perhaps indicative of addiction, prompted men's frequent and continued use of prostitutes in spite of the ever increasing risk of experiencing health, legal, relational, family, financial, and career consequences – particularly when many attempted to stop this behavior without success. Such practices were highlighted in the book, *LT: Over the Edge,* when NFL Hall of Fame linebacker Lawrence Taylor estimated that he had spent $70,000-$90,000 on female escorts during one particular three-month drug binge.[49] Moreover, Taylor's extreme expenses were followed by his assertion, "I was averaging about six [females] a day, six a night," and it was apparent that his drug addiction had become intertwined with an out-of-control sex addiction that involved the compulsive use of prostitutes.[50]

Along with the ever-present risk of contracting a variety of sexually transmitted infections, using prostitutes also promotes non-relational attitudes that compartmentalize and reduce sex to a physical act that is separate from love, intimacy, and commitment. One minor league basketball player supported these notions by saying, "I think guys have the mentality that a lot of women are just prostitutes and not getting paid for it, I think that's the mentality." Such beliefs reduce women to the role of sexual objects while encouraging prostitution as an acceptable option. Ultimately, these practices can negatively influence an individual's ability to engage in a healthy relationship since infidelity creates barriers to intimacy by depleting honesty and trust. Although engaging with a prostitute might seem like a worry-free business transaction on the surface, athletes inadvertently compromise their well-being on multiple levels in the process.

Prostitution is not the victimless crime that many believe because it has resulted in a variety of consequences for athletes as well as harm to the female prostitutes, who in this study were cheated of out money and taken advantage of sexually by numerous athletes. Childhood trauma may also contribute to becoming a prostitute because 59% noted they were physically abused to the point of physical injury and while a majority experienced childhood sexual abuse, 63% were sexually abused by an average of four different predators per child.[51] It is also an erroneous belief that most sex workers enter the industry to support their drug habits because various studies revealed that 39-60% of individuals reported that prostitution preceded their drug abuse, which was used to cope with the negative feelings related to their profession.[52] Finally and perhaps the strongest evidence illustrating the harmful nature of prostitution involves the estimated 1 million children worldwide, most of whom are females, who are forced each year into the sex industry although the actual total may be as high as 10 million.[53] Such pathological practices targeting children show no sign of slowing down in lieu of soaring profits, infrequent prosecutions, and the steady demand for illegal services.[54] In the end, many athletes rationalize their use of prostitutes as an activity that is harming no one and yet, whenever athletes pay for sex, they are contributing – often without realizing it – to the re-victimization of these and countless other sex workers.

ATHLETES' CORNER: POINTS TO PONDER

1. Strippers and strip clubs provide frequent entertainment for numerous collegiate and professional athletes who too often overlook an array of potential consequences that have negatively impacted athletes and coaches at all levels. Like pornography, some athletes use this pastime to bond with each other so you must carefully consider whether this activity is worth the potential costs that have damaged numerous lives and athletic careers. Such entertainment is potentially more addictive than pornography because live women provide actual sexual stimulation that can readily blur the line between exotic dancing and prostitution.

2. Know that if you choose to hire prostitutes for individual and/or group sexual encounters despite the many dangers associated with these practices, you risk experiencing an array of negative outcomes for yourself and the female(s) as well. Involvement with prostitutes may result in damage to personal reputations and well-being, disease and infections, infidelity, family and relational issues, abuse and violence, addiction, and legal consequences. In short, using such services has the potential to negatively impact your life years after they have occurred.

3. Athlete involvement with strippers and/or prostitutes has also resulted in a variety of consequences that have put players' careers in jeopardy. Athletes have experienced team suspensions, loss of athletic careers and/or salaries, damage to team reputation, false accusations, and incarceration. Always consider the worst case scenario *before* engaging in any activity because certain events cannot be changed and involve consequences that linger long after an athletic career ends.

Chapter 4
The Practice of Picking Up Women

The pastime of meeting and then convincing a newly acquainted woman to engage in some type of sexual activity on that same evening, which is often referred to as a hook-up or a pick-up, is a common phenomenon among males in all walks of life. Athletes are no strangers to these practices which are among the most common sexual behaviors found within this study. While it could be argued that picking-up females is a male activity more than an athlete-related practice, not every male wanting to have sex with a female he met earlier in the evening has the ability to succeed in this type of activity consistently – if at all. In her book, *Hooking Up: Sex, Dating, and Relationships on Campus,* Dr. Kathleen Bogle discovered college men and women engaging in casual hook-ups which often took the place of dating.[1] Both genders agreed that men were much more free to hook-up as often as they could because unlike women, there was no stigma for engaging in numerous sexual encounters.[2] Men were, however, stigmatized for not "getting any" sex, and this encouraged males to try to be promiscuous because even the descriptive names for such behaviors (i.e., player, male-slut, or man-whore) were free from negative connotations and viewed as a joke by many.[3]

In this study, over 95% of the participants revealed a high prevalence of involvement in the pick-up scene among athletes on their particular teams that could reach almost daily participation for some players. Over 50% of the participants also admitted that they had personally engaged in picking up women at high frequencies during their collegiate, minor, and/or major league careers. Athletes who competed in the 1960s, 1970s, and 1980s were just as likely to report high frequencies of picking up women as those who competed from 1990-2010 and for some players even more so, because their promiscuity occurred before the emergence of more serious sexually transmitted diseases such as herpes, HIV, and AIDS. While professional athletes from various sports have noted such practices in their memoirs, this chapter will provide an in-depth view into elite-level athletes' involvement in the pick-up scene that supersedes this glimpse.[4] In addition, athletes' participation in the pick-up scene can be very different from what most non-athlete males experience with women.

My experiences picking-up women began slowly and rather unexpectedly during my junior hockey career in Canada and steadily increased as my athletic career continued. In contrast to my hometown where hockey had nominal status compared to other sports, Canadian junior hockey was very popular because this was Canada's national sport. This enabled our team to meet and hook-up with local women fairly easily. Hockey also happened to be among the most popular sports at my first university and the school's higher ratio of females to males encouraged me, along with other athletes and non-athletes alike, to engage in the pick-up scene. Although hockey was not the most prominent sport at the second university I transferred to, the team's popularity combined with the school's greater enrollment provided ample opportunity to meet and pick-up women. My participation in the pick-up scene continued throughout college and into my professional career particularly when I was not involved in a steady relationship. Because my hockey teams provided the most popular form of entertainment in most of the cities that I competed in professionally and particularly in the United States, this resulted in a steady supply of females who were readily available to hook-up with if one so desired. Overall, I would rate my participation in the pick-up scene as average compared to other athletes. While I had my share of one-night stands and casual sex, I was nowhere near the level of certain teammates whose reputations with women bordered on legendary since some made this their major focus. Shortly after my 27th birthday, which was just after the start of my final two seasons as a professional hockey player overseas, I ended my participation in the pick-up scene permanently because these sexual pursuits became more and more unsatisfying for me.

IS IT "GAME," MANIPULATION, OR COERCION?

Despite the fact that numerous participants insisted that the use of pressure was unnecessary with women because so many were sexually available, over 80% of the sample representing every sport and level described athletes, including themselves, using "game," manipulation, and/or coercion to gain females' sexual compliance. Participants were in agreement that "game" was a universal practice that involved trying to "smooze" (i.e., charm and convince) a woman into having casual sex through conversation and drinking. While athletes differed in their approach, having "game" was the difference between picking-up a woman versus going home alone and having sexual intercourse or not if you took a female home. Essentially, "game," manipulation, and coercion were used to achieve the goal of having casual sex although they could involve different tactics that ranged from "relaxed and casual" and "straight-forward" to conniving and "more aggressive." However, because every athlete had their own definition of what "game" could involve and this could change with each new woman they encountered, "game," manipulation, and coercion often described the same practices rather than different behaviors on a continuum. As a result, participants revealed that often there was little distinction between having "game" and the use of more depreciating behaviors such as manipulation and/or coercion since more often than not, these practices were used to secure a casual sexual encounter on a given evening rather than involvement in a dating situation.

One collegiate basketball player discussed the importance of having "game" by saying, "When you meet somebody and sleep with them, and you just met them two or three hours ago...you know most girls just won't go sleep with you, just, 'Oh hi, you're such and such, you're a big star, come on and let's go have sex' – it's not that easy but...it's not that hard, but it's not *that* easy, I mean you have to put [in] some conversation." This participant noted that for many athletes, certain protocol was needed in order to convince a female to have sex because most women required more than simply knowing that someone was an athlete. There are definite exceptions to this depending on an athlete's persona, social status, and his sport and team's reputation. At the same time, certain collegiate athletes from lower status programs or sports revealed that there was little or no female availability for their teams unless it was promoted individually. Consequently, this made having "game" and the "gift of gab" essential for sexual success with many college women. Numerous participants discussed the different versions of "game" they observed including a minor league basketball player who explained:

> They call it pimping, hey, I'm going to get this female to give as much as I can get out of her, and I aien't going to give her nothing, you know I'm going to sell her a dream, a dream that you know that would never come to reality...that's how some guys go about approaching it.

This participant referred to "game" as "pimping," and it basically involved collegiate and/or professional athletes lying "every chance they get" by selling a reluctant female a false "dream" in an effort to gain her sexual compliance. Some athletes found a lot satisfaction in the process of convincing an unfamiliar female to have sex according to a MLB player who revealed, "I think it's the game of it actually more than anything." A wrestler further elaborated by saying, "I mean you know trying to convince them was probably more of the challenge than anything else...like trying to convince them that they should go home with you, more than the actual sex itself was probably more important – it was that bragging right." Success with women established a "pecking order" that was a "big thing" because it dictated "where you stand" among your peers according to the previous basketball player. Other participants including a minor league hockey player detailed what "game" could involve during their athletic careers:

> ...you know, you're about to get laid and she's like, "I can't do this...my roommate is out there, I got to go. We have this policy where all five girls go home together." And you're like, "No." You're like trying to sell it on Stan and you know, "Come on, I'll give you a back rub" or whatever. You

got to be a salesman. You're a guy trying to get laid. You know, just like if you're on break away [in a hockey game] and you miss the first shot, but you're going to stuff the second one in – it's the same thing. So, I definitely had to pull that one off saying, "You know, you're drunk, stick around, let's hang out." And the next thing you know, you'll have to coerce her... and you might have to sell her a little bit but in college, it's all about that. These girls are naive, they're young. They haven't experienced anything yet, so you have to give them the crash over. You have to sell it, but that happens all the time. They come back for more, they might, the next day, be upset, like, "I'm so upset, I can't believe we did it. What are my friends going to think?" "Don't tell anybody." I mean, that happens all the time..."I can't believe it, you know, this was wrong" – or whatever. As long as you're nice and you play the game and they play the game... they're going to be back and have fun. They're going to tell their friends they had a great time and he's a great guy and that's how it is. It's a big game because girls don't want to have a bad rep [reputation]...I just think that hey, you have to play the game and tell them what they want to hear – and tell everybody else the same...

For this athlete, having "game" essentially involved manipulating a woman into having sex by telling her "what they wanted to hear" because it was all part of playing – and winning – at "the game." While this participant subsequently noted that he never had a female say, "No and stop and all those crazy stuff," perhaps his manipulation and/or coercion superseded an intoxicated woman's resistance because the female's regret he observed from having sex the night before prompted him "to basically try to get them out of your bed as fast as possible." Such practices were not relegated to the collegiate level because they also appeared at the professional level as an NFL player revealed by saying, "Well guys are pigs man, we'll lie to a woman [laughing] you know, I mean the biggest lie ever to a woman is, 'I love you'...[but] when you're pressuring a woman to have sex with you, you'll tell them anything and so how prevalent is it? You know it's as prevalent as it needs to be." Similarly, a minor league basketball player revealed "the latest one" that his NFL friends were using was to tell a teammate, "I think that I met 'wifey'" in the presence of a woman in order to give her the false impression that she had a chance for a long-term relationship with a professional athlete who only wanted sex from her. It is apparent that although many females are often willing to engage in casual sexual encounters, not every woman complied with every athlete's sexual desires on every occasion. Consequently, this encouraged some athletes to use alcohol, different manipulative tactics, physically enticing behaviors, and coercion to accomplish their goal of having casual sex. In the end, such practices raise the intriguing question: How far will certain athletes take their "game," manipulation, and/or coercion in order to have sex with a woman?

WHEN ATHLETE PRIVILEGE AND WOMEN COLLIDE

Throughout this study, athletes have routinely noted that their greater attention and popularity has translated into preferential treatment and privilege since they are considered celebrities in certain settings. One need not look far to see that athletes are often glorified in society for their skills and talents, and because certain females are among those who partake in this admiration, some are willing to provide special privileges to athletes.[5] As a result, numerous participants, including a minor league hockey player and an NBA player, attributed success in picking-up women to the phenomenon of athlete privilege which, at times, created vast differences between athletes and non-athletes both in and out of college:

> You had a lot of easier chance of picking your girl up...if you were a varsity player...than the guys who are going to the library every night... we probably should have went to the library a little bit more ourselves you know [laughs] and let the other guys go out [and get with the women]...but I mean you take any, any sport that's...at a higher level, it's going to be there.

> Ah man...me and a friend we laugh and joke about it all the time, he went to a university where he wasn't an athlete, he was a decent high school athlete but when we went off to college, he was just, I don't want to say just a student, but he was a student and he'd you know say this all the time, "You know when you went to school, you didn't have to use your 'game' the way I did, I had to talk up on everything, all you had to do was go out and shoot a couple of buckets," you know we laugh about that all the time. But not much game you had to present in college or pros if they knew that you were you know part of the team. All it was you know, "I'm so and so, so and so, and I want to get to know you" and you know that was it, not much game, no.

These participants, like others, realized that sports participation opened a wider door to both women and sex that most athletes would never experience otherwise, and many had no problem taking advantage of this unique status during their athletic careers. One minor league hockey player noted such privileges and pampering were "a perk of the job," while an NFL player thought this resulted from "being put up on a pedestal." Because their unique status afforded special privileges, a variety of athletes provided specific examples of how picking-up women, at times, could be a relatively simple process at the collegiate level. For example, a minor league baseball player revealed, "It wasn't even an effort, I didn't even try you know...I went out to a party, and a bunch of us were getting ready to leave and a girl comes up to me and goes, 'Hey, where you going?' 'I'm going back to my apartment,' and she asked if she could come with me, and she did, and one thing led to the next and that was the same way actually both times." While factors including status, level of attractiveness, personality, and a female's level of intoxication can all play a role in determining a male's ability to hook-up, an athlete's looks – or lack thereof – did not always determine success with women.[6] For example, various participants including a wrestler revealed, "I would see guys that were, you know just dog ugly with some great looking girls...just because they were part of the team so yea, I mean...when you're a wrestler, you're going to come home with somebody." Nicole Berti, author and wife of former NFL player, Tony Berti, was so amazed at this phenomenon in professional football that she referred to it as "the ugly factor."[7] As a result, pick-up practices could become even easier as athletes progressed to higher levels of competition as one minor league football player recalled by saying, "I really don't think guys look to pick them up, I think just the opportunity presents itself...most of the time you know when they find out you're a football player." This athlete, like others, discovered it was not always necessary to actively engage in the pick-up scene because so many women pursued professional athletes. This was an even greater reality for many major leaguers as an NBA player revealed by saying, "Oh man, it's real easy as long as you had, you know, a jersey number and as long as you was on a roster or a program." Furthermore, an NHL player elaborated on how picking-up women, at times, could be an effortless process during his major league career:

> I'd say post game, every game at home if you were at a venue that you hung out [at]...with your group...opportunity was always there...I would say easier than you would ever imagine, it was almost like the snap of the finger, it would be just a matter of what you're [wanting] – if you're picky and choosy...it usually went your way – if you were a person that, you know, say some guys would sleep with anything, and other guys they wanted the girl that was the "10," but that was also attainable.

It is evident that collegiate, minor, and major league athletes' unique status and privilege often afforded them with effortless success when it came to picking up women. However, such abounding opportunities can make it increasingly difficult for some athletes to differentiate between actual consent and their use of coercion, pressure, or force to promote sex with a reluctant female who agrees to some, but not all of his sexual requests. With so many athletes being accustomed to getting whatever they want sexually with countless women, how will this impact the athlete who is finally told to stop – and the women he is currently pursuing sexually?

SPORTS INFLUENCES, MASCULINITY, AND PEER PRESSURE

Numerous participants within this study including a wrestler noted the practice of picking up women as "normal, constant unless you were dating someone seriously at the time." For many athletes, once competition between men in practices and games is finished, women become next in line to conquer. A minor league basketball player revealed, "You know [it's] the mentality of an athlete like always wanting to win or always wanting to be the best" while an NFL player observed, "It was a game and just kind of what was expected I guess in your college days number one, and then number two being an athlete even more so." Expectations to sexually conquer women increased for athletes because their competitive nature carried off the playing field into their sexual behaviors with women. Such practices were not limited to the collegiate level because these sports cultural influences could be just as prevalent as athletes progressed to the professional level as one NBA player revealed. "The fact that you're in the league and you know some of the guys thought that this is what we're supposed to do, we're supposed to go to practice, supposed to go to games, and we're supposed to lay every chick that we can." Because collegiate and professional athletes viewed picking up women as "normal" and "expected" behavior, some took these pursuits as seriously as their athletic participation. For example, one wrestler recalled, "I remember the first day that I went to [XXX University]...one of the first practices after a weekend being on campus, and one of the first questions was, 'Did you get laid?'...[as if] that's your goal for the weekend." For many athletes, the practice of picking up women does, in fact, become a competitive pursuit which another wrestler confirmed by saying, "It was the goal [laughs] pretty much every night...for most of the guys." Another NBA player similarly commented on major league teammates' competitive nature with women by saying, "In the pros, probably just as much [as college], you know it was...more of a sport, more of a one-upsman type of thing, you know you see your teammate he got a girl, one in L.A. and you're like, 'Okay, I'm going to get me a hook up in L.A. too.'" As a result, "the chase," which is the process of picking up a female, becomes a competitive, pressure-filled event because success brings status and recognition which can be as satisfying and rewarding – sometimes even more so – than the actual sexual encounter itself. This also means that picking up women is not only about the sex because as one collegiate football player noted, "Some of its pride, some of it's knowing you can do it." Despite a variety of motives, the pick-up scene teaches men to separate sex from love, and this causes some to disengage emotionally from women and any feelings they might be experiencing because women become nothing more than sex tools for men to use.

Sexual pursuits also become the source of frequent story-telling, bragging rights, and bravado which often takes the form of locker room talk. Such conversations are filled with humor and highlight perceptions of athletes' manliness as a collegiate hockey player, a minor leaguer, and a professional hockey coach discussed in this way:

> Oh, anything and everything is said. How many times she's ever fucked this, that, every time – they embellish a lot of times…usually it's the truth, cause you can't take the stories much further than what we actually did [laughs] and if you can, they should be an author, not a hockey player…but, just anything you can imagine gets said and is talked about…everything that I've mentioned so far, plus three times more and…guys will embellish, but they won't make up an entire scenario. They'll say, well…I fucked the living shit out of this girl, she was moaning eight ways from Sunday and she couldn't get enough, and then the next morning she came on top of me and we went at it again, so I'm going to have a real shitty practice. One story I really like, our goalie, a little absent-minded, great kid, we're leaving for practice…we're late as it is and we're like, "Where's [so and so]?" We go in his room, we think he's going to be napping, he's tagging some girl [laughs]…and he goes, "Oh, I totally forgot about practice," so…that was the story of stories in the locker room, cause this kid, I mean [laughs] you know once we're out to the car…he's still half erect.

> I would say in the world of hockey, women are objectified quite a bit no question. They're a piece of meat as opposed to a human being. There are exceptions to that of course, but I mean you have heard locker room talk centers around a lot of that – how big tits Brenda has and how big a box [vagina] Julie has and this and that – how many guys are rolled up in it. You never hear guys talking about in locker rooms how nice Jennie is and that kind of thing. That kind of thing is not, is not going on – certainly objectified in the locker room. Even when you go to the bars, especially with hockey buddies, it still continues. It's like yeah, "Where can we find the next one?" "Who is going to be the next victim?" Victim in a light-hearted sense not victim of rape or anything like that. You know, basically it was not a successful weekend on Monday afternoon unless you scored. There is no other world that I have been in that more objectified women than they are in hockey. I have been in a lot of different organizations of sports and even the work environment and business environment is pretty bad for that…but nothing in comparison…

> As far as one guy banging a broad and then coming into the locker room the next morning and telling the guys, I'm not in the locker room per se anymore, so I miss those stories, but I used to enjoy them when I was

playing. I used to find good humor in them, but that happens all the time...you know, it's no big deal to fuck the shit out of a girl every way possible and then come to the locker room and tell all the boys how it was and how she was, how she felt, what she smelled like, and in fine detail... he could just do his job and do what he did to her [and] kept to himself. [But] he's got to come in and tell the other guys. Or you know, he may bring a buddy in, they may two-on-one her. Or it may be the situation where she ends up fucking five guys in a gang bang...the soldier crawl is a common thing in hockey where one guy is maybe in his room banging a broad [and a] couple of buddies crawl on the floor and come in and watch him...[but] especially the one-night stand I mean if they were with regular girlfriends, live-in girlfriend, or wives obviously, it's a different situation you know, [but] for a pick-up one night and bang the shit out of them, [it's] another story, another notch on the belt and you can better believe a lot of other guys are gonna hear about it, and then when they do, they hear this story, and so somebody else is gonna try to bang her too...so I think the respect level is very low.

It is evident that some collegiate and professional athletes view sex with women as a sport of its own, and deviant sexual behaviors become a way to display masculinity to their peers. The first participant believed that "85%" of athletes' deviant sexual behaviors with females were motivated by the locker room stories because teammates wanted to "see who can top whose story, who can do something better." This prompted some athletes to be constantly on the look out for their next sexual conquest since it provided a continuous flow of entertaining stories and greater prestige. Because female objectification in combination with athletes' deviant sexual behaviors can be rampant among certain teams, it is easy to see why women who have sexual encounters with athletes fear being the subject of conversation in a locker room.

At the same time, locker room conversations can be a source of peer pressure that is responsible for influencing certain athletes' sexual behaviors with women as one minor league basketball explained, "You want to be the big man in the locker room you know, so I think quite a bit peer pressure [of] wanting to come back [and] tell a story to the team, yea, you know it always worked for me...part of the quest of being on the road trips [was] you go out and find a chick and if you got one in your room, you were the cool guy." This participant felt self-induced pressure as well as stress from being in an athlete culture that promoted acceptance and recognition for engaging in sexual conquests on collegiate road trips. Interestingly, a minor league baseball player discussed his awareness of the culture's silent pressures in this way:

Nobody ever came out and said it, [but] I mean...do guys think that way? Yeah, I really think they do, I mean I know I did, definitely there was a time where it was like...if you weren't having sex, you know then you weren't manly...it was expected you know what I mean, you better be hooking up.

Unspoken beliefs and expectations create pressure by challenging players' masculinity and despite more than a 25-year age difference, such pressures were as prevalent during these participants' collegiate and professional careers in the early 1970s and the early 2000s. Furthermore, such pressures increased whenever teammates verbalized these expectations, and various participants including a collegiate hockey player discussed these pressures in this way:

...I guess at times there's pressure because...I remember last year every morning my roommate would walk into my room on the weekends and see if I had anybody in my bed, and he would laugh and joke and say, "Oh, you didn't get any again...last night huh?" [Of] course, he had a girlfriend. So, that was all in fun, it was never like you know, "Oh you're a fag"...but I guess at a party, you're hanging out with some girl, [and] you see one of your teammates working on a girl, you know you're going to bust his balls and make fun of him if he doesn't score at the end of the night. I guess, I see that all the time.

Various participants noted such attitudes promoted peer pressure and attempts at promiscuity because peer influences are particularly strong among athletes whose primary friendships revolve exclusively around their teammates. Peer influences have also been linked to sexual aggression.[8] In study of date rape, Dr. Eugene Kanin discovered that college men who experienced pressure from their male friends to engage in sexual activity were more likely to rape female acquaintances.[9] In the end, the problem is not that athletes engage in picking-up women like other males in or out of college, but rather that their ultra competitive nature in combination with the previously noted influences kick in and create tremendous pressure to "score" with women. This has caused some athletes to attack the pick-up scene with a vengeance and will to succeed at all costs. It will become evident that this mentality can create an array of problems for both athletes and the females they target not only during collegiate careers but during professional careers as well.

PRACTICE AND PREVALENCE AMONG COLLEGIATE ATHLETES

Because women and committed relationships can take a lot of time and energy that many athletes do not want to give, casual sex is another alternative to steady relationships. Moreover, it was no surprise to find athletes with such mindsets gravitating to settings that promoted such interests. Numerous participants noted the link between the bar scene and picking up women including a collegiate hockey player who explained, "Happens all the time...I like to go out to bars, I like to talk to girls, so I'd say you know three, four nights a week [laughs]...picking up girls." Environments such as parties and bars are prime socializing locations because the presence of alcohol acts as an effective social lubricant that breaks down barriers and inhibitions which can lead to casual sex with unfamiliar partners.[10] Furthermore, numerous college students have recognized that alcohol intoxication was a major factor that promoted their participation in sexual behaviors that they would never have done if sober.[11] Under such circumstances, it is easy to understand how such encounters can escalate into conflict whenever two newly acquainted and intoxicated people are involved in sexual intimacies that may have very different agendas.

At the same time, drinking establishments are certainly not the only places athletes go to meet and pick-up women. Plus, the prevalence of hooking up can relate to specific times of the year for some athletes. For instance, a wrestler discussed the manner in which seasonal influences impacted sexual pursuits during his career as well as among the collegiate wrestlers he coached in the late 2000s:

> Probably more prevalent off season...in season maybe, depending on the schedule and everything else, you know maybe once a week, maybe twice a week. But...out of season it could be three, four times a week... it seems pretty much the same [among current collegiate wrestlers], it doesn't seem like much has [laughs] changed there...I was a little more laid back and a little more shy, but I had a fair share of one night stands...

Numerous participants, like the previous wrestler, also revealed that socializing, partying, picking up women, and deviancy of all kinds increased dramatically during the off season because athletes had more time, energy, and suspensions carried little impact in the off season. However, the time of the year did not influence the sexual pursuits of all athletes as a collegiate basketball player revealed by saying, "Oh I mean that was just constant, I mean that was an everyday thing [when] you were 18-23 years old, you got that on your mind all the time." This participant, along with others, noted that youth combined with peak conditioning through constant physical training increased testosterone and "sexual energy" exponentially so that athletes were always looking for sexual outlets. Certain athletes made socializing with women a priority that could rate as high as their athletic participation, and a minor league basketball player elaborated on athletes' opportunistic nature by saying, "Every night, every chance from the desk clerk, waitress, to whoever, to the reporter interviewing you...every night, every city, they'd try to pick up the maids just cleaning the rooms [if] she looked good...every chance I got [when] I was single [laughs], there was no sense having no partner, that was a waste of time." It is evident that for some collegiate athletes, no one, no time, or no place was considered off limits when it came to meeting females, and this afforded athletes with constant opportunities to pick-up women which was often met with success. For example, a collegiate hockey player observed that his teammates experienced a "15-20% success ratio" which amounted to "a lot of sex" while a minor league baseball player revealed, "College world probably at least a girl a week I'd say on average, at least." A wrestler recalled, "Pretty much every time we went out we'd pick up something...probably like three or four different girls a week." This participant highlighted a common theme among athletes because although he and his teammates were consistent in picking up "something" when they went out, this "something" referred to a young woman – not a thing or an object as many athletes believe. A collegiate hockey player and a minor league basketball player continued to elaborate on hook up practices in the 1990s and 2000s in this way:

...playing hockey in college it happens a lot, I'd have to say realistically if you were a single guy and you went out, you could probably pick-up a girl every weekend I would think depending on how good looking you were...before I started dating [a long-term girlfriend], it was like pretty much [I] picked up a girl about every weekend...and that's not to say that...you had sex with all of those girls...but anything from making out with them to having sex with them did happen on a very regular basis.

Oh pretty much on nightly basis if guys went out, if they could get one to go [home], they would...so it wouldn't be like, "Nothing for me tonight," it was a lot of guys would say, "You know let's see what happens, let's see what happens tonight"...and you know if things go well, I'll be leaving early"...in college it was very easy...[and] it had a lot to do with, a lot of times there were people that you might not have even recognized on campus before, but they definitely know who you are, but when you're out, everybody's inhibitions are a little bit different now that you've been drinking for awhile, so there were a lot of situations where a girl, you might not have even realized you passed on campus one day, completely knows who you are, and...next thing you know you've been hanging out with them for the last hour and a half at the bar, and you know then you're taking them home.

While numerous athletes have noted their success with women, others admitted that they or their teammates lacked "game," and therefore struggled to "close the deal" by taking home a woman. One wrestler even recalled being tutored by an older wrestler who was legendary with women by saying, "I don't want to call him my mentor, but he would always call me his student and so he would always try to teach me how he would pick-up women." It is apparent that pressures to succeed in the pick-up scene were indeed a reality within certain athlete cultures, and this caused some athletes to resort to more drastic measures that a collegiate football player revealed:

> ...it's funny the guys always talk about "The Mad Dash," and "The Mad Dash" is at 2 a.m. and any girl that's still at the bar or after last call after people start filing out, the girls who sort of linger there, they're the ones that usually get taken home and it's like the known fact that if you wait long enough after they start kicking people out of the bar, the girls who don't make for the exit are the ones that are looking to go home and get fucked, so that's always been sort of like the unwritten rule if you just wanted to take home some strange pussy and get some...

Because most males and females are heavily intoxicated and do not know each other well at this point – if at all, it is easy to understand how such scenarios and assumptions about a woman's sexual desire can create a recipe for disaster (i.e., sexual assault) whenever sex is added to the mix. Athletes displaying little conscience by choosing any female that they could find for casual sex were often referred to as "dogs" or "pigs," and a collegiate football player commented on their attitudes by saying, "[To] a guy who's a 'dog,' everything's a piece of meat and everything's you know a conquest, a trophy hunt, versus you know talking to the guy with a serious girl, well he doesn't look at it like that because hey if he did, he wouldn't keep a serious girl." Indeed, some athletes are all about conquest and compared to non-athletes, it was not surprising to discover members of athletic teams reported significantly more sexual partners.[12] However, unbridled promiscuity has ramifications because researchers also found that the more sexual partners a man had, the greater the likelihood that he will have sexually assaulted at least one female.[13] Interestingly, a collegiate baseball player supported these findings by saying, "Some guys would fuck anyone at any time and place and they'd fuck them if they were passed out, and I heard of an event like that cause there were those who had no moral standards even though most moral standards get lowered in college or with that age group." Behind the façade that believes all athletes are admirable role models stands the reality that within the athlete culture, some choose to satisfy their sexual desires at the expense others. Furthermore, this can include any manner that suits them regardless of whether the behavior is legal or illegal.

PRACTICE AND PREVALENCE AMONG PROFESSIONAL ATHLETES

It is not difficult to fathom that if collegiate athletes were constantly on the look out to meet and pick-up females despite busier schedules filled with classes, studies, and athletic training, professional athletes who are into such pursuits can invest even more effort because they have more resources to do so. Minor leaguers attributed higher participation in the pick-up scene to an abundance of free time, having money, high alcohol consumption, frequent time spent in bars, a benefit of their occupation, frequent road trips, having a conquer mentality, easy access to sexually available females, and the mindset that athletes were supposed to have sex with women constantly. Interestingly, certain athletes discussed the differences between the pick-up scene during their collegiate and professional careers including a minor league football player who revealed, "I would say they're a lot easier in my pro career...I mean there's a lot more college athletes and...with being a professional athlete...some girls get into that kind of a thing." Because professionals held a unique status to some women who were usually a little older and more assertive than college-aged women, this athlete, like others, found that "the girls come out to where you're hanging out...they'll just come up and start talking and kind of put it out there" which implied some women were quite open about wanting sex with an athlete. Similarly, a minor league baseball player revealed his awareness by saying, "In the pro world it happened like that, I mean it was just 'boom' you know, you go to the bar and automatically there's 10 girls and they know what you're there for and you know what they're there for...on a 15-day road trip, we were in five different cities, probably a girl in every city...absolutely." The previous participants, like numerous professional athletes, discovered that the practice of picking up women could supersede their collegiate experiences because older women made themselves "more available" to professional athletes.

In addition, other professionals including a minor league hockey player revealed the prevalence of the pick-up scene during his career in this way:

> Oh god...in the [A level minor leagues] that was almost nightly. That was the thing...I mean, it was every night going to a bar. And I mean, I look back on that now, now that I'm married – I don't go out at all... but there's no motivation to go out. And so that leads me to believe that like when I was younger, you were going out *just* to meet women.

This participant's realization, after the fact, that some athletes' primary motive for their frequent bar visits came with the purpose of meeting and picking-up women appeared as no surprise because I made similar observations from going to bars six or seven nights per week during my first minor league season.

Moreover, these practices were not relegated to the sport of hockey, or to all athletes, as other professionals including a minor league baseball player recalled, "For some guys though it was every night go out to the bar and try to come home with a girl." While some athletes' sexual pursuits were confined to bars, this was not always the case as a minor league basketball player revealed in this way:

It went on all the time, I mean that was their thing, I mean a lot of guys did that, I mean if you have 15 guys on the team, there's about six or seven that's doing that [and] they're trying to get anything they can, some people are like that, some people aren't, it just depends, I've seen it happening too much you know...like in my last team I played with, a lot of the young guys were just constantly on the prowl, it didn't matter if it was at the airport, if it was Big Lots, or...the grocery store or whatever, they was always on the prowl...

It is evident that some athletes took advantage of every opportunity to pick-up women in virtually any location they chanced upon, and this participant further elaborated on certain teammates' practices by saying, "They'll do anything they have to, to get that next one...to conquer, to conquer, to conquer, to conquer you know what I'm saying." This participant's reactions to some of his teammates' excessive behaviors highlighted the possibility that he was observing sexually compulsive behaviors and addictions in process. Furthermore, having a conquer mindset becomes problematic whenever an athlete encounters a woman, however rare, who is not willing to accommodate his sexual goals. When this occurs, only two choices exist: Stop the sexual advance or sexually assault the female.

Like minor league athletes, major leaguers also revealed frequent participation in the pick-up scene although a small percentage thought this occurred less often than in the minor leagues or college because players were shielded by more security, spent less time together, traveled by chartered flights, were more likely to be married, and had more to lose for poor sports performances that resulted from too much partying with women. On the other hand, major leaguers reporting frequent participation in the pick-up scene attributed this to being on a higher pedestal, more frequent travel with greater time away from their families, having a prominent profile and income, access to more sexually available females, a desire to one-up teammates, and the incredible ease with which these practices could occur. For example, certain participants compared the ease of the pick-up scene during their minor and major league careers including a MLB player who revealed:

[It's] much easier at the big league level and a lot, probably quality is a lot better [laughing] as far as that goes. Put it this way, I had more girlfriends in the major leagues than I did in the minor leagues...because of who you are and the money involved, and let's face it, there's girls out there that want to grab onto a ball player and they'd rather grab a big leaguer than a minor leaguer.

While most participants from the various sports found that picking-up women, who were often higher caliber, was easier to do in the major leagues compared to their minor league careers, other participants noted the frequency of the pick-up scene during their major leaguers careers. For example, another MLB player revealed, "Oh it depends who they were, it could be every night for them I think...depends on the guy, a couple [days a week] maybe, [and] some are out there all the time." Moreover, an NFL player recalled, "I would say that's a daily quest...[that] wasn't hard at all" while an NBA player revealed, "How often? Every day." An NHL player elaborated on the prevalence of such practices by saying, "I would say it was pretty routine, it was just you know the goal I guess... [and] the way to put it would be is you know most people are going to get up and brush their teeth in the morning...[in the same way] that guys are going to go on the road and try to get laid – that's probably the chances of it happening." Interestingly, an NFL player happened to reveal players' success rate in the pick-up scene by saying, "I mean you could literally go every night and pick-up somebody in a bar in the pros, I mean it was just easy, you know you already got five or six sets of eyes on you when you walk in the door." Overall, participants found women were attracted to their perceptions of professional athletes as well as to their physical traits including size, increased earnings, fame, and popularity regardless of players' martial status. Plus, it was not beyond certain females to try to steal athletes from their partners as a MLB player revealed by saying, "It's actually crazier at that [major league] level as well because these girls are you know out there trying to trap guys and take them away from their spouses so it's pretty common." In contrast to being targeted by athletes, this was but one of the different ways that women tried to use and trap athletes.

While the vast majority of participants (96%) noted frequent participation in the pick-up scene among teammates at all levels, approximately 45% of the athletes revealed their own participation was average, infrequent, or nonexistent. This was often attributed to having a meaningful relationship with a steady partner. Some athletes admitted they had conversational deficiencies which prevented them from even trying to pick-up a female including a MLB player who revealed, "I had no game, no verbal game." Spiritual beliefs and/ or guilt prevented others from pursuing casual sex while a small minority of conscientious athletes noted that they had no desire to have sex with promiscuous females often out of fear of contracting sexually transmitted diseases, getting someone pregnant, or meeting a "fatal attraction" type of woman that would not let go of them.

THE DARKER SIDE OF "GAME"

It is evident that females are often viewed as sport and something to conquer rather than people with feelings and consequently, some athletes treat them as such by saying virtually anything in order to have sex. Unfortunately, such practices are not uncommon since some athletes considered this to be a part of having "game." As previously noted, "game" can be as different as the athletes themselves, and it has a darker side that turns the pick-up scene into nothing more than a nefarious act of manipulation which disregards bonding and intimacy and relies instead on various types of deceit, pressure, or abuse. A collegiate basketball player revealed how these practices worked for him by saying, "You just talk them into it or try to make 'em feel bad if they don't, you know something like...'You know I thought you cared for me, you know here I am, you know spending this time and I'm all into you,' and you could be telling the truth – or you could be lying." Moreover, this participant admitted that he used manipulation to convince reluctant women to have sex 50% of the time because athletes, like himself, were often proficient in preying upon a female's "weakness." Similarly, a collegiate football player observed certain teammates targeting female weaknesses by saying, "They go up to a girl with low self-esteem and they're like, 'Come on...no one else would want to get with you, you know, I'm the only one who'd want to do that with you,' but...that was their way they'd pick up girls...that was their 'game,' they would pick-up girls with low self-esteem." Interestingly, an NFL player observed that 25% of athletes' "game" during his collegiate career involved negative or demeaning language toward females, and an NBA player elaborated on what this could entail:

> Ah yea, I had one teammate I just thought that he was just the raunchiest...
> [and] I didn't think that he respected the females at all you know...he was
> a yeller, he would snatch them, he would you know do anything just to
> get them back to the room with him, but yea that was the only incident
> you know that sticks out with me because I, you know, started to – not
> dislike him – but I looked at him different you know after I would hear his
> conversation with the women and what and not...[in] college...yea, [he
> was] pressuring them to leave with him, but not the [sex] act, just to get
> them somewhere by themselves...but no not to have sex with him.

Because this athlete acted aggressively enough in public to shock this participant, one can only wonder what he was capable of doing behind closed doors should a female reject his sexual advances. Other participants' "game" took on a different approach that was not relegated to the collegiate level as major leaguers from baseball and hockey revealed in this way:

> I mean you see it, I mean it's out there, you're sitting in a bullpen... as a player and a girl leans over and you know sticks her chest out and winks at you, and you know what she wants, and you might say, "Hey you know" the famous line is, "Hey, you like pizza?" you know to a girl standing away, you know, "Hey you like pizza?" "Yea" "Want to go to my room and get a pizza and fuck?" "No? What's a matter, you don't like pizza?" You know what I mean stupid stuff like that, I mean...most young guys, single guys, they're not going to find the woman of their dreams...at the baseball field, you know what I'm saying, and so you don't [look] in your own environment, you're not looking to find your life partner sitting in the second row...there's a pretty good chance she's there for a reason, she's looking to hook up with somebody and you're just looking to hook up with somebody for one night.

> ...I seen it happen where you know guys have said, "Hey look you know, I think you're hot and I'm fucking horny, so I don't know how you feel about this, but you know why don't you come up with me, you know, let's get it on you know"...[and] you got guys that are at one extreme that say, "Fuck it, I'm not going to sit there and try to work this girl for an hour and a half and you know spend 30 bucks on drinks and...then finally pop the question and try to [leave with her] – you know it's either we're going to do it or we're not," then you got other guys that will just say, "Hey you know what, I think you're pretty hot and I want to fuck your brains out and let's go," and if not, "See you later."

Both participants noted major league athletes using different versions of "game" that were sexually offensive to some women. The first participant noted young, single major leaguers making sexually insulting remarks to flirtatious women at the ball park because he believed these women, like the players, were looking for casual sex. Such attitudes can be harmful because they have prompted certain athletes to sexual assault women they believed were promiscuous groupies when this was not the case.[14] The second participant noted that because some major leaguers efforts did not always result in casual sex, they decided to take a more direct approach by asking females for sex at nightclubs even though this tactless approach was more likely to disgust women than promote a sexual encounter. Other participants noted collegiate athletes' "game" included asking different females for "a blow job" in bars although this was thought to be motivated more by alcohol and players' desire to entertain teammates than a serious quest for sex. Another NHL player expressed disgust rather than amusement whenever teammates verbally pressured unfamiliar women for sex, and he was convinced that such character deficits were the predominant reason these athletes never became bona fide major leaguers. In either case, the use of sexually demeaning innuendos is a poor representation of collegiate and/or professional athletes as individuals and role models as well as their teams. Some athletes' unwanted sexual advances as well as their rejection became even more apparent when it required teammate intervention as an NFL player revealed in this way:

> Yea...I have done this in college and pro cause if I see that a guy is taking this too far you know you have to nudge him or whatever, call someone over, "Hey man you too drunk, man, shit you tripping" you know whatever, you know girls usually give you a sign, you know you can tell if you're observant, you can usually tell a sign when a girl is starting to get irritated or whatever, and you know with this person with this gal whatever, I might go over there and be like, "Hey man, you know, you leave this chick alone man, there's other fish in the sea" or..."Let's get out of here, time to go"...or something you know so...not a lot, maybe let's say two and two, that didn't happen a lot in four years of college, and five years of pros maybe three times...

Nearly 17% of participants noted athletes, including themselves, intervening to stop a teammate's use of sexual pressure during their collegiate and/or professional career. This included athletes from MLB and the NHL who discussed intervention with teammates who became verbally aggressive toward a woman after experiencing rejection; for example:

> I've had teammates intervene where a guy had had too much to drink out at a bar and was getting vulgar with a particular woman...and before either her or her boyfriend or her friends would make a scene, somebody would have to grab the guy and say, "Hey we're getting out of here before this gets out of hand."

> I think only two times...well I mean I think both of those times were similar because the girls were telling the player to leave her alone, stop touching me, you know, and when you start hearing you know vulgar words and things, you know, getting a little out of hand...you just try to get in the middle of it so it doesn't go any farther than that, so I mean it was two similar situations and you know nothing else happened from there, and again alcohol and sex, and it was kind of...not a great combination when you know the answer is "no," or it doesn't go the way you want.

Each of the above participants noted intoxicated major league athletes' sexual advances being rejected, and this resulted in teammate intervention when these athletes became blatantly abusive to the women. Because major leaguers have

123

much to lose in terms of their prestigious careers and high salaries, teammates reacted differently than certain collegiate athletes in similar situations by removing the player. This protected the athlete and the woman as well as their team's reputation from becoming tarnished through negative publicity. The NHL player in the previous narrative subsequently discussed his teammate's reaction to his intervention by saying, "At first abrasive, pissed off, combative, you know more times than not, don't you know remember [it] anyways... [but] you're family and...you would hope the guy would do the same thing for you if you ever got in the situation or...could become dangerous per se." Family-like bonds caused this participant to intervene even though he knew this could cause a physical confrontation with his teammate. This was in contrast to several narratives which depicted collegiate and minor league players withdrawing their support from a teammate following an attempted sexual assault on a female. Like other athletes who engaged in abusive behaviors with women, this participant found in most cases the players were so intoxicated that they were perhaps experiencing an alcohol-induced blackout because they did not remember their actions the next day. While this participant intervened in two incidences, he was aware of other major league teammates intervening in approximately six events that were virtually the same scenario.

Participants representing every competitive level and sport similarly revealed that they or their teammates had to intervene – sometimes with regularity – to stop an athlete's verbal aggression toward a woman following their rejection. For example, one minor league baseball player admitted he and his teammates intervened to stop intoxicated athletes unwanted sexual advances in bars "15" times during his collegiate career and "20-30" times in the minor leagues. Similarly, a collegiate football player recalled stepping in to defuse his teammates' unwanted sexual advances "probably you know 10-20 of 'em in my career." Although these participants were separated in age by over 30 years, coercive behaviors and intervention occurred among certain athletes as readily in the late 1960s/early 1970s as it did in the mid-2000s. Moreover, a wrestler revealed, "I've had to do it on at least two occasions as a coach to a wrestler like, "You know calm down, leave her alone, she said, 'No' [and] as a teammate, maybe one time...where I felt like it was going to get out of [control] – just for his protection and hers." This situation is noteworthy because if some athletes are making enough unwanted sexual advances to warrant their collegiate coach's intervention in the mid-2000s, one can only wonder how much these advances would escalate if the athlete was not stopped or in the presence of a coach or his teammates. It is apparent that collegiate and professional athletes experience rejection from females, and both have reacted in similar ways that can include verbal aggression and abuse of women as well as teammates who intervene. An NFL player attempted to explain these behaviors by saying, "I think there's athletes out there who when they are rebuffed by a girl, they take it like it's an affront to them and they get belligerent about it...I've seen stuff like that happen. I've also seen athletes think that their shit doesn't stink and they are above and beyond all, you know like all the world owes whoever a living type of thing." Such attitudes and player reactions are a major concern because if certain intoxicated athletes become this volatile in public establishments when they experience rejection, how will they react behind closed doors when they are sexually rejected and no one is there to intervene?

CONSEQUENCES OF THE PICK-UP SCENE

Compromising Character, Integrity, and Personal Well-being

In spite of its higher prevalence and numerous athletes' nonchalant approach toward unfettered, casual sex, the practice of picking up women has the potential to produce an array of consequences for athletes as well as the women involved. This reality challenged one minor league hockey player's assertion, "What do you have to lose you know? You want to get laid." Indeed, for those engaging in the pick-up scene there is always the potential "to lose" in a variety of ways that are both hidden as well as more obvious, and an NHL player revealed one of the less conspicuous consequences that impacted individual character in this way:

> ...it just elicits very egotistical and very, I guess, expectant behavior, you know guys expect women just to come to them...whereas in real life, that just doesn't happen [laughs]...I think it's more of you know [a], "What can you do for me?" attitude...you know they are the celebrity, you should be kissing their ass, and do whatever they want type of thing.

Inflated egos are problematic because individuals with self-centered mindsets often have little or no concern for the welfare of others, and this includes women who are very casual sexual partners. At the same time, it becomes a rude awakening when athletes realize that their fame and privilege can be as fleeting as smoke because the unpredictable nature of elite-level sports participation means that careers can end at any time. This can cause any inflated sense of self to suffer tremendously particularly when athletes' figure out that many so-called fans, including females, are often attracted not to who they are as individuals, but rather what they represent and do as athletes.

In addition to its negative effect on players' attitudes, 98% of the participants in this study noted collegiate and/or professional athletes, including themselves, compromising their integrity as boyfriends or husbands by participating in the pick-up scene despite being involved in committed relationships with women.

One minor league hockey player happened to discuss his own infidelities as well as his rationale for engaging in these practices in this way:

> My experience personally? It all depended on how I was feeling. What kind of cycle I was going through with relationship to my girlfriend at the time. If I was unhappy, of course I was out messing around. If I was happy, I tapered off a bit, really did. I went through a phase too where I thought, "You know what, I need to have fun now while I am in college because this is all going to come to an end." Sow my wild oats so to speak and get it out of my system because I was afraid of being the middle-aged guy in midlife crisis who never got it out of his system when he was younger. I did not want to be that guy. Sometimes it's like, "Let's do it now and get her done, get the hormones a flowing."

This athlete's behavior was fear-based because he was "afraid" of experiencing a midlife crisis as a result of not being promiscuous enough in his younger years. This prompted him to try to remove such inclinations from his system while he was still young even though this meant cheating and constantly seeking out sexual conquests. Consequently, this participant was asked if his prolonged cheating and engagement in the pick-up scene eliminated these urges and desires:

> Some days, but some days no. Some days I question if you can ever get it out of your system. As I get older it seems like I can. Then some days I'm like, you know these are fun times. I do not know if I can ever get rid of that. I don't think I can get rid of the "grass is greener" attitude. I think I eventually will but I guess as I get a little older, things that used to entertain me when I was 19 don't entertain me as much now. You spend a lot of time in nudie bars, chasing women around when I was 19 and doing all that crap and then I find myself when I go out that I could care less sometimes if women are around or not, I just want to be with my buddies. If one falls in my lap, well hey that's fine, I'm not going out of my way to chase it…I'm not doing any work for it. But, at a younger age, that wasn't the case [with] chasing around, I did as much as I could [so] I think from that perspective, I'm getting a little more mature. I don't know, it just doesn't seem to be as much as a chase anymore or conquest.

Individuals with a "grass is greener" mindset find that no partner is satisfying, and they continuously search for their next partner by convincing themselves that someone better is available for them. In this way, individuals move from partner to partner without being able to fully commit themselves to anyone for long because they sabotage relationships by magnifying their partner's flaws to insure that no one is ever good enough for them. Although this participant realized his interest in "conquest" and the "chase" practices of his youth had lessened, he also admitted he would still accommodate a female "if one falls in my lap." Such limiting attitudes and practices do not always end because of age, and this was further highlighted in pro football Hall of Fame running back Jim Brown's book, *Out of Bounds*.[15] Brown's teammates referred to him as "the hawk" because of his success "chasing women," and at age 53 he dated a 19 year-old female because he wanted his partner's body to be ripe like a piece of fruit, but not "overripe."[16] Such attitudes are harmful to developing intimate long-term relationships with one partner because they reduce females to body parts and enable men like Brown to discard an aging woman for an endless supply of younger, firmer bodies.[17]

While a "grass is greener" mindset is certainly a potential consequence of prolonged participation in the pick-up scene because of the way it sabotages perceptions of a partner, it is not the only problem athletes face since these behaviors can sometimes spiral out of control. An NFL player revealed his experiences with such issues by saying, "At one point in time I was a sex addict…a sex maniac, I mean I just wanted to have sex so you know at every opportunity…[and] I really, really didn't care who she was, what her name was, or whatever." Because this participant was subjugated by this particular mindset, women were viewed, not as people, but rather as objects that were needed to satisfy his sexual urge and craving. Such addictions can create major problems for an athlete and a female who is not willing to satisfy another's sexual requests. And as this participant eventually realized, sex provided only a temporary fix and solution to a much greater problem that had emerged from what he thought was sexually recreational behaviors with women.

Contracting Diseases

Another consequence of the pick-up scene and engaging in casual sex is the potential for contracting sexually transmitted diseases (STDs) or sexually transmitted infections (STIs) which is the more common term used today.[18] STIs comprise the most commonly reported infectious diseases in the United States today and by age 25, one in two persons will contract an STI.[19] Such widespread rates of disease suggest that the chances of contracting an STI from engaging in risky sexual practices is almost like flipping a coin. Furthermore, the fact that most STIs produce little or no noticeable symptoms means that carriers often have no idea that they are even infected, and therefore unknowingly infect others.[20] The often used cliché, "No glove, no love" can give athletes a false sense of safety and security from condom use; however, certain STI's including incurable ones such as genital herpes and genital warts can result from skin-to-skin contact rather than through exchange of bodily fluids.[21] This means that condoms would only be completely effective in preventing certain STIs when they cover an entire body like a jump suit.

Los Angeles Lakers Hall of Fame guard, Earvin "Magic" Johnson, was among the first athletes to become an outspoken advocate warning others about the dangers of engaging in heterosexual promiscuity after he contracted the human immunodeficiency virus (HIV).[22] Following a brief return to the NBA after announcing his illness, Johnson retired permanently from basketball in November of 1992 when opponents feared that they might contract the virus from him during competition.[23] Although HIV is among the more serious STIs since it can lead to acquired immunodeficiency syndrome (AIDS), it is certainly not the only type of infection that athletes have contracted from the pick-up scene. For example, a collegiate football player revealed his awareness by saying, "Oh god, I've only known of one guy who admitted it...one guy having it, some gonorrhea, but his mom was a nurse so she got him some penicillin or whatever, but...that's the only case I've ever heard of cause I guess if a guy gets an STD, he's not going to be too open about it." While engaging in promiscuity is something most athletes boast about since it is status-producing, contracting an STD often brings ridicule upon an athlete because it is viewed as a humorous and embarrassing situation as a minor league baseball player revealed:

> ...this guy is one of the top relievers in baseball, one time [laughing] and when he came up, he was real young, and he ended up being my roommate and we were roommates in fall ball, an instructional league in [a certain city], and he ended up getting the crabs...and one day I'm sitting around and...he said, "Something showed up in the toilet or something," and he goes to the trainer and...he's got crabs, so I'm like, "You got to be kidding me," so I'd been rooming with him for the last few days you know, so I had to get out of his room and they had to get all of his sheets and everything out and he had to put that powder on him for a few days and he was the only guy that I know that ever caught anything from anybody.

STIs are always a potential risk and consequence when participating in casual sex and because their impact can range from inconvenience to financially costly to incurable and/or lethal, athletes often avoid discussing their infections out of fear that teammates will ridicule or reject them. However, in his book, *Bad As I Wanna Be,* former NBA star Dennis Rodman openly discussed how he was falsely accused of giving a female cheerleader herpes and was subsequently sued for $1.5 million.[24] Although Rodman refused to settle out of court and was proven innocent because he did not have herpes, it cost him nearly a quarter of a million dollars in legal fees.[25] In contrast, health care worker Sonya Elliot charged former Atlanta Falcon quarterback, Michael Vick, with a lawsuit claiming that he knowingly gave her herpes in April of 2003 after she allegedly tested positive following an unprotected sexual encounter with him.[26] Vick's attorney noted that the woman agreed to an undisclosed resolution to the case in April of 2006.[27] In the end, casual sex with unfamiliar partners is indeed a high risk behavior for both partners, and women are at greater risk for contracting disease because STIs are transmitted more easily from a male to a female than vice versa.[28]

When Abuse, Pain, and Regret Overtake Pleasure

A variety of participants at all levels noted athletes inflicting pressure as well as ridicule on teammates to engage (and succeed) in the pick-up scene since such pursuits are valued as a way to prove one's masculinity. While such pressure tactics are thought to be harmless, sometimes they produce out of control behaviors and abuse that target not only athletes, but females as one collegiate hockey player recalled:

> Well, [the pick-up scene] it was happening everywhere – every weekend somebody was... walking by with your arm around a girl, high-fiving your teammate and making some snide comment about her ass or her tits or something and then you know the next day everybody at practice wanted to know what happened you know, "Does she have any friends you know?" – and my junior year here was just awful and I still think that it had everything to do with the fact that we were back on campus – you know for the first two years I played here we played in obscurity because we played all games on the road...nobody knew about us and those were the two closest knit teams I'd ever been on. My junior year we came here had a brand new rink started playing in front of standing room only crowds and all of a sudden everybody went Hollywood – and there was this like real abuse thing that you know people just giving each other shit – [it] started off as a joke kind of a thing – [and] it got to the point where people started taking it personal and people started meaning it – and it got ugly, it got ugly – you know guys would find out you were with a girl and just go and torture the girl and the girl would then come back and be pissed at you like, "What are you telling your buddies?" and you know, I didn't say anything to my buddies, they're making all this shit up you know, and there's a girl you might have had a decent shot at a relationship with and she's telling you to fuck off because she thinks you went and told all your buddies [intimate details about her] because they think they're being funny – they go, "Just joking," but it didn't matter, it ruined a relationship.

It is likely that some athletes felt threatened by the possibility that a teammate's deeper involvement with a woman would be a potential threat to their team bonding and camaraderie. Consequently, sabotaging the early formation of intimate relationships was a practical solution that could easily be played off as a joke that hid certain athletes' true underlying fear of intimate relationships replacing their close team friendships. Unfortunately, these practices created hostility between teammates, and its impact on females was no less devastating since those who were victimized, once again learned not to trust athletes because their affections were used for ridicule and team entertainment.

While it is evident that some athletes took pleasure in abusing teammates and women who engaged in the pick-up scene, not all athletes' displayed such character deficiencies and behaviors. Furthermore, certain participants observed athletes experiencing emotional pain and regret that was tied to their participation in the pick-up scene as a collegiate baseball player and a collegiate hockey coach discussed in this way:

> ...there were guys that went out three nights a week to get laid and these guys actually worked at it whereas others didn't and had the attitude of if it happened it happened but...there was another group of guys I saw who felt bad [if] they were with a female who was drunk and maybe didn't know what was going on in hindsight of looking back on the situation and these guys were regretful – if they thought they might be interested in seeing her again – then they had some concern in hindsight...

> I've watched a lot of our guys go through a lot hurting – you know I've seen guys come to me crying their eyes out because they don't want to be part of that culture anymore – they had this reputation of being a stud, reputation of being a woman's man, you know the whole bit...and they come to me and they cry their eyes out about all they really want is one girl that they admire, respect, and can trust – and that's what they want, a relationship – they don't want all the whoring and the, just the gratuitous sex – and two weeks later they're right back at it...they get back with their buddies and it's easier to fall back into that cultural thing – you know where it's just an accepted part of being an athlete... in the last 10 years more and more – you can just tell they crave a steady relationship and I think they almost regret that they have that...

The first participant observed that alcohol promoted 70% of the sex because "it gave the guys courage and the women no inhibitions," and he saw this as "a dangerous combination" that could result in sexual aggression. The second participant found that despite certain players' best intentions, they were not able to give up "all the whoring" and quickly succumbed to the cultural pressures that promoted promiscuity and were "part of being an athlete." It is apparent that when some athletes relinquish their decision-making, this can result in inner turmoil because giving up control of your desires to teammates is essentially prostituting yourself. This coach also observed that some of his collegiate players avoided alumni events because they did not want their female partners to know the extent of the sexual practices they engaged in as athletes. One newly married wife, who was not aware of her husband's seedy background, experienced shock when his teammates began revealing various "war" stories at one particular gathering. Because the past does catch up with most people sooner or later, it is wise for players to conduct themselves in such a way that they do not have to fear or worry about explaining participation in behaviors that will eventually surface and potentially damage reputations as well as significant relationships.

While the previous narrative noted certain athletes' unsuccessful attempts to stop their involvement in the pick-up scene, a minor league hockey player elaborated on his womanizing experiences and its subsequent ending during his career in this way:

> Picking up women in a bar...I'd say quite a few in the whole – in the only real full year that I was involved in it. And, I recall going back the next year in training camp, and I never did continue with that...that was my main goal to cut that crap out because it was a non-satisfying practice. I recall having conversations with a friend of mine who was my goaltending partner in high school, you know, saying how that kind of thing was very unfulfilling. Like you'd go out and you'd be lonely and looking to hook up. And afterwards, whether you might have had sex with that woman or not, a one-night stand situation, it certainly wasn't fulfilling. It wasn't, it wasn't what you intended it to be.

Although this athlete noted loneliness prompted his desire to "hook up," such experiences were continuously lacking perhaps because the both participants were trying to find deeper intimacy with someone they did not know and were using sex as a way to do this. In time, this participant came to the realization that intimacy must precede sex in order for it to be fulfilling and more than just a physical act. Such notions were supported in *The Hite Report on Male Sexuality* because men found sex much better when they loved someone.[29]

When Athletes Become the Target

Previous player narratives provide ample evidence that athletes engage in a variety of negative behaviors that target women for sex. At the same time, it would be naive to believe that athletes are exempt from experiencing similar behaviors at the hands of females who turn the tables by targeting them. This fact has caused athletes to become wary of women as one NBA player noted by saying, "You know a woman can sure make you feel good, but they can sure as hell 'damage' you too." Similarly, a minor league basketball player observed, "In watching other guys go through the whole pick-up scene and they end up picking up the wrong one, and then you know attitudes flair and publicity, you know things get out, and that just didn't seem like that was something that I wanted to get involved in." Both participants mentioned that sexual involvement with the wrong woman could result in negative consequences although they did not elaborate on the actual "damage" or what the "publicity" involved. This was in contrast to another NBA player who revealed, "These women aren't here...to you know figure out our likes or dislikes so much, it's mainly a physical attraction or a monetary attraction, you know, 'Maybe I can get pregnant by this guy and I'll be set for life, I can have his baby and be set for life.'" This participant, like others, found that females trying to get pregnant without an athletes' consent or awareness was a very real consequence of the pick-up scene. Furthermore, this life-impacting consequence affected professionals as well as collegiate athletes who similarly observed female "gold diggers" looking to latch onto them as a "meal ticket" for long-term financial security once they turned professional.

NBA star Earvin "Magic" Johnson recalled one teammate hooked up with a female who made herself sexually available and upon waking up the next morning, the player realized that the female had left and stolen his wallet along with his pants.[30] Such experiences provide evidence that casual sexual encounters with unfamiliar women can be risky, and a minor league basketball player in this study revealed an even greater reason to beware by saying, "It's the women that videotape, and they do it as a scheme or scam of blackmailing, especially when there's money involved." While this participant noted females videotaping sexual encounters with high paid minor league basketball players overseas in order to extort money from them, a MLB player elaborated on other practices he encountered during his major league career:

> When I first got to the big leagues there was a situation going on where a man would hire women to you know seduce players, the woman would somehow sedate the man...the player would be passed out in a hotel room and you know they'd have all their clothes off with a woman and the man would take pictures and then use that down the road for you know monetary reasons.

Players in committed relationships were especially at risk because their marriages and families could be jeopardized whenever these kinds of practices in conjunction with the athletes' sexual behaviors were disclosed. Like MLB players and minor league basketball players, NHL players were targeted as well. It is apparent that while athletes used different manipulative practices that targeted women for sex, women used various sexual practices to target athletes for their money. In the end, it is not an individual's gender or athletic participation that determines whether someone targeted another for money or sex, but rather a lack of scruples, morals, and/or deeper emotional connection.

False Accusations or Forced Sex?

Sexual assault and rape as well as false accusations of such crimes are among the most serious consequences resulting from the pick-up scene. For example, two NBA players, Derrick Coleman, formerly of the New Jersey Nets, and former Washington Wizards Juwan Howard, were both accused of sexually assaulting different women and after thorough investigations that even involved DNA testing in Coleman's case, police found no basis for charges in either case.[31] Howard even filed a lawsuit after his case was dismissed to publicly declare his innocence and in November of 1998, a Maryland judge ordered his female accuser to pay Howard $100,000 in damages.[32] More recently, the Duke University Lacrosse Team had its 2006 season cancelled when team members were falsely accused of gang raping a female stripper they had hired.[33] This highly publicized case highlighted the problem that some athletes face when people and prosecutors jump to conclusions by presuming guilt before an incident is thoroughly investigated and/or proven in a court of law. In this study, approximately 10% of the participants revealed their awareness of false sexual assault and/or rape accusations that targeted individuals and groups of athletes even more so because group sex was prevalent in certain athlete cultures. For example, a minor league football player revealed, "I got a buddy that was accused of it, actually him and some other players were accused by an individual of having done that and she was actually arrested after that allegation was found to be…no basis for it, no foundation for it, but that almost destroyed his marriage." While this false rape allegation related to the woman's desire to extort money from professional athletes, other participants attributed false claims to a female's desire for power and control as well as her regret over sexual behaviors perhaps while under the influence of alcohol. One minor league basketball player felt underlying guilt from having sex with an athlete from a different race often caused women to tell authorities a sexual encounter was nonconsensual – even if it was. A wrestler revealed his awareness of false rape accusations that targeted a group of athletes in this way:

> Actually yea, but fortunately they were taking pictures, one girl called rape and filed a police report and a complaint and everything, and when the police came and collected the bed sheets and all that stuff, and the

cop asked, [since] he wanted to hear both sides of the story, so he came to this guy and said, "Do you have...a position on this?" and both these guys...called it bullshit, it was consensual, and he goes, "How can you prove it?" and they're like, "Well, we have pictures," so when the cop got the film developed, she was sitting on top with her hands in the air, and this wasn't the first time she's called rape, so it was bullshit and they threw it out. And they asked our wrestlers if they wanted to press charges against her and they said, "No."

Despite this outcome, athletes need to ask themselves if justice would have been served without pictures in this case. And, is picking up a woman in order to engage in group sex worth the risk of losing an athletic career, scholarship, reputation, and time and money spent proving your innocence in the legal system? Several other participants representing hockey, football, and wrestling similarly noted females claiming gang rape following seemingly consensual group sexual encounters with multiple athletes that became disrespectful and/ or abusive to the woman after the experience had ended. In such cases, the female felt used and disrespected and because it appeared she wanted revenge against the athletes, she told police she was raped. While certain participants admitted their teammates' behavior was rude and wrong, they also noted the implications of rape charges are life altering even when they are proven false. This prompted one collegiate football player to declare that if he were a coach, he would immediately teach athletes the importance of avoiding risky sexual behaviors and situations including group sex. This is sound thinking because what may appear to be consensual group sex while a situation is in progress can be readily recanted whenever an unfamiliar female becomes sober, disrespected, or regretful of her sexual behavior. This is not to say that group sexual assaults do not happen because they do; however, this study has uncovered ample evidence that women have falsely accused athletes of individual as well as group sexual assaults. In the end, athletes must ask themselves if putting themselves in compromising sexual situations is worth the risk of experiencing an array of consequences regardless of whether they are found innocent or guilty.

Although false accusations are always a potential consequence whenever an athlete has an intimate encounter with a female he does not know, FBI crime statistics reveal that only about 2% of rape reports are false because women face an intense screening process before an offender is brought to trial and convicted.[34] False accusations cause harm not only by impacting the targeted athlete(s) and their families in tremendous ways, but they create great injustice for women who are actually sexually assaulted and may not be taken seriously or believed.[35] However, the percentage of false rape reports is minute compared to the number of females who are, in fact, sexually assaulted each year, and this makes sexual assault a much more likely outcome and a very real consequence for women participating in the pick-up scene compared to false accusations targeting athletes.

Such notions are highlighted by the fact that athlete sexual assault is usually not a random act of violence, but more of an exploitative event akin to acquaintance rape that occurs because many women make themselves sexually available for brief encounters by freely entering an athlete's residence, hotel, and bedroom.[36] When such assaults occur, there is often no sign of physical struggle or confrontation, the use of weapons, or eyewitnesses to support the claim of sexual aggression because often the athlete and woman were engaging in a sexual encounter prior to the assault accusations.[37] In such instances, the problem and sexual assault often occur because the athlete refuses to stop his sexual advances and engages in certain sexual behaviors without the woman's consent. Collegiate and professional athletes' superior size and strength often in combination with alcohol intoxication enable an athlete to easily overpower a woman during an intimate encounter and have their way sexually.[38] While countless women have experienced one-night stands without any incident or problem, promiscuous women face fierce scrutiny that would seriously challenge their credibility should they become the victim of sexual assault since they pursued the athlete for sex.[39] Under such circumstances, acquaintance rape provides prosecutors with the formidable challenge of proving that a rape occurred "beyond reasonable doubt" as opposed to the situation being a consensual sexual experience that defense lawyers and their athlete-clients often claim.[40]

Approximately 50% of participants representing every sport were able to discuss their awareness, observation, and/or participation in athlete sexual assault allegations and/or incidences that occurred within their own collegiate and/or professional teams during playing and/or coaching careers spanning the 1960s through 2010. As a result, numerous participants discussed the phenomenon of athlete sexual assault including a collegiate hockey player who revealed:

> ...I've had girlfriends that have told me about people that had done things to them...had sexually assaulted them...you know that they were at a party or a bar and then they went home with someone...and were making out or consensually making out or whatever – and it escalated to the point where something the woman didn't want to happen – happened...I would say it's more prone to be athletes, more athletic people definitely – I'm not sure why...

This participant believed "date rape is prevalent among the jock culture" and he attributed this to athletes' "misogynistic group mentality" that resulted from athlete cultures which promoted aggression in combination with negative attitudes toward women. While athletes in this study often differed in their definition of what constituted sexual force with females, researchers who conducted a national study found that 88% of college men who self-reported an assault that met the legal definition of rape were unwavering in their belief that their behavior was definitely not rape.[41] This does not mean all rapists are liars, but rather it implies that some men interpret their sexual behaviors as consensual – even when it involves the use of coercion and physical force.[42] Interestingly, various researchers also found that the group norms and behaviors that the previous athlete referred to were strong predictors for the kinds of sexual practices – including aggression – that some males find acceptable to use with women.[43] A wrestler supported these notions when he said, "From my personal experiences, whoever I was friends with or whatever, it wasn't...that bad, it may happen, you know kind of like forcing them a little bit or maybe just a handful of times I probably seen it happen." This participant noted teammates' use of force was not "that bad," and it is evident that because sexual assaults can happen without being defined as such, athletes cannot allow certain peer groups to determine right from wrong sexual behavior. In the end, sexual assault is a very real consequence of the pick-up scene that athletes seem to overlook because they are the perpetrators rather than victims in these cases. However, such apathy regarding sexual aggression can quickly change whenever a close female an athlete knows is assaulted, or when an athlete himself faces a host of potential consequences resulting from sexual assault accusations that threaten to change his life and the lives of others in a striking fashion.

ATHLETES' CORNER: POINTS TO PONDER

1. "Game" is a universal practice among males, including athletes, which involves the use of alcohol and conversation to convince a reluctant female to leave with you to engage in casual sex. While "game" is thought to be a skill, it has a darker side since some athletes are willing to say or do virtually anything to engage in causal sex. This reduces picking up women to nothing more than an act of deception that disregards authentic bonding, communication, and moral/ethical behavior in favor of self-serving sexual gratification.

2. Athletes' status and privilege, competitive nature, bravado, and peer pressure encourage involvement in the pick-up scene since women are viewed as sex objects and a sport to conquer. Athletes have rightfully intervened to protect both females and teammates from escalating and abusive situations when an unwanted sexual advance was rejected causing an athlete to become openly hostile. This raises questions about how far some athletes are willing to go in order to experience and/or force casual sex particularly when teammates are not around to stop an aggressive sexual advance.

3. Know that participating in the pick-up scene has consequences that have caused some athletes to compromise their character, integrity, and well-being through engaging in infidelity, poor relational practices, addictive and/or compulsive sexual behaviors, allowing others to dictate their lifestyle, and contracting STDs/STIs. Although athletes use females for sex, women target athletes by trying to get pregnant without an athletes' awareness; other females attempt to extort athletes' money by luring them with sex. Sexual assault and false accusations of such crimes are among the most serious consequences of the pick-up scene although the former is much more likely to occur and victimize women than the latter which have targeted male athletes to a far lesser extent.

Chapter 5

Examining the Other Half of the Equation: Sexually Available Women

One of the most apparent factors enabling the pick-up scene to flourish is the manner in which women make themselves available to athletes. Without female sexual availability, athletes arguably would not be able to pick up women or engage in deviant behaviors to the extent that some do. This research reveals there is no shortage of women who often go to great lengths to be with athletes, and this was highlighted by the fact that 90% of the participants noted high female availability during collegiate and/or professional careers spanning the 1960s through 2010.

My first observations of female availability occurred during my junior hockey career in Canada. After my team in Quebec folded in mid-season, I arrived at my next junior team in Ontario just as players were preparing for a formal dance. My teammates told me that if I wanted to attend, I could go to the high school and with their help, I could choose virtually any female to take to the dance without really knowing her at all – and I did. It was evident that my instant status as a hockey player opened doors to opportunities with women that would have been previously closed for me. Such female availability only increased during my collegiate as well as professional career. While opportunities for sexual encounters were readily available, some players would make this a sure bet by seeking out female followers or team "groupies" whenever they experienced rejection, had no other options, or did not want to put forth any effort to have sex. Together, these situations showed me there were plenty of women who made no qualms about being sexually available to athletes and sometimes in amazing ways.

THE PHENOMENON OF FEMALE GROUPIES

Most athletes were very aware of the fact that their athletic participation attracted an abundant supply of women that expressed their higher loyalty, support, and sexual availability to certain athletic teams. Such female followers were often referred to as groupies or super groupies, freaks, cleat chasers, bat girls, hangers-ons, baseball Annie's or junkies, mat maids, jock or jersey chasers, puck bunnies, puck fucks, buffarillos, or dirties. Former MLB star Jose Canseco revealed that the women athletes had sex with on road trips were considered "road beef," while the unattractive females that athletes had sex with were called "slump busters."[1] Regardless of the different labels used, such nicknames essentially highlighted the lower status these ever-present women often held among many athletes. In her book, *Wedded to the Game: The Real Lives of NFL Women,* Shannon O'Toole noted one collegiate coach's wife was responsible for monitoring the football dormitory and locking the doors at a certain time in order "to keep the maniac girls out."[2] Moreover, such female availability could exist for both high profile sports as well as the sports that lacked such prestige on campus as a collegiate baseball player revealed by saying, "We weren't as high profile...so people didn't know our faces as much...but you had your own set of groupies and...set of people who knew who you were...if I didn't play baseball...I would have probably gotten 50% less attention." Like other participants, this athlete noted female followers often had very specific team interests that an NFL player and a minor league basketball player elaborated upon in this way:

> ...at the collegiate level just bars, there were specific bars that you would go to, football players went to three or four different places, and if you wanted to hook up with a football player you would go to those three or four places, if it was a basketball groupie that was hanging around, they went to the bars that the basketball players went to, so it was very much a sport-by-sport thing, wrestling parties you had a different set of girls typically that went to the wrestling party, and likewise with baseball, pretty much a whole separate group of young ladies who were around baseball players, and there was some guys from all those sports that were able to go between the four to all the parties and be accepted and it was not a problem, so it was pretty much at the bars and restaurants at the collegiate level.

> The groupies or the women, they follow their sports [and] are the same in my opinion, it's just where you happen to be...soccer is huge and [in XXX], in Europe, so those guys got the top pick of the females, basketball was second so there's a nice little hierarchy there, and it went down and we get our nice share, but there was very little crossover between the two, they were segmented – this is what they like and that's who they're going to try to be with – and I think that's the same, you don't see too many women that are in for basketball and football players or football and baseball, it's just not what they do, so I think they're very specific in who they choose to do these things with...that's been my experience.

Although the second participant observed female followers gravitating to professionals from one particular sport only, this did not hold true in all cases because other participants noted certain females' sexual involvement with collegiate athletes from a variety of sports. Participants, however, were in agreement that female followers were often persistent in their pursuit of athletes as another minor league basketball player noted by saying, "Overseas, I mean shoot I've played places where you come home from practice and there's three or four women waiting for you where you live...[and] girls would come to different cities to follow you to play and watch you play with the hope of meeting you, and I mean they're basically there, everywhere you turn." This participant found women who were little more than distant acquaintances showing up at his residence often for the purpose of having a sexual encounter. A wrestler also noted engaging in casual sex with females, who were "willing to literally be your sex toy," was an attractive alternative because women can be "very needy" and committed relationships took a lot of time and energy that many athletes did not want to give. A minor league basketball player discussed various factors that he believed motivated female groupies' sexual behavior:

> ...when I was in [a particular NBA] camp, I mean you come out after a practice and there were...just amazing women you know just waiting outside to talk to an athlete – that was the same way in the [minor league]. I used to laugh and tell people that the groupies in the [minors] were the same as the players in the [minors] trying to move up, trying to get to the next level – you know they want to meet a guy who is going to get to the NBA and see if they can string along during that – it was the same thing overseas, [women] loved...the athletes, especially the Americans, especially the African Americans, and that's who they want to hang out with.

Another minor leaguer from baseball offered another observation by saying, "We were dealing with girls that were...I don't know, don't want to say [it] but almost using us, almost using the players in some ways, it's almost like a game for them too." One wrestler even revealed his awareness of an actual game by saying, "They always had a game where it was if a girl hooked up with one guy, how you could really say she hooked up with these other guys. It was kind of a weird game they had going on. The girls just wanted to see how they were all connected together in some way." And, this could be a source of pride for certain women as an NFL player recalled:

> ...I've heard of girls that have stepped up and said, "Yea, I've slept with him, I've screwed him, I blew him, I did whatever to him" you know... [and] I've heard girls go as far as to say, "You know I'm going to have something to tell my kids when I have kids," and I think...I'm not sure I'd want to tell my kids that I, you know, I screwed you know whomever.

Like numerous participants who reported that athletes, including themselves, used female followers for sex and stories, women also bragged that their sexual encounters with athletes were noteworthy experiences. However, such behaviors, like the females involved, were seldom respected according to a collegiate hockey player:

> ...I've talked to female friends of mine and told them about what happened and they sit there and they're like, "Where do you find these girls?" Like these girls just have no self-esteem, no self-respect, you know nothing, and for some reason or another, they just try and look for it in hockey players or in lacrosse players or in football players or something. And...maybe they think people are going to like them afterwards because they're giving them sex, where in actuality most guys are going to look down upon them. So, I think it's just a mix up in the mind, looking for one thing but actually getting the exact opposite.

The above participant observed that although some women believed their sexual availability for both individual as well as group sexual encounters would bring them popularity, it had the opposite effect by alienating the athletes they had sex with. Female observers were equally disgusted with promiscuous women and in the book, *Fast Girls: Teenage Tribes and the Myth of the Slut,* author Emily White found women were far more vicious toward each other for such behaviors than males.[3] Such practices carried repercussions for women that this participant elaborated upon by saying, "Somebody just wants to feel important for a night and just figures you know, 'Oh...let's just do whatever you guys want' and the next day wakes up and just feels like a whore and walks away." Indeed, promiscuity can have a definite impact on a female's reputation, the way she feels about herself, and the peer pressure she experiences. Various participants, including a MLB player, also believed promiscuity assisted in promoting negative attitudes toward women in general:

> I think that generally guys looked at females like sexual objects, opportunities to self gratify, [and] why did they look at them that way? Because that's the way the females presented themselves, so I'm not going to just throw all the blame on the guys there, you know when the girls are presenting themselves that way and making themselves available that way, why would they look at them any differently?

It is apparent that the double standard continues to exist by rewarding males, including athletes, for all kinds of sexual conquests while women who engage in the same practices become quickly dismissed often with their reputations in ruin. Some collegiate and professional athletes have even noted females experiencing more blatant disrespect and ridicule immediately following their sexual encounters with athletes which further shows that females are not free to engage in causal sex like their male counterparts without being shunned in many cases. One collegiate basketball player recalled athletes saying, "Let's go" whenever casual sex was offered although this was quickly followed by, "Get out" as soon as the sexual encounter ended.

While casual sex with an athlete could certainly result in a woman being ostracized, some professionals kept female team followers at a distance without even having sex with them as a minor league football player revealed in this way:

> …you had your groupies that came to the game and things like that, but this is my experiences, those girls were people that you just stayed away from, they were kind of the nutty ones that were going to run around town and tell everyone that you were their boyfriend or whatever, so the groupie girls did not get a lot of attention physically, they got a lot of attention, they would hang out with us, they would go you know if we had a party or whatever, they would call, and come over and hang with us, but they didn't get a lot of attention physically in my opinion… which is probably the opposite of what they actually wanted…

This participant also revealed the differences in women that he became sexually involved with during his collegiate and professional career related to whether or not he knew the female. Consequently, encounters with sexually available collegiate females were described as "friends with privileges" whereas sex during his professional career involved one-night stands with unfamiliar sexually available women rather than the team's female followers that he knew.

Previous narratives provide ample evidence that female followers are not accepted or respected even though athletes use these women for sex. Perhaps this is why some women developed unique strategies that camouflaged their true nature and agendas from the athletes they were targeting; a minor league basketball player revealed his observations in this way:

> On the professional side, the groupies so to speak are professional groupies, you would never know it now, usually the way they dress and the funky type of style that they have that you would know, most groupies these days they don't travel in packs anymore, it used to be where there were people that would hang out and you know exactly who they are, you don't know them anymore, they're high skilled professionals, they're corporately inclined, you know they're very, very calculating women and they know exactly how to get the attention of the guys, so…the guys are unaware of it, and they're very good at disguising themselves…

Camouflage enabled such women to penetrate the athlete culture more readily and be accepted since they were not suspected of being groupies with ulterior motives. Although professional athletes' higher profile and salaries provide primary motives that fuel such females' time and attention, there are other motives that fuel their interest and sometimes create turmoil as well.

FEMALE AVAILABILITY AMONG COLLEGIATE ATHLETES

Team success in combination with a sport's popularity were predominant factors that influenced female availability for collegiate athletes competing at universities of all sizes. This was evident when certain team sports with prestige at one university had little status and female following at another institution of equal size. The opposite also held true as a collegiate football player found an incredible difference in female availability once he transferred from a Division II program to Division I because moving to a higher division translated into thousands more available women. Non-revenue producing sports such as baseball and wrestling sometimes were identified as having lower status and a limited female following which a minor league baseball player observed, "I don't think the baseball players were in big demand at all...there wasn't like groupies hanging out for baseball players...like on 0 to 10 [scale], it'd be a one...the higher level would have been for a football or basketball player, not a baseball player." In contrast, other baseball players including another minor leaguer revealed that female availability was never an issue for 20% of his collegiate teammates since sex with "three or four different girls" was "a phone call away." Such arrangements were not uncommon because collegiate athletes representing every sport in this study as well as professionals similarly noted players summoning women for individual as well as group sexual encounters through a quick phone call. At other times, certain females took more initiative to have sex as a collegiate baseball player explained:

> After college or [during] the summers when I'd play in the semi-pro tournaments...you know you'll sit in the bull pen and [the females] they'll give you their hotel room keys and they'll follow you around and basically do whatever you want...it was kind of shocking how, how aggressive they'd get in pursuing, like come into your room and just ready to throw down [have sex]...it was pretty amazing, it was pretty shocking that that would happen.

While some baseball players expressed disappointment with their female following at certain universities, this was certainly not the case in all players' experiences. Furthermore, such availability was observed as a "competitive thing" between women because athletes were viewed as a potential "meal ticket" out of a certain town. In addition, athletes from other non-revenue sports, including a wrestler, noted the impact of team popularity on female availability:

> We weren't the biggest wrestling school, we ended up being pretty good by the time I was done, but you know I've heard at other bigger time schools it was easily available, at [XX University] you had to work more for it like to get a girlfriend, or you know I don't remember too many situations where girls coming over, "Oh you guys are wrestlers, here you go." I don't remember that, not at [XX University], it's a more conservative school, we weren't really known for wrestling so...somebody getting a girl at a bar and a lot of times she may not even know that you're an athlete, she's just maybe so drunk that that's whoever that happened to be.

This account was in contrast to other wrestlers who noted high female availability at their universities. For example, one wrestler recalled, "[Laughing] actually they were quite a bit, women seemed to throw themselves at us" while another noted, "I think pretty prevalent, pretty available." This participant also revealed that female availability remained unchanged for the collegiate wrestlers he coached in the late 2000s compared to his own career at this university in the early 1980s. Another wrestler commented on differences in female availability between sports by saying, "How easy? – on a scale of what like 1-10 (10 is very available) I'd say a seven probably, but the hockey players are like a 12 at [XXX University] I'm sure, those guys had it all...the wrestlers not as much." At the same time, not all athletes took advantage of the female availability they could access because for 25% of this wrestler's teammates who were referred to as the "God Squad," their stronger religious beliefs meant they had no interest in casual sex.

Athletes from a variety of sports noted that while women were certainly attracted to the perceived "mystique" and popularity of high profile collegiate athletes, this also worked against them whenever females held negative preconceptions. For example, a minor league baseball player recalled, "Yea they kind of don't want to talk to you cause...we had a bad reputation as far as with the girls...you know guys would sleep around and they would still have girlfriends where they were from...they managed to upset a lot of women down there." However, notorious team reputations do not always produce lower female availability because although a minor league hockey player recalled academic counselors warning incoming freshmen women to avoid hockey players at his university, this made his team even more alluring to some women.

Collegiate basketball and football are often the most prestigious sports at universities because they attract the largest crowds and the most attention. Consequently, it was no surprise to find these athletes often discussing experiences with high female availability. A minor league basketball player discussed this by saying, "At your disposal, at your disposal cause…if it's a highly talented team like we were you know on the news already, you know people calling your room, some chicks who knew a guy's going to be a potential first rounder…[they] let you know that they were there." An NBA player also noted, "The college level like I said for some it was one big orgy, so you had your pick throughout the university especially if you were a popular player." In a similar fashion, various football players noted high female availability including one collegiate player who revealed, "Very available…and again is it because you're a football player? It could have been I, I don't know, you like to think it probably wasn't, but nonetheless you know, yeah, there was a ton of activity."

A variety of athletes recalled certain events involving female availability that even surprised them, and this occurred at home as well as on road trips during their collegiate careers. For example, a collegiate hockey player recalled, "In the parking lot of McDonalds that we stopped at half way home from a game [against a rival university] – I mean we're all looking for him [a teammate] and here we find him in some car getting a blow job from some girl that he had met five minutes ago." Other participants including a collegiate baseball player, a minor league basketball player, and a collegiate football player elaborated on their unique collegiate experiences involving female availability in this way:

> …I never did anything personally that was crazy…but I can remember girls coming over, you know to my apartment, and taking their clothes off and jumping into bed with me uninvited, and just kind of say, "Whatever you want me to do I'll do"…you know pretty regularly especially I mean, whew, I don't know I'm trying to think of…how to describe the time frame, you know, I'd say…over three years, over four years of college I'd say 10, 15 different times…they were pretty aggressive actually.

> Very available, very available in college at any of the schools that I played at, there were always women around, there were some that would make themselves available at two or three o'clock in the morning, there was one girl, one group of girls that would like make rounds, they'd you know knock on doors and see who was home at two or three in the morning after being out all night, stuff like that…it was about two or three times when like at one point, one of my roommates he might have been out and he came back with a couple of girls or something like that, and there were some times when I was just in there, you know taking a shower for bed, and he came back and you know pushed a girl into the bathroom with me and I didn't even know her name.

I have one situation that I'll probably never forget...we had just gotten to [the university] and...we were starting you know for the season, it was like in August and...my roommate had a convertible and you know we didn't have school, you know we were out driving around...we had the top down and we ran into, in the car, like three or four girls and... started talking to them at a stop light...[and] that led to coming back and a sexual encounter, just on a situation like that...I mean they knew we were football players, whether or not they were patrolling...but you know three or four guys in one car and three or four girls in another car and...the next thing you know we were in the room so...it was like pretty much my first experience of [XXX University] life and...I'd been [an athlete at another university], I'd been to other colleges and...as far as in a bar and picking up a girl on a one-nighter, I mean that, that happened a lot...but that specific situation...on a Friday you know early afternoon, and...the next thing you know, you're having sex in your room that was kind of bizarre to me and unusual in that it had never happened before.

It is easy to understand that when women make themselves that sexually available, most athletes will accommodate their request for casual sex, but nothing more. Such behaviors also help to explain why certain participants from larger universities with high profile sports programs found female availability was comparable to or even surpassed their major league experiences because thousands of college females were readily available and accessible on campus. It is also equally important to note that women had easy access to collegiate athletes as well. While it is evident that team success and a sport's status are among the most impacting elements that determine collegiate athletes' access to women, this is often amplified even more at the professional level.

FEMALE AVAILBILITY AMONG PROFESSIONAL ATHLETES

Minor League Athletes

Only a small minority of athletes failed to find an abundance of female availability during their professional careers although these circumstances could change from team to team, city to city, and league to league. For example, a minor league baseball player revealed, "I would say fairly available, I mean not so much in rookie ball, but once you get up into...playing a little bit of the higher levels I think pretty much available." Such differences also appeared at the major league level as an NFL player revealed:

I think this changes from place to place, and to give you some dynamics that were involved, when I came to [my first NFL team] from college, I went to training camp, there's 20,000 people a day at training camp… okay, now I also played for [a second NFL team] and [a third NFL team]. They might have had 10 people at those training camps. So, especially here [on my first pro team], it was, I mean, it's almost hard to even, to even tell you what it was like. I mean there was just people everywhere. And whatever you kind of were looking for…you could get.

Like certain minor leaguers, the previous participant found tremendous differences in female availability during his career with several different NFL teams which was often linked to team success. One minor league football player admitted that although women were readily sexually available for his team, this could include certain limitations:

I guess that kind of depends on your standards, so I mean there were always girls available, it just depended on how far you wanted to go down in your ratings I guess [laughs], so…I mean if I wanted to go out and hook up with a girl, it was going to happen you know, it…just depended on how good looking a girl I wanted to wait out or hold out for I guess, and if I wanted to risk hanging out with the good-looking girls to wait for a maybe, or go for a sure thing with a girl that wasn't so good looking.

Some athletes have no qualms about choosing less attractive females because they believe sex will be a sure thing more times than not. However, this can pave the way for conflict and potential aggression to occur whenever an athlete's expectations and agenda do not coincide with a woman's desires and sexual behavior.

Some minor leaguers compared the female availability they observed in their professional experiences with their collegiate careers. One minor league basketball player noted, "Europe I would say [is] similar to my college career… pretty easily accessible" while another mentioned, "I think more on the professional side, it's just a bigger pond." Because professional athletes often experience greater exposure through more frequent playing and traveling schedules and their free time is not supervised to the same extent as collegiate athletes, this can translate into greater female availability that various minor leaguers noted. For example, a minor league football player recalled, "I would say very available, I don't think there's ever been a team that I've been on professionally that there hasn't been a group of girls around us." Similarly, a minor league baseball player elaborated in this way:

I don't think baseball in college attracted the females that much to the baseball players – in the minor leagues I think it was just the opposite, they were there at the games, they were there at the practices, and they were quite available...when I was in spring training in [XXX], it was just unreal that I would see so many women line up at the different fields... so it was not a problem I think for a lot of athletes.

Another minor league baseball player noted the impact of competition by saying, "[In] college you had to work a little bit harder for the girls I think due to...how many guys and girls are running around...[but] certainly more readily available in the pro world." Other participants, including another minor league baseball player, explained how minor leaguers' status could impact female availability:

...in the minors though, I think when you're in hick-town America and you're not making any money but you're the star, you're the main attraction in that town for the summer...again there's a certain cachet involved with that – in other words...even though you're not making six figures, you're a celebrity to the people of that town and...I think that opens a lot more doors than just for the regular Joe.

As the only entertainment and "show" in certain towns where a minor league team had no competition, females ranging in age from "15-50" were readily available for single and married players alike at home and on road trips. And unlike collegiate athletes, professionals had no classes to attend which enabled them to experience the bar scene and women on a nightly basis. However, female availability was not always dependent upon the bar scene as two minor league hockey players revealed:

In [XXX] it was like, it was amazing. I remember sitting on the bench all the time and if you'd look at one girl for a while in the stands and you thought that she was attractive, I mean there were several instances where I'd come out of the locker room and that girl would just be standing there. And, you know, she'd talk to you. It was very easy to pick-up women...

...we were in playing in [another city] and somebody told me the stories about [XXX] and they said after the game you can just walk down the hallway and nod and she'll jump in behind you, you can take her to the bar and do whatever – I'm like, "Yea right," and I got scratched that game (did not play) so I'm looking around the building, I'm like, "There's no women in here" – with about three minutes left in the game in down by the one corner it starts filling up and all these girls started to show up...they don't even watch the game anymore, just come in the end, so we head up and we're walking up and I'm looking straight ahead, I'm married, I aien't – not looking any ways, I don't want anybody to get the wrong idea...

Although the first participant found that simply gazing at a woman during a minor league game could promote a meeting afterward, he questioned the depth of this attraction by saying, "I never felt that they were really attracted to me – they were attracted to the celebrity because...you just don't do that in a normal situation." With this kind of female availability being offered to professional and collegiate athletes alike, it is easy to understand how many get caught up in overindulgent sexual practices as well as deviancy since sexual encounters can be virtually effortless at times. Interestingly, another minor league hockey player commented on how female availability could influence deviant sexual practices in this way:

I mean there's gotta be something to fuel the fire...[and] I think that the women are so in abundance...it's like, "Put a sign on me, fuck me, I'm here guys," you know. Pretty easy to fall in that trap...I mean if it's there, just like a damn fish, if the bait's there, take it you know. I think that has a lot to do with why these guys are so crazy and wild as they can get, you know I don't know what else, you're young, you're full of spunk, you know, I mean, it's male, you're a male, it's instinct. By god, if it's sitting out there to grab, if you don't grab it, it's your own fault. Probably that's the attitude you cop. You know hell, she's sitting there, let's go boys...

Unrestrained female availability was believed to play an important role in certain athletes' overindulgent sexual practices as well as their deviancy perhaps because women and sex were available to the point that normal sex could become unsatisfying after awhile. When this happens, certain individuals feel the need to increase their sexual thrills in an attempt to gain at least temporary satisfaction since they are falling into a "trap" of potentially addictive behavior. One NFL player supported these notions by revealing, "I've seen just as many, you know just as many, you know orgies in college as in the pros, I mean it was going down" which implied some athletes' boredom with one-on-one sexual encounters and some females willingness to do anything to remain in their company. Another minor league hockey player elaborated by saying, "You're popular in that city or that town or wherever you're at and...[women] they feel that you're an important person, and they want to be part of that...and they don't want to say, 'No' to anything so that's why I think you can get away with a lot more." Although certain athletes can act like "kids in a candy store" when it involves women and sex, females also need to take responsibility by evaluating their sexual practices to determine why they are allowing themselves to be sexually available to the point that conversation is not a requirement before engaging in sex with one or more athletes. Such practices place participants at extreme risk for experiencing an array of consequences that can include disease, unwanted pregnancy, and sexual assault particularly when an athlete, who has never heard "no," encounters a woman who does not want to have certain kinds of casual sex.

Major League Athletes

As athletes continued to advance in their careers, it became apparent to most players that female availability increased exponentially once they reached the major leagues. One NFL player elaborated by saying, "In pros [it's] more available...in college you had to be the superstar whatever, you had to be one of the top guys in order to get it as available, as easily as you wanted to." One minor leaguer with nominal NBA experience compared female availability during his minor and major league career by saying, "I'd say a lot more available [in the NBA]...and girls would go up to them whether they was married or not...it's sort of like the rock groups and stuff like that I mean...you got that power behind you as far as like you know being a superstar." Another minor league basketball player elaborated on what this involved during his career:

> You know when I was trying out for the NBA, you would come up outside and there were 200, 250 just incredible women outside, and here I am, I wasn't drafted, I'm a free agent, and...I could pick on half of them because they can't all get with [one star player] and [another star player]...and all those guys – so they got to settle, well that's fine by me so...when you have that much opportunity at that age, you're going to dabble.

The above participant noted that players would converse with women to get phone numbers and/or arrange to meet later at various nightclubs. Because players had so many women to choose from, they would quickly move onto the next whenever they realized someone may not be interested in casual sex. Consequently, this screening process enabled an athlete to experience "some sex acts" with a woman "every time" during the ride from the nightclub back to the hotel. This participant also found it "just amazing" that women offered him sex whenever he went out to nightclubs with NBA players after returning from playing overseas. He attributed such perks to "looking like" an NBA player while in their company and "because I could."

In addition, a minor league baseball player, after closely observing a relative's major league baseball career, compared the female availability and reported, "There's more women that want to attach to you if you're from the big leagues cause they know you got the money, in the minor leagues it's more of...the chase kind of thing." This participant admitted that minor leaguers had to engage in "the chase" more often to have casual sex than major leaguers who were often pursued by women who had already educated themselves to the details of major leaguers' salaries. Still, major leaguers, like minor leaguers, used females for sex, while women attempted to use the athletes for their money and status since "they already have an idea of what they're looking for, [and] who they're looking for," according to an NBA player. Major leaguers, however, resented this fact even though some would use their higher profile, money, and possessions to attract women. Certain minor and major leaguers also noted that rampant female availability could come with a heavy price because some women tried to get pregnant or use male accomplices to extort money from professional athletes in a variety of ways. In short, most participants found female availability greater at the major league level compared to their collegiate and minor league careers, although certain exceptions resulted from chartered flights, which meant athletes left immediately after a game, playing at high profile collegiate programs with large student enrollments, and because tighter security prevented women from accessing major leaguers.

Even with such obstacles, female availability was often rampant as an NHL player explained, "At home for a home player, it was easily accessible 24 hours of the day." A MLB player revealed. "About as easy as spelling your first name, I mean let's put it this way, if you want it, you know where it's at, and it's available...I mean there are plenty of women that...know where the team bus is...the team hotel is...the bars that the guys go to, and they're not going there to get an autograph." Another MLB player admitted, "Very available [laughing] can I check that box?...certainly at the college, minor league, and even at the major league level sex, at times, could be you know pretty promiscuous and you know it was available if you wanted it, there was no doubt about that." Similarly, an NBA player recalled, "Ah man, we used to have, it's a [saying] you know the NBA, the acronym for NBA was 'Nothing But Ass.'" Another NBA player elaborated on what this could mean, "Women were like underwear, you know you'd change them everyday...[so] they were constantly you know ushering in one or two and then getting them out and bringing in the next." Women allowed themselves to be part of this turnover by holding onto the hope and belief that they would be treated differently than the others and possibly end up marrying a player someday. In reality, most women found they were dismissed and replaced by another hopeful sooner or later. Dennis Rodman highlighted such practices in his book, *Bad as I Wanna Be,* as he observed the NBA uniform attracted higher female availability that promoted "the ticket to whoreville and fuckville and slutville."[4] Moreover, Rodman noted sex often occurred without the use of condoms; however, even when players used condoms, an NFL wife recalled a situation where a female groupie stashed the used condom following sex because she planned to reinsert the sperm later to get pregnant and collect large child support payments from the athlete.[5]

In this study, professionals who competed in the early 1970s were just as likely to report access to high female availability as those who competed in 2010, and certain participants revealed what female availability could mean at the major league level. For example, one self-proclaimed "average" NFL player revealed that he received "nude photos" and "underwear" in the mail just like the superstars of the team. Former MLB player, Jose Canseco, noted women chasing the team bus in their cars while "flashing their boobs or throwing their underwear," and sometimes these females would be in their cars naked.[6] Other participants from this study, including another NFL and an NBA player, elaborated on the details of what female availability could mean during their career:

> Readily available and...at the professional level, I was very fortunate to have a couple of teammates who had been around for awhile and their leftovers were always very good [laughs]...[so] when we went on road trips, I always was able to have access to a nice looking young lady if I wanted to – absolutely [laughing], there have been instances where I've come home from a night out and there's been someone waiting on me that sort of thing both collegiately and professionally, given cars to drive, and bills paid for by [women] just to be associated with me... professionally it was after the game at the tunnel when you came out regardless of what city you went to, that's where they would go to meet the players and you sign an autograph, they would say some things, and you either hook up with them, get some numbers, and plan for the next time that you're in town...depends on the city, but professionally I would say 30-50 [women were available].

> ...I have been in a situation where a guy had a girl and it was weird, I helped him get out of some issue he had financially, and this was the guy who actually let his career go down the toilet using drugs and he was short some money for his rent or whatever, so I actually gave him money for his rent and we just happened to be on the road, and I wasn't actually looking to be reimbursed or you know have to pay you back or whatever, but...[laughs] he felt that I was the only one to reach out to help him, so he ends up calling me in the hotel one time and I was like, "Yea what's up man, what's going on?" he said, "Hey man I wanted to say I really appreciate you helping me out with that situation cause you know I got some issues and I was kind of in a spot and you helped me out man, I got a favor that I want to do for you," and I said, "What is it man, I'm tired and I want to go to sleep" and he says, "You know just hold on...just hold on," and he hung up and the next thing I know is

someone's knocking on the door and it was some girl he knew...yea he set me up, but I wasn't expecting it, didn't you know anticipate it, but when that [happened], I mean it was a drop dead gorgeous girl.

Sexual perks such as women showing up unexpectedly at night were also reported by other participants from football and basketball at the minor and/or major league levels. The first participant was subsequently asked if he knew the females who would wait for him late night at his residence, and he admitted, "Sometimes yes and sometimes no," which implied these events occurred on multiple occasions. In her book, *A Face in the Crowd: My Life as an NFL Wife*, Nicole Berti similarly observed various females going room to room looking for sex by knocking on players' hotel doors during her husband's playing career in NFL Europe.[7] Women who provide sex on demand reinforce the notion that they are indeed sexual objects and consequently, certain major leaguers had no problem passing such females to their teammates as gifts. It will become apparent that the practice of passing women onto teammates is one that can flourish within certain collegiate and professional teams.

WOMEN GOING THROUGH ATHLETES, ATHLETES PASSING AROUND FEMALES

Females' unbridled sexual availability further manifests itself when women actively engage in sexual encounters with multiple players from the same team. Because these events are one-on-one sexual encounters that occur at different times over the course of an evening, season, year, or a career, they are not to be confused with group sex which involves multiple athletes sexually engaging with one or more women simultaneously or in quick succession during an encounter. The phenomenon of women going through a team is not recent because collegiate and professional athletes who competed in the 1960s were as likely to report these practices as those who competed in every decade through 2010. This suggests that nothing has changed in this time frame regarding such practices. While certain women have no problem sexually engaging with multiple players on a team, numerous athletes were equally willing to sexually accommodate them despite having an awareness of the females and their teammates' past sexual experiences together. Consequently, this section will explore females' sexual involvement with certain teams as much as it will examine athletes who figuratively pass women among teammates since these behaviors are virtually identical by having the goal of engaging casual sex. Over 95% of the participants in this study were aware of these practices and two thirds revealed a higher prevalence during their careers. Exploring this phenomenon provides a continuation of athletes' perceptions of female sexual availability as it relates to multiple players within a team as well as their own sexual behaviors.

I became aware of the phenomenon of female fans passing through teams when certain collegiate teammates revealed their sexual encounters with a particular female. One woman in college even told me that she had a friendly competition with her friend to see who could "hook up" with me first. Although I found this both flattering and disturbing since I did not know women had such inclinations before this situation, this was the first time that I experienced what it was like to be objectified as a sexual conquest. Later, I discovered teammates had sexually engaged with certain women I had been with both before and after the fact. These situations caused me to avoid encounters with any woman that I remotely suspected of being a groupie. This was in contrast to other collegiate and professional teammates who found passing female fans from player to player an ideal situation for no-effort sexual experiences regardless of the number of teammates who had previous sexual encounters with the woman.

WHEN FEMALES TRY TO SEXUALLY CONQUER A TEAM

Participants representing all sports and levels were able to discuss females' sexual involvement within their teams and sometimes in a striking fashion. Numerous participants identified females for their promiscuity including a collegiate baseball player who observed certain women would "run the circuit" by having sex with multiple players on his collegiate teams. Moreover, a minor league baseball player recalled, "In college it almost seemed organized, it seemed like they had their own little sorority, the little baseball girls' sorority." A wrestler who observed these practices during his career revealed, "I'd say 90% of the girls that hook up with a wrestler hook up with another wrestler, at least one other guy, maybe not actually having sex but at least you know doing something with them at some point was pretty much normal." A summary of participants' disclosures revealed that athletes believed women were motivated to have sexual involvement with multiple players on a team because of female bravado and bragging rights, low self-esteem and insecurities, different tastes in partners, attempting to get a player to fall in love with them, a desire for increased status and/or money, desperation to leave a certain town, players leaving teams, and gaining satisfaction and perhaps revenge by manipulating players and creating havoc within a team. Numerous participants, including a wrestler and a minor league baseball player, elaborated on the manner in which females would sexually assert themselves with athletes; for example:

> ...like any wrestling program, we had a group of girls who loved wrestlers just because we were wrestlers and I know when we lived in the house...

the one girl had sex with at least six guys in the house and she came in once and she said, "Well I haven't had sex with you yet," and she was pointing at me and my roommate had a girlfriend and she was there and of course that caused problems, but she came over because we were wrestlers and she liked to have sex and it just worked out well for us...she would go almost like a weekend thing and then I remember one night cause their room was right below ours, she was having [group] sex with two guys on the team, and we would open up the vents and kind of watch and listen but she was very much, I would call her whorish, but I know she had to have sex with more guys, but those were the guys that lived in the house, so she probably was up to 10 wrestlers on the team... she just sticks out in my mind because she was so open about it and so she didn't try to cover it up, she was just throwing it out there.

...there was a spring training incident where some girls came down from [another city] and I think this was a group of about four girls and they came to our spring training complex and their goal was to screw as many of the baseball players as they could, and...what they were doing was they would come to the hotel and they were just going room to room and that's what happened, I think I might have been golfing that day...I wasn't involved in that situation...there was a lot of them [laughing] I couldn't really tell you [how many players were involved] it was quite a few, a lot of guys that I knew too...that was the only time that ever happened that I can remember...

Such incidences showed that some women, like certain athletes, were competitive in their sexual behavior, and a collegiate basketball player supported this by saying, "I think it's like a sport to them, you know a sport, a sexual craving, a compulsion with numbers to see how many you can actually sleep with." While it is apparent that certain women can be subject to compulsive sexual behaviors as well as indifference to their promiscuity, this was a two-way street according to an NBA player who revealed:

Oh you knew it goes on I mean god if she's with you this night, tomorrow night she's going to be with the guy with the [next NBA team] coming in, so you knew what was going on I mean, but you didn't care because you didn't care about her. You cared about her for the time that she was there with you, but other than that, once you leave, it's onto the next city.

This participant was also asked how many NBA players a woman might become involved with in a season and he replied, "Depends on how good she looks [laughs] and what she has to offer, I mean she can go through the whole team, they wouldn't care." Because women were considered sexual objects and their behaviors often reinforced this notion, physical attractiveness and sexual prowess often determined their value among numerous players that could include teammates as well as athletes from other NBA teams. Earvin "Magic" Johnson recalled a story about one gorgeous woman who arranged an intimate evening with a high profile NBA player and requested that he bring an autographed pair of gym shoes with him.[8] Following the encounter, the athlete saw the woman's closet contained about 100 pairs of shoes that were arranged alphabetically by team.[9] Such behaviors confirm negative stereotypes that an NFL player revealed by saying, "I think to a great extent and I speak for myself, they're objects you know...they need to satisfy us, me...I don't know how much more specific you can get you know...they could be used." In the end, promiscuous practices highlight the self-centered mindset that exists within certain athlete cultures and engulfs both the players and their female followers because both look to take whatever they can get from a partner while apparently having little concern for the other once a sexual encounter ended.

PASSING FEMALES BETWEEN ATHLETES

At the same time that women were being scrutinized for their promiscuity within teams, numerous participants implicated athletes for their role in these same practices. For example, a collegiate hockey player admitted, "We're very incestuous by nature for some reason," and his team's motto to "keep it within the family" highlighted his team's acceptance of passing women from one player to another. Similarly, a wrestler revealed, "It was the culture of the team, [within] groups of the team...[so] it's not unusual to try to share a chick, pass a chick around, the groupie kinds of chicks. Now someone's girlfriend...that wasn't the case, you had to respect her...[but] that shit wasn't uncommon." Another collegiate hockey player elaborated on his personal experience with these practices in this way:

> Most unusual was the way we, you know, pass our girls around. There's girls that four, five, six of us all knew – kind of a big rotating door. There's a bunch of girls like that. One time [a teammate] was with a girl and he had been sleeping with her for awhile and one night he just couldn't stand it and she came over all drunk and he didn't want to hook up with her. She was sitting on our doorstep crying so I went in and I said, "[Player's name] thumbs up, thumbs down?" He goes, "Thumbs up so I took her home." That was probably the most unusual thing. A lot of guys won't do that, but we never had a problem like that at all.

A summary of participants' disclosures revealed that although this was often encouraged within various team cultures, athletes were also motivated to sexually engage with the same female(s) because of their desire to tell captivating stories, have additional sexual conquests, one-upmanship, viewing a woman as a sexual challenge, and the desire to have a quick, no-effort sexual experience. A different collegiate hockey player also thought these practices were "a kind of bonding thing," and he elaborated on its extent:

> ...I remember one time we sat in the locker room someplace and went through and every guy was somehow, I don't know how to say [it], [but] related to another guy, meaning that either they had slept with the same girl or slept with the same girl with someone else and...it was all intermixed in the circle and I don't think there was one guy in the dressing room that was out of that circle that didn't somehow sleep with another girl that a guy on our team did, and that's how I guess if you look at it that way, it's really prevalent...that was in college, in juniors, there was probably some of that, but I don't think it was anywhere close to what it was like in college.

Despite the health risks, this participant revealed that virtually all of the 26 players on his college team shared a connection by sexually engaging with one or more women in an individual and/or group sexual encounter at some point. This participant, like other athletes, also found that a female's sexual availability increased once teammates knew a player had sex with her because she would meet other players who would try to have sex with her as well. This could result in a one-time sexual encounter or in some cases even dating situations that a minor league football player recalled, "I had one girlfriend that I used to date and then [she] dated all my roommates that played football [laughs], yea I'd say you get a lot of that and even in the pros too." Such liaisons were not limited to athletes from a particular sport as a collegiate basketball player revealed:

> ...there were probably a handful of those [females] on the college campuses, it doesn't take long to figure out who they are and guys know, guys talk...I don't know about just one-night standing everybody, but... there were a couple girls who had you know two or three football players and one or two basketball players over the course of, you know, a couple years...and that actually was not unusual. I would say there was probably quite a few in that boat of girls who tried to be the girlfriend of a football or basketball player and went through a couple of them a year.

This participant subsequently revealed that although women who constantly sought athletes for boyfriends could still be considered "a groupie" of sort, they would not be relegated to the same lowly status given to females who only engaged in one night of casual sex with athletes. Many athletes would agree that females who became someone's girlfriend improved their standing immensely provided they did not revert to their former ways.

Dating multiple athletes at different times provided women with the most favorable status from the athletes' perspective, although these situations were also the least common when compared to the different types of liaisons that occur. For example, sexual involvement with multiple women or players on a team could occur at different times in an evening, as a collegiate hockey player revealed by saying, "I've seen two different girls sleep with the same guy in one night knowing that both of them had slept with him. Like, just strange stuff like that, you see it." In contrast, a collegiate baseball player noted, "I've heard of two [players] on the same night at different times [with a female]." Individual sexual encounters that occurred at different times on a given evening with different athletes or females were less common and involved lower numbers of participants when compared to the number of women and athletes who were involved sexually over the course of a season. One minor league football player revealed, "Happens quite a bit, I'd say every team that I've ever been on there's been a couple, a couple girls...[that] have had sex with quite a few different guys on the team. That happens pretty much every year...that I've played football." Moreover, a collegiate football player reported, "This number might even be low, [but] I'd say there was a good 9-10 girls that...whew, I would say some of those girls would've gone through 10 guys [in a season]." Such numbers were the work of a "super groupie" according to one minor league football player while a minor league hockey player recalled, "In college because you're there for like four years and guys graduated and the new guys come in, I'd say probably about 10-12 [players]...yea, yea [it happened] a lot." A wrestler revealed the highest number of athletes by saying, "[Laughing] actually quite a few, oh geez...maybe 15-20 [females]...some of them [with] maybe half the team, oh...I'd say double digits yea, I'd say 10-15 [wrestlers] maybe yea, before the season was over, yea." This participant was one of two wrestlers who revealed that anywhere from 15-20 female team followers were known to engage in individual sexual encounters with as many as 10-15 wrestlers during a season. Similar practices were also found among Olympic wrestlers and involved "three or four girls that kind of made the rounds" with "anywhere from 5-10 guys."

Other participants compared these practices during their careers, including a minor league basketball player who revealed, "It could be as few as two or three guys [in a season]...[or] you know majority of the team [12-15 players]... some in the same night." While this participant found the number of players who were sexually involved with a particular woman in individual and/or group sexual encounters were "a little bit higher" during his collegiate career compared to his professional experience, other professionals found the exact opposite to be true. For example, one minor league football player noted, "I've seen that quite a bit...[more common] hard to say...probably [in] pro" while a MLB player revealed his awareness by saying, "In college I didn't see as much, in the minor leagues there was one [female] that was like that [laughing]... probably 12 [players] yea...the one year we were there."

Major leaguers from every sport noted similar experiences despite greater scrutiny and the possibility of negative publicity at this level. One MLB player mentioned, "I'd say more in the minor leagues and some in the major leagues" while another revealed, "College level I didn't see that at all, very rarely at the major league level, I'd say occasionally...two or three [players] maybe...[with] just a couple [females]." Similarly, an NBA player recalled, "Oh yea, there's some of those – whew, I don't really know her track record, but I would say probably three or four [teammates]... probably more common in the pros" because close-knit college communities would crucify such females with gossip. Likewise, an NHL player revealed, "You know what, I think pretty much every team I was on there was that situation, I would say every year of my career... [and] it could be anywhere from 2-5 or 6 [players]." While this participant noted such practices occurred on every team in which he competed including the junior, minor, and the major league levels, an NFL player elaborated on his own personal awareness and experiences in this way:

> Aw man, four or five [players] maybe I think [with] this one particular girl, like I guess maybe I might have sucked like three dicks I guess [laughs] was the little joke going around, so yea, they pass them around and in college we did too...the first white girl I ever slept with we would pass around yea, yea, so I mean we did it in college...probably more in pros but it's really on the same level, I mean we passed them all the time in college, passed them all around in the pros, so it's about equal really, not too much difference...

It is apparent that such practices are not uncommon among major leaguers, and they are not recent either. In his book, *Thunder and Lightning: A No-B.S. Hockey Memoir*, NHL Hall of Fame center Phil Esposito recalled convincing one very loyal female team follower to have sex with the late, gargantuan wrestler, Andre the Giant, in the early 1970s.[10] At this same time, fellow teammate and NHL superstar Bobby Orr had so many sexually available women wanting him that he often sent them to "go screw my buddy over there," and they would agree to it.[11] Such attitudes and behaviors have the potential to change quickly because after NBA superstar Earvin "Magic" Johnson acquired his HIV diagnosis, his former agent George Andrews revealed, "About five or six other players are puking in the sinks right now, what with the way some of these guys share women."[12] Indeed, such practices certainly frightened many athletes for a time because they realized their behaviors put them at risk for contracting a sexually transmitted disease. In the end, there is no shortage of participants to provide ample evidence that numerous collegiate, minor, and major league athletes continue to sexually share women into 2010. While participants noted that as many as 100 females could have sexual involvement with anywhere from two athletes to an entire team, these practices were not without repercussions for both the women and the athletes.

CONSEQUENCES OF PASSING FEMALES BETWEEN ATHLETES

Ruined Reputations, Rejection of Women

Previous narratives provided ample evidence that female sexual availability can take a heavy toll on a woman's reputation, and this can increase exponentially when promiscuity involves athletes from the same team. Various athletes including a collegiate hockey player discussed these notions by saying, "It's this cultural thing that people get involved [in] and...[women] they want a social scene, they want to be part of something and...I don't know how it starts off, but some of them get themselves in over their head and before they know it... they've ruined their reputation." As a collegiate coach, this participant observed numerous females ruining their reputations by having sex with multiple players on his team while athletes were applauded for their promiscuity. Another collegiate hockey player elaborated upon these ideas in this way:

> ...obviously if a girl's scored a hat trick with the team (sex with three players), she's going to be viewed one way as opposed to a girl who... maybe she slept with one guy on the team and she's hooked up (without having intercourse) with a lot of other guys on the team, but since she's really only slept with one guy, it's different. And yeah, it also depends on who the girl is too. I mean there's favoritism towards certain girls that we really like, or a lot of guys like, and if a girl's disliked, she's going to be talked about in a different way and...more than likely, she'll be out of the loop eventually or...sooner than later.

Athletes can be highly critical of females' promiscuity even though they engage in similar behaviors. It is interesting to note that group consensus strongly influenced which sexually available women were talked about and rejected or accepted by a team. Other participants also noted rejection could occur in a limited fashion. For example, one minor league baseball player described a woman who was sexually available to players on his professional team as "cool" and "nice," although "nobody ever dated her." Furthermore, the previous collegiate hockey player provided one explanation for this by saying, "You'd never want to date a girl like that cause you know peer pressure...was pretty tough." Indeed, engaging in sex with promiscuous women is acceptable and even encouraged within many athlete cultures while attempting to date a woman with this type of past is often taboo and can result in harsh ridicule. In the end, one thing is for certain: the double standard is alive and well because the sexual behaviors that athletes are praised for can result in women being depreciated and even ostracized from the players they are trying to bond with.

When Female Availability Leads to Female Abuse

The practice of passing women from one athlete to the next was common within many athlete cultures, and such practices also had a darker side that included ridicule and even abuse. Various participants including a collegiate football player elaborated in this way:

> [Laughing loudly] I can think of a couple names yea, yea…that happens like the one cheerleader she was one of those types, there was one volleyball player who was one of those types, and then you always see the girls at the bar [and hear], "I knew like three or four guys on the team who banged that chick so stay away from that" – there was always stuff like that going on yea, or you'll even hear guys talk like, "Hey, you fucked that one girl didn't you?" "Like yea," and the girl's still there and they talk about it you know, I mean it happens definitely.

Athletes in this narrative gave the clear message by embarrassing a female publicly that casual sex was okay for them, but improper for women. Moreover, sexually available women were sometimes taken advantage of in other ways as another collegiate football player revealed, "I think you can get away with a lot more especially with groupies, I mean, you can get away with you know 'double teaming' them…just to say she hooked up with a star and then you know once you get that, you can get them to do a lot of different things." This participant, like others, noted players testing females to see what they would do for them because certain women were eager to win their approval and be involved in athletes' social lives. Such tests and tasks included doing athletes' school work, laundry, shopping, and cooking as well as engaging in sexual activities such being "double teamed," which involved a sexual encounter with two athletes at the same time. It is apparent that certain athletes have no problem using fame and positions of power to take advantage of women, who allow themselves to be manipulated because of their desire to remain in the company of high profile athletes. In addition, a collegiate basketball player revealed the manner in which female availability could result in other types of abuse:

> …one time I know my teammates handcuffed the girl, they were doing something behind the closed doors and then he had a pair of handcuffs

and...she passed out, and he handcuffed her to the outside of the dorm so she was facing the hallway...she actually was one of the girls that was always around the team...most of the guys knew about it, the coaches didn't know about it...it never got [revealed], she wasn't found, and it never got in a public domain, so it was the guys knew about it on the team and then she continued to hang out with them with the team.... [but] she was in her underwear...she was handcuffed to the door handle on the outside of the dorm so the dorm has a hallway, so she was handcuffed outside of the room to the door...I think she was left there for four hours cause she passed out, so it was probably my best guess it was a 3 a.m. to a 7 a.m. deal, so I don't know how many people in the dorm would have seen her at that time cause most people weren't up...I think he just kind of came out and uncuffed her.

Although this event did not result in severe harm to the woman who was later released, it could very easily have resulted in a variety of negative outcomes for everyone involved. While women have a definite role in keeping themselves safe by avoiding excessive intoxication, athletes are responsible for their predator-like actions which have the potential to inflict harm in a variety of ways. Interestingly, one wrestler elaborated on athletes' role in such abuse as well as the women who could be victimized in this way:

...certainly there were girls who would go through multiple guys, so there's a mixture between the sexual prowess in guys, some certainly more sexually aggressive and disrespectful, but no matter where they lie on that continuum, there's a type of woman that is attracted to that type of guy. And then not only would [she] be abused by one guy, but by multiple guys on the team. We could talk and speculate about what those characteristics are in the history of those women, but nonetheless, I think there's a potential piece. Not all women, there are certainly really some very healthy women out there that have been abused and taken advantage of whether it's through alcohol or drugs or just straight out malintentions of a guy.

Although some athletes victimized healthy females, women with specific characteristics were more likely to be victimized and then revictimized by others in this athlete's experiences. These notions were supported by researchers who discovered that two out of three individuals who were sexually victimized were revictimized at a later time.[13] Women who were revictimized experienced difficulties in their families, interpersonal relationships, coping skills, self representation, and managing their emotional states in addition to exhibiting greater self-blame, powerlessness, and shame.[14] Revictimization also related to females having multiple sexual partners, higher frequency of sex, substance abuse, and shorter relationships.[15] Such factors were frequently noted among athletes in this study, and they raised questions regarding the kinds of trauma some women may have experienced. One wrestler validated these notions by recalling how an extremely promiscuous female athlete was declared sexually off limits to all the male athletes at his university. This occurred when her coaches sent her to counseling in an effort to help her resolve her personal issues after she was discovered having sex with numerous athletes on multiple teams and engaged in one of the largest group sexual encounters in this study. Past traumas particularly involving childhood sexual abuse can have residual effects on a woman's personality, and this impacts her choice of partners, decision-making, and a variety of behaviors affecting her victimization as well as revictimization. Unfortunately, there are athletes without a sense of right and wrong who see an easy target in such women and have no problem repeatedly using and abusing them in a variety of ways.

Mocking and Abusing Teammates

Athletes were not immune from experiencing ridicule and abuse at the hands of their own teammates after they sexually engaged with women who were passed within their teams. One NFL player elaborated on his observations in this way:

> ...one of our guys got, they were at a party, got a blow job from a girl, actually as he's leaving the party he told me the story, as he's leaving the party and saw another teammate kissing this girl and walked by and just whispered, "How do I taste?" and yet I know the other teammate went home with her that night and once again that was a training camp deal, that was a training camp party, that was pro, so two I remember...and like I said it was one on each level.

This participant observed these practices during both his collegiate and major league career, and it is apparent that some players are quick to reveal their sexual encounters with the same woman particularly when the disclosure could be used to ridicule the next teammate who had sex with her. This was in contrast to another NFL player who revealed his teammates used a different strategy that produced even greater mistreatment:

> ...one of the more candid stories was my rookie year I met this girl, you know beautiful girl whatever, and you know I was like, "Yea you know I met this chick whatever" talking to one of my, you know position mates, "Yea...she's fine, she's fine, whatever" "What's her name?" "Her name is [XXX]" "Okay, yea [XXX], what she look like?" Okay so then, they don't

tell you, they don't, you know the whole thing is they want you to fall in love with her, so then they can tear you down...but once you finally, you know...recognize the female for who she is, then you know they kind of razz you a little bit, "Aw yea, you sucked my dick, you sucked my dick, you sucked his dick, you sucked his dick too, you know I know you kissed her," you know one of those deals, so that was a big thing not telling the guy that you've already slept with the girl and of course she knows...and of course all his guys know because he going to tell his guys...nobody's going to tell you, you know nobody's going to say, "Hey man, don't fall in love with that chick" you know they just going to let you go out for what you go out for, and then they going to razz you to death that you clown around, and that you messing around, and fall in love with her or something like that you know, so it's kind of like an unwritten rule that you don't tell the guy that you slept with her, let him find out on his own.

The above participant subsequently revealed that the woman he was involved with had prior sexual involvement with four or five of his NFL teammates. Unlike the previous narrative that revealed ridicule, this participant experienced abuse from his teammates that was both overt and covert because no one would tell him about their sexual experiences with this woman. Moreover, this participant experienced the taboo and repercussions firsthand that could result from dating a woman who had previous sexual involvement with other players. While sex and/or dating situations with such women are common in many athlete cultures, peer groups always determine what is acceptable from what is not. This participant elaborated on other cultural observations involving women and relationships in this way:

...when I first got to professional ball, you know, because everybody been through almost every woman, it's very rare that you're going to find a woman that somebody on the team hasn't slept with, I used to think that the guy would be jealous, "Yea I got her, you didn't" you know one of those type of things, but...if you're really, really in love with somebody, they will break you down, they will come out with a video, come out with a panty, come out with a monogrammed underwear, whatever they have to come out with, you know with the videos, the pictures, the taped messages on the phone, whatever [and say], "Nigger...I can't believe you falling for this ho, man she called me last night, I fucked her last night nigger straight up, I'm serious, our relationship wasn't there when she called me and told me to come by and fuck the shit out of her," you know stuff like that I mean the girls, they never was treated equal, never...they was always you know inferior, like I said bitches or gold diggers, or never really taken serious.

While collegiate teammates often ridicule players with girlfriends for being "pussy whipped" when they do not go out with the guys, it is apparent that professionals were much less tolerant of deeper relationships with women who had previous sexual involvement with teammates. As a result, teammates would literally "break you down" by saying and doing whatever they could to discourage deeper attachments to certain females who had a sexual history within a team. This participant attempted to explain players' anti-relational attitudes and their subsequent behaviors:

> I think a lot of it has to do with the insecurity where, you know, the males are kind of insecure and they have to protect...everybody like, you know they don't want to get taken for, taken for a sucker...made to feel like they were played or taken advantage of or used, you know, because... even though I had a love for the game...in the pros you know the whole thing is...I got to make money, I got to check my money you know so...it's hard to separate you know reality from finance and the chick in reality might be a good chick, a wholesome chick, she might have made some mistake – just like you made – but society said that if you done two of my guys (by having sex with them), then you're not the one for me, and she might be a great girl – she just was young, dumb, you know caught up [in] whatever, but you can't allow yourself knowing [that] as an athlete, you can't allow yourself to fall into that thing...unless you have enough coat on you, on your back, enough pain coat on your back then that you can take it cause you're going to definitely get shot at, "Have your superman dress on," they used to say, "You know have your superman dress on cause we going to shoot at you, because you know we going to shoot all kinds of stuff at you – can you take it?"...

In the end, women who had a sexual history within a team were sometimes declared off limits for deeper involvement because as this participant discovered, it would be too much to bear teammates' constant abuse, sexual innuendos, and relentless peer pressure to conform to their beliefs and expectations.

Women Who Extort or Play Athletes Against Each Other

One reoccurring theme among professional athletes related to the fact that many were wary of women who made themselves sexually available because this could accompany an array of ulterior motives. Females were often stereotyped as "bitches" and "gold diggers" for the simple fact that both minor and major leaguers experienced and/or observed athletes being targeted as well as taken for their money. For example, an NHL player discussed these notions by saying,

"You know who knows what the ultimate goal is, the reason why somebody would want to be with somebody whether it's sexually or financially or you know looking at [it like], 'You know if I could get hooked up with this guy, then I'll be set and I don't have to work.'" This participant elaborated on how female availability changed during the course of his career and why athletes had good reason to be cautious of sexually available women:

> Well I think it's changed...I know there's always somebody available, guys always knew where to go to find girls available, girls always knew where to go to find the players, I think now that leads to gold diggers to black mail to broads trying to get stolen identities from you know former lovers, to a broad picking up one of the players and having her boyfriend in the closet and having a camera there to take pictures and then black mailing the player that's picking up a broad, I think now guys are very, very selective, I think that they have [to be]...[so] that's really changed...

The above participant recalled "four or five" instances of athletes being targeted for extortion during his NHL career, and these practices were noted by professional baseball and basketball players as well. These events often required intervention from legal authorities including the FBI because once a player would give in to extortionists' demands for money, it was never a one-time payoff since extortionists would subsequently return to try to collect more money.

While it is evident that certain females used extortion to target athletes' pocketbooks, not all women had the goal of using athletes for their money. Some women were found engaging in more calculated behavior that was meant to create dissension and wreak havoc within certain professional teams as a minor league football player and an NBA player revealed in this way:

> Shit man...yea, you see that all the time that's called a "freak" [laughs], that's a "freak," she's hopping...shit I've seen one young broad she had about four or five of our guys, damn near broke [us] up, she tried to tell us she was going to break up our team, and she damn near did her best... that was professional football...she went through guys yep, in different parts of the season...you know she had a couple of guys that went after each other, you know that didn't speak to each other, and you know why they didn't speak because they were with that gal but...shit, [she was] just getting her thrills, if the man can do it, she can do it too.

> Yea, that was pretty much an unwritten rule that [women would go through teams] you know, there was a couple, there was a couple, whew man...there was a group out west that you know wreaked havoc on this one particular team...there was about five of them, they called

themselves "The Starting Five," and you know they just wreaked havoc on a couple of teams, so that was the only situation where I knew that you know a couple of girls had been with you know more than six, seven, eight guys on a team.

The second participant elaborated on the manner in which a group of women caused problems for certain NBA teams by saying, "Oh man they created turmoil, they had all these guys who thought they were exclusively seeing them and that wasn't the case...she would leave one room, go to the next, you know [it] just created a lot of tension and a lot of animosity among the team and teammates and yea, she was pretty good I heard." Similar to the "juggling" behaviors of certain athletes who had numerous sexual partners at the same time, these women also used athletes sexually and then played one against another by making various players believe they were sexually exclusive when, in fact, this was not the case. This created jealousy and anger because the athletes' egos and competitive nature had taken an unexpected hit from what they believed was another teammate who appeared to have "won" over one of their prized female's affections. While this participant found females' involvement with multiple players more prevalent during his collegiate career, it is unlikely that the women's sexual involvement with his collegiate team was as calculated and controversial as the previous situation. In the end, these practices appeared to be particularly disturbing to these athletes because for once the women, not the athletes, were in control of the sexual agenda and behaviors.

ATHLETES' CORNER: POINTS TO PONDER

1. High status groups, including athletic teams, attract their share of female followers. Such women provide an array of perks although they are recognized predominantly for the way in which they make themselves sexually available to athletes. Athletes readily use such females for casual sex, while some women, in turn, try to use the athletes for their higher status and/or money. Regardless of the motive, using others for sex, privilege, money, or anything else is a poor practice that depreciates oneself as well as the others involved. While individuals engage in casual sexual encounters to experience various types of fulfillment and positive outcomes, this is often short-lived and followed by a sense of emptiness since this is the true nature of such experiences more often than not.

2. Promiscuous women are demeaned because the societal double standard favors males, including athletes, by rewarding their promiscuity while simultaneously rejecting females for the same behaviors. This has perpetuated a hypocritical point of view that needs to change because its basic premise is flawed and carries no credibility or honor. In short, athletes have no right to judge, criticize, and condemn certain females for their promiscuity when they are engaging in the same behavior. Promiscuous behaviors have resulted in harsh repercussions that have ruined females' reputations and ostracized them in addition to exposing partners to sexually transmitted diseases, unwanted pregnancy, extortion, abuse, and sexual assault.

3. Females who make themselves blatantly sexually available to athletes often do so because they have unresolved issues and lack wholeness. The same is true for athletes who stroke their egos by engaging in one meaningless sexual encounter after another. Females' unbridled promiscuity is often the result of experiencing trauma such as childhood sexual abuse because adults, who violate a young woman's sexual boundaries, leave her with no boundaries for her sexual behavior with age-appropriate males. Athletes must examine why they are taking advantage of such situations which negatively impact their female partners as well as numerous aspects of their own well-being.

Chapter 6
Athlete Infidelity and Juggling Women

Golf legend, Tiger Woods, and University of Louisville men's basketball coach, Rick Pitino, are among the latest of a long list of sportsmen to invite unwanted media attention into their personal, professional, and family lives by way of their indiscriminant sexual activities with extramarital partners.[1] Tiger Woods' infidelity shocked the nation and made constant headlines particularly because his public image as a world-class husband and family man turned out to be a façade that disappointed many fans who saw him as a role model. Woods and Pitino join major leaguers from a variety of sports including MLB star, Jose Canseco, NBA star, Earvin "Magic" Johnson, NFL star, Lawrence Taylor, and NHL star, Phil Esposito, who similarly admitted to cheating on their wives or significant partners during their professional careers.[2] While high profile athletes attract extraordinary media attention whenever their infidelity becomes public knowledge, these practices reveal merely the tip of the iceberg in the sports world. Consequently, this chapter will provide a unique look into an all too common phenomenon because a culture of cheating exists within numerous collegiate and professional sports teams.

Revelations involving infidelity do not imply that this behavior only occurs among athletes because non-athletes cheat on marital partners too. One national study involving 3,432 Americans ages 18-59 revealed that although 94% indicated they were faithful within the past year, 25% of the married men and 15% of the married women reported extramarital involvement at some point during their marriage.[3] While these findings suggest that extramarital sex is the exception rather than the rule for those in the general population, this is in stark contrast to elite-level athletes' sexual behaviors revealed in this study.

During my career as a collegiate and professional player and coach, I was aware of various athletes' infidelity as it related to girlfriends and fiancées, but not among the few players I competed with who were married. However, I have known various collegiate and professional coaches who actively pursued other female partners despite being in committed relationships including marriage. Personally, I engaged in a number of instances of infidelity on one steady girlfriend just prior to playing professionally in Europe and during the preseason as well. Basically, I told my girlfriend to date whoever she wanted to without actually telling her that I would do the same. The uncertainty of our future combined with the long distance motivated my actions and allowed me to rationalize them. Almost immediately, the stress apparently resulting from my infidelity produced incredibly painful back spasms that had no clear explanation at the time. My condition, which did not result from an injury, actually made me wonder if I would have to retire early because the pain was that debilitating. Interestingly, about four months later I decided to permanently end my sexual misconduct and my back pain ended completely within a week. Although this was a hard way to learn that stress from incongruent behavior can produce severe physical reactions, the experience turned out to be a very effective teacher that promoted personal change and increased awareness that was very positive.

INFIDELITY AMONG COLLEGIATE AND PROFESSIONAL ATHLETES

Participants in this study were asked to discuss the prevalence of sexual infidelity during their athletic career as it related to themselves and their teammates. Because approximately 40% of the participants were single at the time of their interview, infidelity could involve sexual activity with another female outside of any committed relationship that included a girlfriend, fiancé, or wife. Having a broader definition was also necessary because most collegiate athletes are not married, and those playing professionally – particularly in the minor leagues – often choose not to marry until after their career ends. The uncertainty of a minor league career along with its lower salary, frequent travel, and constant roster changes make it difficult to include a marital partner. In contrast, major leaguers are more readily able to afford a marital partner particularly when they command large salaries and have more stable careers.

Virtually all of the participants (98%) were aware of infidelity among collegiate and/or professional players during their careers. Although about one quarter of the athletes noted a lower prevalence of cheating that involved 10-30% of their teammates, three quarters of the athletes revealed higher frequencies of cheating that involved at least 40% of their teammates. Even more surprising is the fact that about one third of the participants revealed that cheating occurred more often than not among most (70-100%) of their teammates. In addition, 55% of the athletes admitted they were unfaithful to a significant female partner or had involvement with a married female at some point during their elite-level athletic career, 37% said they were faithful or did not have a steady partner to cheat on during their career, and 8% were not asked the question. While it can be argued that cheating on a marital partner is different from cheating on a girlfriend or fiancé, I know various athletes who cheated on their girlfriends and their unfaithfulness carried into their marriages because exchanging wedding vows does not end these practices for everyone.

With infidelity occurring during most (98%) participants' athletic careers, an overwhelming majority of collegiate athletes (nearly 80%) also revealed higher frequencies of cheating during their collegiate careers. For example, a two-sport collegiate athlete revealed that when it came to cheating among both wrestlers and football players "about everyone of them did." "I'm saying that with all honesty – I probably cheated on every girl that I've ever been with, except for my wife and that's probably why I married her...but yeah...there was not a whole lot of loyalty when it came to girls." An Olympic wrestler similarly revealed infidelity among "60%" of his teammates, which means athletes at this level were not immune to hero-worshipping women overseas that made casual sex "just too easy for some guys." Baseball emerged as the only collegiate sport that was the close to being equally divided between athletes who revealed a lower and higher prevalence of cheating. One minor league baseball player representing the higher end of the continuum recalled, "There was no one married in college when I was there. Most of us had girlfriends and so I would say most of us were with someone else even when we had girlfriends; I think that went on a majority of the time." In addition, an NBA player noted, "Oh god, probably 90%...both [in college and pros]" while another NBA player who responded with a big sigh said, "If I had to put a number on it...I would say out of 100 college or professional athletes, I would say at least 85-90% of those guys cheated on their significant other, spouse, whatever you want to call it." Similarly, a minor league hockey player noted, "In college, I would say of the people who had significant others, 90%, probably 85-90% were messing around," while a collegiate hockey player elaborated on team infidelity:

> A lot more times than not, it's unfortunate. I remember, [and] this will answer this for you. In college we had a hockey house. There was 12 of us my senior year who lived in this one house. Probably eight of us had girlfriends away from college at home or either graduated and went on elsewhere. My girlfriend would come up and three or four of those other eight guys that had girlfriends would be cheating on the girlfriends. And the following week, my buddy, [his] girlfriend would come up and the other three or four [cheated]...[laughs] and it happens all the time... you're young, you think that's what you do out there.

This participant also observed certain teammates transitioned away from being "a player" with women when they got married because cheating "gets old and you move on from that." While this may be true for some athletes, others continue their pattern of cheating by taking it into their professional careers.

Like the collegiate athletes, approximately 70% of professional athletes representing every sport also revealed higher frequencies of infidelity during their minor and/or major league careers. For example, the majority of NFL players indicated that "at least half" of their teammates were unfaithful while minor league football players revealed even higher percentages of cheating. One minor league football player noted, "Boy the pro level's real tough… probably be more [cheating than in college] – 85% in the pros" while a current minor leaguer recalled, "At the pro game, man it's sad…it seems like everybody's going out messing around so I would say 100%." Moreover, these participants, like others, thought "seeing if he's still got it" with other women and being apart from significant partners created insecurities as well as a void that players would try to fill by cheating. Because players' infidelity on road trips had little to no chance of being discovered, this made infidelity all the more attractive to certain athletes.

A majority of professional hockey players also revealed higher frequencies of cheating at both the minor and major league levels. One NHL player observed "about 80%" cheated during his minor league career, while a minor leaguer elaborated by saying, "50% of the guys will whenever they can – 50%. Well 25% of the guys…it might happen a couple times, and then the other 25% aren't going to do it no matter what." Various NHL players also revealed higher frequencies of cheating at the major league level including one who said, "I would say 80%…like one time or more…yea, 80% for sure." Similarly, an NBA player recalled, "95% – that's the minor and the majors…in college I didn't have a girlfriend, so you know I was free to do whatever, in the pros I did have a couple [girlfriends] but I still went ahead and had my fun." Another NBA player revealed even higher frequencies by saying, "Whew man, 98%, 99% of the guys that I hung out with."

Among baseball players, a MLB player discussed infidelity by saying, "50%…I think it was just as prevalent in the majors as the minors" while another elaborated in this way:

> …all I can say is I know that there's some guys that were very faithful to their wives and partners and I know that there's some guys that were very, very unfaithful taking every opportunity that they could to be unfaithful, and then there were some guys in between that felt like you know they really didn't want to be just looking for it all the time, but when it was easy and the time was right, you know they ended up giving into the temptation. I don't really want to put numbers or percentages on that.

Higher frequencies emerged at the minor league level as one minor leaguer explained, "I would say 80% of the single of the betrothed men that are playing in a town where their girlfriends for sure aren't, they're cheating at least once in a summer."

In the end, infidelity is a thriving phenomenon that happens more often than not within many collegiate and/or professional teams that competed in the 1960s – 2010. Such practices raise questions such as: How does elite-level sports participation promote a culture of cheating within certain teams? And secondly, what factors contribute to higher frequencies of cheating? In order to answer these questions, it is necessary to examine the culture within the different sports and to listen carefully to what athletes themselves have to say on this subject.

HOW TO PROMOTE A CULTURE OF CHEATING

When attempting to understand athletes rampant cheating patterns, it is important to first realize that many athletes rank their sports participation as their main priority with everything else, including relationships with partners, being of secondary importance.[4] This may be because many athletes have a very strong passion for their sports participation, and there are vast differences in the time commitment they dedicated to reaching higher sports levels when compared to the time invested in most intimate relationships during an athletic career. This fact readily reduces some athletes' partners to a lower status and priority which a collegiate baseball player supported by saying, "I knew people that had girlfriends and...wouldn't even give it a second thought if they were cheating on their girlfriend." Indeed, athletes from various sports cultures may learn to devalue intimate relationships and cheat because elite-level athletic participation perhaps promoted a self-centered mentality that many felt was necessary to succeed. Women could be easily replaced since they were so accessible, and an NFL player noted such attitudes permeated "the mindset of the entire sport" enabling athletes to rationalize their infidelity and succumb to the "temptation" to "conquer" women. Nearly 25% of the participants cited female availability and easy sexual opportunity as the major reason for athletes' infidelity, and former MLB star, Jose Canseco, thought this was the reason that 60% of the players cheated during his career.[5]

In addition, some groups of athletes defined cheating in such a way that not all deviant sexual behaviors would be classified as such. Or rather – at least not among their teammates – as a minor league hockey player revealed:

> ...you've heard, played, and heard about "The Hockey Players' Handbook" where blow jobs don't count, so that's not considered screwing around you know, [but] it depends who you ask because I'm pretty sure if I was to go out and get a blow job, my wife would be really pissed off so you have to take all that into consideration with a wife and three kids – Is that what you want to ruin it all over that or don't you?

> So is it worth it? You're better off snapping one off [by masturbating] and going to sleep – save yourself all the bullshit attorney's fees...

While some athletes define various sexual behaviors like cheating to support their own agendas, this would hold little influence with a female partner, who viewed oral sex as cheating and was willing to hold her partner accountable.

Keeping the Code of Silence

One of the major ways that sexually deviant behaviors, including infidelity, are allowed to perpetuate lies in the fact that they often exist within a code of silence. This means that players do whatever they can to preserve deviant practices by keeping their behaviors hidden from those who would protest and try to stop them. When such behaviors and secrets are upheld by more teammates than not, one may assume a team has evolved into a deviant culture. Adhering to slogans such as, "What happens on the road stays on the road" is one way sexual deviancy occurs according to a minor league hockey player because it gives players "a security blanket" which assures them that even "the most crooked of guys will not say anything." A wrestler noted such practices within his team by saying, "The culture of the team and again not everybody, I'm speaking as a team, but...there were groups that I know of that cheating upon your partner was the fucking norm, and you would cover for teammates, this was just common practice." Interestingly, a collegiate hockey player describing a similar culture within his team further elaborated on his participation in these practices:

> ...I would say a lot [of cheating]...there are some guys that will cheat on their girlfriend every weekend, and it's the team's duty to make sure the secret never gets out, and the team always knows about it, but it's a secret...whatever's said in the locker room stays in the locker room pretty much...if you know something happened, it's usually you don't say it...but yeah, I've seen people cheat on girlfriends numerous times, while their girlfriend's at the house...I've seen a guy go say he's going to the supermarket cause he just got in a fight with his girlfriend and go hook up with a girl while his girlfriend's sitting in the backyard talking to me about how much she loves the person, and I know what the guy's doing and I have to say, "Oh, you know, it's alright, he loves you, blah, blah, blah," because...I'm not going to, you know stab my teammate in the back. If the girl happened to be a good friend of mine, then I wouldn't let it happen. But, as it was, I don't know the girl very well, I figured I'm not going to hurt my teammate.

This participant further revealed that there were consequences for players who broke the team's code of silence because "you won't just have the guy you ratted out on your ass, you'll have the entire team on your ass." In this way, team norms required that players followed such codes, or they would experience negative consequences. One athlete, who broke the code by revealing infidelity to another teammate's girlfriend, "lost a lot of respect," was denied access to confidential team information, and was even shunned by certain teammates. Indeed, the seriousness of such consequences prevented many athletes from identifying cheating teammates because their primary friendships involve their teammates rather than someone's girlfriend. Plus, players have to deal with their teammates on a daily basis throughout the year, so they cannot easily get away from unified negative scrutiny without leaving a team.

Athletes were not the only individuals who remained silent because participants noted that girlfriends and even wives upheld such codes despite having knowledge that some athletes were cheating on their partners. Such practices were puzzling to observe according to a minor league hockey player who elaborated in this way:

> ...another thing about it that's kind of funny, all the crooked girlfriends that stay in town with the players and even the girlfriends know that this guy is fooling around on his girlfriend, but yet when that girlfriend comes into town, those girls will not say anything to that real girlfriend like, "Hey, he's cheating on you." [Instead], they'll be like, "Hey nice to meet you and we'll show you around town" kind of thing, so I don't understand and I asked my wife once and she's like, "It's probably not my place to, you know say something," and I'm like well if you were doing that on me, I would hope someone would come up to me and say, "Hey your wife is fucking around...you know," but for whatever reason they felt that it wasn't their job to do that.

A wrestler also noted that while numerous athletes "enjoyed that game" of cheating, "sneaking around, and just being that way," certain girlfriends "accepted it and some of them didn't."

Similar practices appeared among married athletes and their wives because infidelity was thought to be "an accepted part" of the professional game to the point that another minor league hockey player believed the wives were aware of its occurrence as "one of the things that happens." Dr. Steven Ortiz supported such notions through his study of major league baseball players' wives when he found teams pressured players' wives to follow an unwritten code of conduct that preserved athlete privileges such as team-sanctioned infidelity whenever a wife happened to travel with the club to an away game.[6] Essentially, the code insisted that certain bars and restaurants and particularly the team's hotel bar and even the lobby were off limits to wives because this is where many players, including those who were married, would go to meet and mingle with female admirers, groupies, and/or their girlfriends.[7] Married players socialized in these public settings rather than secluded locations because it provided them with an audience in which to flaunt their extramarital dalliances and perceived masculinity.[8]

Certain teams, including those from the NFL and NBA, had even stricter codes that prohibited wives from traveling with a team at all.[9] Interestingly, an NBA player from this study supported such findings and elaborated on his awareness in this way:

> I mean it [cheating and juggling] definitely went on I mean and some guys are ashamed of it because they're like, "What happens on the road, stays on the road" – it's like that commercial, "What happens in Vegas, stays in Vegas," guys have that attitude and if you got your wife at the hotel, they ask that you – it's a written rule – you go to another [place] or have her stay in another hotel and you go over there or you know you just let everybody know what the situation is like, "Hey my wife's here, so you all just be careful."

Similar to the findings from Dr. Ortiz's study, the above participant noted that if a wife went on a road trip, the player and his wife were not allowed to stay in the same hotel as the team because no one wanted someone's wife reporting back to the other wives suspicious behaviors that suggested infidelity.[10] Wives who noticed a married player with another woman were expected to make themselves invisible by not acknowledging him because seeing such an event defined the observing wife as a potential threat to the athlete.[11] This often caused wives stress, rather than the unfaithful athlete, because wives did not want to jeopardize their husband's status, career, or friendships within his team by observing forbidden behavior.[12] Sometimes these wives felt like co-conspirators from having to conceal behaviors they strongly disapproved of because it was in the best interest of their husband and his career.[13] Such codes enabled athlete infidelity to flourish while it kept many wives who happened to observe such behaviors quiet and angry.[14] Interestingly, a minor league basketball player in this study discussed other practices within his sports culture that enabled infidelity to thrive:

> ...nine times out of ten, the wives know this too – yes, and that's the quiet undercover thing about basketball, the wives know that their husbands are "out there." A number of years back Patrick Ewing's wife wrote a book (i.e., Home Court Advantage) about basically what I'm saying and there's a group of wives that knew what was going on –

they say..."We're in it for the money as well at that point" – that's why they don't want to leave when they're so comfortable...[but] there's an unspoken rule: Just don't disrespect me, don't let it get in the press, don't let the public know what's going on with this – as long as they don't know then I can go about my business and pretend I don't know. The book was a big stinker because here it was, again basketball's a very tight community just like all sports, but basketball [is] very small and you've got an insider who is part of this telling our business – and yea there was a lot of upset players because of that...[but] now – well, it gets quickly swept under the rug, "Okay let's go back to business as usual" – but for awhile there was a little look in for society if they wanted to pay attention to see how it really works...and all the things I'm saying now I know for fact – not because of hearsay or anything like that – this was common knowledge that most wives know their guys are stepping out and there are those wives who will call every 10 minutes and you have to call back, and if not, "I'm gone," and those guys are true to their women because they don't have time not to be – and the ones that are like, "Our marriage is just a marriage in terms of we signed on the dotted lines, but we're both leading separate lives" – that's basketball, that's the professional athlete that I know of in basketball – and that's what I wanted so badly not to be that way...when I was married I became a professional basketball player – well you smoke marijuana, you cheat on your wife if you don't beat her – that's the way it kind of goes with the perception of basketball players, and I'm a black guy too, so that all kind of goes together too and I wanted so badly not to be that guy.

Wives have various reasons, besides love, for staying in marriages where infidelity exists because for some, marriage was a sort of business arrangement involving children that provided long-term security. Others enjoyed the affluent lifestyle and prestige that accompanied life with a professional athlete. This participant also noted that periodically various high profile basketball players would appear in the media because they were being sued by former mistresses and sometimes for child support. When this occurred, infidelity now impacted the athlete's wife and as well as their marriage because cheating was no longer a secret.

Peer Pressure and Cheating

Keeping infidelity a secret allows it to flourish because it is allowed to go on unchallenged. While secrecy may be considered passive behavior promoting infidelity, approximately 5% of participants revealed active behaviors that involved pressuring teammates to cheat on their partners. Moreover, this can happen in a variety of ways as a collegiate baseball player recalled, "I think there's probably a little bit of competition from that standpoint too. You know to see who can tell the best story and...have the most notches on their... bedpost. So I think there's a little bit of competitiveness to that too, I mean I know there is." This participant highlighted the fact that elite-level athletes reach higher levels because they are very competitive individuals. Consequently, when competitiveness occurs between peers, it can carry into sexual behaviors with women regardless of whether an athlete is in a relationship or not. Approximately 12% of participants noted phrases such as "it's the thrill of the hunt" and "the chase" to describe athletes' competitive sexual urges that could result in infidelity. One participant as a collegiate hockey coach discussed other ways that peer pressure influenced cheating:

> ...a lot of our guys have steady girlfriends, but they fuck around on them all the time whether they be at home or they're here [at college]...again, the peer pressure, the group, the mentality that you know, "It's okay" your buddies say, "It's okay, so it must be okay" – they're doing it so it's okay for you to do it – you know even though they're risking ruining their own relationship, you don't care because you're caught up in the moment – you know and it's a momentum thing – no different than camaraderie or winning and it's you go with the flow – that mob, group mentality...it's that sense of invincibility that sense of entitlement like, "Hey, don't all athletes do this? Isn't this part of the gig? Doesn't this come with part of the territory? It's cool to do that," and again so many of them come from divorced families where the dad left...[so] they don't have any sense of you know sticking it out...

In other instances, hockey participants, including a married minor leaguer and a collegiate player, noted peer pressure that went beyond expectations and beliefs to include more active pressure to engage in infidelity:

> ...I mean I can honestly say and a lot of people go, "Aw bullshit"...[but] I behaved myself pretty much – I had a lot of pissed off roommates, "Ah you got to." "I ain't touching her – forget it, you want her that's fine, but I ain't having nothing to do with the other one – I won't do it – my standards are way up there and I ain't doing it forget it." "Well, just talk to [her]." "I ain't even talking to her don't even bring her back – so just forget it...I'm going to bed leave me alone."

> ...I told [a roommate] that if she calls don't tell her I'm here – I got to get some sleep. This was Thursday night, I'd been with her Monday night, Tuesday night, Wednesday night, and I mean my dick was raw – I couldn't have taken much more...and finally she called up and [my roommate] he answered the phone and she was like, "Come on...I

know he's there – you know I just want to talk to him," so finally, "Oh yea, he just happened to walk in" – I'm like, "I'll kill you," so I get on the phone and I said, "Naw," I said, "Look I'm on the ice the first thing…[and] I got this to do…" She said, "Aw it's just a shame, I really was hoping you'd come over cause I picked up some ice cream and I was going to pour it all over me and have you lick it off." I said, "What time do you what me to be there?" [laughs] – it's like the guys all along are listening to this conversation take place – they're all urging me on and everything – I knew better, I mean I was wiped out, you know I had a girlfriend back home…I didn't want to – this was just insane.

Together, these narratives show that athletes' competitive nature in combination with teammates' expectations, beliefs, and modeled behaviors created the pressure that prompted some athletes to cheat on their partners.

Coaching That Influences Cheating

Coaches are often held in high esteem, and therefore, their words and actions can make a lasting impression on their players. For instance, coaches who take personal interest in their athletes or promote good citizenship both in and out of sport make a positive impact that is fondly remembered long after a sports career is finished. On the other hand, coaches have also been known to negatively impact their players through careless words and actions which also become deeply etched into a player's memory, but for the wrong reason. A collegiate baseball player recalled one such event in which his collegiate coach inadvertently encouraged different types of cheating early in his career which made a lasting impression:

> …I can remember specifically that our coach…I can remember a speech by him when I was a freshman that was…like, "I don't care if you cheat in school and I don't care if you cheat on your girlfriend, but you don't cheat out here on the baseball field," and what he meant by that was not necessarily scuffing the ball [as a pitcher], he meant you get out here on time and you work hard when you're out here, you lift weights, and you do all the things you have to do to prepare and…you know, "I don't care if you have to miss a class, but you're out here and you make sure you practice and put your work in out here."

While this message essentially gave the team license to do whatever they felt was necessary to succeed in their sports participation, it is unlikely that their dishonesty could be contained in only certain areas of life without seeping into others. A much better message would have stressed honesty in school and in personal relationships because failing in these areas will ultimately impact an athlete's sports performance. Indeed, athletes who cheat in school and get caught and/or fail classes usually do not see much playing time. More importantly, this is a poor message to give to a team of developing collegiate players particularly when it comes from an influential role model such as a collegiate coach. Finally, deviant behaviors including infidelity thrive with some coach's attention and/or silence whenever such behaviors are not confronted.

CHEATING THAT TARGETS A TEAMMATE'S PARTNER

Few will disagree that high levels of trust are essential for team success among elite-level athletes. At the same time, athletes' trust in one another can be compromised whenever players observe teammates cheating on their partners. This was highlighted when a minor league football player questioned his teammates' integrity as well as their ability to support him under all conditions during competition after he observed certain married players cheating on their wives. This participant reasoned that if someone would cheat on his own wife and family, essentially the people you were supposed to be the closest to, how could a player trust a teammate to support him when he was not as connected as a family member? This participant believed trust carried into all aspects of life and could not be compartmentalized to fit into specific times, places, or situations. Furthermore, if trust can be depreciated by observing teammates' random acts of infidelity, this raises the question of what happens when an athlete finds out a teammate has become sexually involved with his girlfriend, fiancé, or wife.

In his book, *Juiced: Wild Times, Rampant 'Roids, Smash Hits, and How Baseball Got Big*, former MLB star Jose Canseco noted that it was not at all unusual for baseball major leaguers to sleep with other players' partners, and some players were only too happy to take on another's wife or fiancé when she came onto them while feeling neglected or intoxicated.[15] Canseco noted this happened "a lot in baseball" especially when a female partner wanted revenge against her husband or fiancé for sleeping with other women, although he chose not to provide names of players or the females involved.[16] Because there was no follow-up or discussion of the repercussions to such events, the reader was left wondering whether the recipient player was angry or not with his teammate for having sex with his partner – if he knew this occurred.[17]

In this study, numerous participants previously noted that passing females between teammates for the purpose of engaging in casual sex with the same woman was common and not a big deal for many athletes; however, cheating with a teammate's steady partner can be a very different situation for certain athletes. One collegiate hockey coach noted that infidelity involving teammates' partners "happens frequently because they all know one another – they're all friends" although sometimes these relationships were ambiguous particularly when certain players along with their female partners were equally promiscuous. Moreover, when this type of infidelity occurred, this participant discovered his players were quick to forgive the offender because they did not want these indiscretions to affect the team chemistry. It is also possible that infidelity produced little upset because some players viewed their friendships with teammates as a priority while their relationships with certain girlfriends were seen as short-term situations or conveniences. Despite this, the frequency of such occurrences forced this collegiate coach to intervene in some instances. This also caused him to consider implementing "a morals clause" which he hoped would deter a variety of deviant behaviors including infidelity with teammates' partners and having sex with married women. Although having players sign a morals clause was intended to end sexual behaviors that were "deemed detrimental to the image of the program, [and] you pay a price for it," the idea never materialized during this coach's career.

The previous participant noted infidelity involving his athletes' partners sometimes involved undefined relationships; however, this was not always the case as a collegiate hockey player revealed:

> It wasn't uncommon. If it happened, it was usually just brushed off, it wasn't a big deal. Guys really didn't hold grudges against one another and that mentality just continued, and guys, I think who would kind of be put off by this when it did happen, were forced to accept what the team thought of this and it was the culture of the group...one guy, years before me, was engaged to a girl, and one guy on the team used to date her, [he] came down to town and walked into the two sleeping with each other. And the guy said, "You know, keep it within the team... [but] please don't do this again," sat down with both of them, [the] guy was still best man in his wedding...and he was pissed obviously, understandably, but he forgave him and they moved on...[but] yes, it happened so often that it wasn't that big of a deal unless...certain guys had real serious girlfriends and stuff, but most of the guys didn't and you had three or four guys on the team who did, and that was kind of off-limits and usually the girl wouldn't get involved in that kind of activity and were girls you take home to mom. But the other guys, yeah, it was kind of I'm dating her, she's my girlfriend, it's not very serious, and if one of the guys was hooking up with them, [okay]...

While previous participants noted infidelity occurring among collegiate teammates and their female partners, these practices were not relegated to the collegiate level because they were found among minor league players as well.

For example, two minor leaguers from hockey and basketball discussed their awareness as well as experience with this phenomenon:

> ...it was a rude awakening when I left college, because to see a lot of the stuff, you know especially like in the [AA level] league and...you know fucking one of those league-leading goal scorers that played on our team's wife [was] fucking everybody on the team and him not knowing it. Now that's pretty fucking rude there...I remember because I was laying in bed one night and the broad comes into my room and wanted to give me a blow job. I said, "What the fuck, you a groupie or what?" you know. [Then] I said, "You're damn married to a guy on my team and you want to suck my dick?" And I mean a lot of guys were fucking her, it was kind of, kind of sad really, you know. And that was...a good hockey player, been playing...there a long time, getting [to the] [AAA level] and stuff. The whole time his wife's doing everybody else, and this poor bastard don't even know it...or if he did, he didn't care, you know. But...that was one of the rudest, rude awakenings of [all]... this is your buddy you're playing with and you're fucking his wife...she'd come right to the houses...or he'd be passed out drinking, and she'd be upstairs fucking somebody, you know pretty scary, pretty scary there...I mean that was the extreme I seen right there...

> When I was [playing overseas] last year, you know I'm over there and we only had actually eight guys on the team, so you know we were real close, so everybody would hang out after the game cause it was a pretty small town, so there weren't that many people like our age, two of the guys were just best friends on the team, and you know their friendship was kind of you know on and off it looked [like], you know throughout the season a little bit because you know the one guy starts suspecting that his wife is cheating on him, you know with you know his teammate here, but...nothing's ever really said and all of a sudden the last week of the season, all of a sudden it comes out, that the wife has been cheating with the teammate for like six or seven months I guess it was, and like she was telling the husband, "Yea I'm going to work till 6:30 p.m." and she'd be like getting off at 5:30 p.m. and then she'd go over and visit the teammate and you know have sex with him, you know hang out for an hour, and then you know go home and then just say that, "You know I came directly home from work." That was one of the craziest things that I've heard where it was actually a teammate and a teammate you know – especially you know – cheating on him with his best friend there [laughs].

Although bonding and camaraderie were prominent influences in many of the sexually deviant behaviors discovered in this research, no one expects their teammates, as a group, to behave like they did in the first narrative. It is evident that certain teammate bonds can be very shallow particularly when some athletes place greater importance on satisfying their own self-serving desires rather than maintaining ethical boundaries and friendships. Moreover, it appears that this athlete's wife was sexually acting out to get revenge against a husband who perhaps had a drinking problem since he was often found "passed out." As a result, team bonding was a façade in this example since it did not extend to all players, and this was all too apparent when so many teammates had no problem sexually accommodating their leading scorer's cheating wife.

This participant also noted a player on another minor league team he was on that was having sex with his best friend and teammate's wife, which prompted a divorce as well as a remarriage to the player with whom she was cheating. Once again, this event caused this participant to question the depth of the "best buddy" friendship these athletes were supposed to have shared. He also questioned the cheating athlete's behavior by saying, "I'd have a hard time fucking my best buddy's wife you know, especially if I was playing on the same line...but...everybody is different, everybody has their own morals." Another minor leaguer commenting on this event noted such occurrences were not always the cheating player's fault because in this instance, the recipient athlete's troubled marriage in combination with his wife's desire to perhaps leave him played a significant part in promoting her infidelity, divorce, and remarriage to the player she became involved with.

The second participant described a similar situation in which a player on his team was having sex with a best friend and teammate's wife, and the deterioration of their friendship became evident when the one player began suspecting something was wrong in his marriage. This participant elaborated on the overall atmosphere within his team as well as the manner in which this situation culminated:

> Basically the two guys just acted like the other one wasn't even on the team, it was always till the last week of the season, the practices that week were absolutely horrible, the one guy didn't show up for two or three [practices], he only came once or twice that week to practice and you know actually the funny thing is we won pretty easily that Saturday night, we won that last game and it was weird, the girl didn't come to the last game and basically those two just didn't speak at all, you know after the game...the woman who was cheating and the new boyfriend I guess just took off right after the game...you know there wasn't really any fights or any really [aggressive behavior] you know cause that's what I thought was going to happen especially because the guy, who you know got through it or whatever, he was pretty crazy, he wouldn't

necessarily fight with other people but...we'd lose a game and he'll throw something through the locker room door, you know throw a chair, kick this, kick that, so I expected him to go off, but he really just didn't, but...now this year they're both on different teams and you know I assume they won't really speak to each other at all...

Although this participant noted the recipient of the infidelity was an explosive, unpredictable player, there was silence but surprisingly no physical confrontations between these two teammates. This was in contrast to a collegiate hockey coach who discussed a similar event involving a girlfriend that resulted in a confrontation between two players:

...it's happened enough times that I've had to get involved...I thought that [one player] was going to kill [a teammate]...for some things that [he] said to [the player's] girlfriend and some inappropriate touching... she never gave in to him but he made the pass at her, he made the attempt, he got his feel in and he took advantage of her in a drunk state...yea, but she was sober enough to recognize what was happening and went and told [her boyfriend] – and I was there when [he] went up to [the teammate] and told him if he ever heard him talking like that to his girlfriend [again]...and [the offending player] not only didn't back down, but he was like, "If you had any balls, you'd beat my ass – you're too big a pussy to even stick up for your own girlfriend," but they were roommates...and you know again, they weren't going to let it come between them as teammates...

The above participant noted plenty of situations involving infidelity among players and their girlfriends on his team, and this was an incident where he felt it was necessary to intervene as a coach. Furthermore, cheating with a teammate's significant female partner can have a definite impact on players' trust and bonding with one another which in turn influences team chemistry and success. This would also explain why some coaches choose to intervene in such instances because preserving team harmony can also mean keeping their job.

In addition, participants identified a variety of influences that related to their teammates' infidelity as well as their own. These influences included: loneliness, boredom, excessive spare time, dissatisfaction in a relationship, apathy or anger toward a partner, long distance relationships and time apart, being in a less than serious relationship, not understanding commitment, being on a road trip, a desire for freedom and non-committed sex, youth and immaturity, curiosity, the thrill of someone different, having a competitive and conquer mindset, sexually available females, opportunity for easy no-effort sex, invincibility (i.e., will not get caught), satisfying the ego (i.e., cheating because you can), selfishness, a sense of power and entitlement, desire for increased masculinity (i.e., cheating is manly), cheating as normative practices (i.e., accepted and expected within a team), sexual drive and/or addiction, peer pressure and story-telling, alcohol, coaching and peer influences, a lack of conscience, disconnected from spirituality, temptation, and poor impulse control (i.e., desire for immediate sexual indulgence and gratification). Finally, infidelity can involve a one-time sexual encounter, or it can continue over time so that an athlete has sexual involvement simultaneously with more than one partner. When this occurs, athletes are now engaged in the practice of juggling which will be discussed next.

THE PRACTICE OF JUGGLING WOMEN

Juggling refers to the practice of simultaneous involvement (often translated to mean: having sex with) two or more women with or without their awareness. Athletes can be single and involved in multiple relationships when they juggle different women, and juggling is not cheating for single athletes who make it clear they are not committed to anyone. Other athletes are married or in committed relationships when they engage in these practices, so for them juggling is also infidelity. Moreover, juggling differs from one-night stands with various women because athletes' involvement with two or more females continues for an extended period of time. Juggling practices often originate from a casual sexual encounter when both parties agree to continue their involvement. Although athletes may enjoy their involvement with different women, more often than not, these relationships are more sexual in nature and do not evolve into deeper long-term situations – particularly if an athlete is already involved in a committed relationship or marriage.

Golf superstar Tiger Woods' infidelity provided one of the more recent and documented examples of juggling because at least seven different women have alleged sexual involvement with Woods during affairs that went beyond one-night stands by continuing for months or even years.[18] One study comparing the prevalence of multiple sexual partners in college males and females aged 18-24 revealed that the young men were nearly four times more likely than the women to report multiple sexual partners in the two months preceding the survey; this was in agreement with outcomes from other studies.[19] Such findings suggest that men were less likely than women to view sex as a significant way to establish closeness with a partner, and men were less invested in their primary relationships.[20]

I practiced juggling during different periods of my collegiate and professional career as an alternative to participation in more meaningless one-night stands.

Since I was not looking for a deeper relationship with a woman, juggling offered a practical solution and middle ground between these two options. Consequently, I would juggle anywhere from two to four women by letting them know that I was "seeing" others. Most were fine with this probably because I did not detail the particulars of these arrangements which included sexual involvement with each one. For the most part, I was not involved in a committed relationship while I was juggling and when I was, this was short-lived because as I mentioned previously, it resulted in stress and back pain.

JUGGLING AMONG COLLEGIATE ATHLETES

Surveys of the general population report that about 11% of men in the United States engaged in partner concurrency (juggling) in the past year.[21] This was in contrast to over 50% of the participants in this study who were aware of and/ or experienced juggling during their collegiate and/or professional careers. This juggling percentage might be low because it was influenced by the fact that this question emerged during the study, so not everyone was asked it. This was particularly true for athletes at the collegiate level, however, various participants still revealed an array of juggling frequencies involving collegiate teammates as well as themselves. For example, one minor league basketball player noted, "I think [in] college it doesn't happen because of course you can't financially do it and it's a little more closely watched" by some coaches. In contrast, other participants representing every sport noted a range of juggling behaviors that could involve a lower prevalence of "10-15%" up to "30%," of the players while other participants including a minor league baseball player noted, "Oh absolutely, I mean most of the [college] guys – probably three or four girls – 50-60% of the guys [on the team] were [juggling]." Similarly, a wrestler who recently finished his career observed "60-70%" of his single, collegiate teammates juggled up to several women. Another minor league basketball player revealed an even higher prevalence of juggling within his teams during the 1990s/2000s:

> Almost all of them at both levels [college and minors] – that's very common, I'd say for a team roster of you know let's say 12 guys, I would say at least 10 of them had multiple options...some guys liked to keep two or three [women], some guys preferred five you know but...guys always had plenty of options and opportunities...roughly 3-5 was kind of the going number for me.

While juggling was a normal practice within the above participant's teams, a current minor league basketball player found juggling was much more prevalent among collegiate teammates, including himself, than among his minor league teammates because "90%" of collegiate players on his teams juggled anywhere from 2-7 women. Additionally, a wrestler observed juggling was "very prevalent" within his team and could involve anywhere from "2-10" females although these were not all sexual relationships. Personally, this wrestler noted his juggling practices involved "seven or eight" females with "two or three" being sexual relationships.

Other participants revealed more extreme juggling practices among teammates including a minor league football player who said, "I had a college roommate… and shit he had a girl every single day, a different girl came to our door every single day, and I have no idea to this day how he did it, but he did it, I'm like, 'Man, how in the hell do you have sex with every damn type?' [laughing]…[but] yea, I mean that's going to go down." A wrestler similarly noted that juggling was "huge" on his team and particularly among "five or six" of the "ladies men" who would be "hooking up with a different girl every night, twice a day…and they just loved it [because] you know they could pull it off." A minor league hockey player observed even more extreme practices in the new millennium:

> In college…this one guy in particular, I mean this guy was unbelievable, he'd have a girl for every hour and a half to the point where like the one girl was leaving at 8:20 and the other one was coming in at 8:30 and they'd cross paths…and then his real girlfriend would come in from his home town and…these other girls knew that he had a girlfriend, but it never seemed to bother them…[but] I mean every hour, hour and a half, this went on Monday, this went on Wednesday, and then these two on Saturday you know kind of thing…

While some players' juggled different females without their knowing it, certain women were fully aware of these practices and an athlete's steady partner and yet choose to ignore them. Participants representing every sport observed that juggling was especially common among collegiate athletes who had girlfriends that were living in their hometown or at another college. Other participants found juggling was common in college because no one established real relationships, and athletes had such an easy time meeting and picking up females. One minor league baseball player noted observing "a lot" of situations where teammates would "just play the girls" by having sex with "two, three girls" at a time because having regular sex with certain females caused some to mistakenly think they were an athlete's special partner. Similarly, a collegiate basketball player attributed the common practice of having a steady girlfriend along with "multiple partners" to the "power of your status," "age," "hormones," greater "access to women," and "because we could." Athletes let their "natural urges run wild" because as a collegiate basketball player noted, "Nobody ever said that was wrong." This participant highlighted an important point because when coaches and/or staff choose not to address certain issues such as juggling, players can interpret this to mean they have a "green light" for engaging in deviant behaviors which can produce problems for both sexes. This became apparent among certain athletes, who engaged in extreme juggling practices, because it appeared that some were on the path to developing sexual compulsions and addictions. A minor league basketball player supported these notions by saying, "I think that there are guys who get addicted to the attention and of course the sexual activity...I've seen some guys they misuse sex to relax them...from a stressful standpoint...but the end result of it is not positive and that's something that's always kept me away from it." About 10% of participants believed sexual drive and/or addiction prompted athletes' cheating behavior. In addition, addictions can emerge insidiously whenever habitual behaviors are rewarding and offer high levels of physical pleasure and comfort – similar to the feeling and high accompanying the use of drugs, alcohol, or gambling.

I found juggling to be invigorating at times because sex with a variety of partners was a definite ego boost. At the same time, juggling was also depleting because I was constantly on the go deciding who I would see next, when, and where. This also prevented deeper attachments from developing, which is what I desired, because I could not give any woman a whole lot of time and priority. Even though most women I was with realized that these relationships were time-limited with some being more sexual in nature, this did not change the fact that certain women still developed attachments and feelings during our time together. Consequently, some women got hurt inadvertently when the relationship ended. Observing this fact made me carefully examine and reflect upon my motives and behaviors since I did not want to play with people's feelings. In the end, juggling soon took a greater toll on my time, energy, and my peace of mind, and this prevented me from engaging in these practices long-term.

JUGGLING AMONG PROFESSIONAL ATHLETES

Like collegiate athletes, minor and major league athletes representing every sport also engaged in juggling practices that included a wide range of frequencies at both levels. Because professional athletes have more resources than collegiate athletes, greater time, money, and access to females means that juggling practices can be even more prevalent among certain athletes at this level. Moreover, juggling was discovered as readily among players who competed in the early 1970s as it was among those who competed in every decade through 2010. While certain participants observed juggling was nonexistent or involved lower percentages of players (10-30%) who had involvement with females in up to several cities, others noted that 40-90% of teammates or more juggled one to three females in virtually every city in which they competed.

At the lower end of the spectrum, various participants including minor league baseball players revealed there were obstacles to juggling women at the minor league level because their teams would not play certain opponents enough to establish females in rival cities. Other minor leaguers found constant team changes prevented players from reconnecting with females who were one-night stands that had the potential to be part of an athlete's juggling practice. Some hockey and football major leaguers noted low or nonexistent juggling practices because of time limitations on road trips while other participants recalled teammates "went out that night and found somebody" without any desire to reconnect with the woman at a later time. Players who did not engage in juggling attributed this to being in a committed relationship, prioritizing their sports participation, religious beliefs, fearing the repercussions of such practices, limited time on road trips because of chartered flights, getting cut, traded, or simply not playing long enough to establish female contacts at home or in other cities.

Despite certain obstacles, juggling thrived among many professional athletes because it was a relatively simple process that a minor league football player explained, "It's really easy, I think if you end up hooking up with somebody and you end up having a good time then they end up giving you their phone number and just telling you, 'Hey next time you're in town, call me,' which happened to me on a couple of occasions." Older, veteran players representing every sport were particularly known for juggling females because longer careers meant they had more time to establish additional female contacts both in and out of season. For example, a minor league baseball player revealed, "Most of them [juggled], the veterans all did, the rookies that was their whole goal was to make that happen, that was the whole goal of going out at night was to find one so that the next time you come back, you're ready to go." Moreover, there could be vast differences in players' personalities and juggling behaviors within teams as a minor league hockey player observed, "Some guys were loyal as hell, other guys had a different girl in every city." As time went on, certain players' juggling practices grew to include more and more women. Athletes would meet women at games, bars and restaurants, networking through others, and The Internet. Some players expanded their juggling practices when they were traded by continuing to see females from previous cities they lived in along with any additional women they would meet in their new location. One NFL player observed these practices by saying, "There was guys who had girls that they could just call when the urge hit them. They probably weren't like out in the singles scene you know actively probing…I got the feeling they more or less had this whole thing kind of set up for awhile, and you know they were just going with that."

Other participants including a minor league baseball player discussed the manner in which juggling practices flourished during road trips:

[It was] very prevalent, oh they'd call ahead, meet a gal at this town, go out with them once or twice, keep their number, go to the next town, they'd already have some gal in the next town that they had met or gone out with...[women] just keep rotating through...so they kept everyone on the line so to speak...oh 8-10 or 8-12 [females].

Juggling females in other cities made road trips much more enjoyable, and this allowed players' to keep their sex lives secretive from partners back home according to a minor league basketball player. Various participants with minor league experience from hockey, football, and basketball observed "about 80%" and "at least" 85% of teammates' juggled different women often on road trips. Another minor league football player elaborated on the extent of these practices by saying, "Oh yea that's a professional thing, some guys had a woman in every city they go to, 16 cities that's 16 different women, sometimes two or three at a time in [a home city]...it happens man, it's crazy shit, I mean I see it happen right here in [this city]...[as] I was sitting in a little ass." As a result, juggling appeared to have a practical side to it since it conserved athletes' time and energy particularly on road trips as another minor league football player revealed, "You have an itinerary so you're on a real tight schedule so you really don't have time to get out and do much, so it's real easy to make a phone call, you know for somebody you already met previously."

Like the codes that were previously revealed which enabled infidelity to thrive among major league baseball players, a baseball minor leaguer revealed the "unspoken" codes that enabled both cheating and juggling to exist within his sports culture at the minor league level:

...it was kind of an unspoken rule whenever you go away...you may be in town for you know five days or five months who knows, but whenever you're hooking up on a regular basis with a girl, you either come out and say [it] explicitly or in a better case scenario, it's implied that what happens here is going to end as soon as the summer's over, and as soon as the summer's over I'm leaving, I'm going back home where I may have a wife or a girlfriend or a fiancé or whatever and under no circumstances [do] you try to contact me. It's like I said an unspoken rule that it's kind of like the Las Vegas commercial...[but], "What happens in the minor league town, stays there" – unless one of the two parties decides to come out and say something different, than what the situation is supposed to be...

Such situations enabled athletes to experience the luxury of uncommitted sex and female companionship while also being involved in a steady relationship. However, various participants including an NHL player revealed another side to juggling that appeared to empower some women despite health-related concerns, "There were a lot of guys that had girls in different ports and a lot of [them were] regulars and...when the guys would leave, a new team would come in and those girls would have other guys on other teams so I mean it just became... like a Ferris Wheel you know that just kept turning and turning." This participant, like others, noted plenty of women juggled just like the athletes because they were able to reap benefits such as "room service," "shopping," being "paid close attention to," and sitting in the "VIP" section at games.

A MLB player compared the prevalence of juggling during his minor and major league career by saying, "I would say major leagues [has more], minor leagues is too – you're in a different league every year and you're going different places where in the big leagues you're pretty much going to the same cities every year." Likewise, an NFL player observed juggling practices were more prevalent at the NFL level than in college because more away games allowed players to meet more women. Another NFL player noted "money, power" and "just being able to do it" was reason enough for "a good percentage of guys" to have "mistresses," and nearly 20% of participants believed ego and power fueled athletes' cheating. Recently retired major leaguers from baseball and football similarly noted that 50% or more of teammates, which could include themselves and baseball minor leaguers as well, juggled anywhere from "7-10" women. An NHL player noted juggling by saying, "Yea...that's prevalent too," while another who juggled himself observed up to 50% of his teammates entertained females in "four or five" different cities. Various NBA players revealed juggling practices occurred "quite often, there's a lot of that" and "all the time," and one player explained this by saying, "Oh man, [just] machismo you know, 'I got more than you do' just competitive nature." Another NBA player with recent professional experience elaborated on the extent of such practices including his own by saying, "In the majors, every major city that you play in, you could have a different woman there...maybe several...[you] didn't really have to [do much], [for] most guys, the women set it up themselves...I had at least three in every city." Interestingly, over 20% of participants believed that athletes' desire for conquest and increased manliness prompted cheating while almost 30% cited female availability, opportunity, and temptation as the cause of the behavior.

In contrast, an NFL player noted that unlike NBA or MLB players who stayed in cities for longer periods of time and/or played multiple games, football road trips were much shorter in duration, so this caused players to actively pursue females at other times:

...setting up off season contacts, I mean I definitely would...no doubt, no doubt it's going on, I mean that's huge, that's a must, everybody's doing it and see that's the whole thing you know when we go up, when the plan comes down, you know we head into the malls, we head into the spots, wherever the spot is you know we headed there, and we're looking [for] females, we're looking for numbers, so we call them area codes, we're looking for area codes, so we can just collect area codes and then you know who knows? You know your guy's going to camp you know, and they see you, and they might fly down you know, everyone's got relatives and everywhere you know...and you're going [to] want some legs when you come back you know so, "When I come back, we'll go get some dinner or whatever and take you and hang out."

This participant mentioned that he still had "a diary" that contained women who were available in every city in which he competed as well as places he did not. Indeed, certain players, including this participant, became proficient at "the numbers game," because more female contacts meant a greater likelihood that it would lead to subsequent encounters as well as sex. One NBA player revealed the number of women that certain players, including himself, would juggle, "Oh shoot, wow, 20s, 30s, depends on how long they've been in the league, the longer, the more [females]...I have done it but again, it was in my youth and I was single...but I did have 'a friend' in just about every city and if I didn't, I would fly my friend from one city to the next." Because players knew the whereabouts of their wives on a particular day, this player also noted, "It's easy for you to have somebody there waiting [in another city]...give them a hotel key, they'd be in your room waiting for you, I mean it's very easy [to cheat]...[the women] make themselves very accessible." Athletes representing a variety of sports including high paid minor leaguers who played overseas noted similar practices during their careers. While certain participants noted teammates' "extra partners" were taken care of "extremely well," no one knew any teammates who were paying their girlfriends' bills or acting as "sugar daddies."

While juggling thrived among many minor and major leaguers, some professionals saw the risks involved which ended or reduced certain athletes' juggling practices. A minor league basketball player who juggled women during his collegiate career avoided these practices as a high paid professional overseas because he saw the financial risks involving unwanted pregnancy, divorce, and even extortion. Similar caution was expressed by an NHL player who discussed how juggling had changed over the years for certain athletes:

Well I think it's changed...I think now guys are very, very selective, I think that they have their you know one or two girls that they have that they know that they can so-call trust and be with them whenever they want, bring them on the road, fly them here, fly them there, I think that it's...really changed, where you might have had 25 different girls in 25 different cities, but now it's you know you got maybe one or two at the most, you know whether you're married or not.

JUGGLING THAT LEADS TO DEEPER INVOLVEMENT, SECOND FAMILIES

Various MLB players in this study noted teammates who juggled women were "just a lot more discreet." One logical rationale for this is that certain athletes did not want to risk being discovered since it could ruin their primary relationship or marriage and cost them their family and money. Another explanation for concealing infidelity and juggling may be that an athlete does not want his secondary relationship to be discovered because it had evolved into more than just a casual sexual relationship. While cheating and juggling other women is certainly heartbreaking when many wives discover this, such practices are arguably more impacting whenever juggling leads to deeper involvement. For example, a minor league football player observed, "I would say probably in professional football...the biggest thing that stands out in my mind is just the amount of infidelity that there is...guys going out with strippers and having full blown relationships...and here they got a wife and three kids back home you know 500 miles away." Participants from various sports noted that athletes' girlfriends and fiancés as well as wives and families did not always live in the same city where their partner's team was based. Consequently, this may help to explain why nearly 25% of athletes attributed infidelity to issues such as loneliness, boredom, long distance, and dissatisfaction with their relationship.

Athletes' involvement in deeper relationships with females they juggled was not limited to the minor league level. Moreover, sometimes these relationships evolved into second families for certain major leaguers who were obviously not as discreet as some participants had suggested. Two MLB players elaborated on their awareness:

> Oh those are a lot of the Dominican players actually, they always seemed to have two or three wives...we had one guy that he had, we knew his wife and kids and then at the other cities every time we were on a road trip, there was another lady with kids that was always with him and then they actually made a mural, a guy drew a mural of him, of his family, and it was of this lady, not of his wife, so I don't know how they arrange those things...[but] we pretty much always liked to sit back and watch, it was quite amusing...

> There's only a few different instances of that, couple guys that I know of just had their little organizer where, you know, when we got off the

plane and onto the bus in whatever city we were in, they would pull that one up and they'd have somebody to hang out with, I knew of a couple of situations where actually even married guys had had partners in different cities that actually, some of them actually had children with these other ladies and almost like a second life, I know of a couple instances where you know that person and the child ended up coming to the home town and actually one time I remember a wife showed up on the road, and you know to surprise her husband, and she found the other woman and the child and it was a little bit of a shocker...

Ninety percent of athlete-related paternity cases are settled before they reach public awareness; however, it appeared that the situation in the second narrative was being handled without any court involvement because the player's wife was shocked at discovering her husband's second family.[22] Whether or not the children in the previous narratives were planned is not known, although it is unlikely because such situations only complicate an athlete's already complex lifestyle. Plus, the fact that these athletes already had families and traveled frequently because of their sports participation means their time as a father in a second family would be very limited. Nevertheless, such situations have become an all too common phenomenon among present-day athletes who often seem oblivious to the legal, financial, and emotional ramifications of fathering children out-of-wedlock.[23] A *Sports Illustrated* article, "Paternity Ward" revealed that numerous athletes from every sport were subject to paternity suits with some fathering numerous children with different females.[24] For example, former New England Patriots running back, Dave Meggett, fathered five children out-of-wedlock with four women while former New York Knicks forward, Larry Johnson, supported five children by four women, which included two he had with his wife.[25] By the age of 28, former Cleveland Cavaliers forward, Shawn Kemp, had fathered seven children with six different women and then experienced a "well-publicized meltdown" resulting from the financial and emotional pressures related to paternity and child support obligations.[26] Such situations can take a tremendous toll on everyone involved, and this is particularly true for the child and the woman who is left to raise her family alone. This occurs because unlike the previous narratives, certain athletes choose to have little or no personal contact with their out-of-wedlock children, which means many kids grow up without having their high profile fathers involved in their lives at all.[27]

CONSEQUENCES OF INFIDELITY/JUGGLING

Out-of-wedlock pregnancy with its high financial and emotional costs is one of the more visible and lasting consequences of athletes' infidelity and juggling. Additionally, minor and major leaguers from a variety of sports previously noted females working with a male accomplice to try to extort money from an athlete who had a cheated on a partner and did not want this revealed. These situations often required law enforcement intervention since the extortionists would return for more money even after an athlete paid them off. However, these are not the only examples of negative outcomes associated with infidelity and juggling.

Sexually Transmitted Diseases

Los Angeles Lakers Hall of Fame guard, Earvin "Magic" Johnson, was among the first athletes to warn others about the consequences of unbridled promiscuity after he contracted the human immunodeficiency virus (HIV) while juggling numerous females during his NBA career.[28] As an unmarried player who had cheated on his girlfriend, Johnson paid a high price for his actions by contracting a potentially fatal sexually transmitted infection (STI) in addition to losing his NBA career at the height of his stardom.[29] Furthermore, there is little doubt that Johnson's stress (and possible remorse) regarding his behavior would have been amplified much more if his innocent girlfriend Cookie had tested positive for the virus. Indeed, STI's can be very difficult to deal with for the individual contracting the illness, however, this is magnified exponentially when a cheating player is discovered after infecting both himself and his partner as a minor league hockey player recalled:

> ...a buddy of mine that actually happened to him, he actually took his wife "a little package" home with him and got her infected and turned out that me and my wife went to visit them when they were going through the middle of it – and they weren't speaking real well, so we were trying to be friendly and I was asking them what was going on, so, "I was in such and such...and I picked up something – and she got it"...

Various participants recalled collegiate or professional players, including themselves, contracting STI's after they had casual sex with a female they picked up; however, the previous scenario was the only one of its kind to involve a player passing an infection to a partner, who in this case was his wife. This incident created understandable upset and relational stress because discovering a married partner's infidelity is difficult enough without finding this out through contracting an infection from them. While this athlete had contracted the infection from a female he picked up on a road trip rather than from a woman he was juggling regularly in a particular city, this was in contrast to a collegiate hockey player who cheated with his best friend's girlfriend and contracted an STI in his mouth after performing oral sex on her. Although medical treatment cured the infection, the memory of this event prevented him from going "down on a girl for many, many years after that." In the end, STI's are a definite consequence that should come as no surprise to the numerous athletes and the women they hook up with because both sexes frequently engage in high risk sexual activities with others who are doing the same.

Experiencing Personal and Relational Pain

Another consequence of infidelity and juggling relates to the high personal cost of such activities. For example, a minor league hockey player recalled a married teammate trying to seduce their coach's wife. After several days of dealing with the player's unwanted sexual advances, the wife told her husband prompting this player's immediate trade to another team.

Infidelity also caused personal pain and relational damage that various participants recalled including a minor league baseball player who told how he "lost" his girlfriend for awhile by cheating on her in college. Although this event had a happy ending because he eventually married the woman, this is not always the case as another minor league baseball player revealed:

> [I] didn't think about my consequences. All I knew was, "Man, look at all the ladies out there, boy, this could be fun"…and it was. In the process I did hurt one person that was very, you know, near and dear to me and that would never be repaired, so that was a consequence for that action…that was something that I had to deal with.

A wrestler expressed similar regret which was an uncommon reaction among his unfaithful teammates and like 6% of participants, he attributed cheating to alcohol's negative impact on "good judgment." While infidelity and juggling can be painful when athletes realize their cheating hurt their partners and ended their relationships, sometimes this produced long-term grief and remorse that an NFL player revealed in this way:

> Oh yea, that's why I'm not married right now, my college girlfriend, we were together in my sophomore year, and then when I went pro…I asked her to marry me, and she at the time was still in college and wanted to finish school, but you know in doing that you know I thought it would be, you know cool for me to clear the air [by revealing past cheating], so there were things that I have done, I don't want us to be married for four or five years and then it come back alive that this happened or that happened…I just don't want that to be you know [an issue] and I want you to know and…she flipped out on that, and I never married my high school or my college sweetheart because of that, I mean we're cool with it to this day…and like we're really good

friends, but you know that episode literally caused me, the things that I had done in the dark, literally caused me you know to lose a marriage to the girl that I probably loved the most in my entire lifetime – even at this point...years later, you know I still compare everybody that I meet to her...

Deep regret and pain resulting from infidelity is noteworthy because it can be life threatening – even for the athlete guilty of cheating. For example, a minor league hockey player revealed that he "hung out" with a teammate, whose wife and family lived in another state, until this player found "a girlfriend" that "he hit it off" with. Eventually, the wife discovered her husband's infidelity and juggling which prompted her to end their relationship. Just as quickly, the athlete discovered "his girlfriend didn't want him either and he tried to kill himself." This athlete learned a difficult lesson after losing his family that some women, like many athletes, do not want deeper involvement. Furthermore, it is apparent that cheaters need to closely evaluate the potential consequences of their actions because while juggling may produce euphoric feelings while it is happening undiscovered, these feelings can quickly turn into extreme despair.

Previous player disclosures focused on the pain and problems various cheating athletes experienced that many observers believe is well deserved. At the same time, athletes' cheating can have a tremendous impact on their girlfriend or wife which can result in a backlash of negative emotions and behaviors that an NFL player observed on two different occasions:

...we've had females come to dog gone practice once they find out, I mean it's always happening shoot, but...one of my best guys was living in the same complex, a condo complex you know, his girl she was going through his stuff one day, and found pictures or whatever she found, she found incriminating evidence, she ransacked his crib, calls me, I don't know what's going on, "Hey you know," she's calm and cool, "Hey...I know you got the key to his crib or whatever, you know can you just lock it up for me, I'm going to be downstairs, you know come take me to the airport, you know my mom said I got to go home." And now this is a superstar I'm talking about now, "I'm like okay," so you know I go pick her up whatever, take her to the airport you know, she got a big time like eight piece big time luggage set you know...catches a flight whatever, and you know so he gets home...[and] he's ready to fight me you know because I given away all his shit, I was like, "I didn't know"...she called me, you was gone like you know you was out working, so you know she caught me and asked me, "Can you come up alright?" I didn't see any harm in it...but that kind of stuff happened all the time...in pros.

This participant described another instance that he observed during a road trip in this way:

> ...one time it was in [XXX]...so you know I've been out gift shopping that day whatever, so I'm going to let my guys go ahead and go on up to the room and I'm going to get to the gift shop cause one of my big things is sending post cards, I would send post cards to my children, to my mom, to my school teachers, and to my high school coach...so...I go the gift shop, so I go down the elevator and like my guy's wife was on the elevator, I'm like, "What the hell?" so she [laughs] you know [she] found out he had...a little dip you know on the side in [XXX], so she's about to you know let loose fire in the hotel in [XXX], you know [she wanted to] come back up with me, trying to get clearance to get up to the hotel room with me, so she can get into the room and you know get at him, because...I guess she knew what was going on, you know she had...flew down there, spied on him, followed him around, you know while he was with this other chick in [XXX]...so I mean just all kind of stuff was going on [like] all that...

While some women's response is to quietly leave a relationship and sometimes with a cheating partner's prized possessions, other wives prefer confrontation once they gain access to their husband. Certain participants, including NFL players, noted time constraints during road trips suppressed players cheating and/or juggling behaviors; however, this does not hold true for all athletes since many make such practices a priority during their limited spare time.

Children are often the innocent victims of their athlete-fathers' infidelity and juggling particularly when these events damage and divide their families permanently. An NHL player with current professional experience observed this and said, "I'd say it goes on a lot, it sucks to see it, sucks to say it, especially when you see guys with kids and I think that's the most disappointing thing when you see a guy who's got kids go out and throw it away for nothing...I think it's pretty damn foolish." Because this participant prided himself on being a dedicated family man, it was particularly disturbing for him to witness teammates risking relationships with their wives as well as their children's well-being by cheating with women who meant little to them. Children of divorce are often forced to adjust to a lower standard of living that is prevalent among single-parent families, and few escape the long-term physical, mental-emotional, and spiritual anguish that impacts virtually everyone in these cases.[30] In the end, I am certain that the athlete, who lost his wife and family and almost took his own life because of his infidelity with a girlfriend that was quick to abandon him, would have much to say on this subject. Perhaps his message would focus on why it is best to resist the temptation to cheat because although athletic careers and affairs are often exciting in the moment, both can be brief in duration while family-life is a fulfilling experience for many people.

INFIDELITY AS A SOURCE OF VIOLENCE

A theme of indifference to infidelity was apparent within many player narratives because cheating was accepted and more common than not within many athlete cultures. Various participants, including a wrestler, highlighted their belief in the seemingly harmless nature of such practices by saying, "So, what harm could it cause?" Although some athletes rationalized infidelity as being a risk-free activity – at least for the person doing the cheating, previous narratives proved otherwise. Moreover, cheating could also result in violence, and a collegiate baseball player feared this by warning numerous collegiate teammates who were having sex with married women that they could get "shot" since this was a very dangerous act in his college town. Many victims of infidelity would agree that discovering these hurtful behaviors can produce an array of unbridled negative emotions that, at times, can lead to physical aggression as a minor league hockey player elaborated upon:

> ...in college, that [physical aggression] happens a lot because of a lot of infidelity going on. No one is married and there is a lot of screwing around going on which always seems to be at the root of what was going on. My roommate, actually this was another kind of reverse violence, he got smacked over the head with a racketball racket with the wooden protector still on. She came in and she caught him red handed screwing around with some girl which is in my house. She comes in grabs the racket right out of his closet and walks over and whack, right over his head, knees buckled, went down on the ground, and didn't know what hit him. She threw the racket down and left. It was probably the most violent thing that I have seen. It was funny because usually it is the opposite way with a guy beating up on the girl, but in that case it was the girl hitting him with the racket...[just] ugly.

The above participant noted "a lot of infidelity" during his collegiate career was responsible for different acts of aggression including one female fighting another, male athletes physically assaulting their girlfriends, and in this case, a sober girlfriend physically assaulting her athlete-boyfriend. This was not the first time this couple had engaged in a physical confrontation during their "roller coaster type relationship" because according to this participant, aggression during "weekly" low points made it "the worst thing you ever saw in your life." Surprisingly, this woman acted as the primary aggressor because "she was bigger than he was" and when "they would just go at it...he actually took the worst of it, but he would fight back sometimes." While this case may appear unique, nearly 60% of participants in this study were aware of females using physical aggression against an athlete and 20% were personally assaulted by a woman. Such assaults targeted collegiate, minor, and major league athletes and sometimes involved the use of objects which caused observable physical injury; however, female assaults did not relate to athletes' infidelity in every case.

Wife assaults targeting their high profile athlete-husbands have appeared in the media periodically. For instance, on April 1, 2002, former actress and sex symbol, Tawny Kitaen, was arrested on charges of attacking her husband, former Cleveland Indian pitcher Chuck Finley.[31] Finley filed for divorce three days later, and Kitaen's plea bargain included avoiding contact with Finley and entering a spousal battery counseling program.[32] In January of 2006, Daniell Harper, the wife of former Indianapolis Colts defensive back Nick Harper, was arrested on preliminary felony charges of battery with a deadly weapon and criminal recklessness after she stabbed her husband in the knee with a knife inflicting a wound that required several stitches.[33] Harper was no stranger to incidences of domestic violence himself because he was arrested six months earlier on a domestic battery charge after police said he hit his wife in the face.[34]

Such findings are not surprising according to various studies including two representative national surveys which revealed that women assault their male partners at similar rates to men.[35] Furthermore, the majority of studies examining dating violence in college students revealed that women engaged in more violent acts than men.[36] Another study that compared the rates of physical assault between partners in 526 dating couples, 237 couples who lived together, and 5,005 married couples revealed the most frequent pattern of violence was for both partners to be violent, followed by female only violence, and the least frequent pattern was male only violence.[37] However, because men typically have greater size and strength than women, their aggression is more dangerous since they were six times more likely to inflict serious injury on a female during an assault.[38]

Physical size and strength are traits that often distinguish male athletes from non-athlete males. Consequently, when athletes react to infidelity by using physical aggression, the outcomes can be devastating as two wrestlers and a collegiate football player revealed:

> I remember going in a group into this fucking house and these poor kids lived in this house and for some reason I think this one guy was cheating...with another wrestler's girlfriend, there was some motive there...[we] marched in the team, maybe five guys as back up, walked into this poor bastard's house, he was laying on the sofa, and this guy unleashed on his ass, I just stood back there thinking, "Holy shit man,

this is out of control." This guy just got pummeled man. He didn't know what hit him. It would be like you fucking relaxing on your sofa and a young fucking stud, powerhouse coming in and just whaling on you.

I actually came to [this state and university] because of a fight...an old girlfriend of mine was hanging out with a wrestler that was a friend of mine and I found out and...I did $3000 worth of damage to his face, so I had to pay that and then pretty much I just left there because I had like 13 counts of assault and whatever else against me because of that so that was a pretty memorable one...that was probably the reason why I exited [the state] yea...I was with a girl for six years and then we went out on a break I guess and cause...we were both deciding on like what we were both going to do with the rest of our lives and we were together all through college and...maybe a little bit after, and the kid that used to live with me that I was good friends with started hooking up with her, and then I found out so I just pretty much just walked into his house and just beat the shit out of him in his own bedroom...I threw him through a window also so he had some stitches in his back and in his foot and then whatever – it cost me $3000 in the emergency room for all the cuts and lacerations and stitches and everything else in his face.

...it was an innocent type of situation as far as the girlfriend and the other guy was concerned they had known each other from high school and they were in the dorms and he was in her dorm room – actually he and another guy were in her dorm room, and you know [the football player] comes up and he doesn't know anybody's in there, he's just going to his girlfriend's dorm room and so he gets there, knocks on the door, and opens it up and sees two guys in there with her and he just, he was kind of a loose cannon anyway, but he's a really nice guy, but in that type of situation I could see him snapping and that's what happened, he got in there and he didn't really ask any questions, he just you know saw his girlfriend and two guys and he attacked the two guys and beat up both of them really...he didn't rough her up, but he like was grabbing her and shaking her and stuff you know what I'm saying...ah man, he got in trouble for that...because of the police did come and [coach] did find out.

The first participant was subsequently asked if there were any injuries from this event and he replied, "Oh fuck, I'm sure. There's no way there couldn't have been, I don't know what they were but...that's one that speaks out in my mind." Because the wrestler who acted as the primary aggressor suffered no consequences for his assault, this means the situation went unreported, and therefore, it is likely that he will continue to solve problems using aggression in the future.

As a collegiate coach, one of my players physically assaulted an athlete from another sport while teammates provided him with similar backup. This was a poor decision because rather than teammates removing him from the situation, my player's actions resulted in legal problems, medical fees from injuring the other athlete, and an expulsion from the university.

The second participant noted leaving one state in order to take a collegiate coaching position in another state following a financially costly assault on a former roommate/teammate. Surprisingly, this participant did not receive any legal consequences because his teammate told him if he "paid for all his medical bills, then he wasn't going to press charges." Although certain collegiate players and teams did not consider infidelity with a teammate's girlfriend to be problematic, it is evident that not all athletes subscribe to these beliefs. This participant's previous friendship with his teammate coupled with perhaps this teammate's guilt for his role in igniting this assault prevented this incident from resulting in serious legal consequences.

The third participant noted a teammate also experienced harsh consequences when he was suspended from the football team and university and lost his scholarship after physically attacking two male students and assaulting his girlfriend in the process when he thought she was cheating on him. It is apparent that regardless of whether infidelity is perceived or occurs as an actual event, few will argue that it can be an extremely hurtful experience that can result in fierce emotions as well as aggression. Given the consequences and major life changes these events produced in most cases, I am certain that if the athletes could replay their situation a second time, all would gladly choose to talk and exercise different options rather than using aggression which proved to be a very costly decision.

The fact that over 95% of participants in this study had awareness of out-of-sport athlete aggression targeting other males, including teammates, during their careers means fighting is all too common. Approximately two thirds of participants revealed engaging in a physical confrontation during their collegiate and/or professional career, over 80% witnessed a fight involving an athlete, almost 20% intervened to stop an athlete's fight, and 15% knew teammates who did the same. One wrestler recalled that he had engaged in over 100 out-of-sport fights during his collegiate career while another admitted his team averaged 10-15 fights per month.

While the previous narratives revealed physical assaults that were predominantly directed against the male who was thought to be cheating with an athlete's girlfriend, sometimes an athlete's aggression targeted his girlfriend exclusively as a collegiate football player revealed:

[Physical aggression against a female] that happens more, that happens with some frequency...[and] it almost always involved you know some sort of infidelity on the girl's part, or on the part of the guy and...the girl would come after him and he'd have to do something to calm her down and grab up and do something, but the one big story that we heard where the guy got really physical with his girl was [that] he was living with his girlfriend and she cheated on him, and he like found out she cheated on him, and he got home that day and like he slapped her around, and then you know bruised her up a little bit, and he got in some trouble for that, but it was sort of like the hush, hush trouble, it wasn't like the big newspaper trouble...

The previous participant revealed that his premier collegiate football program had an unwritten policy that enabled certain players to avoid team suspensions for physical assaults against females during the later 2000s – if their aggression was not publicly exposed through the media. In this case, the offending player received help and various consequences because "he had to go to some sort of diversion program and an alcohol program, and he had to do some sort of service type of thing." However, because this incident was handled exclusively through the team, the coaches did not end up losing a key player during the season. Therefore, even though the female victim was "bruised up," "there were some threats to press charges," "the cops came, but they didn't charge him, and she didn't press charges," this participant noted "somebody handled something" which enabled his teammate to avoid negative media coverage, formal legal charges, and a team/university suspension because this athlete's assault included police involvement.

Unfortunately, such events were not uncommon because about two thirds of the participants had awareness of athletes' physical assaults targeting females during their careers, although this did not always involve infidelity. Over 30% of the participants witnessed an actual assault on a female, 30% had teammates intervene to stop an incident, and 30% personally intervened themselves. Furthermore, over 15% of the participants noted their own physical confrontation with a female at some point, although this was not necessarily related to cheating; this figure increased to nearly 20% when it included striking an object that was near the female. In all, about 3% experienced legal consequences from personal physical assaults involving a female.

CONFRONTING A CULTURE OF CHEATING

Not all athletes accepted the norms of cheating that often accompanied their elite-level sports participation. For example, a married minor league hockey player previously described how he repeatedly turned down his roommates' attempts to set him up on road trips with an extra female who often accompanied the women they were trying to have sex with. Similarly, a minor league basketball player found his team's pro-family culture refreshing because the married players were faithful and even warned him about the consequences of cheating that they observed during their professional careers. While mentoring practices were rarely found during players' collegiate careers – much less at the professional level, this player found his teammates' experiences were impacting so he "took their words to heart" since they had previously been where he was now during his rookie season. Essentially, teammates told him that female attention and temptation increased as athletes progressed in their careers and although it was "too easy" to accept sex from "anybody who's just willing to throw it at you," these situations were "not real" and could not compare to being with a "special someone...who's been with you through the thick and thin." Another minor league basketball player revealed that although his sport and teams were steeped in a culture where cheating was the norm, he saw through this façade and even tried to challenge its underlying belief system:

> [Infidelity] this is a lot – I wouldn't put a number on it – but I'm more surprised by guys who don't cheat on their wives or girlfriends and are faithful. No, I did not [cheat] because I had made a conscious effort that that while I'm single I'm going to be out there doing what I'm doing and if and when I find the person that I'm going to be with, that means that I'm going to be with her and I'm done. I made that commitment to myself before I ever met my ex...I want to be that voice that says it's okay to say, "I love my wife" or the person I'm with and not have that be seen negatively – the fact that I didn't cheat on my wife was seen as a bad thing in my culture, yea, it wasn't seen as normal – when we were dating and trying to get back together and I was [playing in the minors] and I didn't take part in some of these things that were going on (i.e., picking up women, infidelity, group sex) – that was seen negatively as well...I was part of the culture, but I was never really that into it...I didn't necessarily agree with all the things you were allowed to do and could do...I was in my mid-twenties and was like, "This is great and I can't believe that I could do all this stuff," but then you [get] a little older and you're like, "I can't believe that I could do all that stuff, there's something wrong with that cause it's not exactly the most healthy thing to be able to do" – that's why I said that it's more, it's getting to guys early enough and really making them understand the danger...it doesn't have to necessarily be the way you read about – it doesn't have to [be] – hey...it's a great thing to be young, have money, and have all these advantages but at the same time, understand the responsibility of the human being in some situations and I think if you can get them to

just think about [it] for a half of second before acting on some of those things, it could solve – not solve – [but] cut back a lot of the stupidity that ends up happening – I think you'll see less incidence of rape and violence if guys take that extra second to think about it – we have way too much to lose…

This participant further acknowledged the difficulty of changing the athlete culture because "it's a completely different mindset" to understand unless someone has walked in the shoes of an elite-level athlete in order to see where they are coming from and what they are experiencing. He also thought that teaching athletes early could help them understand that just because a culture has accepted certain beliefs and behaviors as normal does not mean they are right. While this participant admitted that he experienced the sexually promiscuous lifestyle of a professional athlete for a time, he also realized that such behaviors needed to be addressed and changed since they were not healthy practices. In the end, cheating and juggling practices are learned and take root during many athletic careers. Furthermore, many coaches believe that athletes play games just like they practice, and if this is true, cheating is, in fact, practicing negative attitudes and behavior that are certain to damage relationships with significant partners and family members as long as these practices remain active.

ATHLETES' CORNER: POINTS TO PONDER

1. Athlete infidelity is an undeniable fact within many athlete cultures that more often than not involves the majority of a team. These practices become firmly established because they are learned, accepted as normal, and even promoted within certain teams. However, the consequences and harm they produce far outweigh the excitement these practices provide in the moment. Because athletes' competitive nature, peer pressure, unwritten codes encouraging silence, female availability, and even coaching influences combine to promote a culture of cheating, each player must decide to either perpetuate this culture or take a stand against the errors that many have painfully revealed.

2. For certain cheating athletes, no woman was off limits, and this included teammates' girlfriends, fiancés, and even wives. While infidelity could involve a one-night stand, longer affairs with one or more mistresses turned into juggling practices in which the majority of players on a team often participated. Be aware that such behaviors teach athletes to become proficient at deceiving others. This raises questions about whether athletes can be trusted in other areas of life since they lack integrity with partners they are supposed to be closest to. Know that excellence as well as its opposite is demonstrated within close relationships like no where else whenever personal integrity is challenged and tested through an opportunity to cheat on a partner.

3. Both infidelity and juggling were the underlying cause of a variety of consequences that included unwanted pregnancies, sexually transmitted infections, extortion, and attempted suicide. These practices also created high levels of human suffering that impacted athletes, women, and children during relationship and/or family break-ups. Cheating also resulted in physical violence that targeted non-athlete males, teammates, significant female partners, the athletes themselves, and often included additional consequences. Various athletes revealed that they would gladly trade their pain and regret for another chance with a special partner they hurt and permanently alienated through infidelity. In the end, know that each athlete must decide whether short-term sexual gratification is worth the potential long-term consequences that often accompany infidelity and juggling.

Chapter 7

Competitions, Contests, and Conquests

Athletes as a group are extremely competitive because this characteristic is essential for athletic success. This fundamental premise to be a strong competitor is promoted early at the little league levels and continues full force in higher level sports participation. Having strong desire to compete and succeed is also a major reason corporations like to hire former athletes. Regardless of whether this is the result of biological influences, learned behavior, or a combination of both, one thing is for certain: athletes who lack drive seldom reach elite levels because they are weeded out in favor of more spirited and competitive athletes. Consequently as a coach, it was no surprise for me to observe that competitiveness often differentiated athletes and the levels and success they achieved. Being highly competitive is also a trait that does not turn itself off easily just because an athlete leaves the sports arena or retires.

While athletes' competitive drive is desirable, this becomes problematic in sport whenever athletes try to win at all cost and in the process harm themselves or others by using performance enhancing drugs, competing when they are injured, or intentionally trying to hurt another during practice or games.[1] At the same time, competitive drive can be just as problematic when it merges into athletes' social and sexual behaviors with females as a collegiate baseball player discussed in this way:

> ...you know you're in the middle of a game and...you want to win it and so you're resorting to those kind of [aggressive] tactics to make sure that you win...that's an instinctual kind of thing, and then you know there's a sexual drive, and then it seems to me that guys have, typically have, a pretty strong sexual drive especially at that age...maybe I'm kind of casting my opinions on the rest of the population but...I was sexually motivated, and then I don't know which was more motivating... [because] the competitive thing that you want to [win] – that this is what you wanted to have happen...it's kind of almost a game and...you want to kind a push the edges wherever you can – to win.

While this participant noted his strong sexual drive in college combined with an equally powerful competitive drive that made sex "almost a game" which athletes, like himself, wanted to win, he was unsure which drive had strongest influence on his sexual behavior with women. Other athletes including an NBA player also noted "chasing girls was the thing to do" besides studying since it was "definitely a priority." Because certain athletes already viewed sex with women as "a game," this may help to explain why some choose to formalize such practices.

Competitive behaviors involving sex, females, and high school athletes received national attention in March of 1993 when members of the self-proclaimed "Spur Posse" from Lakewood High School just outside of Los Angeles, California were discovered tabulating their sexual conquests.[2] While 20-30 core group members, who received a point for having sex did not see their long-standing competition as a big deal, police arrested nine on suspicion of raping and molesting at least seven girls, including one who was 10-years old.[3] The subsequent investigation revealed the girls were sexually preyed upon – not because of desire for sex, love, or affection – but for a point, and the 19-year old leader of the competition boasted that he had accumulated 66 points.[4] All but one of the group was later released when the district attorney concluded the sexual activity was consensual; however one 16-year old member was formally accused of lewd conduct with the 10-year old girl.[5] Still, various females who were victimized sought justice because they felt the group used threats, persuasion, and even forced sex to score points in both individual as well as group sexual encounters.[6] Group members along with certain parents claimed innocence of any wrongdoing because it was not illegal to have sex with "sluts," while others called attention to the question of common decency regarding morals, values, and ethical behavior.[7] Such practices are perhaps more universal that expected because a minor league baseball player in this study recalled similar competitions that involved "a point system" at his religious-affiliated high school although this only involved his non-athlete friends. In the end, discussions and competitions related to "scoring" with high school females are nothing new; however, such practices that once centered around getting to "second or third base" by feeling a girl's breasts or genitals have changed dramatically in recent times because it now appears that only "home runs" involving sexual intercourse count.[8]

The previous incident involving the "Spur Posse" revealed that many people, including some of the boys' parents, dismissed their sexual behaviors as age-appropriate and "boys being boys."[9] However, if such practices gained acceptance among certain adults while they occurred among high school athletes and students, this raises an interesting question: When athletes reach the collegiate and/or professional level, do they engage in similar competitions? Previous narratives already revealed the pick-up scene with its surplus of sexually available women thrived at both the collegiate and professional levels. Although I recall brief discussions that appeared to be more urban legend during my collegiate and professional career, I did not know anyone who participated in contests and competitions involving females. If any of my teammates were in competition to have sex with women, such events would have been unspoken. In contrast, approximately 75% of participants in this study, who were asked this question, revealed their awareness of competitions and contests involving women while approximately one third personally participated. Such practices may be even more common because approximately one third of the participants were not asked this question since it emerged later during the study. Elite-level athletes, who competed in careers spanning the 1970s-2010 and represented every sport and level revealed an array of sexual competitions and contests targeting women who often had no idea they were involved in such events.

COMPETITIONS AND CONTESTS INVOLVING WOMEN

Vying for Phone Numbers

Compared to all the different types of competitions that emerged in this study, perhaps the most harmless event involved both collegiate and professional athletes who competed to gather the most phone numbers by the end of the evening. For example, a minor league basketball player revealed that he and his collegiate teammates participated, "I think the occasional thing was how many numbers you get, I think there are a lot of guys that do, you know, with your buddies if you go to a party you're like...'I got five numbers today or I got six or I only got two' that [was] the most we ever went through." Although this kind of competition could bring disappointment to certain females whenever athletes had no real intention of ever calling, it did not involve the direct sexual exploitation of women the way other competitions did. In contrast, other minor leaguers including a football player found these practices could become more competitive whenever he heard his professional teammates say, "I'll bet I can get more numbers than you can tonight." Betting obviously increased the athletes' competitive urge and fueled these competitions because now their pride, reputation, and perceived manliness was on the line, and together this mattered much more than losing a sum of money or buying drinks for everyone. It will become evident that most elite-level athletes take losing at anything very seriously because in the world of sports, this is often the difference between having higher status and being virtually unknown.

Timed Competitions

Unlike the previous narratives revealing less harmful practices, collegiate and professional athletes representing every sport also engaged in competitions to see who could have sex with the most women within a certain period of time. A wrestler noted that his "ultra competitive" teammates competed to see "who could pick up the girl first," whenever "somebody threw out [a challenge]... to see if somebody could outdo them." An NHL player with recent playing experience similarly recalled timed competitions for women during his major league career. While picking up a female the fastest did not always come with specifics, a minor league football player recalled that it could at the professional level, "Yea, I mean you basically like...'I'll bet you I could fuck her first' and then you'll make a bet...we bet on everything." One collegiate hockey player recalled competitions to see "how many girls you could hook up with by ten o'clock," and larger parties provided the best setting for this since "you could meet your goal a lot quicker there." Other participants including a collegiate basketball player revealed, "There were time tests to see how many different people you could be with in a day...one day constituting 24 hours." Basically, this event was described as "just an ego thing" where guys would sit around, "brag about it," and "compare" their numbers that typically did not exceed "more than four...different people." A wrestler discussed his involvement in one such event that resulted in three sexual encounters while a minor league basketball player recalling two of these events noted "the record is like nine" since his collegiate teammates would actually schedule "appointments" with women to insure their success.

Various professional athletes and coaches representing different sports thought such competitions were more of "a college thing" because professional athletes were thought to be "a little older, a little wiser," and there was less interest and camaraderie on certain teams. However, other participants who compared the frequency of these competitions during their career including an NFL player recalled, "We had competitions like that in college, but not to the scale [as] in the pros [because] I mean it's pretty hard to sleep with multiple girls in one day in college." It is apparent that some collegiate athletes are extremely resourceful and conduct outrageous sexual competitions; however, professional athletes have even more time and resources to devote to such practices which flourished on certain teams even more so than at the college level. Such competitions at the minor and major league level involving "bets" at bars sometimes took place during a single evening. For instance, players would go to a club to find a woman to "shag" either in their car or at their residence if they lived nearby, and they simply returned to "get another one and shag" her according to a minor league hockey player. One NHL player revealed participating in such events with major league teammates, and this involved sex with as many as three females in an evening. When asked if he won any of the competitions, this participant declined to answer perhaps because of modesty, embarrassment, or regret over his past behavior. It is apparent that athletes view these practices as fun contests; however, such events can inadvertently promote forced sex whenever athletes focus on having sex at all cost and women are reduced to nothing more than sexual objects that are necessary for scoring points.

Some competitions involving sex with women had longer time frames. For example, a minor league baseball player discussed his collegiate team's annual event by saying, "We always had the one week where we [saw] who banged the most broads in a week, I mean...that was a fun week...some guys were up in the 20s...[laughs] [I was] probably about 10." Moreover, a minor league football player recalled a "gentlemen's bet" between two collegiate teammates "to see who could sleep with the most girls in one semester," while an NFL player observed a similar competition "topped out at like you know 30-35 [females]" during a particular semester in college. A wrestler elaborated on the frequencies of his team's competitions by saying, "Oh that went on a lot, a lot...I tried to pick up a girl every week that semester so 15 different girls yea...[I] was probably middle of the road I would think [compared to other teammates]." Numerous professionals including a minor league baseball player with recent playing experience noted his professional teammates also competed for "numbers" that involved "how many [women] per season." It is apparent that competitions abounded within certain athlete cultures because for many athletes, sexual conquests with women enabled them to show off their perceptions of masculinity and manliness to teammates off the playing field.

Competitions Targeting Specific Females or Physical Characteristics

Numerous participants also described an array of specialized competitions that targeted specific women or types of women. Collegiate and professional athletes representing every sport and era participated and as a wrestler explained, "I know they made basically a sport out of it." Indeed, such competitions were "very prevalent on pro teams" as far back as the early 1970s according to a minor league baseball player who observed teammates with too much free time competed for "the best looking" woman, "how many blondes, how many brunettes, so on so forth, and they'd have all kinds of games." A current minor league basketball player noted competitions at the collegiate and professional level targeted "the funniest," the freakiest," or "the sluttiest girl." Another minor leaguer from football recalled "between 8-10" professional teammates competed weekly in another specialized event by saying, "We had what was called 'Cougar Night,' and it was always the best-looking older lady." While numerous participants including a minor league basketball player noted more generalized events such as "the who can get one to go [have sex] competition," a wrestler recalled the dialogue that usually fueled a competition by saying, "There's always that issue of 'I was with her and you know so she won't go with you,' so that guy's got to prove that she will." In these instances, athletes will target a specific woman that a teammate had sex with – not because they found her appealing or wanted to date her, but rather because she presented them with a sexual challenge.

Collegiate and professional athletes representing every sport also discussed competitions where athletes would try to pick-up "the ugliest girl and the fattest girl" which was often referred to as "hogging" or "heifer night." A wrestler recalled such competitions involved "crazy things" during his collegiate career like seeing "who could bring the ugliest girl back to a party you know and winner take the pot – just about everything [laughing]." While betting and money fueled certain competitions, various participants recalled discussions of competitions without participating because as one collegiate hockey player noted, "I don't think none of us had the balls to go through with it." In contrast, another wrestler revealed such practices were mandatory on his college team because they involved "initiation and competition [for] any incoming freshman and the older guys on the team...just a one time thing, some of those guys took it to the extreme with you know 350, 400 pounders." A collegiate football player recalled his participation in one such event by saying, "I remember my roommate and I one night we were bored, and you know we went out with the intention of to see who can pick up the fattest chick and bring her back to the room and he won...pretty convincingly, but probably by 40 pounds." Other participants including minor leaguers from baseball and hockey elaborated on their awareness and/or participation in different variations of such competitions:

> Yea, we played the 2 a.m. game in the college world, that was the game where...before 2 a.m. your job was to take home the best-looking girl in the bar – absolutely, after 2 a.m...whoever didn't have somebody to take home...the object was to take home the fattest girl. The winner got their drinks paid for the next night, so that was the game...[and] that was an every night thing... because you know the fat one needs loving, I mean that's...what happened.

> Oh yeah...there was two guys in juniors that had that contest going on. They actually had to one way or another...get the girl on the scale. It was one of those guess games, so they'd say... ridiculous things to the girls they were with to get them on the scale. I mean, they're fat. They generally don't want to get on the scale anyway, but they'd say, "Come on, baby. Let's get on it together." Kind of thing to see what they weigh together and then you'd obviously subtract what he weighed from what he saw on the scale – round about ways to get a girl on a scale. I don't know how they did it, but the prize in that situation was a case of beer. First guy to a 1000 pounds with the least number of women [wins],

of course you could do ten 100 pound girls or you could do two 500 pound girls, but the less the better...so yeah, I've been around those. I never personally [entered]...them.

There is little question that the women in the previous competitions were highly dehumanized because they were used for sex because of their specific physical characteristics. Competitions targeting heavier and less attractive women were arguably crueler because many of these women already suffer from low self-esteem. Indeed, such females receive constant media messages telling them they do not fit society's stereotypical idea of physical attractiveness, and this can negatively impact their image and self confidence. Furthermore, a minor league basketball player observed some teammates were "aggressive and rude" in their approach to pick up certain women, and it is likely that athletes acted this way with women they had less respect for. Other athletes often ridiculed the women used in these competitions both covertly and openly while likening them to animals. Competitors convinced women to have sex – not because they were likable or intelligent – but "more or less for his buddies to laugh about it" according to a collegiate hockey player. This means that story-telling and entertainment fueled many athletes' sexual encounters that occurred at a woman's expense simply because teammates wanted to see this happen.

Various participants including an NFL player discussed the contests in which his professional teammates would compete for a specific female, "Oh yeah, there would be situations where guys would go and...you know try and crack on the same girl and see you know which guy she decides to leave with...they just do it for the competition, you know, 'I can do better than you with this.'" Similarly, a wrestler revealed an array of competitions that included teammates placing "bets on different girls – maybe a mat maid or you know a cheerleader or pom pom girl or whatever, there were tons of them." Other participants including an NBA player observed that "ego and pride" prompted many professionals athletes' unspoken competitions because "you hear about one guy that's obviously a ladies man, you got another guy that thinks he's a ladies man...I mean you're dealing with competitors, these are guys that gamble, they compete at a high level, so it's good friendly competition." In reality, competitions that athletes perceive as "good" and "friendly" are anything but this because women are used for selfish purposes. This also raises questions about the true character of certain athletes and teammates who encouraged these types of competitions. Such notions were further highlighted when various athletes including another NBA player revealed that the competitions he saw during his collegiate and professional career targeting "the best-looking girl" essentially had the athletes competing for a woman – regardless of whether she was with her boyfriend or husband. These types of behaviors epitomize ego and risk-taking and are potentially a disaster waiting to happen.

Competitions Involving Specific Sexual Behaviors

Other contests centered upon specific types of sexual behavior with females. For example, a wrestler recalled that his teammates "would strictly go out for anal sex" since this was the only sexual behavior that would satisfy the contest criteria. Interestingly, a participant discussed the mentality that encouraged these and other competitions during his career as a collegiate hockey player and coach. "Women, suddenly they're objects, they're simply conquests. They joke around about, you know, that everybody thinks that girl's ugly and whatever – you know the idea is: 'Who's going to get her tonight?' Somebody asks, 'Who's going to be the first to bang her?' – and then [there's] the two-on-ones, three-on-ones, the four-on-ones." This participant clearly observed that females were frequently depreciated while athletes continuously pursued them as sexual partners for individual competitions. At the same time, group sexual encounters were also prevalent among his collegiate players in the new millennium although these events were not related to competitions to his knowledge. In contrast, other participants including an NFL player revealed, "We might have a competition to see who [could] get a group sex going on, you know nobody taking a one-night stand home unless we all going home, you know it was one of those type of deals, we had them competitions and games like that would be going on no doubt." Such competitions were understandable given the fact that this participant noted group sex involving "two guys and a girl was always going on," and it was more prevalent in his NFL career compared to his collegiate career. In addition, this participant noted that larger group sexual experiences involving more than three people occurred in season at a rate of approximately one encounter per month.

This was not the only reference to competitions involving group sex because a minor league football player revealed that "threesomes, you know with two girls and one guy" were among the competitions his teammates participated in. These competitions differed from the previous NFL player's disclosure because the minor leaguers competed to have sex with two women rather than a group of athletes engaging with one woman. Furthermore, this participant revealed that competitions to have sex with two women occurred "sometimes" because "some people don't like that, some people didn't really care for it, so it all depends on the person." Still, it is apparent that certain minor and major league athletes compete to engage in group sex in the same way they do for other sexual practices. In this study, the practice of engaging in group sex apart from competitions flourished because approximately 95% of participants representing every sport were aware of its occurrence during their collegiate and/or professional careers. During my elite-level career, I also knew athletes that engaged in group sex with various women, and one group even asked me to participate although I declined their invitation. In the end, group attitudes and practices dictate the kinds of sexual behaviors that are acceptable from those that are not, so athletes hold this power of authority exclusively within their select groups.

Male-Female Contests Promoting Sex

Not all contests involved only athletes because some included women along with alcohol and had the purpose of promoting sexual activity. For example, a collegiate hockey player described one such event by saying, "[We were] playing cards and drinking and it just happened, you know we're playing strip poker and a guy starts kissing and next thing you know, there was sex going on." While playing strip poker and drinking led to one of this participant's group sexual encounters, another collegiate hockey player and minor league hockey player revealed other co-ed contests that promoted drinking and sex in this way:

> I remember once we were spinning a bottle. We started to kiss and it started leading to a kissing contest. It led to multi-person sex with a girl, but again, it never seemed awkward or too severe because it was always consensual and everyone was having a good time. I don't think it so much tied into the [sport of] hockey...some people are into that certain type of thing...just know the girl, talk about it before, and let's give it a try. We would spin the bottle and then start making out and then all of a sudden we're having sex and that's the point where we didn't turn back...I think that it would have happened both nights even if we weren't drinking, so I don't think that was a big influence on it, but it helps...

> Well drinking games, the specific situation was we had this...game that we set up on an old tray, a lazy Susan. We put a coat hanger and nailed it in and put a couple of words on there like basically, kiss the girl to the left of you. You know, strip to your boxers for guys. Strip to your underwear for girls, your bra and panties, whatever. It was crazy. I didn't know about any of this personally. It was on our hockey team. One of the houses had this thing called The Spin Game. At the time, I was captain of the team. The coach came in and took me out for a one-on-one meeting and said, "What is it with this Spin Game?" I said, "I don't know what it is." He said, "Oh come on you're a senior, you have to know about The Spin Game." I have no clue what's going on here. He said that the freshmen and the sophomores in this team are getting out of hand with this Spin Game and...the women's [XXX] team coach came into my office and said, "Coach, your hockey guys have this game called The Spin Game where my girls are getting naked and laid because of it." "Drunk, naked

and laid"…Coach was like, "Why didn't I have this game when I was in college?" So he comes to me and tells me to find out more about it. So obviously I'm intrigued. So I go to the house where it's alleged, allegedly had The Spin Game. So I walk in and I see a long table with this lazy-Susan Spin Game that was made by one of the boys at the [hockey] house. And when I walked in there were five naked girls and three naked guys. And one guy was spinning it with a hard on as I walked in. So apparently it was [true]…so I called coach and said, "Yeah it exists, I saw it and it's pretty cool." So those games, I mean, you're talking a drinking game that has a sexual connotation. They bring sex in…in college everything goes around on the weekend and sex and booze and having fun and partying and that's what it is. These drinking games, you're chugging beer and if you lose the game you either have to drink some more or whip something out. That's the way it was. I mean, we played…I've been a part of beer pong games. I see a girl trying to distract you from sinking a ping-pong ball in a beer cup, she whips her chunk [vagina] out on the table. She's got her beaver [vagina] right in your face, and that's completely real, that's real life. It happens all the time. And if you lose, if you get swept, you have to drop your pants and run around the party. I've seen girls pass out and guys have to give them a frappe. We came up with that. A frappe is when you get a semi hard-on and you bang your dick against the first girl who passes out. You bang it against her forehead three or four times. I mean, that's happened. I've seen crazy, crazy shit at all these parties. And it's real. It happens. It's crazy. These girls are partying it up and they're coming back…

Each of the above participants discussed different games and contests that included males and females along with alcohol consumption that resulted in nudity and/or a variety of sexual encounters or acts which sometimes targeted passed-out women (i.e., frappe). In the end, the coach in the previous narrative was responsible for banning "The Spin Game" as a form of entertainment among players he coached in the new millennium.

Competing for Personal Bests

Not all competitions occurred between teammates because some involved athletes competing against themselves in an effort to accomplish a sexual preference or personal best with women. For example, a minor league basketball player recalled, "There's a lot of guys would say, 'Like…let's see if I can get at least two [women] for the day' or 'You know it's been a long road trip, I need to make up' you know stuff like that…was a discussion, not necessarily a competition." Such perceived accomplishments brought pride to numerous athletes including a minor league baseball player who revealed his own best by saying, "I personally had a situation where I was with three different girls in one day, but not together...[so] I kind of rested my college hat on that one." Other participants, including a collegiate hockey player, found having sex in unusual places such as "public places, on top of buildings, over of the side of a parking garage" brought prestige although he admitted it was "one of the dumber things" he would not repeat because it was exhilarating as well as dangerous to the point that he awoke the next morning thinking, "Oh my God, I can't believe I'm alive." He further elaborated on other sexual goals occurring within his team that were not related to formal competitions:

> ...after we'd won a championship we were out for a month straight and didn't stop, so...you'd hook up, not necessarily have intercourse, with 30 girls in a month. Not saying a girl every night, maybe two one night, three one Saturday at an all-day party, all-day event, something like a tailgate, for instance. You'd like hook up with a girl at the stadium, have a different girl right that afternoon...and then take your girlfriend home that night, so I mean...30 a month out of season, you could do it. I know guys that have, I have so...definitely attainable...anything is attainable – one of our mottos.

Numerous athletes noted that partying and getting in trouble out-of-sport increased exponentially in the off season because athletes had fewer team-related obligations and much more time and energy to do as they pleased. And like the previous participant revealed, athletes' time and energy could also include focusing on achieving more sexual conquests with women.

Such practices were not limited to the collegiate level as a minor league hockey player told how a teammate during his professional career would "hang panties from the ceiling [for] every different one he got" since this was his way of showing off the number of women he slept with. Moreover, an NBA player with recent pro experience proudly highlighted his personal best by saying, "I've had eight different women come through you know back-to-back-to-back... no it wasn't [a game day], but there's nothing wrong with it on a game day either, some guys can handle it some guys can't." This participant revealed he was able to accomplish his feat because picking up women was constant during his major league career and more prevalent compared to his collegiate or minor league career even though this was not part of any formalized competition. Sexual conquest played an important role in many athletes' self-esteem and perceived masculinity because as a MLB player observed, "I wouldn't go so far as to say it was a competition, [but] in some cases certainly there was braggadocio." In addition, a minor league baseball player elaborated on other types of practices he observed that served this very purpose:

> Yea, there was times in college when we had one guy in particular who…it was his thing to take home the biggest girl or the ugliest girl in the bar, and another guy was always trying to take home…the hottest chick in the bar, there wasn't necessarily a competition between this guy and that guy, but that's what this guy's going to do and you knew it, he'd tell you like, "We're going to walk in here and I'm leaving with the hottest chick in here I don't care who she's with" and the other guy says, "I'm taking home the biggest, fattest thing I can find" but it wasn't competition…it was kind of statement by [them]…

This participant's collegiate teammates were not in competition to pick-up a particular female; however, they were in fact engaged in a personal competition that involved attention-seeking or else they would have kept their intentions to themselves. Furthermore, these athletes' sexual agendas highlighted a kind of bravado that differentiated them from others. Minor and MLB players with recent playing experience similarly noted their professional teammates periodically "going out and getting a fat girl" which they considered to be a "slump buster." In addition, an NHL player observed certain major league teammates made it their personal quest to "just pick up the fat one at the end of the night because that's what they did" even though this did not involve any kind of formal competition.

Participants at the collegiate and professional levels previously revealed that personal challenges intensified whenever bets were attached to a proposed sexual quest. For instance, a wrestler recalled, "I doubled a shot on this girl, I bet the guy I could pick her up, so I picked her up." This participant felt confident that the odds of winning his bet were in his favor because he knew "they love wrestlers in [XXX]." While collegiate athletes' bets often included drinks or winning "the pot" everyone contributed to because money was limited at this level, this was not the case at the professional level as an NBA player revealed:

> …you know some guy would…get you know a bug up himself and say like, "Alright I'm going to get me [some], I'm going to get somebody tonight" and you'd be to the point then like, "You know man, $100 says you ain't going to, you ain't doing nothing"…and that's in the pros obviously we weren't gambling like that in college [laughing] we wouldn't have any money, but you know…I got involved in the competitions where I bet that the guy wouldn't close the deal and lost some money, yea, I lost $100 [in pros]…you ain't going to lose it in college, no man.

Competitions between Different Sports or Teams

Not all competitions for women involved teammates or striving to achieve a personal best with women because sometimes athletes' competitive nature manifested through both spoken and unspoken rivalries against other collegiate teams on campus. For example, an NFL player and a wrestler discussed their experiences in this way:

> ...for me, it was between sports, not necessarily teammates, it was football against basketball – who had the best-looking [woman], the finest, and then also who had the most money...it was kind of both [spoken and unspoken] [laughing] both, who had the best-looking girls from sport to sport and typically of those girls, who did things the best, and then who treated the player the best, and...gives cooking, all that kind of stuff, I don't think it was a competition like, "Well I have to go find the best" but just in general, who attracted the best and so when you did attract that one that was better...then you made it a point to point it out to the basketball players or present that to them, so that they could see it firsthand.

> ...I guess there's always jokes about that...in [XXX University] I know that there was a couple of guys that had a competition going...that [was] on like a month basis or something like that – how many different girls – and they were right [there] when that Adult Friend Finder stuff came out, I mean...it was almost disgusting and wrong, they were getting girls that I mean were like 18-years old that were driving like from two hours away to come and hang out in [the city], and they would, I wouldn't say they were getting them drunk and having [sex] with them [all], but I mean these girls definitely were up to the challenge, most of them I guess...[but] that was pretty crazy for a month there...it was between the wrestling team and the swimming and diving team, but I don't really know much about it, I wasn't involved in it... they probably had some sort of pointing system...but yea [sex] pretty much that was the goal...[a teammate/roommate] actually was in that competition and won...

The second participant was not aware of any competitions among the collegiate wrestlers he coached at a Bible Belt university; however, his wrestling teammates along with the swimming and diving teams attracted females for their competition by going to parties and bars and using Internet resources such as Instant Messenger and Facebook in the new millennium. Swimmers and divers' involvement in these competitions was an unexpected finding because like athletes from men's gymnastics, tennis, track and field, and lacrosse who were found engaging in different types of sexually deviant and/ or aggressive behaviors, they were not interviewed for this study. Although participation in more aggressive sports has been linked to different types of out-of-sport aggression targeting both men and women, it is evident that athletes representing virtually every sport engage in different types of sexual deviancy and/or aggression.[10]

Previous narratives provided ample evidence that competitions between athletes from different sports on campus occurred when they wanted to showcase their perceived superiority. However, sometimes competitions for women included athletes from different universities who competed in the same sport and engaged in actual physical competition as a wrestler revealed:

> ...I saw [when] we wrestled against [XXX] State and then of course they would have like an after [tournament] party after because that team would stay in town, and you know wrestlers are pretty friendly off the mat, and these two guys wrestled on a pool table and whoever won, you know got to spend the night with this one girl, and she was like right there, you know ready for the results, you know just sitting there waiting for the winner...I mean you know, they were pretty much hitting on her pretty hard and you know and they said, "Well let's have a competition to see who gets her you know," and they're like, "Well, what do you want to do?" "Well, we'll wrestle for her you know," so they cleared the balls off the table and what they were trying to do is throw one another off the table you know and then whoever threw the other one off, you know got to go with the girl, and she was like all for it, you know she knew what was going to happen, and she just stood there and was like cheering and you know all excited about you know getting to get one of these wrestlers so...there was two, one from our team and one from the other team, both [XXX] pounders...and they were both you know wrestling for this girl...our guy did [win] yea, he couldn't win in the dual, but he did win that...

It is interesting to note that this woman had no problem allowing herself to be objectified as the trophy, and she had no real preference for which of the two wrestlers she would be with because she allowed a wrestling match to determine her sexual partner for the evening. It is likely this woman felt very desirable since two athletes were literally fighting for her in an organized spectacle. Because wrestling is all about physical confrontation, this was probably not big a deal to these athletes who were simply trying to resolve their dilemma and get to the female the easiest way they knew how.

Competitions Involving Rules and Tallying Systems

Various participants made references to competitions that made use of rules and even point systems although these events were not elaborated upon in any detail. And like other athletes, a collegiate baseball player believed these competitions were fueled by athletes' desire to see "who can tell the best story," "who can kind a have the most notches...on their bedpost, so I think there's a little bit of competitiveness to that too – I mean, I know there is." While this participant observed athletes competitiveness with females often manifested through bragging and story-telling that provided entertainment as well as prestige, another collegiate baseball player revealed his awareness of the previous competitive practices by saying, "I know two guys that literally made notches in the bedpost when they slept with a girl, but it had to be in that bed because those were the rules." For these collegiate athletes, the practice of making visible notches into their bedposts created a permanent "score board" for tracking the number of females each had sex with, and these practices probably brought higher recognition to these competitors because their stories obviously lived on long after their playing days were over. In addition, a minor league baseball player discussed a more systematic approach to recording sexual conquests that occurred during competitions in his collegiate career:

> In college, most of the guys did [tally their sexual conquests]...[but] on a college level [it was] a little bit different, you know...I can remember that my senior year we had seven of us living in a house and five of us were baseball players, and there was a "Tang Chart" in our house. I mean that was just something that guys kept the score of, and there was rules [laughs]...rules were you know, you couldn't put the same girl up there twice. So if you were with someone more than one time, well, that didn't count you know. Only new girls could go up there...[sighs] let's see you know, myself it was probably 10 [women]...we had one guy that was pretty well known on campus for his size and so I think he ended up with like 25, and everyone was kind of scattered between 5-15...[triple digits were] not in that group...but again, some of these guys had, you know had girlfriends for part of the time or they dated someone for part of the time and so no one in that group was you know Wilt Chamberlain type [or] Casanova. And again, we were a small school so you know, word kind of got out there that – I don't know that it got out that there was a chart up for say at our house, but...with 4 or 5,000 students, you know it doesn't take long for the female population to figure out that, you know [laughs]...these guys are sluts.

The previous participant revealed that he and his teammates along with their non-athlete roommates made a "Tang Chart," which was short for "poo tang"

223

or female genitalia, to record their sexual competition with women. Moreover, the rules that governed placing a female on the chart were certain to increase the contestants' promiscuity because sex with the same woman did not count. It is apparent that this activity provided both the competitors and observers with entertainment, competition, and bragging rights while women were valued only for their ability to provide sexual release and an increased score. While the previous events occurred in the mid 1980s, a wrestling coach discussed similar practices among the collegiate wrestlers he coached in the mid to late 2000s by saying, "Yea, yea, yea our guys now particularly have a bracketed format, kind of like 'The Sweet 16' that type of tournament setting, [so] they'll do that."

Other participants revealed that competitions often occurred throughout the season but only on road trips because both collegiate and professional athletes often had steady partners and serious relationships. Consequently, athletes would be less likely to get caught cheating while they were competing out-of-town as opposed to in the vicinity in which they lived. Moreover, a wrestler recalled the frequency of these events during his career by saying, "Oh yeah, I mean in college...competitions on away trips for the year, things like that so yea, I've experienced that, I never won [laughs] but...I remember that was a big thing." A minor league basketball player and another wrestler elaborated on their tabulating systems in this way:

> ...on the road, it was always a thing to get sexual conquests, how many women could you sleep with on the road, what's your record? If we went on 10 road trips were you three for ten? Or were you nine for ten? Seven for ten? So guys kept tabs on stuff like that you know and were straight up about it, ain't no sense in lying you know if it didn't happen, it didn't happen, but you know guys coming back from the bar wanted to know who scored.

> ...like I said we used to have contests to see who could get the most girls on [road] trips, you know where if you got laid you get a point, a blow job was half a point, a hand job was a quarter point, if you screwed the same girl on the same trip, the second time you would only get a quarter of a point the second time, and we would actually keep track...

The first participant revealed road trip competitions were cumulative and recorded because both collegiate and professional players during his career wanted to know who scored with women and who did not. In each of the previous cases, such practices were certain to create pressure whenever athletes did not score because they had to face their peers and any accompanying ridicule. These practices are also dangerous because they can promote sexual pressure, coercion, or even force to achieve certain sexual goals since athletes were rewarded with the pleasure that accompanied sexual activities as well as points for their competition. Interestingly, the second participant discussed one such incident among his teammates that showed this theory was more than simply a possibility; for example:

> ...[after] everybody did her, and then mind you this is one of the trips so we're keeping track too [of points] you know, so another one of the guys came late, we were all done just sitting around bull shitting around, you know talking, and everybody's naked and you know just sitting in the room you know talking to the girl and talking to each other, and he comes in and wants to do her too because he wanted to get a point, she didn't want [to], so he starts wrestling around with her and finally and we says, "Hey, you know if you don't want to do this you know you don't have to do it" and she says, "No I don't want to do it" and then he stopped and left so...five guys did her that night and almost six [laughs].

The previous participant discussed the ending of a larger group sexual encounter involving five wrestlers and a female that resulted in every wrestler earning a point for their particular competition. In this study, participation in group sex was not uncommon because approximately one third of the participants experienced this and nearly 70% of this group also engaged in a larger group sexual encounter involving more than three people. Following the previous encounter, a sixth wrestler attempted to have sex with the woman because he also wanted to earn "a point" for their competition, and this resulted in a wrestling match that ended only when other wrestlers told the woman she was not obligated to have sex with him. While these wrestlers insisted their group encounter was consensual, the next day they were fearful the woman was going to press gang rape charges following a discussion concerning her alcohol consumption and the aggressive manner in which the event had ended. This event provided strong evidence that competitions can encourage sexual pressure and/or force because excessive competitive drive compels certain athletes to want "a point" at all costs. In addition, it is easy to understand how a seemingly consensual group sexual encounter can result in everyone being charged with a sex crime because it only takes an intoxicated woman and/or one male disregarding a female's sexual limits during group sex to change the event into a group sexual assault or rape.[11]

SEXUAL CONQUEST AS A WAY OF LIFE

Previous narratives revealed an array of competitions that some athletes proudly discussed which occurred throughout their collegiate and/or professional career. While these competitions often included time limitations that lasted for an evening, 24 hours, a week, semester, or a season, it appeared that some athletes engage in their own personal competitions for sexual conquests with women that had no end. These notions were highlighted whenever certain high profile athletes' sexual conquests were revealed regardless of whether this was believable to the casual observer or not. For example, Jose Torres, a friend and sparring partner of former world boxing champion, Mike Tyson, recalled one occasion where Tyson had sexual intercourse with 24 women in a single night.[12] Other athletes including former MLB star Jose Canseco estimated his sexual exploits involved "a couple hundred" women during his career while former NFL playboy, Joe Namath, confessed to having "300 sexual conquests – before his graduation" from college.[13] A *Sports Illustrated* article, "Dangerous Games," noted an NBA player, who was under 30 years old and did not have all-star status, estimated that he had sex with 2,500 different women at the time and was still counting.[14] Although NBA superstar Earvin "Magic" Johnson's chose not to reveal the number of women he had sex with in his book, *My Life*, out of respect for his wife, an alleged estimate of 2,550 women was linked to Johnson.[15] Unquestionably, the most famous athlete to report an exorbitant number of sexual conquests was NBA legend, Wilt Chamberlain.[16] In his autobiography, *A View From Above*, Chamberlain reported that since the age of 15 he had sex with 20,000 different women which averaged out to be 1.37 women a day for 40 years.[17] Even if his estimate is off by a few thousand, Chamberlain was easily one of the more visible elite-level athletes at the height of the American sexual revolution.[18]

In this study, athletes' intensity and competitive drive for women and sexual conquests became strikingly apparent when participants were directly asked if they or their teammates were in triple digits (i.e., meaning over 100) with regard to the number of women they had sex with. Clues to such questions appeared in part when certain athletes previously revealed the number of different females that certain time-limited competitions involved. Once again, not everyone was asked this question because it emerged later on during the study. Nevertheless, nearly one third of participants admitted they knew one or more athletes, which could include themselves, that had sex with over 100 females during their collegiate and/or professional careers. In addition, approximately 7% revealed their own sexual conquests numbered in the triple digits – and in one case higher. Examining sexual conquest estimates was not intended to provoke athletes' bravado, but rather to provide a more complete picture of how deeply ingrained sexual promiscuity can become within certain athletes and their sports cultures. And as one wrestler revealed, "Most people know your numbers, I mean…hopefully you can remember every girl that you had sex with…if not – then you might need to chill out a bit I guess or at least go get tested." This assumption is particularly true for males because there's no stigma attached to their sexual activity – only admiration for the number of women athletes slept with.

Such praise can raise speculation about whether athletes inflate their numbers; however, my observations and participation in the social life that many elite-level athletes experience gives me no reason to believe these athletes are lying about their disclosures. Although I was not close to being as sexually active as certain teammates, I still had sex with about 35 different women during my collegiate and professional playing and coaching career despite my involvement in a handful of long-term relationships lasting at least a year. Such numbers are indeed modest compared to the sexual conquests I observed among certain athletes, teammates, and/or coaches which included one individual who showed me some of the 360 pictures collected from the different women he had sex with. I had no reason to doubt his word on this because most of the women in the photographs were naked. Based on findings from this study, numerous collegiate and/or professional athletes, who competed from the 1960s through 2010, revealed startling numbers of their own sexual conquests with women as well as those of their teammates.

TALLYING SEXUAL CONQUESTS AMONG COLLEGIATE ATHLETES

Collegiate athletes were among the first athletes to discuss the practice of tabulating their sexual conquests. For example, two wrestlers who competed before the emergence of AIDS revealed that because their teams had a strong female following along with a "wham bam thank you ma'am" attitude toward sex, this means "everybody was doing everybody back in the early 70's" so it was not unusual for some athletes to have sex with "50 or 60...different women" in a year. Similarly, a collegiate baseball player observed a teammate during his collegiate career in the 1990s was with "something like 65 different girls that year." While sex with 50-65 women during a college year would easily put someone into triple digits during their career, a collegiate football player who competed in the mid 2000s noted certain players "came into college already in double digits," and he compared a younger teammate's sexual behavior to "a revolving door." It is likely that athletes who are very promiscuous under parental supervision in high school will continue or even increase their practices during collegiate athletic careers unless they experience a major shift in their thinking because sexual freedom and experimentation along with female availability abound in college.

Certain athlete cultures appeared to encourage rampant promiscuity because higher numbers of sexual conquests seemed to be normal. For example, a wrestler supported these notions by saying, "Yea I was over 100, and I'm sure there was probably about four or five other guys that got up that high" while another recalled, "Oh yea, usually within a team maybe half a dozen to a dozen" were in triple digits. Similarly, various minor leaguers from hockey, baseball, football, and basketball noted "a lot of guys" in both their collegiate and professional careers had lists of sexual conquests that were "scary" because they were so extensive. One current minor league basketball player who estimated he had sex with "probably like around 150" women also noted "about 50%" of his collegiate teammates were in triple digits as well. Often, collegiate athletes recalled their numbers through "a black book," memory, or even "pictures" of all their "female conquests." At the collegiate level, several participants representing different sports revealed sexual conquests that could involve "157 or something crazy like that," "165 last time I knew," and "close to 300" different women. Moreover, a minor league baseball player believed "the whole point of the college world was to fire your numbers up and to get them up there," so it was not surprising when he revealed, "We had guys probably 300-400 in the college world, I mean that's a lot for college [laughs]…I probably have about a 100, yea." Milestones for reaching a certain number of sexual conquests could be a celebrated occasion in some athlete cultures as a minor league hockey player recalled:

> [Picking up women happened] a lot. I think it's a game. It's a game amongst a game basically. I played with a guy in college who kept track of his numbers. When he hit a 100, he sent an e-mail out. People sent him cards, you know. People were sending him birthday cards that said, "Happy 100th Birthday" on it with birthday scratched and put "Happy 100th whatever" [laughs] stuff like that. So, it literally becomes a game, a numbers game for a lot of guys. Who can get the most, sort of a physical prowess to all their buddies basically. It's just another type of circumstance where, "I'm the silver back (dominant male gorilla) of this group, and I'm the man."

As this participant and others have revealed, sexual conquest is considered to be a competitive game where athletes could demonstrate their "physical prowess" and masculinity which often determined social status within a group. The fact that people sent cards celebrating this athlete's 100th sexual conquest showed the manner in which competitive sexual behaviors were rewarded. Interestingly, this athlete used the metaphor of a "silver back" gorilla to describe an athlete's dominance over women and his teammates through sexual behaviors that might be considered animalistic since they are performed without any thought of establishing an emotional bond with the woman. In contrast, women are depreciated by both genders when they have sex with a higher number of partners because even though our society has become more sexually permissive, the double standard still exists.[19] This was without a doubt a significant reason that a collegiate hockey player believed that different women he was with minimized their number of sexual partners; however, some females can be as competitive as males when it pertains to sexual behaviors. For instance, a minor league basketball player observed that some woman viewed sex with an athlete as "a notch on their belt as well" while a wrestler elaborated on college women he knew who tabulated their sexual conquests in this way:

> ...I think some of the girls were worse about that [keeping tallies] than some of us guys...they always had a game where it was if a girl hooked up with one guy, how you could really say she hooked up with these other guys. It was kind of a weird game they had going on. The girls just wanted to see how they were all connected together in some way.

Previous information relating to female availability and promiscuity revealed that some female team followers had sex with a substantial number of athletes within a particular team; however, these estimates do not come close to the number of sexual conquests that many male athletes in this study revealed. This included athletes who did not report triple-digit sexual conquests on their teams but still noted players, including themselves, having sex with numerous women. One collegiate hockey player said, "I don't think there was anybody on the team who hadn't slept with at least 10 women through college" while he and other athletes noted sex with anywhere from "40 or 50 girls" to "over 70" different females was common. This participant further clarified his thoughts by revealing that a teammate "cleared 100 his senior year...and that's sex... we're not talking oral sex, hooking up, having a hand job, we're talking you know sexual intercourse – now if you try to quantify hook-ups, whether oral or hand job, I have no idea." Such numbers among collegiate athletes are indeed alarming and are put into better perspective when compared to a national study that revealed the median number of sexual partners for adult men in the United States since the age of 18 is six while the corresponding number for women is two.[20] Another more recent national study reported the average number of female sexual partners for U.S. men 30-44 over their lifetime is six to eight while the corresponding number for women the same age is about four.[21] A 2006 survey of over 94,000 college students from 117 campuses revealed that within the last school year, approximately 70% of college men and women were sexually active with at least one partner.[22] While most students (43% of men and 49% of women) had one sexual partner, 11% of men and 6% of women had four or more partners.[23] Based on the findings in this study, it is apparent that numerous collegiate athletes have sex with many more female partners compared to the average number of partners most non-athlete males experience. And, these numbers can be even higher among certain professional athletes who have more time and resources to devote to their sexual pursuits.

TALLYING SEXUAL CONQUESTS AMONG PROFESSIONAL ATHLETES

Like the collegiate athletes, professional athletes also had competitive tendencies with females that resulted in certain players tallying sexual conquests during their minor and/or major league careers. This was not universal because some professionals noted players did not reveal their numbers of sexual conquests perhaps because they were beyond this sort of ego exercise or wanted to avoid being judged while those with higher sexual conquests perhaps felt no need to elaborate. However, various minor leaguers from hockey, baseball, football, and basketball noted numerous players, which could include themselves, engaging in sexual conquests that numbered in the triple digits during both their collegiate and professional careers. One minor league hockey player observed "a lot of the same tactics were going on with the single guys" because that "doesn't really change" just by reaching the professional level. While overall competitive sexual behavior could be less frequent on teams which carried more married athletes as this participant discovered, this was not the case on certain teams where infidelity and juggling thrived. Furthermore, fewer players competing for sexual conquests because of their marital status could mean greater female availability for single athletes. This was perhaps one reason the previous participant estimated that he had sex with "about 120" different women during his collegiate and professional hockey career while another minor leaguer revealed, "I counted about 300 different women...you know not 3000 like Magic [Johnson] or anything, but holy shit...I'll never tell her [a significant partner] that."

Other minor leaguers felt triple digits were "easy" to achieve when players juggled one or more females in every city they played in, were "always on the prowl" for women wherever they went, competed in the same city for "three or four years," and went out to bars "as much as three, four times a week easy." Furthermore, finding sex at the professional level was "very easy" because women were older, more mature, and "know what you're there for and they know what they're there for." Consequently, some females made themselves "a little bit more available," which enabled one minor league basketball player to have sex with approximately 200 different women during his career in the 2000s. A current minor league football player recalled "at least 50%" of his professional teammates noted they were in triple digits. Indeed, certain minor leaguers are no strangers to logging high numbers of sexual conquests because as various athletes revealed, their sport is often the only show in the towns they play in which gives them greater prestige and access to women.

Certain participants were asked to compare the number of sexual conquests that occurred during their minor and major league careers. This included a MLB player who said, "Triple digits...yes that was more common in the major leagues, well shoot...I'm sitting here thinking of some guys that I know that did that, and some of the guys I know that came to mind were in the minor leagues." Another MLB player making similar comparisons explained, "Major leagues just because there's more travel...it's a lot easier, and you're making more money and that makes it easier." An NHL player also found this to be true during his career as he revealed, "Yea, one year in particular for sure, my first year pro there was a guy that kept track of every name...I don't think he was at 100, but I think he was close." Other major leaguers including a different MLB player with recent playing experience supported such notions by revealing his own numbers, "You know something I don't even know anymore, I'm being truthful too, if I had to make a guess I would say...probably 120" different women. An NFL player similarly recalled, "Oh yea lots of guys, lots of guys [in triple digits], 100 is like just a beginner level seriously, I'm serious, lots of guys have slept with more than 100 girls... but honestly I probably slept with like 150, 160 myself I mean and I was like an average guy." This participant further estimated that certain superstars perhaps had sex with anywhere from 250-500 females during their career.

In addition, an NBA player recalled the prevalence of higher numbers within his teams by saying, "I knew there were some Romeos on each team that I played on and if I had to bet...I'd say at least 20 could have been close to triple digits." Another NBA player believed that although "length of time in the league" impacted players' numbers, he also revealed that "you can get over 100 girls in two years." Indeed, sexual conquest thrived within many athlete cultures because according to an NFL player, those who were having sex with numerous females received "kind of the gold star that you'd put on their head" which essentially rewarded them for these behaviors. Such reinforcement can result in some athletes taking their sexual behaviors to extremes as we have seen. This was further highlighted when another NBA player with recent professional experience was asked if he had sex with over 100 females and revealed, "Way over, I'm about 1,500 strong [laughs] yea." Although previous collegiate and minor league players noted certain athletes, including themselves, experiencing higher numbers ranging anywhere from 100-500 sexual encounters, this participant's 1,500 sexual conquests perhaps revealed one of the striking differences regarding athletes' heightened competitive nature that also separated the various levels of competition. Additionally, it showed females' greater willingness to sexually engage with major league athletes for any number of reasons including their higher salaries, social status, and/or prestige.

WHY DO THEY DO IT?

By now, it is all too apparent that numerous elite-level athletes representing every sport engage in a variety of competitions involving sex with women and have for over 40 years. This raises the question of why certain athletes, including many of whom already enjoy a healthy social and sexual life with women, choose to participate in outrageous competitions that encourage rampant promiscuity and tallying sexual conquests. In order to understand these behaviors, it is necessary to look at certain reoccurring themes among participants which highlight athletes' competitive nature as a significant factor fueling their contests. For example, numerous participants including a collegiate hockey player revealed, "I think you're so used to challenges, you're really used to being challenged in hockey and that carries over, you like a good challenge, like guys going to bars...to try and bring a girl home – and it's fun and somewhat of a conquest." An NBA player observed competing for women was "more of a one-upsman type of thing" where players tried to outdo one another while a wrestler further elaborated on athletes' competitive nature in this way:

> There's something at high level athletics that raises the intensity level of everything, someone that makes it to a high level sport is [a] pretty fucking intense person, and you think that would generalize across all behaviors and perhaps it does...but you wrestle hard and you can be the best [so] you're gonna wrestle hard, you're gonna fucking drink, [so] you're gonna drink hard, you're gonna fuck, [so] you're gonna fuck hard, you're gonna study – well that didn't happen much – but you're gonna do things hard...

Most athletes are very proud individuals with big egos who want to be the best at virtually everything they do. No athlete wants to be seen as weak or second rate because failing with women can open the door to peer ridicule which can be both demeaning and merciless at times. Athletes who are successful with women often enjoy higher status among their peers so their efforts pay high returns. Therefore, such notions highlight the fact that peer pressure also plays a big part in these behaviors because teammates provide the rewards and the extra competitors for contests with women. One minor league baseball player explained how peers encouraged promiscuity by saying, "When I look back on it, it was almost like...that's where your acceptance came from" because teammates "would look up to you...if you was getting women." This was further evident when this participant observed players "patting" a teammate "on the back" and saying, "Hey man, he's awesome" which served to reward and encourage promiscuity even more. As a result, this participant found that athletes, including himself, often treated women "almost like a sport" rather than human beings with feelings because they derived so much of their acceptance and validation from teammates by having sex with numerous females.

"Bragging rights," story-telling, and entertainment were also part of this peer pressure that combined to promote competitions for women. One wrestler speaking for others revealed that he and his teammates enjoyed a lot of "humor" and "entertainment" when teammates would "make asses" out of themselves by competing to see who could pick up "the ugliest girl and the fattest girl," because they would "sit around and talk about it." Such events involved the presence of alcohol "100%" of the time according to a collegiate hockey player because "I think alcohol gives you the balls to do stuff you wouldn't normally do – like I said the fat girl thing…a lot of things you talk about and you wouldn't do them unless you were pretty well banged up [drunk]." Such notions are supported in the literature as various researchers have shown that alcohol consumption is linked with the decision to have sexual intercourse in addition to engaging in risky sexual practices.[24]

Other participants attributed competitive practices with women to youth, immaturity, boredom, another way to prove dominance and masculinity, having sex "on your mind all the time," "because you can," and athletes' heightened sexual drive from sports participation that caused "hormones" to go "crazy." Numerous participants including a wrestler observed that teammates often sought out females who were "willing to literally be your sex toy" because higher level sports demanded a lot of time and energy that some athletes were not willing to invest in a deeper relationship with one woman. Athletes from all sports noted these kinds of sexually appealing arrangements were common, easy to find, and satisfied their sexual appetites without including any type of commitment. However, in time it appears that certain athletes become "bored" with their sexual pursuits, and some attempt to enhance the thrill and intensity by adding a competitive twist to their sexual behavior.

WHEN CONQUEST LEADS TO CONSEQUENCES

Like any habit that becomes solidified from years of routine behavior, sexual promiscuity or compulsion is not always easily reversed even when it creates personal, relational, and/or family problems that can bring athletes to the brink of emotional breakdown. This was evident when golf superstar, Tiger Woods, checked himself into long-term rehabilitation to address his long-standing issues with sexual promiscuity and/or addiction.[25] It is evident Woods realized on some level that he could not permanently overcome his behavior by himself and was wise to seek professional assistance. In contrast, it is safe to say that most athletes who engage in rampant promiscuity do not seek similar help because observing more athletes than not participating in these practices gives the false belief that they have no problem. This included former world boxing champion Mike Tyson who was previously noted for having sexual intercourse with 24 women in a single night according to his friend and former sparring partner Jose Torres.[26] Interestingly, Torres did not view this behavior as admirable, but rather to Tyson's inability to control his lust for sex coupled with his access to unlimited females.[27] This is a dangerous combination that warranted concern because Tyson's unbridled appetite for sex – and/or addiction – resulted in numerous women filing charges and civil lawsuits against him.[28] In these cases, women alleged that Tyson had fondled them, engaged in sexual harassment, and even rape which was highlighted when Tyson was convicted in March of 1992 for raping Desiree Washington and sentenced to six years in prison.[29] Numerous athletes, including Tyson, learned the hard way that rampant sexual promiscuity could also result in out-of-wedlock fatherhood and paternity suits that accompanied emotional and financial obligations that are costly.[30]

At the same time, heavyweight boxer Tommy Morrison and basketball legend Earvin "Magic" Johnson discovered too late the health-related consequences that could occur from engaging in unbridled heterosexual promiscuity.[31] During the pinnacle of their careers, both athletes contracted HIV from female sexual partners and had to prematurely and permanently retire from their professional sports participation.[32] In this study, a minor league basketball player noted that rampant promiscuity took its toll on certain teammates' health because "those were the same guys seeing the doctor, you know every couple of weeks." It is not known whether these doctor visits related to sexually transmitted diseases, lowered immune systems resulting in other illnesses, injuries, or a combination of problems but one thing is for certain, excessive nightlife and promiscuity depleted these athletes' physical health and probably their sports performance as well.

Some of the more insidious consequences that may not manifest immediately relate to the manner in which unrestrained promiscuity teaches athletes that it is okay to use women. As men continue to engage in sexual conquest and view women as nothing more than tools for their sexual pleasure, they can develop a mindset that suppresses their emotional and caring nature. In short, men learn to turn off their feelings toward women and sex, and this can include the woman they feel closest to. Such men become skilled at keeping a partner at a safe and emotionally distant arm's length even though this negatively impacts the quality of their lives by making intimate relationships superficial at best. These men may want to experience greater closeness with an intimate partner yet become frustrated when they cannot because they have damaged their emotional and feeling self by suppressing it over time. Years of using women as sex objects can also mean that some men do not know how to relate to women as individuals and friends or let a woman get close to them. Consequently, they can lack the personal and communication skills needed for healthy long-term relationships.

Rampant promiscuity also teaches men to believe that cheating, juggling, and using women are normal since females can be easily replaced. Although this may be true when women are viewed as only casual sexual partners, various athletes previously revealed pain and regret because they believed these lies and permanently damaged relationships with women they truly loved. Certain athletes come to realize – too late – that scores of female team followers were not attracted to them as individuals, but rather to their occupation, higher status, and salary. Consequently, when athletes retire from their sports participation, many find it to be a rude awakening that they are no longer sought after by adoring, sexually available female fans, and they lost the love of their life in the process. The belief that fame is vapor: visible one moment and gone the next highlights the harsh reality that slams many athletes, who are not ready or willing to cope with the cold, hard fact that athletes who used women were also being used in return. One minor league baseball player discussed his experience with this darker side of promiscuity by saying, "There's consequences, terrible consequences for those things, you know things I still deal with today you know that nobody tells you about at that time." This player further noted the importance of positive role models in helping athletes make good choices. This included athletes' sexual behavior and treatment of women because promiscuity during this player's career resulted in consequences, including guilt and remorse, that he was still dealing with years later. In the end, this player, like others, regretted his actions and not encountering more positive people that could have led him on a very different path than the one he had chosen with women during his career.

ATHLETES' CORNER: POINTS TO PONDER

1. Having a strong competitive nature is essential to success in elite-level sports, and this can be positive when it is confined to sports participation and activities that do not harm oneself or others. Athletes will know when their competitive nature has crossed the line to being a liability whenever this trait is allowed to dictate sexual behavior of any kind that targets women for selfish purposes or gain. Make it your daily discipline to practice behaviors that only uplift others while avoiding those who use people or encourage others to do so – particularly when it involves becoming a sexual predator.

2. The fact that sexual competitions are normal and prevalent within many athlete cultures needs to change because this so-called form of entertainment is harmful. Athletes who engage in contests dehumanize women by reducing them to sexual objects and numbers. Athletes need to be aware that negative behaviors that are modeled also get imitated by younger, impressionable athletes. In addition, athletes need to ask themselves how they would feel if a close female friend or family member was treated simply as a conquest or prize. Because sexual conquest teaches men how to use women and turn off their emotions, many athletes never learn how to relate to women as people and friends and have healthy long-term relationships.

3. Let's be clear about why athletes compete with teammates for sex with women. Such competitions show off athletes sexual conquests so they can boast and gather points. This means that pride, arrogance, stroking one's ego, and trying to prove that someone is more manly and dominant through their sexual behavior are the real reasons that sexual encounters occur at a woman's expense. Aside from strengthening these and other negative character traits, there is no benefit to engaging in sexual contests – only harm. Rampant promiscuity accompanies an array of negative consequences that have resulted in personal and family problems and break downs, addictions resulting in unbridled sexual behavior, sexual harassment and assaults, lawsuits, unwanted children, therapy, and sexually transmitted diseases that ended sports careers. In the end, the pursuit of excellence is not relegated to the sports arena because it carries into all aspects of athletes' lives including sexual behavior and treatment of women.

Chapter 8
Sex in the Recruiting Process

The process of recruiting and signing exceptional athletes is one of the most important elements of any athletic program at elite levels of competition. This is particularly true at the collegiate level where recruiting is an ongoing process in which coaches, current players, university staff, alumni, and other supporters all play an active role. It is no secret that competition to attract a constant stream of quality student-athletes each year can be fierce among universities because coaches' jobs along with the program's future success depend upon recruiting. This makes the recruiting visit a vital part of the process because athletes often decide whether to attend a particular university based on their on-campus experience. This fact has caused certain collegiate programs and/or their affiliates to use every available resource – including sexually available women – to attract the best athletes because memorable visits are thought to encourage a permanent return to the university.

While such perks may be appealing to some highly recruited high school athletes, sometimes they come with a heavy price. This was highlighted when Southern Methodist University gained national attention in 1987 when the NCAA imposed the "death penalty" by suspending its football program after it was discovered that boosters paid sorority women up to $400 a weekend to have sex with high school football recruits.[1] More recently, the University of Colorado's football program under former coach Gary Barnett experienced similar scrutiny when allegations surfaced in 2001 that Colorado football players set-up recruits to have sex with female students and as many as nine sexual assault accusations emerged among players and/or recruits since 1997.[2] It appears that certain collegiate programs do whatever it takes to convince recruits that playing for their university is the best choice by flaunting promises of sex along with athletic success.

During my collegiate and professional playing career, I had no awareness of sex in the recruiting process so I never bothered to ask other athletes in hockey or any other sport about such experiences. However, I came across these practices later while I was coaching when a former teammate told me they occurred with certain players' assistance when I was no longer on a particular team. While previously noted sex scandals involving recruits resulted in negative media attention and severe NCAA sanctions for SMU, these were not isolated incidences according to over 50% of the participants in this study who were aware of the use of sex in the recruiting process. This percentage is even more significant given the fact that nearly 25% of the participants comprised predominantly of hockey players were not asked this question because 40% never attended college and those who did were interviewed before this question was added to the study. At the same time, approximately one third who responded to this question noted that they personally experienced and/or promoted sex of one kind or another in the recruiting process during their collegiate careers. In addition, sex in the recruiting process was discovered as readily among collegiate athletes who competed in the late 1960s/early 1970s as it was in every other decade through 2010. Although a small number of universities have been disciplined for allegedly using sex in the recruiting process; they represent a minute percentage of the numerous collegiate programs that engage in similar practices based on this research.

DISCUSSIONS ABOUT SEX IN THE RECRUITING PROCESS

Participants were asked to discuss the phenomenon of sex in the recruiting process during collegiate recruiting weekends, and this included specific awareness and/or experiences of sexual encounters occurring "by chance" as well as those intentionally planned by team members or staff. For example, a minor league football player recalled, "When we were recruited…there were always parties and there were always girls around, but there was never you know, 'Here have sex with this girl to come here' that I witnessed." Similarly, an NBA player recalled, "I've heard obviously they'll take them to a party and then introduce them to a lot of girls, but nothing where you know giving them a girl for the whole weekend or anything like that." Various participants including a minor league baseball player noted he and his teammates made sure that females "were always around" during recruiting weekends; however, any recruits who happened to hook up with them did so strictly as "their own deal." Moreover, a collegiate baseball player who had never heard of baseball recruits being set-up with sex thought such practices would only involve high profile sports such as collegiate football because they had access to greater resources including female availability.

Although 48% of the participants who were asked to discuss sex in the recruiting process had no personal awareness of such practices, discussions and rumors surrounding such practices persisted. For instance, a minor league basketball player recalled, "I heard like people talking about it, but I never did it and I never saw it" while other athletes including an NFL player revealed, "I had heard of things like that happening and actually as a senior in high school going to some of these places, you kind of dream about that." One minor league basketball player similarly supported such notions by saying, "I'm sure it goes on like I've heard stories" while another elaborated in this way:

Absolutely – not I think that that happens – of course it does across college campuses in America where you want the guy and willing [to] do anything that you can do to get that guy but no...I've never experienced that as a college recruit and I've never taken a recruit into a situation like that so, but it happens all the [time], it happens more times than you know on a campus because that's the only thing that can separate one recruit at one school from another. You know if one school goes out to do that for him, then he's thinking as a young man that's going to be an everyday, every week thing so...you're breaking the line and that should be considered a violation you know of recruiting.

Although certain participants believed that pre-arranged sexual encounters were prevalent without experiencing them firsthand, participants also revealed a variety of alternative methods that collegiate athletes used to entertain recruits that also raised ethical concerns.

SETTING STAGE BY ENTERTAINING RECRUITS WITH A VARIETY OF VICES

One practice that collegiate athletes routinely use to entertain incoming recruits involved the use of alcohol which is a rampant activity on college campuses today.[3] This is problematic for a variety of reasons including the most significant fact that high school athletes are underage and are not legally permitted to drink. This means that law enforcement officials can easily ruin the weekend for a recruit, the hosting collegiate athletes, and particularly the coaches anytime a high school athlete is arrested for being under the influence of alcohol. As a result, collegiate athletes unwittingly promote a negative lifestyle choice by making drinking appear harmless when this is certainly not the case. This is compounded by the fact that alcohol more than any other drug has been linked with all types of aggression and violence and even death.[4] For example, Matt James, a highly recruited offensive lineman, who was the University of Notre Dame's first big signing under new coach Brian Kelly, was killed in April of 2010 from an alcohol-related fall from a fifth-floor hotel balcony during his high school senior-year spring break in Florida.[5]

Nevertheless, alcohol consumption flourished during recruiting weekends according to numerous participants including a minor league baseball player who recalled, "I've been...on recruiting trips where you know a coach might say" to the players who were going to entertain them, "'Hey, here's some money...show him a good time,' you know wink, wink, and then they go buy booze with it and stuff like that, but nothing really for girls." Such practices were even more intense according to wrestler who revealed, "I went to [XXX

University] and had parties, went to big parties, there were drugs, alcohol, there were girls there, but nothing set up for me." One minor league baseball player recalled experiencing an "uneventful" recruiting weekend other than being "left at the coach's door at two o'clock in the morning, you know drunk."

Another alternative form of female-centered entertainment that collegiate athletes routinely used to occupy time with recruits involved excursions to bars or strip clubs. This was another risky endeavor because high school athletes were usually under the legal drinking age and not permitted in bars. Nevertheless, such practices flourished on certain campuses, and one wrestler discussed his experiences by saying, "It was easy to take those guys out and get them into bars and get them drunk and that's what happened to me, I went on my recruiting trip and I thought you know, 'This is pretty cool.'" This participant also noted that he only took recruits to the bars if they wanted to drink and because he "never pushed anybody into doing that," he would simply leave the recruits who were not into partying with teammates who were more "mellow and religious." Other participants representing a variety of sports noted athletes taking recruits to strip clubs, and this included a collegiate football player who elaborated in this way:

> No [pre-arranged sexual encounters], they'd have to do it themselves, I mean we'd give them the opportunities you know, definitely give them the opportunities and you know that's probably where we hit the strip clubs...you know give them a little bit of a taste of a naked girl and then we'd get onto [the bars] you know, and like I said, we knew all the bouncers so getting an 18-year old kid in was no big deal...[because] it's recruiting week, the bouncers would say, "No problem, just watch him," and then you'd end up trying to score yourself, and then if he kind of saw something where it could lead to something [sexual] for the recruit then great, maybe he'll come to school there...if the coach told you that he was a blue chipper (i.e., high profile recruit).

It is safe to say that many high school athletes have not been inside a college bar, and the same can be said for strip clubs. Because such venues offer naked women along with alcohol, they can readily surpass the glamour of the college bar scene. These notions were supported by a wrestler who recalled that he had all his lap dances paid for when collegiate wrestlers took him to a strip club during his recruiting trip in the late 2000s. This excursion became even more memorable when one wrestler from the group paid $1000 to have sex with a stripper in a private room in the club. Because strip clubs put underage recruits in contact with an array of illegal activities including substance abuse, they are risk-filled places that can result in a variety of problems.

Interestingly, the previous football participant used strip club attendance as warm up for bar hopping because this was a way for the collegiate athletes and recruits to "wet their appetite" prior to their quest to find sexual partners for the evening. Furthermore, this combination of alcohol, bars and strip clubs, and the hunt for female sexual partners was thought to be a major factor that could influence recruits to sign with – or reject – a particular university. Such beliefs were supported when a collegiate basketball player revealed that his team's "puritanical recruiting process" did little to enhance their program while it depleted the collegiate players' own resources since they ended up spending more of their own money on recruits than they received. In contrast, a wrestler reported:

> I would take them to the topless bars more than anything else because I knew that's what hooked me when I got recruited there, and you know depending on the kid and who he was, [it] just opened their eyes up to a world that they may not have seen before was something that I thought was important…for them to see.

This participant went on to say that he was one of his coach's "better recruiters" because he had good sense for what to do and not to do when he entertained recruits. While this may be true as far as the recruits and certain coaching staff were concerned, taking recruits to strip clubs where they served women and alcohol would raise a lot of questions regarding good judgment, values, ethics, and role modeling.

Allegations surfaced in 2001 that University of Colorado football players entertained recruits though the use of homemade pornography, alcohol and drugs, strippers, and/or strip club attendance.[6] Former lineman, Chris Leeder, who was one of Coach Gary Barnett's players at Northwestern University from 1994-97, challenged any finger pointing at his former coach by noting the practice of selling sex to recruits, which could include the use of strippers, was universal among all schools and not something that was invented at Colorado.[7] Such notions were supported when the *Rocky Mountain News* reported that Steve Lower, the owner of Hardbodies Entertainment in Denver, had been sending strippers to recruiting parties at University of Colorado and other universities for the past 20 years.[8] Lower went on to say that players or friends of players (but never the coaches) arranged for the women, and sometimes the agency was told to send their "best girls" because it was for a recruiting party.[9] In the end, it is evident that certain collegiate programs and/or their affiliates alike believe that providing recruits with access to women and alcohol is a practical way to entertain and perhaps secure a recruit's decision to attend their university. And, access to women can mean more than simply talking to females or watching naked bodies at strip clubs.

STEERING RECRUITS TOWARD CERTAIN FEMALES

Providing recruits with access to alcohol, bars, and strip clubs could certainly encourage the desire for female sexual partners; however, participants identified other informal arrangements in this process that were normal occurrences. For example, a wrestler noted how teams would have parties specifically for their "high caliber recruits," and he told how he was "real flattered" by this and the fact that the females would "talk to you" because "they know who you are...so you kind of get suckered into all that." While this wrestler was unsure whether these women would "take it that far" by sexually engaging with "a recruit," he found "once you're on campus...it would definitely be taken further than just the hellos." A collegiate baseball player also noted there were parties for recruits from different teams although "nine times out of ten the women were...a lot more into the football guys than they would be [for baseball] because these guys looked more higher profile [laughs]." Like the previous wrestler, this participant also noted that "the baseball girls" at the recruiting parties "weren't so much into the kids...the recruits." On the other hand, the football recruits were quite vocal about "who they were" and the fact that sex was not "a given" despite being in the company of many attractive women at these parties. While sexual challenges and/or rejection do not happen in all cases, it is evident that sometimes highly touted recruits from various sports struggled to find sexual encounters with college students who appeared eager to talk with them at parties without going beyond this. Such findings help to explain why some collegiate athletes feel it is necessary to intervene and assist high school recruits in finding a female partner for sex during the recruiting weekend. After all, this is particularly important for some high profile recruits who expect sex and judge the quality of their weekend and a collegiate program by whether or not they hooked up with a college woman. Consequently, recruits are conditioned to believe that sex with women is part of the fringe benefits that they will receive as star athletes.

Numerous participants noted introducing recruits to as many college women as possible wherever they went. This included a wrestler, who as a collegiate coach in charge of recruiting, discussed his philosophy and practice of introducing recruits to female college students:

> Oh yea...you try to get the guys to get introduced to girls, you try to do that so they get to meet them – I mean if you're talking about like what Gary Barnett [former University of Colorado football coach] did – then no, but...I'll ask a guy you know what kind of girl a guy likes, we had a kid in the other day and said he liked volleyball players, I said, "Well, we'll be sure you get to meet some of the girls on the volleyball team." I make sure stuff like that happens but I don't encourage [sex]...like Gary Barnett basically, just getting guys to meet you know the type of girl they want

to meet...if they like cheerleaders, I will introduce them to cheerleaders... [now] if a guy does that [hooks up] that's his own business but...I don't encourage that because once that kid gets down here...I don't want a kid to get the wrong impression, like when I do a recruiting trip...I want it to be as close to what regular school would be like, you know I don't want to bring him down from a big party and have him thinking that this is what college is all about you know, but I do want him to meet this girl who's around and stuff like that and if she takes a liking to him, so be it, but not directly set up for the purpose of sex no.

By asking his recruits "what kind of girl a guy likes" and then making these introductions, this coach, knowingly or unknowingly, assisted in reducing college women to sexual stereotypes rather than people with unique athletic talents and individuality. Another wrestler supported these ideas as it related to recruits by saying, "We would introduce them to some girls, but there were no like 'standby sluts' that we could just hook them with...wrestling really didn't have any groupies." While this participant's team lacked access to women who were willing to sexually accommodate them or incoming recruits, he also suggested that greater female availability increased the likelihood that these practices could occur with higher profile teams like football since some women may be eager to help their team in anyway they could.

Previous narratives revealed collegiate athletes and/or coaches using a variety of methods to entertain recruits although this stopped short of pre-arranging actual sexual encounters. However, not all athletes took this perspective with the recruits they were responsible for entertaining. For example, a MLB player recalled, "I was on a recruiting trip after my senior year in high school to a college and ended up at a party with some seniors and I was directed to some girls and some girls were directed back towards me and we basically just partied all night long." Although "nothing" sexual resulted during the evening, this was a common practice that a minor league baseball player further explained. "I think...they steered you towards girls but it wasn't...'this girl's gonna take care of you and...that's why you should come to [XXX University]' type [of] thing." This participant, like others, noted collegiate athletes steering recruits toward certain women and then if a recruit happened to hook up, the thinking was "more power to him" but it was not an actual "set up" – at least not in these cases. At the same time, there were collegiate athletes from certain cultures that took a more vocal role in promoting sexual encounters. For example, a wrestler recalled, "I mean...they were encouraged to try to a have a lady friend for the night when they came on a recruiting visit" while a minor league football player elaborated on how this could occur:

[Laughing] of course they always, always let you know who the easy targets are, I mean who's who, or she does this, or she does that, just kind of give you an idea of maybe who you might want to mess with that night, or who you might want to stay away from once you do finally attend your school...I mean if the recruit specifically asked me, I mean for something like that – or something that night – then I definitely would give him an idea of who is a better chance for that night, so yea that definitely does go on.

Revealing the women who were "easy targets" for sex was a common practice among athletes from every sport and era because collegiate players were eager to assist recruits anyway they could in an effort to better their team and bond with a new athlete. Such practices in combination with female availability caused one wrestler to notice that women were "a lot more friendly" when he was being recruited although he was not sure if this was because the collegiate wrestlers encouraged them or not. Furthermore, he observed "a lot of female activity" to the point that he thought, "It just made you feel like man, you know this (sex) could definitely happen." One collegiate football player revealed taking a more assertive role because "you grab" a woman "you knew that would be interested" in sex and introduce her to a recruit in order to assist him in finding a potential sexual partner. While it is apparent that certain collegiate athletes took a more active role "in showing a recruit a good time," this participant also noticed that some recruits arrived with "their heads so big cause they're getting recruited" to a big-time program that they needed "no coaxing" or assistance with college women. Another collegiate athlete who played basketball noted that although no one ever pre-arranged recruits sexual encounters, he found that just being out with his team provided recruits with ample opportunities to hook up with various women. He also noted that "sometimes nothing would happen and they wouldn't care" because "to have sex with a girl" was like "gravy" and an added bonus to being out with his team because he believed recruits had a lot of fun whether they engaged in sex or not. Although it is apparent that many collegiate athletes indirectly assist recruits in finding sexual partners since it created a bond and helped their teams, it is not uncommon for some athletes to go above and beyond simply assisting recruits in connecting with sexual partners during recruiting weekends.

SETTING UP RECRUITS WITH SEXUAL ENCOUNTERS

Previous player narratives revealed visits to strip clubs and bars as well as recruiting parties where alcohol, drugs, and friendly women flourished along with certain collegiate athletes who encouraged sexual encounters by steering recruits toward promiscuous female students. While these elements contributed to the greater likelihood that a recruit might experience a casual sexual encounter during his recruiting visit, sexual experiences were not previously arranged according to these participants. At the same time, this is not to say that collegiate athletes have not pre-arranged sexual encounters for recruits because they have. In fact, collegiate athletes representing every sport who competed from the late 1960s through 2010 were equally aware of these practices on teams in which they competed. For example, a wrestler recalled, "We would always set them up with girls and that was a necessity, you had to do that" in order to insure success in recruiting. Moreover, his team boasted a "100%" success rate because friendships with "the loose girls" in combination with "a few parties" and "a few beers" was all that was needed to promote sex in the 1970s before the emergence of "AIDS."

Similarly, a minor league basketball player from this era revealed, "We were known for that at our school" because athletes would target "looser" women they knew who were not receiving "a lot of attention" and pair them with a recruit "who knows nothing about her." Such females were encouraged to sexually engage with recruits because the collegiate athletes made these women believe it was in their best interest to connect with a potential "star" now in order to gain a potential relational advantage over other college women later. As a result, certain collegiate athletes became skilled at manipulating promiscuous women to have sex with their recruits. These practices also highlighted the fact that athletes' desire to bond quickly and take care of their recruits superseded any concern for their female supporters who were used as a means of signing their recruits by having sex with them. And, this occurred even though there was no guarantee these high school recruits would become future teammates.

Another participant who played in the NFL recalled that such practices were not an exact science during the 1980s, and he provided an example of the type of salesmanship that targeted both college females and recruits:

> ...like I said that there was no guarantees you know, and we might have tried to prep the girl, "Hey you know this guy he handsome, he cute, he thinks he digs you" or whatever, you know there was never nothing mandated, but it was always kind of inferred like, "Hey, you think he cute then holler at him cause we want him to come here and he's one of the top running backs in the state of [XXX]" – you know something like that, we would prep the girl and stuff like that yea, and then...we'd have some dorm mates that we knew that was you know promiscuous and stuff, we would try to field the guy a female, we would tell him, "You know actually you could get that, do you want to hit that tonight? – yea you can get that" you know so yea, we did that.

This participant, like others, noted the uncertainty associated with trying to pre-arrange sexual encounters for recruits. This was further highlighted when a collegiate football player noted that although "it's not hard to talk the guy up," another revealed, "I think even 'a slut' has her own standards" which implied that even promiscuous women had to be talked into having sex with a high school athlete. This realization prompted certain collegiate football players who competed in the later part of 2000 to address this concern by doing one of two things: "Either they go out...like the older guys will have the recruits out and they'll actually get some girls and pick them up [together], or the [collegiate] guys will have some girls already sort of in their stable so to speak that they can call at any moment and get what they want out of them." Both options enabled players and recruits to accomplish their all-important goal because athletes often believed that recruiting success depended upon whether or not a recruit had sex during his visit. Such notions were supported by a wrestler who revealed, "Yea...you're setting him up and talking the girl into doing it so you could get this recruit...yea, I've done that before... actually it was a lot of times that kind of made their decision where they were going, they just thought, 'Yea, this place is pretty wild and crazy, and this is where I want to be [laughs]." And, one of the previous collegiate football players also added:

> ...the recruits will always be there the next day after their night out and you'd be like, "Well did you have fun out last night?" and they'd be like, "Yea dude, I got drunk and this chick, I banged this chick yada yada," so they're always getting some, and that's why recruits go on recruiting visits, you know to have a good time and do those kind of things.

It is easy to understand how positive responses from recruits enable sex in the recruiting process to flourish because collegiate athletes from every era felt they were providing valuable assistance to both recruits, who get what they think they want by having sex, and their collegiate program as well.

At the same time, not every woman needs encouragement before becoming sexually involved with a recruit. For example, a collegiate basketball player recalled a female college student who took a sexually assertive approach with a recruit she was already acquainted with, and therefore, needed no flattery and/or manipulation from other athletes. A minor league baseball player revealed his team had no shortage of helpful women in the late 1990s by saying, "Yea, yea we had about five or six girls that we knew...could take care of [recruits], we could just tell them that, 'Hey, there's a new guy coming in and we really want him and...boom," these college females were willing to assist the team by having sex with them. Similarly, a minor league basketball player explained it was "not really a lot" of effort to convince his female college friends to have sex with recruits in the 2000s. Basically, he and his teammates would say, "Hey, take care of them," or, "Will you look after him for us while we're gone?" Then, the women "do the rest of the calculations on their own, so...if they agree to it, they kind of understand to what they're agreeing to, if they're going to be involved." This assumption that college women know what they are agreeing to can create major problems when, in fact, certain females do not fully realize that they are supposed to have sex with a recruit. This participant further revealed that his female college friends were never paid to have sex, but did so because they simply enjoyed hanging out and getting to know both the players on the team as well as the recruits. It is apparent that "getting to know some of the players" is defined very differently for certain athletes and women because it could involve casual sex with recruits for the asking. In addition, it is likely that certain women felt they had a definite role in the recruiting process by agreeing to have sex with one or more recruits during this athlete-centered process. While females' sexual participation in this process could be explained in a variety of ways, it is likely that their fear of being excluded or shunned would rank high on this list. This means that certain women could feel pressure to have sex with a recruit particularly if they felt this was the only way to continue experiencing a sense of belonging with collegiate team members – even if it was often a shallow and false sense of belonging. In the end, some participants mentioned that although recruits' sexual encounters could never be assured with one estimating this likelihood at 10%, it is apparent that others, including the previous participants, noted success rates for pre-arranging recruits' sexual encounters were 50% and even 100%.

Setting Up Recruits with Prostitutes

The process of pre-arranged sexual encounters for high school recruits was not relegated to the use of female college students because sometimes it involved prostitutes who were hired with or without a collegiate athletic program's awareness and approval. Such practices were substantiated when the University of Colorado disclosed that a phone-record audit traced a series of calls from an athletic department cell phone to a Boulder escort service called Best Variety between June 2002 and July 2003.[10] At the time, the cell phone was assigned to football recruiting coordinator Nathan Maxcey, who acknowledged making calls to the $250-an-hour escort service for his own personal use and no one else at the university.[11] However, this was challenged by a lawyer for Pasha Cowan, a former manager for the Best Variety escort service, who told the *Boulder Daily Camera* that Maxcey set up the service for others, and this specifically involved "some young and very athletic men."[12] A university investigation subsequently determined that although football Coach Gary Barnett and athletic director Dick Tharp showed lax oversight without knowingly sanctioning the use of sex, alcohol, and drugs as recruiting tools, both were allowed to keep their positions and no one was held accountable.[13]

Previous findings revealed approximately 55% of the participants had awareness of athletes' use of prostitutes during their collegiate and/or professional playing and/or coaching careers spanning the 1960s through 2010. Furthermore, this could include the use of prostitutes with high school football recruits as an NFL and a current minor league football player revealed:

> ...when I take you know my high school kids on college trips and they meet the hostesses now, they're pretty basic now, but when I was in school...there was prostitutes, I mean they worked for the university, yes they did, they slept with the kids, they tried to get them to come to the school, but we're talking about late '70s, early '80s, now they're more you know just pretty basic for the university but yea that's what happened back when I was being recruited...

> Man, I had a teammate, he just told me this last week it's funny you asked, he ended up going to [XXX University] but he had a recruiting visit to [XYZ University] and he said after they had their dinner with the coaches, they let them leave with the players, and he said the minute they got back to their apartment, they said there was like three stripper-type girls that were in the room playing with each other, and then all they basically had to do was take their clothes off and go handle business and I was like "Wow, I've never experienced anything like that that's crazy," and he said it's happened to him on a couple of his visits cause he took all five of his visits, so I will say this from what I've been hearing, I know it goes on at the Division I level.

While the first participant observed that the hostesses who entertained collegiate recruits today were not prostitutes to his knowledge, the second participant revealed his awareness of stripper-prostitutes accommodating a teammate who was recruited in the late 2000s. This was no surprise since the University of Colorado's disclosures regarding escort services were substantiated in 2002-03 while similar allegations have surfaced at University of Miami in 2011.[14] Such notions were further highlighted when a collegiate football player revealed the option he had available in order to secure a sexual encounter for recruits he entertained during his collegiate career:

> ...there was prostitution if you will, you know by this guy you know just trying to help them out, trying to...[so] during your visit – what would happen is you would sit there and you'd eat dinner...with them and their parents and all that [time] you kind of get the feel of a guy and... what he's all about, if he's coming there to be an engineering student then he could probably care less about going to the bar and getting hammered and you know hooking up...with a girl that night, you know

I mean [if they] had serious girlfriends...and they didn't want to hook up and you know, it's just some guys are wild, some guys aren't, and you know it's probably why I'm good at sales now, I kind of, you know, can greet people...pretty decently and kind of you know take them in the direction they want to go..

Although it is not known whether or not the coaching staff was aware of these practices in the late 1990s, sex with prostitutes always occurred with the hope that it would lead to signing high profile prospects. Furthermore, having the option of accessing prostitutes is one way to insure that a recruit will have a sexual encounter during his visit if he wanted to because the bar scene alone can be a hit or miss endeavor when attempting to secure a sexual encounter with a college woman. In the end, providing recruits with prostitutes sends a poor message that essentially teaches athletes that sex is a reward they are entitled to for being a talented high profile athlete.

PERSONAL EXPERIENCES WITH PRE-ARRANGED SEXUAL ENCOUNTERS

Previous narratives revealed numerous collegiate athletes, who competed from the early 1970s – 2010 and represented every sport in this study, setting up sexual encounters for recruits by using prostitutes and/or promiscuous women they knew who were described as "friends of the program" according to different professional basketball players. Various participants also discussed personal experiences involving sexual encounters with women that raised questions regarding the possibility that these events were set up for them during a recruiting visit. For example, one minor league baseball player recalled, "I went to [XXX University] I was recruited there to play football, baseball, and my host introduced me to a girl and we ended up dancing and kissing and stuff, but then again, I don't know if that was something that they intentionally did or something that just happened." Similarly, a wrestler noted cheerleaders would sit on recruits' laps at one university, and he recalled being fondled on other visits to the point that he thought sexual encounters were possible "if I needed it or wanted it" at two of the "six or seven" schools he visited. In addition, another wrestler believed a hook up that he had on a recruiting visit could have been prearranged because the encounter "happened too fast," and he did not think he was "that good at womanizing to have pulled that off" as a recruit. Furthermore, he thought that this intimate encounter would have resulted in sexual intercourse had he "not gotten so drunk."

While the previous participants wondered whether their sexual encounters were pre-arranged or not, other participants were much more certain after pondering their experience after the fact. This included an NFL player who noticed that the sexual interaction he had with his particular hostess when she invited him to her room was part of a plan that he did not quite understand in his naiveté at the time although it included "a definite line" which she would not cross with him. Other participants including a collegiate and a minor league football player elaborated on their experiences:

> ...I was getting recruited out of high school...and I had an official visit to [XXX University]... and the university pays for everything, the plane flight out of your town...your hotel room for the weekend...your host money to take you out, you know take you to the bars and things...and usually you get off the plane and there's either a coach there waiting to take you back to go get a good meal there [but] Friday night instead of a coach or a player waiting for you at [XXX University], they had girls waiting for you. [XXX] was my hostess for the weekend and...she came out and put her arm out and escorted you out and obviously they used their hostesses to try to lure you into...a commitment to go play at their university...yea they were college students...[and] there was five kids from [XXX] that flew on that same flight getting recruited...so there were five girls...[but] you know for me, it was a peck on the cheek and maybe a make out, it didn't amount to anymore than that...I don't know if they were paid, I couldn't touch upon that...but I know they had obviously...girl hostesses there which you know makes any 18-year old kid kind of you know get excited about it.

> ...I remember when I was coming out of high school...different colleges had different names for the girls that was their hostesses and like... The Bengal Babies...The Garden Golden Girls...The Gator Getters...The Georgia Reps all kind of shit like that, and then you had The Southern Bells and shit like that...so I mean that's back in the days that was easy pickings cause...they have these girls call your house, and you know the next thing you talking, having good conversation with them, and the next thing you know, "Well you come over here I'll show you what I'm going to do for you, you going to come to [our university], you going to 'come' too." "Well shit, okay, let's make it happen then," so you know on your recruiting trip you meet up with that girl and shit, sometimes it happens and sometimes she was just full of shit by the time you get there, she was at her boyfriend's, and I tell the coach, "Your girl lied to me all the time, so I might not come to your school" [laughing].

Although the first participant experienced minimal sexual intimacy with his hostess, he subsequently noted his morals kept him from pursuing a sexual encounter that he thought was possible. In contrast, the second participant recalled female chaperones from a variety of universities making seductive phone calls to recruits like himself. While certain women followed through on promises to sexually engage with this participant, others did not. Whether this participant's anger resulted from being lied to or because he believed he deserved sex as a high profile recruit is not known. What is known is that certain collegiate programs use female hostesses who imply they are sexually available – if a recruit chooses to play for a particular university. Such implications are dangerous and can encourage negative behaviors including sexual aggression when recruits believe they are entitled to sexual encounters which have been advertised before or during their visit. Such notions were supported by an NFL player who said, "I tried to get a blow job when I was in high school on my college visit, yea that happened, you got the hostesses and then when we were in school that's kind of what the hostesses were [doing]." This participant subsequently revealed his attempt to receive oral sex occurred because he discovered that some female hostesses were prostitutes who were hired to assist in the recruiting process. Furthermore, this participant's behavior and beliefs, perhaps combined with his sense of entitlement, revealed how problems involving sexual aggression can occur when athletes' sexual expectations are not met, regardless of whether the woman is a prostitute. In addition, coaches, team affiliates and supporters, and the females themselves who promoted such practices together contribute to teaching athletes to objectify females because women were only used in the recruiting process for their sexual allure, availability, and entertainment value. And in all likelihood, these negative practices occurred without any of these individuals fully understanding the implications of how they promoted negative attitudes toward women. Indeed, these are poor messages to send impressionable high school athletes who will soon encounter an abundance of negative messages targeting women often on a daily basis within their particular sports culture.

While previous participants noted female hostesses limiting their sexual intimacy with recruits, other participants recalled their sexual encounters that resulted in sexual intercourse and were believed to be pre-arranged during recruiting visits. A wrestler recalled being set up to have sex with a female college student on two different recruiting visits although he believed the collegiate wrestlers rather than the coaches were responsible because "they took me up to her room and left." Moreover, a minor league hockey player revealed, "I could remember getting recruited at [XXX University]...there was two or three [women] in the hotel room you know, and if one wouldn't fuck you, the other one would, you know it was no big deal." Similarly, an NBA player remembered his recruiting weekend consisted of seeing "a little bit of the campus," "dinner," and the collegiate players telling him, "Look, so and so's a 'friend of the program' and you know she'll be by and she'll take care of you... you know enjoy, have a good time." Unlike certain participants who thought collegiate players were responsible for promoting their sexual encounters, this player was unsure who set up the women, who were thought to be college students, that would "take care" of the recruits.

In contrast, a minor league baseball player told how he was able to differentiate the women on his recruiting trips that were pre-arranged by a collegiate program to have sex with a recruit as opposed to those that the collegiate athletes tried to arrange themselves. For example, one hostess he was assigned to that greeted him soon after he arrived at a particular university "walked me around the campus, we talked, [and] she said when we toured this part of the lake, 'This is where you're going.'" Moreover, he believed that "she was a whole set-up – absolutely" because they soon had sexual intercourse, and there was no question that her task was to entertain and persuade him to attend the university. In contrast, he observed, "Other ones were set up pretty much [like], 'You know our objective is to get you laid tonight,' and it happened throughout the course of the party...or wherever you went that night, but that [other] one was absolutely set-up right off the get go." Furthermore, such practices thrived according to a minor league basketball player:

> Oh I mean I've never gone on a recruiting visit when there wasn't girls left for you, like the first thing you do when you get with your teammates is I mean they take you to see some girls, and generally they take you to the ones that will end up back at your hotel in a sense...if they're not already there. I mean that's very common, that's almost like a part of the trip.

From the late 1990s through the late 2000s, this participant, as a collegiate athlete and coach, revealed that sex in the recruiting process was as common as campus tours and fine dining because this was the way that collegiate athletes and/or their programs believed they could gain an upper hand on other universities. And it often worked according to various participants including a wrestler who explained the impact of sex during his recruiting visit. "I took my five recruiting trips and [had sex] a couple times I guess...[and] because the other places didn't do that, that was a big difference you know. It's always going to influence an 18-year old kid." On the other hand, another wrestler told how he was introduced to a college woman he "ended up hooking up" with and chose to attend different university which did not provide him with a sexual encounter during his recruiting visit.

Interestingly, not all recruits were interested in sexually engaging with women who were available to them during college visits as a minor league basketball player and an NFL player discussed in this way:

> Every damn trip...you had the campus girls, you know trying to persuade you to go there and get you out to the night club and...there'd be girls

inviting and one thing would lead to another and sometimes you see somebody on your own, you get with a girl, but she might be campus rat, I mean everybody sees she's being passed around...they tried, they tried, they tried [to set me up]...they'd just take you out, they'd be willing to go to the club, or come on by the dorm and knock on your door, or knock on your hotel room at night and if you had nobody with you, you might let them in if that's what you wanted to do.

Yes, you know it's been situations where you know I took a visit to one institution and there was this girl that I guess when recruits came up she was the blow job girl, so they tried to set me up with her and there's been situations where you know kids come up to visit institutions and it's certain girls that guys know that they can call, "You know this is a recruit...make sure [to] show them a good time blah, blah, blah" and you know whatever that means they kind of just make sure they take care of the recruit – [and] does whatever the guy might want to do... you know at some point they [the women] probably...get to hang out with the guys which is probably what they want to do anyway, but...as far as them being paid, I don't think they're paid at all.

It is likely that both athletes decision to reject their pre-arranged sexual encounters was influenced by the possibility of contracting a sexually transmitted disease since they knew certain women were very promiscuous with the athletes. Finally, it is apparent that certain recruits' sexual encounters during their college visits were previously arranged by players as well as other athletic personnel or team supporters. One question remains: Is there any evidence of coaches promoting sexual encounters during recruits' official visits?

COACHES' PROMOTING RECRUITS' SEXUAL ENCOUNTERS

While previous narratives provide ample evidence that certain athletic personnel as well as collegiate athletes previously arranged sexual encounters for incoming recruits, coaches have seldom been mentioned in conjunction with these events. However, some recruits' sexual encounters have been clandestinely encouraged if not promoted by certain coaches according to a minor league hockey player who recalled these events during his collegiate career:

...I wasn't [set up]...and I was never told this by a coach, but I mean that's always [happening], you know you're trying to make them want to come or your coaches are telling you, "We need this guy, we need this guy," but you try to promote like a college atmosphere you know which is like a big party or you try to introduce him to as many girls as possible you know and then maybe he ends up hooking up or not, but I can say for certain that happened, but the intentions were there, and the possibility was there for sure.

The previous participant and his teammates did all they could to promote a recruit's sexual encounter in the 2000s because any implicit goal of the coaching staff became an objective of those entertaining a recruit as well. During this same time period, a collegiate baseball player also recalled a conversation with a teammate who described being "set up" with sex when he walked into his room and found two females waiting to have a group sexual encounter with him during a recruiting trip to a southern university. It is difficult to imagine a collegiate coach being unaware of this type of set up, although proving that a coach promoted such an event would be virtually impossible because no authority figures were present when this occurred. This fact enables a coaching staff to covertly promote sexual encounters and not be held accountable because the collegiate athletes rather than the coaches were responsible for showing recruits their idea of a "good time" whenever sex occurred during recruiting visits. Plus, casual sexual encounters are common among college students which makes it difficult to prove that a recruit's one-night stand happened because of a collegiate coach and/or athletes' intentional prompting rather than simply by chance.[15] However, in situations involving group sex, it would be difficult to believe that two females just happened to desire a sexual encounter with a random male, who happened to be a highly touted recruit, all because they happened to be sitting in the wrong room, by chance, at the exact time that a recruit walked in the room.

The previous pre-arranged sexual encounter with two females is not folklore according to a successful collegiate wrestler and coach who detailed a similar recruiting experience of his own that reinforced the notion that some coaches were directly responsible for promoting certain recruits sexual encounters. For example, this participant recalled, "On one particular recruiting trip I did two cheerleaders...pretty much the entire weekend yea, yea, you know off and on pretty extensively for the whole weekend yea...[even though] I didn't go to school there." Furthermore, this participant elaborated on his experience in this way:

> ...as a senior in high school, it was a pretty memorable experience, actually we got off the plane and met the coach and there was some team members there and some cheerleaders, they handcuffed us immediately when we got off the plane with these cheerleaders, the first establishment we went to was a bar...coach put up a $100 and said, "First couple of drinks are on me" then he said, "If you have any problems, call my home number, I'll come get you"...that evening we

stayed there for dinner and drinks, and then we ended up leaving and one of the team members drove and got pulled over by the cops so he got a DUI, the coach came, talked to the cops, the cops released us to him, he took us back to the hotel with the cheerleaders, picked us up in the morning for breakfast, un-handcuffed us, we ate breakfast with the girls, they stayed with us the entire weekend.

It is apparent that this particular coach had distinct ideas about recruiting methods in the 1990s, and his influence both with law enforcement officials and women who "assisted" the recruiting process was undeniable. Moreover, this situation resulted in this participant and another recruit's first group sexual encounters with two females because they were handcuffed overnight to the women and for the entire weekend. This participant also provided subsequent thoughts about this experience by saying, "Favorable, they were two cheerleaders, [it was] a little difficult getting undressed but we managed... yes [laughing] it was fun...it was quite a memorable experience." Although this wrestler found the experience obviously unforgettable, ironically, he did not attend this particular university because of his suspicions concerning the coach's character and ethics. While this situation perhaps highlighted the pinnacle of decadence that certain coaches promote in order to sign a high profile recruit, this wrestler recalled similar practices that were common in his recruiting experiences. For example, he noted that at "every school, initially five, unofficially just probably five more [universities]" the same thing occurred although usually it involved "just one" woman who would be sexually available for an entire recruiting weekend. It is evident that some coaches implement a "whatever it takes approach" by doing everything they deem as necessary to encourage and influence talented athletes to attend their university. Furthermore, it is likely certain coaches believed that providing a group sexual encounter with two females would make a lasting impression and show the recruit that he was very special and really wanted. Such practices also loudly announce that a program has the guts and resources to go all out by arranging an unforgettable sexual experience that few institutions would dare to facilitate. Unfortunately, this display also included subjecting impressionable high school student-athletes to morally compromising situations and unhealthy behaviors that most had not previously experienced. While certain narratives in this section highlighted sexual extremes that were undoubtedly promoted by coaches, it would be naïve to believe that collegiate coaches in previous sections were unaware that their program's female hostesses were selling sexual allure which had the potential to evolve into sexual encounters with recruits. It is the rare coach who does not know exactly what is going on within every aspect of his program even though many may play ignorant and act surprised when various indiscretions surface.

GROUP SEX AS A PHENOMENON
IN THE RECRUITING PROCESS

Previous narratives revealed indirect as well as direct coaching influences that promoted sex during the recruiting process, and this included the phenomenon of group sex. Although both of these sexual encounters involved the less common type of group sex identified in this research (i.e., two-on-ones involving two females and a male), such events were not the only group sexual encounters that recruits experienced during collegiate visits. For example, a minor league baseball player discussed his awareness of such an event in the mid 2000s by saying, "I knew two guys on their recruiting trip when they came to [my university] they actually slept with a girl but it wasn't like set-up...they met with the girl that night while they were out visiting the school and it was all on them that they ended up sleeping with the girl, it wasn't like we set them up with a girl." In addition, a wrestler elaborated on his awareness of larger group sexual encounters that occurred during his career in the 1990s in a different way:

> I know one repeated event with a group of guys who were current wrestlers...there was this one chick that they would call her up and say, "Hey come over," and four and five guys would go over and just go to fucking town on her. You name it, they did it. In fact, this is really interesting...there would be people coming in, let's say another respected wrestler from another institution or something, or a recruit or something, and they would take him over to that fucking chick. That's pretty crazy, yeah...she was into it...this example wasn't...taking advantage, it wasn't coercive, it wasn't taking advantage [by] using alcohol or drugs. It would be a call, "Yeah, okay, come on over"...

It appeared that this particular team used group sex as a way to bond and build camaraderie with wrestlers that perhaps they did not know so well. Consequently, these events were unlike any other discovered in this study since most athletes engaged in group sex with teammates or other athletes they lived with in a dormitory. Moreover, this participant believed there was nothing coercive about these encounters since the woman was willing to participate without the use of drugs or alcohol whenever his teammates happened to phone her. However, when attempting to explain the prevalence of these behaviors, this participant also noted, "Clearly there's some pathology with this woman, [but] it was the culture of the team, groups of the team was certainly one in that it's not unusual to try to share a chick, pass a chick around, the groupie kinds of chicks." While this participant thought the woman's frequent participation in group sex related to her unresolved issues, perhaps the same could be said for the male athletes. This wrestler was also aware that his team's culture promoted getting "laid" as much as possible and in any manner they could. Such practices were not surprising because collegiate and/ or professional athletes representing every sport and era similarly discussed easy access to certain women who were readily available for individual and/or group sexual encounters. However, the major difference between the previous wrestler's recollections and other athletes' participation in group sex related to the fact that teammates and/or other athletes they were friends with usually participated in group sexual encounters rather than male athletes with whom they were unfamiliar. This is because group sex usually involves higher levels of male bonding and camaraderie.

Like the wrestlers, collegiate hockey players also had experiences promoting recruits' group sexual encounters which were pre-arranged with surprising confidence. For example, one hockey participant described his involvement in one such event by saying, "There was one where...we had a couple kegs done on...like a recruitment weekend, so there was a girl who we knew who would go with a couple guys, so we brought these two recruits here to the house and...she went with both of the recruits." This participant was asked to provide additional details relating to this situation, and he elaborated in this way:

> ...we had a meeting and we had all the kids [recruits] go out and they said, "Where are you guys going?" They said, "Oh, you're staying at the [hockey] house," you know, the whole team was like, "Oooh..." So we...we told the kids, "Come on you know, we're going"...you know the kids were asking, sort of asking, "Why, why is everyone acting like that cause we're staying at your house?" "Ah, don't worry, you're going to have a good time with us." There was a football game that weekend. And we said, "Don't worry, we'll get you laid," and they're like, "How you going to do that?" "Don't worry about it." So we went out to the football game, we had a party at the house, it was you know a good night, then we called this girl to come over, just you know for them guys, and so we had the guys go in a room...it was like two o'clock in the morning, they were going, "When are we going to get laid?" "Don't worry about it," we kept telling them. So we brought the girl over [laughs] [and] says, "Go in, we want you to meet these two guys," so we put them in a room and we waited, we had a couple beers and then we snuck around out onto...the roof and opened the door up and there they were you know, the one kid he had her doggie style, the other kid's getting a blow job at the same time...we were laughing and they're like you know thumbs up, "Hey [laughs] you know." It was pretty good, and the next day you know, they're telling us, "Man that was a great time, we, you know, really liked it"...

It is apparent that the hosting players' reputation along with the reputation of their particular house preceded them, and perhaps this prompted these athletes to show their recruits what they considered to be a "good time" by setting them up with group sex. Years later, this participant happened to have a chance encounter with these recruits and although he had been unsure whether or not the recruiting weekend influenced their decision to attend his university, their subsequent meeting removed any doubts. This was highlighted when one of the recruits noted that not only did both attend the university, but one noted his recruiting visit was "the best weekend" he ever had there since it was "a pretty memorable instance." It is evident that group sexual encounters on a recruiting visit can influence some recruits' decision to play for a particular team. Furthermore, this participant recalled how he and his roommates set up this group encounter for the recruits by saying, "We knew this girl, she had no problem going with more than one guy so we figured, let's show these kids a good time cause they were there for the weekend." This participant was also asked if anyone else participated in the group encounter that night, and he responded, "Nah, not that time no, that was just them. We just wanted them two guys to have a good time." Although "three or four" of these roommates chose to watch the recruits' sexual encounter, this group had other opportunities to experience their own group sexual encounters with this particular female since she was readily available whenever they happened to call. While certain athletes noted that pre-arranged sexual encounters were never a certainty for recruits during their careers, other participants challenged these notions through their ability to pre-arrange sexual encounters for themselves and/or recruits on a consistent basis.

WHEN SEX IN THE RECRUITING PROCESS GOES AWRY

Casual sexual encounters always contain a certain amount of risk for the participants regardless of whether these events occur in the recruiting process or not. While troubles can include unwanted pregnancy, accusations involving sexual coercion or force, and contracting sexually transmitted diseases and/or infections, the later was a basis of concern for previous participants, who as recruits, rejected collegiate athletes' attempts to set them up with a pre-arranged sexual encounter. A minor league football player expressed similar concerns while he and his teammates were in college hosting various recruits when the topic of sex came up:

> ...there was no girl that was automatic plus having been in that recruiting position and in the host position, you know you got to be careful about doing stuff like that because...a kid could come up with a disease you know and the last thing you want is to be trying to recruit him and he's got VD (Venereal Disease) on his recruit trip, you know that don't look too good and we discussed that as players, and I think that some of the guys wanted that (providing recruits with sex)...

This participant noted that teammates who were skilled in the pick-up scene by having the ability to converse with women were usually the ones that were in favor of helping recruits find a sexual partner during their visit. And yet, sexually transmitted diseases and/or infections were always an issue to contend with regardless of whether a condom was used or not during causal sex because skin-to-skin contact provides a suitable means for passing an array of harmful viruses and/or bacteria from one partner to another.[16] These athletes deserve credit for acting with intelligence beyond their years because they examined potential negative outcomes before they occurred rather than experiencing a major problem first and then engaging in haphazard damage control to try to fix it after the fact.

At the same time, attempting to promote sex during a recruiting visit is not always harmless fun because collegiate athletes and/or recruits' belief in their sense of entitlement has led to their use of sexual pressure, coercion, and even sexual assault. A wrestler with recent experience recalled a situation involving sexual pressure and coercion when his girlfriend introduced the recruit he was hosting to her female roommate. This participant then revealed that the recruit told the woman "she might as well just go ahead and sleep with him because if she didn't...he's going to go ahead and tell everyone she did anyway." This would undoubtedly put this college woman in a difficult position because the recruit decided he was going to attend the university, and this meant the woman could be subjected to false rumors about her sexual behavior whether or not she had sex with him. While this was a classic example of a recruit's use of sexual pressure and coercion, a collegiate football player discussed the issue of sexual assault during recruits' quest to have sex during their recruiting visit:

> ...I know there's been issues at the University of Colorado where they
> say like recruits have raped girls, but like I find that hard to believe – not
> maybe that they didn't cross the boundary – but that the girl initially
> said, "I'm not doing this" cause I guarantee a lot of these girls, they're
> there and they know what they're there for, and it happens, I mean...
> they put themselves in that situation so what do you expect the recruit
> to do, not have sex with them?

The previous participant's narrative appeared to epitomize athletes' sense of entitlement since he found it difficult to believe that women were raped during recruiting visits. This was because he believed that most females would not refuse a sexual encounter since "they know what they're there for." Essentially, this participant suggested that women should expect nothing less than sexual intercourse with recruits whenever "they put themselves in that situation." Such beliefs overlook the fact that everyone, including a promiscuous woman, has the right to say "no" to sexual activity at any time during an intimate encounter. While certain athletes and recruits may assume their sexual agenda on a recruiting weekend is public knowledge, this is a dangerous belief when women are not always aware of these unspoken or implied assumptions. Recall that an NFL player previously revealed his attempt to receive oral sex after discovering that some female hostesses were prostitutes who were hired to assist in the recruiting process. Although this participant's attempt, which may or may not have involved sexual pressure, was fueled by his belief that he was with a hired escort, problems involving sexual aggression can and do occur when the woman is not really a prostitute or an athlete's sexual expectations are not met. This was the case with a former Syracuse University basketball recruit who was indicted in 1991 for a sexual assault he allegedly committed during a recruiting visit to the Southern Methodist University campus because he thought the college woman was "one of the team groupies who hang out with the team members and do whatever [the team members/recruits] want."[17] It is apparent that both the female college student and this recruit were unaware of each other's sexual agenda, and this was particularly dreadful for the woman who did not know she was expected to have sex and was allegedly sexually assaulted in the process.

More recently, the University of Colorado's football program under former coach Gary Barnett experienced fierce scrutiny when nine women accused Colorado football players and/or recruits of rape since 1997.[18] This included three alleged sexual assaults related to an off campus party in 2001 where collegiate football players along with recruits were involved in sexual activity that was later described to police as "a big porno."[19] Dr. Michael Kimmel, who served as an expert witness for the defendants, revealed the case was not about female groupies seeking sex from athletes, but rather a group of collegiate athletes who planned a party that was intended to enable several high school recruits to have sex with some college women.[20] Kimmel also noted the problem occurred when no one alerted the women to the athletes' agenda or to the fact that the party was going to be held at their apartment – without prior notice.[21] Boulder County District Attorney Mary Keenan stood by her belief that sex was used as a "recruiting mechanism" to influence recruits even though she decided not to file criminal sexual assault charges since she would have a difficult time proving criminal wrongdoing occurred because of the nature of the party and condition of the participants; this was in spite of one woman's claim that she was raped by two men after she had passed out.[22] The case was eventually resolved when several of the recruits were not admitted to the university, and the collegiate players pleaded guilty to reduced misdemeanor charges (i.e., serving alcohol to minors) that involved "sham" community service consisting of working out in the weight room in case visitors wanted to tour the facility.[23] While the university never admitted to any wrongdoing, eventually they settled the case with the women by paying them over $1 million in an effort to finally end the matter.[24]

It is apparent that the practice of setting up collegiate recruits with sexual encounters commonly occurred between the late 1960s through 2010 among athletes representing every sport in this study. Collegiate athletes, coaches, and other supporters together were responsible for this process which was intended to convince high profile recruits to play for a particular university. Such practices resulted in a variety of negative behaviors and consequences that impacted teams, individual athletes, and women. In addition, a harmful message was conveyed that women could be used as sexual prizes for talented athletes who are entitled to sex whenever they want. In the end, the detrimental practice of pre-arranging recruits' sexual encounters is a longstanding tradition that is likely to continue until such a time when winning, recruiting, and making exorbitant money through sports are brought into proper perspective.

ATHLETES' CORNER: POINTS TO PONDER

1. Collegiate coaches and athletes are role models whether they realize and accept this responsibility or not. This influence not only impacts children and adolescents but also extends to impressionable recruits who are looking to them for guidance. This means that coaches and athletes must be aware of the explicit and implicit messages they are constantly giving because teaching and learning are always occurring. The big question left to ponder is: What kind of teaching are you involved in as an athlete or coach?

2. Athletes and coaches' power to influence brings great responsibility because this produces either admiration, or it reveals a self-centered mentality that is pervasive within certain athlete cultures. In addition, providing vices such as alcohol and sex may impress and attract certain recruits; however, such practices severely compromise the establishment of long-term excellence in favor of deviant traditions that must be concealed to avoid public awareness and an array of negative consequences.

3. Make it a personal and/or team goal to reverse negative traditions that are longstanding. This means refusing to give attention to as well as avoiding participation in any behavior that diminishes personal and team excellence. While this can include various practices involving recruits, it also pertains to the thriving negative behaviors that are perpetuated by influential athletes, observed, and then imitated by younger players who carry on deviant traditions by passing them from one generation to the next. This means always conduct yourself with the highest level of integrity so your behaviors on and off the playing field are respectable rather than regrettable practices that define your career.

Chapter 9

Athlete Voyeurism, Homemade Pornography, and Exhibitionism

One of the dangers associated with strip club attendance and/or pornography usage is that individuals can become desensitized to viewing an array of sexual behaviors, and in time such activities often lose their ability to stimulate and hold the users' interest.[1] The same might be said when athletes have access to high female availability and individual sexual encounters whenever they want. Whenever such activities become routine and boredom strikes, some athletes decide they need to experience something new and more sexually "invigorating." This paves the way for involvement in deviant practices such as voyeurism, homemade porn, and exhibitionism which offer certain athletes the challenge and thrill of involving live participants that they know in events they are able to stage.

The *Diagnostic and Statistical Manual of Mental Disorders* (DSM-IV-TR) classifies voyeurism as a specific paraphilia or uncommon type of sexual expression that involves observing an unsuspecting person who is nude, disrobing, or engaging in sexual activity.[2] Watching people, who know they are being observed such as sexual partners, strippers, or actors in pornography movies, does not constitute voyeurism as a mental health diagnosis.[3] Voyeurs are often men referred to as "peepers" or "peeping Toms," who gain pleasure from repeatedly engaging in these hidden activities which can combine with fantasies of engaging in sex with the observed person and masturbation.[4] In general, data related to voyeurism is scarce; however, a U.S. national study reported that 5% of men and 2% of women revealed it was very appealing to watch others doing sexual things.[5] Although these findings might be interpreted as viewing erotic material or perhaps voyeurism, it is apparent that voyeuristic behaviors were relatively unpopular among the respondents in the previous study.[6] This was certainly not the case according to the participants in this study.

Voyeurism, as defined in this study, relates to one or more athletes secretly observing a teammate and a woman engaging in sexual activity – without her awareness. Often an athlete knows beforehand such events will occur because he allows his teammate(s) to watch his sexual activity; therefore, it is the female's lack of awareness regarding these events that differentiates voyeurism from exhibitionism. Exhibitionism, as defined in this study, involves an athlete and/or his female partner or a group that allows others to observe their nudity and/or sexual activity.

Investigative journalist Bernard Lefkowitz reported voyeuristic practices among a group of high school football players in his book, *Our Guys: The Glen Ridge Rape and the Secret Life of the Perfect Suburb.*[7] In addition, a variety of high profile, former professional athletes including MLB star, Jose Canseco, NBA star, Dennis Rodman, NFL Hall of Fame linebacker, Lawrence Taylor, and NHL Hall of Fame center, Phil Esposito similarly discussed the phenomena of exhibitionism and/or voyeurism in their books or memoirs.[8]

I became aware of athletes engaging in voyeurism during my freshman year of college when I overhead one teammate telling another that some of the team's upperclassmen who lived together off campus were involved in these practices. In this study, over 75% of the participants had awareness of athlete voyeurism during their collegiate and/or professional careers and nearly 30% had personal experience. Collegiate and professional athletes and/or coaches representing every sport provided frequencies, in depth details, and processes pertaining to these events during careers that spanned every decade from the 1960s through 2010.

GIVING NAME AND DESCRIPTION TO VOYEURISM

Voyeurism is the formal term that is used to describe athletes who secretly watch a teammate engaging in sexual activity; however, participants used a variety of names that could include variations of these practices within the different athlete cultures. For example, a wrestler recalled, "Yea that happened quite a bit, we basically just called them 'peek shows'…guys hiding in the closet or maybe the vent on your door was pried where you could see through, there's different ways…it happened [laughing]." While this participant found women were "not very happy" when they discovered they were being observed, a minor leaguer revealed other practices that athletes used at the professional level. "The 'soldier crawl' is a common thing in hockey where one guy is maybe in his room banging a broad, [a] couple of buddies crawl on the floor and come in and watch him." Another minor league hockey player recalled, "We called it 'steamrolled'" as players during his collegiate career would hide in a room and "out of nowhere they would come out and just jump into bed with them." Unlike some events, this did not occur with the purpose of joining in the couple's sexual activity but to be "embarrassing [and] humiliating" before they would leave the scene.

Voyeuristic events could also include specific practices or even rules depending on the particular group that was involved. For example, a minor league baseball player revealed, "Yea, there was a game that a couple of guys called 'rodeo' where they'd be having you know doggie-style sexual intercourse with a woman and then a couple of teammates would bust out of the closet and he's got to try to stay in [her] for eight seconds – that was in college." This participant had awareness of "more than three or four stories about that," and other participants, including a collegiate football player, also used the term "rodeo" to describe similar events. Another wrestler found a group of non-athletes on his dormitory floor used the term "bucking bronco" to describe a variation of their participation in these practices which involved trying to keep a woman from fleeing the sexual encounter while she was on top of the male.

While athletes appeared as the perpetrators of voyeuristic events in virtually every case, a collegiate hockey player recalled an exception in which he was victimized – not at the hands of his teammates – but rather by a group of college women:

> We had this game called "playing through," actually a girl taught me this. I went home with a girl and we were hooking up in her room. Next thing I know, her door opens and her three roommates walk in naked with putters and golf balls, putting through, and they're like, "Oh, do you guys mind if we play through?" Of course the girl I was with just put her pillow over her face and she just [hid], I guess they do that to each other all the time...so then we incorporated that into our daily scheme [laughs]....[after] I went home and told all of my roommates about it. They couldn't believe it, so we started doing that to each other. [If] a guy was with a girl, we'd get naked and take off, putt balls into the room, and play through!

In contrast to females who were victimized by voyeuristic events, this athlete found this incident involving sorority women unique, fun, and entertaining to the point that he shared his experience with teammates so they could implement these practices themselves. Another collegiate hockey player recalled that such practices never involved someone's girlfriend because the "girl gets so embarrassed," and it is likely that few boyfriends would tolerate this type of activity with a woman they cared about. Still, "most girls" this athlete hooked up with could say they were "played through on" because teammates would know that whenever a player brought back a woman for sexual encounter, he would leave his door unlocked for others to "play through."

While the previous collegiate hockey players believed that most women considered "playing through" to be an embarrassing yet humorous event that was not meant to cause fear, upset, or harm, this is not always the case as some of the previous narratives suggest. Ohio State University Sports Sociologist, Dr. Tim Curry, also discovered "a show" and "rodeo" were common voyeuristic practices that were not so benign during his case study-life history interview with one prominent collegiate athlete whose particular sport remained unidentified in the study.[9] According to this participant, once a woman discovered her sexual activity or "show" was being observed, the female would typically attempt to flee the situation.[10] At the same time, the athlete would actually try to prevent her from doing so while his teammates would time the "rodeo" to see how long it took the woman to escape.[11] Athletes who engaged in these practices competed amongst themselves for "rodeo" times and setting records.[12] Once "the show" and "rodeo" ended, the athletes usually "got rid" of the women because the purpose was to entertain teammates rather than to start a meaningful relationship.[13] During these events, there is little doubt that targeted women were shocked and upset by their encounter with a group of predatory athletes that had little regard for their personal well-being. Such events were certain to produce fear because the woman was naked, vulnerable, and in the company of a group of large male athletes who she probably did not know well, if at all. Even more disturbing was the fact that the victimized women were prevented from leaving an embarrassing, humiliating, and frightening situation because this was deemed as entertainment to the athletes.

EXAMINING FREQUENCIES OF VOYEURISM

Athletes who had knowledge of voyeuristic practices during their collegiate and professional careers were often asked to discuss the frequency of these events through their awareness, personal observation, and/or participation. While certain participants noted a lower prevalence of voyeurism that happened "a couple of times" during a career or season at the collegiate and/or professional level, numerous athletes representing every sport and era of competition provided an array of higher frequencies as well. For example, a baseball minor leaguer noted "that was a big thing" occurring "once or twice [per month] in college" and could involve video cameras while a MLB player noted collegiate teammates, including himself, engaged in about "10" voyeuristic events every season during his collegiate career. A collegiate baseball player revealed voyeurism occurred "almost every weekend" but in a seasonal fashion since players had more time to devote to such practices in the fall as opposed to during their official season in the spring. This was not surprising as numerous participants noted higher frequencies of all kinds of negative behaviors during the off season since players had more time and energy to devote to partying and deviancy if they chose to.

In addition, a collegiate football player recalled, "You hear those stories I mean like once every couple of weeks some guy was watching somebody else yea" while a football minor leaguer revealed, "Oh yea, yea...that's a guaranteed college thing [laughing] that happened a lot...I've been involved in that activity myself." Similarly, a minor league basketball player recalled such practices in college by saying, "Oh yea, we did that [laughs]...I'd say every couple of months...I have been involved in that." Another basketball minor leaguer revealed voyeuristic events could be "every weekend," however, they were different and could involve a "very blatant" and "open invitation... without necessarily being spoken" for the observers to become involved. While the previous athletes, who could be separated in age by over 30 years and competed in every decade from the early 1970s through the mid 2000s, revealed voyeuristic practices happened with regularity during their collegiate careers, such events continue to be common occurrences in the present within virtually every sport in this study.

Among wrestlers, one participant noted "15 or 20" voyeuristic events occurred each season during his career although he did not believe that this was a common practice. Such disclosures show that individual perceptions always play an important role in how certain behaviors are processed, quantified, and labeled. A different wrestler recalled, "Oh half a dozen [per month]...basically just a 'peek show' type of thing" while another revealed, "That was quite often, any chance they got they would do it 10, 15 different times [per month]." Because voyeuristic events happened as often as 6-15 times per month, within certain teams, it is apparent that these activities became normalized within various cultures since numerous athletes habitually engaged in these practices whenever possible.

Although there were fewer collegiate hockey players in the study because participants often played juniors rather than collegiate hockey in route to their professional career, a collegiate hockey player who engaged in voyeurism revealed this occurred "whenever the chance arises." Additionally, the collegiate hockey player who was introduced to the practice of "playing through" revealed the prevalence of such events on his team by saying, "How often? Three times a week maybe – pretty much any time a guy brings a girl home." Another collegiate player added, "We'd do that a lot, I mean...when we first learned it, we'd try it every night almost." It is apparent that these particular hockey players differentiated themselves from other athletes by the fact that they had no desire to be discreet with their voyeurism once they decided to "play through" a teammate's sexual encounter.

Like the collegiate players, professional athletes also discussed their awareness and the prevalence of voyeurism among minor and major leaguers who competed in every decade from the 1960s-2010. For example, six different minor league hockey players representing every decade in this time frame noted players, including themselves, participating in anywhere from one to six voyeuristic events during the season. These practices also occurred at the major league level according to an experienced NHL player who revealed, "Yes...I probably say it probably happened half a dozen times [per season]."

Similarly, five MLB players recalled voyeurism during their professional career including one who said, "Occasionally, probably all [levels]...just a couple [in college]...I personally didn't see it in the minors, but I'm sure it happened... [and] a couple of times [per season] yea" in the major leagues. Although this participant lacked awareness of voyeurism during his minor league career, a long-term minor leaguer with recent experience recalled that his professional teammates engaged in approximately four voyeuristic events each season, and this sometimes included his own participation. A MLB player with recent professional experience discussed his awareness of even higher frequencies of voyeurism that included his own participation at every level; this included "probably 10" each season during his collegiate and minor league career in addition to "a handful of times" each season at the major league level.

Among professional football players, several minor leaguers revealed their awareness and/or participation in voyeurism including one who said, "It happened a lot in college and it happened a lot in pro too...let's just say once every two months that would come up...[I] probably been involved in at least five or six...probably equal in [college and pro]." Several NFL players similarly recalled voyeuristic events during their major league careers, and this included one player who revealed his unique awareness as well as participation in this way:

> Yea like I said I did it twice in the pros, but I never, I never became part of it, it happened...I mean if there was a group [sex] session and it was a known group session going on, it probably happened all the time, if it was a known group session somebody probably always hid out, you know was willing to hide out, if...maybe [they] didn't get access, but you know...I think kind of like somebody always wanted to do that, I mean if you get word out that something was going down, somebody going to be wanting to eye it up.

This participant's involvement in two voyeuristic events during his NFL career specifically related to his teammates' participation in group sexual encounters which he did not join in.

Voyeuristic practices were infrequent among professional basketball players in this study compared to collegiate players, and one minor leaguer thought players in college engaged more often because of their immaturity, a lack of intelligence, having roommates, and disregarding the potential consequences of such behavior. In addition, two other minor league basketball players provided other explanations for lower rates of voyeurism among professionals:

...it could be every weekend [in college]...in the pros, not as much like that, you might have you know your roommate, you know the guys you live with...they might, you know, open your door and check out what's going on and nobody really cares, not so much necessarily hiding under the bed stuff, a lot of times...there would be a two-on-one and things like that, it was, it was I mean...just very open, things were very open.

Like I heard a lot about that but that was never my thing, so you know I would hear such and such has got a girl up in his room, and that it was more – it wasn't necessarily so much to watch all the time – it was like that she was probably going to do you too. So that's what it more was in basketball, and "Do you want some too?"...yes, more times than not it would involve more than just watching...if you were going to watch somebody else, you're probably going to be there all only for little while and get involved, or be out and go someplace else, and do what that couple was doing.

Both players explained that a lower prevalence of voyeurism among minor leaguers might be attributed to the fact that certain players and teams within the basketball culture had a very open approach to sexuality. This means that observing players were much more likely to participate in the experience, which resulted in group sex, as opposed to simply hiding to watch another player sexually engage with a female. An NBA player revealed similar thoughts by saying, "I've never done that...[and] I've never run in a situation in the pros or whatever, but when I was in college, there wasn't a whole lot of hiding, the girl man, it was a girl who just decided she wanted to screw three or four guys, and she didn't care who was in the room." This player supported the previous narratives by describing a sexually liberal culture that highlighted exhibitionist practices rather than voyeurism – at least among teammates at the collegiate level. Such practices were not limited to college and pro basketball players because athletes from every sport in this study recalled similar events.

STAGING AN EVENT

Athletes with firsthand knowledge and/or experience involving voyeurism were asked to give additional details that described how players within their particular culture would stage these events since this would provide a better understanding of this phenomenon and its processes. Basically, athletes would watch a teammate having sex with a woman either from a vantage point outside of the room, or they would be inside where the encounter was occurring. Athletes who engaged in voyeurism from outside the room noted a number of different ways this could happen often with the sexually active teammate assisting the process. For example, a minor league basketball player noted collegiate teammates "would say they'd leave a crack in the door open" while a minor league football player revealed that he and his collegiate teammates would "rig the room up" so others could watch. He also recalled, "one time we got kind of clumsy…we were peaking through the door and fell into the room, but the girl wasn't offended by it, she just kept on doing what she was doing [laughing]." In contrast, a minor league hockey player noted a professional teammate had "beads" rather than a door to his room, and this prompted observers, including himself, to regularly watch to see if their teammate could convince the woman to participate in anal sex. A wrestler recalled opening "the vents" of his house in order to "watch and listen" to two teammates, who lived in a room below, engaging in group sex with a female who was sexually active with numerous teammates including those who lived in his house.

Not all voyeurism occurred inside a residence as various participants including a collegiate hockey player explained:

> Sometimes the guy will walk out and be like, "You know I'm going to the room with this girl, I'll leave the window open, tell the guys." And we'll all sit there and eventually somebody will like bang the window and smile at her, or make noise, so the girl finds out and gets all embarrassed, but it doesn't go any further than that. It's just a joke.

It is apparent that while some athletes are content to observe silently, others want the woman to know she is being watched because they enjoy seeing her embarrassed and/or humiliated. Such practices usually were not "a joke" to the woman since they could involve numerous athletes watching a sexual encounter without permission as this participant recalled. "One night there was probably nine guys [that] came inside and they all had their noses black from being pressed up against the screen, and the guy came out and was like, 'Were you guys just watching?' and they were like, 'No,' and their noses were all covered in black [laughs]." A minor league basketball player similarly revealed that a collegiate teammate had hid in a closet in order to watch his sexual activity without permission, which prompted this participant to remove his teammate.

Sometimes voyeuristic events involved strategic planning as a minor league hockey player revealed:

> Yea this one guy, he had like two or three [women] in the city we played in and…my apartment was right across the street and he had sex with the blinds open, so it'd get to a point where he didn't mind if we'd watch, so he left his blinds open and like we would strategize as to what he'd have to do, so we could get a better view so it got to the point

where he ended up rearranging his room, he moved the bed to the window, he ended up turning off the lights and turning on the TV cause the TV lets you see in but you can't see out, and then everyone would come over to my apartment from the apartment across the hall because I was the highest where you could see the most, so it started out just like watching...but then they'd start doing things like, "Okay guys five minutes in look for this" like he'd thrown his hand up or something or he'd start wearing like stupid hats you know so...that was [in] pro...

While this participant unwittingly highlighted his teammate's juggling practices with various women, he also noted that observers tried to inject their own brand of humor during an event by knocking on his door in order to borrow "stupid shit" which was done "more so to piss him off than it was to interrupt the female." It is apparent that these situations, which occurred "four or five" times per season during the 2000s, provided entertainment for both the player who was "on stage" as well as for the observers who watched and then tried to add more humor of their own through creating disruptions. Furthermore, these athletes, like others, essentially bonded with one another through their discussions, laughter, and the entertainment related to this shared event.

Voyeuristic practices were not always viewed from outside a room since some daring athletes chose to set up events in a variety of ways inside the room where the sexual encounter was occurring. For example, an NBA player and a collegiate football player discussed their awareness and/or participation in the different voyeuristic practices they encountered in this way:

[In] college yea...the guy who was inviting the girl over would tell a couple of his guys, "Look, so and so is coming over...why don't you guys stick around?"...and [he'd] plant them different places, you know have a couple in the closet, a couple under the bed...invite her in and you know they would start doing whatever they were doing and the other guys would just be there sitting there watching.

...that happened every other week, a guy would...call up a steady that he knew that he could say, "Ah, I need a paper typed, and I need you to come over to do it" and you know he'd get off the phone, "Alright, she'll be over in 10 minutes, who wants to watch?" and you know you'd get into the closet and you'd get in the wherever [laughing] and he'd do it and you know "high fives" afterwards and...I don't know if she knew it or not, but yea that always kind of...went on.

Both participants revealed different ways to stage voyeuristic events within a room, and the second player narrative noted that "high fives" signified the athletes' excitement, participation, and success in a shared male bonding experience which always occurred at the female's expense. This participant subsequently revealed that he and his collegiate teammates always had one or two women they could call on any given night that were willing to help them with school work and engage in sexual activity as well. This enabled the athletes to set-up frequent voyeuristic events during this player's collegiate career since there was no shortage of helpful women available to take advantage of at a moment's notice. While most athletes communicated in a direct fashion with teammates about what to do when staging a voyeuristic event within the same room, this was in contrast to a collegiate baseball player who discovered a teammate would call his roommates before he arrived to give them "some kind of password or keyword" which alerted them that "he's coming home with a chick." According to this player, this method was very successful because the women "never knew that the guys were in there" watching her and their teammate have sex. An NHL player recalled his minor league teammates giving their room key to other players so they could hide beforehand, and a MLB player revealed this occurred during his big league career as well. In contrast, sometimes voyeurism occurred because of unforeseen and unplanned circumstances as a minor league baseball player recalled:

> ...there was a guy that was my roommate that would once in awhile bring somebody back, and I'd have to act like I was sleeping, you know he'd bring them in and I was sleeping so what am I going to do? – so I just laid there acting like I didn't see nothing going on, so that's a high profile guy too [laughs]...a lot of times you would say, "Hey make sure you're not in the room tonight" or something like that and you wouldn't be there, but once in awhile, it's like three o'clock in the morning, and if you're already sleeping and he comes in, you don't get up and leave so you just act like you're sleeping still so...that would happen once in awhile, not all the time, but once in awhile, most of the time, you'd make sure that you were gone.

As the previous participant noted, most roommates, including himself, would not be willing to give up their bed in the middle of the night while staying in a hotel on a road trip just because a teammate happened to bring back a woman. Such situations are best considered unintentional voyeurism since they were not premeditated like most voyeuristic events. In addition, participants representing a variety of collegiate and professional sports revealed similar events.

ENHANCING ENTERTAINMENT

Like the voyeuristic events that occurred outside a room, entertainment again was the priority whenever athletes hid in a room to watch a teammate having sex with a female. Consequently, various participants including a minor league baseball player and a collegiate basketball player revealed an array of behaviors that further promoted humor during these events:

> We would try to do that as often as possible but it didn't always happen. I can remember one instance though where there was about seven guys in the room where a guy was getting "head" (oral sex) from a girl, there was like two guys that were underneath another bed, one guy was underneath the desk...two guys were in the closet, and there was the guy getting head...well one of the guys that was under the bed couldn't stop laughing, he was like giggling and...the girl heard, and she was [like], "Is somebody else in here?" and the guy getting head was like, "No, there's nobody in here" and then he kept on laughing and he kicked like the bed frame and so when he did that like the other five guys just ran out of the room...

> ...we had a couple of guys that really liked to stage that and I never staged it myself, but I was a participant a couple of times watching, really we had one guy who was prolific on that, "I'm going to have so and so come over here," and the one time he probably had 20 guys down in a room – and the girl was drunk, she was always drunk – and watching and that [event] was where we lived...but to him it was more like, "Hey look at me what I can do, why don't you share in this?" and to be on stage. Most of the time, they stayed quiet in the background, but...the girl was so drunk sometimes they'd go up and pat her on the butt or...he might be saying something just to make them laugh, you know egging on the sexual act or whatever with the girl, just he was being on stage, being a showman...

Similarly, a minor league hockey player recalled that because a female would not suspect that "six" collegiate players could hide in a small dormitory room in order to watch her sexual activity, the engaging athlete would humorously try to convince the woman that any noises she heard were attributed to "a ghost" who lived in the room. Larger events were the "most memorable" according to a wrestler who happened to walk into a room when eight hidden athletes emerged to create "chaos" and all kinds of laughs – for themselves. While the second participant from the previous narratives noted players would go so far as to pat a routinely intoxicated female "on the butt" since this served to increase showmanship and entertainment, a minor league football player recalled "crawling up and grabbing toes or something of the guy just to let him know that...we're there in the room [laughs]." Not all humor occurred only at the woman's expense because another minor league football player revealed that observing collegiate teammates often critiqued and then ridiculed an athlete's sexual performance particularly when "he only lasted 10 seconds ha, ha, ha."

WHO GETS TARGETED, WHO GETS INVOLVED?

The majority of participants, including a minor league football player, recalled that athletes targeted "girls that were just over to have sex" rather than those in committed relationships. Often these women had sexual encounters regularly with various players on a team so they were well known. A collegiate basketball player who noticed targeted women were "real easy" and "would do anything" also added, "You would never do that with your girlfriend because...you don't share that" type of intimacy. Such beliefs are in contrast to a collegiate baseball player who revealed his teammates voyeuristic practices usually involved "another guy's girlfriend, so it wasn't like a girl that he just met or anything." While this participant mentioned that the player's girlfriend had no idea that she was being observed having sex, a minor league baseball player similarly recalled his collegiate teammate and roommate allowed him and "two other roommates" to "come in" to watch him having sex with his girlfriend. This participant also noted, "I would imagine that she probably heard us laughing... [but] I don't think she cared." It is apparent these athletes had stronger allegiance with their teammates than they had with their girlfriends because essentially they chose to entertain others at the expense of their partner.

A collegiate basketball player also noted the type of relationship that he had with the teammates he would stage an event with by saying, "Two or three... that you could fit in the closet of a dorm room. Your closest buddies not just you know irrelevant teammates...you know but you're not that cool with." It is likely that closer friendships were an important prerequisite whenever voyeurism occurred in dormitory rooms since athletes could be together in close quarters for a longer period of time. And like group sex, voyeurism was another kind of bonding experience among athletes. Additionally, this participant was subsequently asked if voyeurism ever occurred in off-campus apartments once the athletes moved out of the dormitories:

> Yeah, yeah, you know you have a roommate and you bring a girl back... and you can see the roommate peeking [laughing]...and like silently cheer you on like...[very softly] "Yeah, go, go, go" [laughing]. Yeah... that actually happened more than in the dorm, but that would be typically with just you and your roommate.

According to this participant, having one or more closely bonded teammate-roommates who were willing to be observers, personal cheerleaders, and even additional sexual partners was more important than the actual location in which athletes decided to stage an event.

REACTIONS TO VOYEURISM

While previous narratives revealed women often became embarrassed, which is an expected reaction when they discovered athletes watching them have sex, a collegiate hockey player and a wrestler noted different reactions by a female as well as the athlete having sex with her:

> A lot of times we're all so hammered [intoxicated] that they don't even care or notice. Sometimes they, depending on the girl, a lot of them, they don't care, they think it's funny, [or] maybe they'll just cover up and laugh, I don't remember a girl ever getting really pissed off about it I don't think, I mean if a girl is going to go home and sleep [with you] on the first date, I don't think she's going to care if your roommate walks in. That's been my experience.

> Probably I want to say the one time we were at [XXX University] there were probably five or six guys hiding in the room when he brought a girl back...that time she didn't [find out], but I think the one time I came up the girl kind of caught on and she threw a fit and then he threw a fit to kind of ease her like, "I didn't know these guys were in here," and after she left, he came out and he laughed about it, he's like, "You guys, dumb asses got caught, blah, blah, blah" so yea I've been in a couple of cases where they did find out and they didn't.

Because the first participant's teammates did not hide in order to observe sexual activity but openly entered by "playing through," it is possible that the women did not feel betrayed or victimized to the same extent as the woman in the second narrative. Moreover, the actions in the second narrative suggested that team camaraderie can supersede a player's bond with a female partner. In fact the theme of camaraderie repeatedly emerged during voyeuristic practices, and another collegiate hockey player revealed that although voyeurism was an accepted "tradition" that increased "team cohesiveness," he also admitted this was something he chose not to participate in. At the same time, even accepted traditions could become annoying since they caused this athlete to respond, "Hey, get the fuck out you know see you later" whenever teammates, who were "playing through" his sexual encounter, were slow to leave.

WHEN ENTERTAINMENT LEADS TO CONSEQUENCES

Too often voyeurism occurs within different athlete cultures without the perpetrators taking the time to consider that such practices can result in severe consequences that are life changing. One participant recalled such an incident involved a collegiate football player who was "arrested and kicked out of school for being a 'Peeping Tom' in women's windows in the city and on campus and masturbating" during these voyeuristic events. As a result, former University of Michigan defensive lineman, Larry Harrison, who was a suspect in 16 indecent exposure incidents that predominantly targeted off campus female students, was convicted of being a sexually deviant person in 2006.[14] Harrison was convicted on the first count of indecent exposure and pleaded no contest to a second count of indecent exposure, which was a felony offense, in exchange for prosecutors dropping two more charges for the same crime.[15] While Harrison received a five-year probation sentence with the possibility of a one-year jail sentence in addition to mandated counseling, he would not have to serve any jail time upon successful completion of his probation.[16]

Similar consequences also appeared at the professional level when a minor league baseball player recalled that two of his teammates who were "high draft picks" were "thrown off the team for doing stupid stuff," which included "hiding in the room" to watch another teammate's "sexual activity." It is unlikely that any of the previous athletes took time to consider the potential team and/or legal consequences they could face because if they had, they could have avoided these negative events. It is also interesting to speculate what these athletes were thinking following their dismissal which unquestionably impacted their athletic careers. One can only wonder that if each athlete had the opportunity to do it over again, would they reconsider their behaviors and decide against them? In the end, it is sad and often traumatic when athletic careers end under the best of circumstances, and these events are likely to produce a lifetime of wondering "what if" for those who chose a harmful path with very bleak outcomes.

WHEN ATHLETES MAKE HOMEMADE PORNOGRAPHY

Technology has produced an amazing array of recording devices including video equipment, digital cameras, cell phones, audio recorders, and web cameras that are available and affordable as never before for recording purposes of all kinds. At the same time, some athletes use these devices in devious ways by recording displays of nudity as well as personal and/or peers' sexual experiences – often without a female's awareness or consent. In her book, *Crossing the Line: Violence and Sexual Assault in Canada's National Sport,* freelance journalist Laura Robinson discovered Major Junior Hockey Coach Graham James of the Swift Current Broncos allegedly paid his players to have sex with girls while he secretly watched and videotaped the events.[17] In this study, a wrestler recalled two boastful high school teammates were "proud" of the fact that one had sex while the other videotaped the act without the girl's awareness or experiencing any negative consequences. In contrast, a collegiate coach recalled a nonconsensual videotaping incident involving one his team's recruits that resulted in the wrestler "getting suspended his senior year" which undoubtedly impacted his career in a negative way. While various participants noted high school athletes, which could include themselves, videotaping nudity and sexual activities both with and without a female's consent, this raises a number of questions about such practices at the collegiate and professional level.

My first exposure to homemade pornography among elite-level athletes involved an individual I previously discussed who showed me some of the 360 nude photographs of the women he had sex with. A second instance involved a female friend whose sexual encounter was videotaped unbeknownst to her by a small group of minor league hockey players. In this study, over 50% of the participants had awareness of athletes, which could include themselves, involvement with consensual and nonconsensual homemade pornography within their specific culture. Collegiate and professional athletes representing every sport and decade from the 1980s through 2010 detailed frequencies, processes, and an array of methods for recording nudity and/or sexual activity. Certain participants who lacked awareness and/or experience with such practices often revealed this related more to athletes' lack of access to certain technology than anything else. In addition, over 40% of the participants noted their awareness of athletes recording nudity and/or sexual activity without a female partner's awareness or consent; 10% from this particular group with awareness revealed personal involvement in such practices.

HOW AND HOW OFTEN DO ELITE–LEVEL ATHLETES RECORD SEX?

Audio Taping Sexual Encounters

Because not every athlete competed at a time when technological advancements in the video industry allowed for equipment accessibility, affordability, and ease of use, certain athletes including a wrestler recalled their use of alternative equipment for recording sexual experiences:

> Well now I think back when we were in college, and technology has changed a lot, we didn't have a whole lot of video cameras just because they were expensive and they were big, but we would audio tape the stuff on cassettes just because that's what was available to us, I'm sure if we had those small camcorders that they have now, I'm sure we would

have, but those video cameras back then were huge and so it would have been hard to kind of hide one.

This participant subsequently discussed the prevalence and entertainment value of audio taping sexual activity:

> A couple of times, it wasn't something that we did every time, but I do remember that we tried to at least have one good one so that everybody could listen to it, and just play it a couple of times and just get some laughs out of it cause you're on tape and you'd say some really stupid shit and try to get them [the women] to respond you know and then everybody would laugh at you because you said something really funny.

Although audio recording sexual encounters with women was an occasional experience during this participant's collegiate career, it served as a source of entertainment just like videotaping in more recent times. A minor league football player also revealed such practices occurred among certain teammates during his collegiate career although they were not very common. In addition, two major leaguers from baseball and hockey found these practices occurred at the professional level among the minor leaguers they coached. Audio recording among certain minor leaguers occurred in the mid 2000s and made use of "MP3 players" instead of cassette tape recorders.

Recording Sex at the Collegiate Level

As technology advanced, so did athletes' methods for recording their sexual encounters with women. Consequently, sexual recordings now included a visual component which a collegiate football player referred to "freak shows." Like any activity, some participants recalled lower frequencies of recordings that could happen anywhere from once to a handful of times over the course of their career. However, observers should not be deceived into thinking because these events did not occur often in certain athlete cultures that they are not a big issue. Visual recordings of sexual activity can create problems for people years after the fact since they can last indefinitely. The emergence of The Internet has served to increase exposure as well as the personal harm such recordings can create whenever the world has access to a posted sexual encounter; this is especially true when high profile celebrities find their sexual intimacies online.

At the same time, certain participants noted higher frequencies of recording nudity and/or sexual activities at the collegiate level, and this included a wrestler who recalled, "Yea, I mean web cams were big for awhile, everybody was doing that...recording on your computer." While this participant was surprised by "the amount of girls that don't mind being videotaped," he also noted some "didn't know" an athlete recorded their sexual activity. Similarly, a MLB player revealed his awareness of collegiate teammates making "probably five" nonconsensual sexual recordings each season, and he elaborated on one way this could be accomplished:

> ...one of the guys I played with had a web cam and every time he would hook up with a girl, he had it set up so it'd stare at his bed and it recorded obviously on his computer and so he had his condoms within the top drawer...and he had the mouse set up where...he had his monitor off and so every time he would get up to get a condom he would just hit the mouse...and it would start recording and so he would grab the condom and go back and obviously it was taped...

Such practices often involved casual sex partners; however, a minor league baseball player noted different instances where a collegiate teammate videotaped "a steady girlfriend" without her consent; this ended the relationship in one case when the woman discovered "other teammates" were shown the tape. Another minor league baseball player revealed that hiding to watch players having sex was "a big thing" that happened "quite often" with "video cameras involved." Such events occurred "once or twice [per month] in college" with females being unaware of being videotaped in "seven or eight of those times." These players also had a practice of recording their group sexual encounters more often than their individual sexual experiences, which suggests that they wanted a keepsake of these popular male bonding experiences to replay and relive.

Recording group sex was not relegated to baseball players because participants representing every collegiate sport in this study revealed athletes using photographs, camera phones, web camera technology, and videotaping to record all types of group sexual experiences. These events ranged from the more common two-on-one experiences to the larger group encounters that could involve anywhere from 3-15 athletes with one or more women. For example, a collegiate coach expressed shock during an early season "team building" exercise when one of his hockey players cheerfully revealed that "he stood in the closet with a video camera and videotaped his two roommates having sex with a girl and then he joined in."

In contrast, a collegiate hockey player recalled, "Not as much as videotaping – but a lot of pictures" because teammates would "run in with a camera and take a picture, you know stand there and watch you until you stop, or until the girl flips out, or which ever comes first." While these athletes were not discreet when they photographed a teammate having casual sex, a collegiate football player, who recalled filming happened "quite a bit," also revealed that teammates videotaped their sexual encounters alone or with another athlete who secretly assisted from a hidden location. Solo filming was easy to set up according to a different collegiate football player who noted players would simply "hide the camera" and "the red dot" when the female "went to the bathroom." Participants who competed at every level recalled teammates showing them "where he hid the camera" as well as saying, "Watch me and this girl have sex." Such practices were not limited to athletes from the sports in this study because a wrestler recalled a collegiate tennis player secretly "filmed" himself "hooking up with a girl" and "showed it around to the whole dorm" without her consent.

Another collegiate football player revealed that although certain teammates would have "the full length computer type videos" each year, other athletes in the 2000s often preferred to make use of a different type of technology:

> ...the big thing is the new cell phone with the cameras...everyday, every frickin day some new guy would have some pictures of some naked girl that he was with or some girl performing some sort of act on him, or just the cell phone pictures were the biggest ones definitely, man I've seen so many naked pictures of girls on guys cell phones it's unbelievable.

This athlete, like other participants including a minor league basketball player, found collegiate teammates were much more likely to use cell phones than camcorders or web cameras to produce homemade pornography. When asked if females knew they were being filmed, the previous football player replied, "Sometimes yes...sometimes definitely they did not know" which was similar to certain basketball player disclosures. Filming also brought out the performer in certain athletes according to this participant who revealed, "They would be more than happy to show it to you like, 'Check this chick out, look at what I was doing to this chick, look you can see me smiling and waving at the camera here watch in a second' stuff like that."

Recording Sex at the Professional Level

Like the collegiate athletes, minor and major leaguers also discussed recording sexual encounters without a woman's awareness. While several professional hockey players noted lower rates of videotaping during their minor and/or major league careers, this was in contrast to a minor leaguer who discovered secretive videotaping was a regular occurrence during his career in the lower minor leagues compared to his experiences in the upper minor leagues. This might be explained by a team having a core of more mature players who took their careers seriously and wanted to get to the next level. An NHL player revealed that although he was not aware of minor leaguers secretly videotaping sex with females, this occurred once during his major league career. In addition, "five" of his teammates at the highest level of minor league hockey took photographs of their group sexual encounters as often as "five" times per season. One of the players referred to as "the Ivy Leaguer" took "disposable cameras" everywhere so he could supply his "scrap book" with their group experiences in addition to close ups of the female's "anatomy." Another hockey minor leaguer noted his awareness of a nonconsensual two-on-one "video floating around" and "still photos" appearing up to "three times a year" during his professional career involving "one girl and three or four" athletes "taking turns" in one instance. Like certain collegiate athletes, it is apparent that some professional athletes also wanted to preserve the memory of their unique group sexual bonding experiences in a more tangible way through pictures or videotapes. These findings also suggest that a group's particular interests rather than their education (i.e., Ivy League) or competing at higher levels (i.e., AAA minor league) determined the frequency and type of deviancy certain players engage in. In short, deviant behaviors that are nonexistent on one team at a particular level of competition can be common or even rampant on another team.

Professionals from other sports including a MLB player similarly recalled secretive videotaping practices occurred "probably 3-5" times per season during his recent experience at the minor league level. Another MLB player revealed, "Yes it does go on...once a year, I'd say 20 times" although his awareness related mostly to teammates' sexual recordings during his long-term big league career. In contrast, a minor league baseball player recalled one of his professional coaches secretly filmed the different women he picked up and had sex with and then proceeded to show the videos to his own players. This raised serious questions regarding this man's ability to be an authentic role model and credible coach because such practices could warrant a player's dismissal from a team, and yet this coach regularly engaged in these behaviors. Eventually, a woman discovered this coach's videotaping which "ended" these practices although this participant was unsure if she ever pressed "charges." Because this coach had to face potential consequences before he stopped filming his sexual activity with women, it is possible that these behaviors were nearing or at the point of becoming an obsession, compulsion, or addiction.

An NBA player with recent professional experience admitted to videotaping his sexual encounters without the women's awareness during both his collegiate and NBA career. Perhaps, this occurred more often in college because this player realized he had more to lose in terms of money and prestige during his professional playing career. This participant further revealed the prevalence and staging of these practices during his career by saying, "Oh yea, all the time guys would have recorders set up, cameras set up in the corner on the entertainment center, or you know on the shelf in the closet and the door just opened you know enough to where...he did get a good shot of what's going on." Similarly, a minor league football player revealed that he and his teammates would get their "camcorders" and "night vision out" to "film themselves" having sex without a female's awareness "probably couple times a season" during both his collegiate and professional career. At the major league level, an NFL player recalled his awareness by saying, "Off season that happened that I know of three to four times a year," and this was more common "professionally" than during his collegiate career. Unlike some of the previous athletes who had access to recording devices during their collegiate careers, this participant, like others, cited financial and/or technological limitations were the main reasons videotaping did not occur during his collegiate career. In addition, a minor league basketball player attempted to explain such practices when they occurred among professionals:

> ...sex is power and I think anytime you're in a situation where you're having multiple sex partners, it's doing a power search and I think that guys fall into that category all the time, they can't get it under control... you've already controlled a person in a particular situation and now you're watching it, so you become a control freak and...that's what motivates guys to do it.

This participant seemed to imply that athletes' greater access to multiple sexual partners essentially enabled players to have complete control over their sexual relationships with women. Videotaping these encounters simply added to this control because sexual conquests were captured for future viewing and/or shared with peers at their leisure. In time, such behaviors can get out of "control" leading to authentic compulsions and addictions which were potential issues for certain athletes and coaches who constantly used and/or created their own pornography.

LOOKING AT HIDDEN AGENDAS AND HARMFUL OUTCOMES

Previous narratives revealed athletes commonly recording their individual as well as group sexual experiences both with and without a female partner's consent. While such activities serve as entertainment to many athletes, they also produce high levels of stress, anxiety, and a sense of outrage, betrayal, and despair that I observed firsthand when a nonconsensual sexual recording of a woman I knew appeared publicly. Female victims often find themselves re-victimized again and again whenever they are not supported, believed, and cannot recover a recording that continues to resurface. Moreover, sexual recordings that occur even with a partner's consent at the time can be equally damaging to someone's reputation, self-esteem, family, relationships, and even their career whenever they are posted on The Internet or shown to others without permission, which is often the case. Indeed, secretive videotaping and/or sharing these recordings without consent is not entertainment to the female and/or athlete victims because such practices can create personal harm and even team dissension. This was illustrated when a minor league hockey player revealed that a team controversy emerged when a collegiate teammate videotaped "getting a blow job" (i.e., oral sex) from a "puck bunny" without her consent, and the woman later became another player's steady girlfriend. Players were divided over what they should tell their teammate – if anything – about the video involving his new girlfriend as well as what they should do about the recording which was never destroyed. A collegiate coach revealed that one of his wrestler's private pictures with his girlfriend were "circulated around" their team, which made this athlete understandably very bitter because an unidentified teammate took the pictures without his permission. In the end, it is apparent that this team bonded through distasteful behavior that showed little respect for their teammate's relationship and girlfriend.

Any time a sexual experience is secretly recorded, it is safe to assume that this is not done in the best interest of the partner who is unaware of these events. A wrestling participant recalled seeing two different "porn" movies that were made before he enrolled in his university by another wrestler, who with the help of his teammates, had his sexual encounters secretly videotaped. This wrestler's pornography making business was discovered after his dismissal from the university and the wrestling team for involvement in an unrelated crime of stealing.

Revenge was also a motive for clandestine videotaping according to a collegiate basketball player with fraternity affiliation who discovered a malicious event involving two fraternity brothers who carefully planned a sexual encounter for the purpose of inflicting emotional pain on a former girlfriend who was unfaithful. Acting in collaboration, one brother targeted the woman for a sexual encounter so that the other could film the event with the intention of sending it to her parents. Although this participant did not follow the legal outcomes resulting from this incident, his awareness of several other nonconsensual videotapes that were shown to as many as "15" fraternity members suggests that homemade pornography is rewarding to the perpetrators and entertainment for the viewers. Similar notions were further highlighted by an NBA player who shared his thoughts on nonconsensual sexual recordings:

> Uh huh, it goes on, you know I guess you have to have a good sense of the female to actually try to pull something like that off, again...as long as

the guy themself is not in the video and it's just the girl...they say it's all good fun and whether she finds out or not, what can she do about it?

This participant subsequently revealed that videotaping occurred more often in his NBA career compared to his collegiate career perhaps because professional athletes often have greater access to women and money. Furthermore, this participant noted players generally considered secret videotaping to be a source of "good fun" – as long as an athlete did not incriminate himself in the process. This self-serving attitude along with this participant's final words: "What can she do about it?" conveys an alarming sense of arrogance as well as apathy for a female partner's feelings and well-being.

At the same time, clandestine videotaping has resulted in a variety of consequences for athletes and non-athletes alike. A minor league basketball player revealed that a collegiate teammate experienced team, relational, and legal problems after he recorded having sex without his girlfriend's consent during the off season and showed the tape to his friends. While star athletes often find that their athletic ability can override stern team consequences, this is not as likely to happen for players with less talent as evidenced by this player being cut from the team the following season. Furthermore, a relatively new federal law, the Video Voyeurism Prevention Act of 2004, provides legal recourse to victims by prohibiting photographing or videotaping a naked person without his or her consent in any place where there can be "a reasonable expectation of privacy."[18]

Not all concealed videotaping had the goal of providing entertainment because sometimes it accompanied serious criminal behavior with legal consequences. For example, now-deceased NFL player, Lewis Billups, was accused in 1992 of drugging, raping, and videotaping his assault on a woman when he tried to extort $20,000 from her in exchange for not sharing the tape with her husband and others.[19] Prosecutors accepted Billups' plea bargain which resulted in probation, but no jail time while he was already serving a one-year jail term for threatening a former girlfriend; however, the penalty for videotaping a sexual assault on unconscious female can be much more severe.[20] This was highlighted in 1999 when two freshmen athletes from Heidelberg College videotaped their rape of an unconscious female student from another college who passed out after drinking.[21] Authorities discovered the incident when the athletes bragged and showed their production in their dorm to other male students who alerted the police.[22] Both Nicholas Klingler, a football player, and wrestler Nelson Pixler were arrested, expelled from the college, pled guilty, and received four-year prison sentences with the requirement to register as a sex offender.[23]

Athletes were not the only ones videotaping with harmful, hidden agendas because such events could involve males and/or females who targeted athletes. For example, a wrestler described a unique situation where members of his collegiate wrestling team became involved in a lawsuit when they discovered their team was secretly videotaped during the weigh-in at a collegiate tournament. Authorities were alerted to the incident when a college coach accidentally discovered the recording was being illegally distributed as "underground porn."

In contrast, a minor league basketball player revealed that he could not "count the amount of times" he heard of videotaping exclusively "at the professional level;" however, "90% of the time it's the women" and "not the guys" that recorded sex to extort money from an athlete. Extortionists not only targeted high paid minor and/or major league basketball players but major leaguers from other sports as well. For example, an NHL player revealed his awareness of about "five" players during his major league career that experienced "black mail" at the hands of "former lovers" or a woman who engaged in casual sex with an athlete and had a "boyfriend in the closet...to take pictures." One victimized NHL player made the mistake of paying his extorters money because they returned "six months later" wanting "to really put the screws to the guy" financially; this forced the athlete to contact "the cops and the FBI" for help. Similarly, a MLB player recalled the FBI alerted them to the occurrence of several "schemes" that involved a female who would seduce and then sedate a player while another male photographed the naked athlete with the women, again to extort money from the athlete.

Not all recordings containing hidden agendas involved those outside of the athlete culture because sometimes teammates targeted each other as a collegiate hockey player recalled:

...I had a teammate who slept with his academic advisor and...she was married and on April Fool's Day we placed a video camera in his room and hid it amongst his clothes and we had one of the assistant coaches call and act as if he were her husband – and the guy [the teammate] was in tears, didn't know what to do, funny as hell, and then he spotted the red light on the video camera and went berserk. It was the greatest April Fool's prank I had ever seen...and it's one of the finest pieces of videotape that we have in college.

While the previous participant felt an older woman sexually targeted and "coerced" his teammate, his prank covertly captured on videotape also ridiculed the player's underlying remorse and regretful reactions for engaging in infidelity with a married woman. It is apparent that as athletes become more comfortable with each other, heightened levels of camaraderie encourage some athletes to push the limits into more shocking behavior. This happens because the more outrageous the event, the more entertainment and status-producing stories emerge for those making victims of practical jokes look foolish. Previous narratives from the first chapter highlighted outrageous sexualized behavior that was photographed in one instance and targeted a teammate who was considered a close and bonded peer. If teammates have little regard for the way they treat each other, this should send a wake-up call to casual female sexual partners that athletes are not bonded to since these women can be targeted just as easily and with no remorse.

MOVING FROM VOYEURISM TO EXHIBITIONISM

Exhibitionism also emerged among certain athletes and/or females who were not concerned that others observed their nudity and/or sexual activity either openly or secretively. While about 50% of participants had awareness of exhibitionism during their careers, nearly one third also had personal involvement in such practices through observation and/or participation. A collegiate hockey player recalled sometimes both girlfriends and the players on the team would "walk around naked" at someone's residence because "nobody seems to be bothered by it, they just think it's normal to do it." Similarly, a minor league baseball player revealed that he and his professional teammates had pool parties with women which included "chicken fights where everybody's naked." In addition, a collegiate hockey coach recalled a particular exhibitionist event that occurred at one of his player's season ending parties which even startled him:

> ...I'm walking around talking to a couple of the seniors, and I come across this beer pong game and there's one of our fathers with one of my assistant coaches and they're playing beer pong against two of the most prominent [XXX] players in the country off the women's [XXX] team... one is like an All-American, all-time leading scorer no pun intended...and during this match the guys are whipping the girls, everybody's crowding around watching this – whooping and yelling – and the one girl just pulls her shirt down exposes her breasts and says, "Let me see you make that shot now" – and the guys are like, "Aw those are nothing, those are itty bitty titties" – you know, "Show us some real breasts if you want to throw us off," so the other girl pulls her pants down and literally puts her pussy right up on the table and says, "Let me see you make that shot now" and the one guy's dad took the ping pong ball and threw it to her and said, "You win." I just stood there and shook my head in disbelief...

The previous participant was shocked to find that such scenarios happened "all the time" among certain athletes in the new millennium, and he believed they were the result of this generation's liberal attitudes toward sex and their obvious intoxication. Various participants felt such behaviors are not surprising when so much of advertising today relies on sex and sexual innuendos to sell products and services of all kinds. Casual and non-committed sexual pursuits, rather than healthy monogamy, are frequent themes within music, media, movies, and television programming of all kinds today. Because young people today are bombarded with sex from all angles, it is apparent that modeled behaviors act as strong teaching tools that get imitated. The question is: Are we teaching youth the types of behaviors we want to see them replicate?

Exhibitionism also involved an athlete and his female partner who together allow others to observe their nudity and/or sexual encounters. Various participants, such as pro basketball players, previously noted that voyeurism was nonexistent and more importantly unnecessary in certain athlete cultures. This also included an NHL player, who during his major league career, revealed, "No, [I] never came across that – not hiding in the room no, I mean there were some forward girls I mean being in the room didn't bother anybody." One minor league hockey player supported such notions when he told how he accidentally interrupted a teammate's sexual activity with a woman in a hotel room and was amazed that the female was not bothered by carrying on a conversation with him while she sat nude. Moreover, a minor league baseball player recalled having a roommate in the minor leagues who brought back a woman to their hotel room during a road trip, and "they were very open" about having sex even though he was there and "didn't appreciate it at all." Another baseball minor leaguer describing similar practices during his collegiate and professional career also found there was no shortage of sexually liberated females because a group of 10-14 women that him and his pro teammates were friends with included certain females that "they'd have sex with a guy and let everybody watch." Players watched teammates having sex "on the beach," "in our pool," "on the lawn, or on the patio." Similarly, a minor league football player who never heard of voyeurism during his career revealed that different teammates would be in the hotel room watching television while a roommate was "doing his thing" with a woman who appeared to have an "objective" that "no one was going to stop her from." The same could also be said for athletes because a minor league hockey player recalled being in a hotel room on a road trip and as he watched television, he also observed six pro teammates come in to have sex with a woman in succession while two more future major leaguers were "heading up" to the room to take their turn as he was leaving.

Various participants including a baseball minor leaguer and a collegiate football player elaborated on their observations of exhibitionist teammates at the professional and collegiate level:

> ...I was playing in...[a southern state], we all had beach houses and there was this one guy he would have a bunch of broads come over

and he was always putting on shows, and I did see that [laughs]... we were outside the house watching and people from the next door, neighbors would always keep an eye out for what's going on, if they'd seen somebody, they'd start yelling and stuff and we'd end up leaving, but this guy and a couple of these girls were exhibitionists and they always wanted to like put a show on for everybody...I seen that happen like maybe once or twice – it was just like a porn show [laughs], they were just doing whatever yea, yea, [within the] screened in porch just for everybody to watch – the two times I did see it, it was just him and the one female...that was [at] the exhibition house, so he would tell some people, "Hey we're going to do it tonight" and they'd come and watch...just that one place, that I can remember.

I've done that, I've done that plenty of times, it's weird almost like how that happens cause the first time I've ever experienced something like that it was with my buddy...and he's like, "Dude, I got this girl coming over, she's a freak dude," and he was like, "Just when I get her down in the basement just come down and sit on the couch dude, she don't care if you watch." He's like, "[another teammate] does it all the time, it's no big deal." I was like, "Really? Are you serious?" He's like, "Really, it's no big deal." I was like, "Okay," so she comes over you know, I'm sitting in my living room and they sit down for a second to talk or whatever and they go down in the basement and I was like, "Well, should I go down there?" I'm debating to myself should I go down there, should I go down there? So I was like, "Whatever" and kind of like walked down the stairs quietly and peeked my head around the corner they were getting it on, they were doing it and I was like, "Wow!" so I walk in and I sit down on the couch like he told me to and she's just fucking, she was on top of him, and she just kind of looked over a shoulder at me and smiled and went about doing her business and I was sitting there with my mouth open like, "What the hell is going on?" I mean this was a good looking girl I was like, "Damn!" but then I watched and I was like, "Okkkay" and they were done and that was cool, I mean...I didn't do anything, I didn't get any, but that was a pretty interesting experience to say the least and like [he] said...another football player, he used to sit there and watch them all the time...now those are stories, you hear... once every couple of weeks...

Because the first participant and his teammates feared legal consequences from having "the police called" on them, this limited their observations to "only a few times." In addition, it is apparent from both of the previous narratives that certain male athletes and their female partners gain additional pleasure and reinforcement by allowing others to observe their sexual activity.

In most instances, previous participants noted exhibitionist events involving sexual activity were viewed by smaller numbers of athletes; however, a minor league hockey player and a wrestler recalled "a dozen" pro hockey players and "20" wrestlers watched a teammate have sex with a stripper/prostitute who was hired for their particular party. The wrestler also noted that another athlete, who briefly left the party, returned with a female cashier he picked up, and he similarly had sex with her while everyone watched the event. Both participants noted heavy alcohol consumption along with marijuana use among the wrestlers contributed to the reduced inhibitions which enabled these events to occur. Larger exhibitionist events did not always involve stripper/prostitutes in private party settings as a collegiate hockey player recalled, "[One player's] girlfriend will give him blow jobs (oral sex) right out on the dance floor at the [bar] and the guys will get around him...so that other people can't see that she's blowing him."

Not all exhibitionism involved sexual activity between an athlete and a woman as a MLB player recalled a unique event by saying, "One time I was called down to a room that had two girls, they were lesbians, and you know I walked in and there's 10 guys in there, so we sit around and watched for awhile." Although this player had no idea who or how his minor league teammates discovered this situation, he was part of the 10 players were "hooting it up" during this unexpected sexual event.

Finally, some exhibitionist events involved more demeaning sexual behaviors and practices that a minor league hockey player highlighted in this way:

> ...a buddy of mine...he was always going into the vacant locker room after the game you know, and she'd give him a blow job and fuck him or whatever you know. Well of course I roomed with that boy, and hell, she'd come over to the hotel at night...well I'd sit there and watch him fuck her with a shampoo bottle or something like that...and then next thing you know, she's on the bus, and that guy that was [with her]...he was done you know, so I kind of initiated that one on the bus...I said, "Well, let's get this girl, I'll get these boys going"...so I brought her in there and hell, they just dropped them (their pants), she made the rounds, you know. It was a big laugh and holler, the whole works, you know. But I mean she was there [with] every, every damn...guy, yeah. Yeah, fucking hell of a woman [laughs]...the bus was parked, coaches weren't on it yet you know.

The previous participant described how he and others would push the limits of exhibitionism into more demeaning behaviors during his minor league career. In addition, it appears that some athletes are motivated to engage in deviant sexual behaviors because it promotes greater male bonding, status, and entertainment for a roommate – or teammates – while simultaneously controlling, degrading, and humiliating a woman in the process.

RECORDING EXHIBITIONISM

Unlike the secreted video voyeurism previously described, over 20% of participants representing every sport and level revealed their awareness of athletes recording nudity and/or sexual activity with a female partner's consent; nearly 25% from this group with awareness noted personal involvement in such practices. Various participants including a collegiate football player found that although "10, 15%" of women were unaware of being videotaped, "a lot" of his teammates were "pretty open" about recording sex since "some of the girls were just into getting videotaped." A wrestler explained his motive for videotaping sex with his girlfriends included bringing fun and excitement to his relationships although unlike many athletes, he did not show any of the videos to his teammates. Similar practices occurred among professional athletes as an NFL player recalled, "They knew more than they didn't know I could tell you that...didn't know did happen, but...two didn't know four knew...a high percentage knew what was going on, they would ask for it." Such recordings enabled athletes to have a permanent record of their sexual experience which they could view and/or show whenever they chose to; this could involve a certain level of showmanship as another collegiate football player revealed:

> Oh yea, on the cell phones they damn near looked like they were posing most of the time and the one girl...she was you know giving the guy oral sex and she was looking right into the damn camera. Yea, it was frickin like – wow!

This participant noted that while females were more likely to be videotaped without consent through small, inconspicuous web cameras mounted on a computer, players consensually photographed naked and/or sexually engaged women vividly on a daily basis using cell phones.

A minor league basketball player similarly recalled "sometimes they didn't know, sometimes they just didn't care" when athletes took "phone" pictures because certain women who were "pretty much willing to do whatever" had few "restrictions so to speak." While these and other participants found numerous females were not camera shy while engaging in sexual acts with athletes, these same women often and understandably experienced outrage whenever they discovered that certain athletes routinely shared these intimate recordings with teammates and in one case a whole fraternity without her consent. Such practices were not surprising according to a collegiate coach who noted his present-day wrestlers' videotaped sex with women for two reasons: "Share them with his teammates and...use them for masturbation."

Participants representing every sport also recalled both collegiate and minor leaguers recording more extreme exhibitionist practices involving group sex. This included a collegiate baseball player who revealed his awareness of two consensual group sex videos which involved two college baseball players and a woman in one and another that showed four of his collegiate football player friends having sex with a "willing" female "video participant." Similarly, a minor league hockey player revealed a unique event involving two of his collegiate teammates who were asked on a road trip to have sex with an older woman while her husband recorded the encounter. Consensual recordings could also involve larger group events as a wrestler recalled, "There's a web cam video going around that there was like 15 wrestlers involved in it and...it was absolutely crazy, it was almost like hard to watch...I saw five minutes of it [and] I was like, 'Oh my gosh'...it's like watching a gang bang porno video, but with people you know." These athletes took the time to write the date of this event as well as the names of everyone present on the wall which suggests they wanted to savor every memory and detail. While the woman appeared to enjoy the attention by "staring" and "talking dirty to the web cam," this participant noted she later received treatment to address the underlying issues influencing her behavior. It is apparent that sexual recordings can be quite common within certain athlete cultures that promote more liberal sexual behaviors; however, these practices are not in the best interest of any of the participants because vivid, distasteful sexual behavior can create a permanent record which can negatively impact someone's life, relationships, and well-being for many years after the fact.

OBSERVING TO PARTICIPATE

Sometimes watching a teammate having sex with a woman either openly or secretively was not satisfying enough for certain athletes. This means that voyeuristic as well as exhibitionist events sometimes were planned with a hidden agenda so that any observing athlete(s) could potentially join the sexual experience either simultaneously or after a teammate was finished having sex with the woman. Various participants representing every sport and era including a minor league basketball player discovered different players "were hiding, trying to watch...because they knew what was gonna happen." Essentially, certain teammates "would want a guy in the closet and try to get him up and get him involved, and they try to set it up that way – there was a select few that did stuff like that." Five different NFL players recalled similar events during their collegiate and/or major league football careers involving one or more observing athletes attempting to participate. While certain participants noted collegiate and/or professional teammates trying to add a single observing player to create a two-on-one sexual encounter with the female, a wrestler recalled such events could result in larger encounters involving as many as six teammates. "Everybody'd hide in the closet and you know you try to watch, a lot of times guys would try to join in." This participant subsequently revealed that while secretive voyeuristic events were often "planned," exhibitionist events "a lot of times" were "not planned" because teammates would filter up to an athlete's room spontaneously when they knew he was engaging in sex with a woman and then try to watch and ultimately join the encounter.

HOW OFTEN DOES THIS HAPPEN?

An NHL player revealed that from the "three or four" voyeuristic events that occurred each season during his collegiate career, certain teammates numbering "maybe, two or three" tried joining "once or twice, [and] usually they were successful if they were in there, yea." A wrestler recalled such events involving "maybe a couple" teammates occurred "five times" during his collegiate career in the new millennium. Another wrestler noted 5-10 events that only involved the "good-looking guys [who] could get the girls to do it" while a different wrestler revealed "50% of the time they tried to jump in." Additionally, a minor league baseball player observed that "five or six" of his collegiate teammates, who were heavily into voyeuristic practices that occurred "once or twice" per month during his career, joined in the sexual encounters "probably about 20-25 times I've seen it happen, yea" because "some girls would let them join in."

In addition, an NFL player noted "it was a common thing" for collegiate as well as professional players to observe a sexual encounter with the hope of getting in on "sloppy seconds." Another NFL player recalled "that happened quite a bit collegiately" because he and certain teammates observed sexual encounters for the sole purpose of bringing in other players to participate in group sex. This athlete further revealed that his participation in about eight experiences resulted from directly communicating his intentions which ultimately made hiding to observe a sexual encounter unnecessary. In short, this athlete would say to a female, "If we do this then...you need to with my friend too, and if not you can leave – that sort of thing." Additionally, he revealed the prevalence of hiding in order to participate in group sex during his NFL career by saying, "None, it was all open, there was no hiding out." As a result, sexual encounters could be very open among certain NFL players with similar interests to the point that teammates did not feel the need to hide in a room in order to participate in group sex since it was usually an open invitation in this participant's career.

As previously noted, an NFL player revealed that group sex occurred among "less than 10%" of his collegiate teammates and "like 20%...6-10 guys on every team were into that" during his recent major league career.

A minor league basketball player recalled collegiate teammates tried to join the sexual encounter they were watching 50% of the time and their success often depended on "if the female was drunk." This participant admitted to engaging in voyeurism without joining any sexual encounters because he questioned an intoxicated woman's ability to give consent to such practices at a time before they were legally considered sexual assault. Another minor league basketball player revealed his collegiate teammates observing a sexual encounter during his career were allowed to participate 80-90% of the time. This again made hiding out in order to observe and ultimately participate in a sexual encounter completely unnecessary – particularly when women would seek out players late night for individual and/or group sexual encounters.

In the end, collegiate and professional athletes representing every sport and decade between the late 1960s and 2010 revealed their awareness of athletes, which could include themselves, observing sexual encounters in order to participate in them. Furthermore, these practices were very common within certain athlete cultures during the past 40 years, and there is no reason to believe these behaviors will diminish anytime soon given the fact that our society continues to push the limits into increasingly liberal sexual behavior.

WHEN ACCESS IS DENIED

Unlike the previous scenarios, not all athletes were allowed to join the sexual encounters they observed. Various participants including two current minor leaguers from football and basketball revealed that each had a collegiate teammate who tried to join in their sexual encounter without success because as one player noted, "the girl, she wasn't having that." A minor league hockey player elaborated on his awareness during his professional career in this way:

> I was at a hockey party...the kid that owned the house played in the NHL a little bit...it was just a group of hockey players, ex-hockey players. These guys picked up two girls from the bar. We were drinking at the bar, came [back to the] home, and were drinking more. The girls are drinking... when my friend and I had gotten there, two of the guys were up in the room with one of the girls, and this one girl's sitting on the couch. And we remembered the two girls and we were like, "What the hell is going on?" So we walked upstairs and we opened the one bedroom and there's the one guy...the girl is laying on the bed. The one guy is on the end of

the bed, and he was having sex with her. The other guy was on the side of the bed leaning his back against the wall, and she was every now and then giving him oral sex. And all the while [with] this other guy…the girl was like having second thoughts. Well, pervertedly enough or whatever, my friend and I watched for a time. Every once in a while she'd be having oral sex with the guy and then stop and be like, "Ah, no no, I can't do that, I can't do that." I guess there came a point where she would and a point where she wouldn't, but he respected that. I mean he would try… he would just stay there, and every once in a while he would try to have her give him oral sex and she would. And all the while this [other] guy is having sex with her. So, my friend and I left…I'd say at least everybody, all the males that were in the house at the time, went upstairs and looked in the room and watched those guys having sex. I remember we came back at the one point and they had moved. This was weird. The guy and the girl moved over to another bed and were having sex. And the one kid, who the girl was giving oral sex [to], he was on the bed and he was pretty much masturbating himself. It was almost like he was a movie director. It was like a porno scene where he's directing the film saying, "Oh, you like that" talking to the girl [laughs] and he didn't see us. We were watching like, "Oh my god." And then he saw us and he was acting like he saw us there the whole time, which he didn't. Then he just started talking more and more trash. So then I had had pretty much enough. I went down stairs and fell asleep. Then I found out the next morning that my friend – he crawled on the floor and went in the closet. He was watching in the closet, apparently passed out, fell asleep in the closet. He woke up the next morning and he was like in bed with all three of them. So it was like four people and they were just sleeping…that was pretty strange.

The presence of alcohol undoubtedly played a role in reducing inhibitions that enabled this event to occur. It is possible that high pornography use within certain athlete cultures becomes normalized to the point that some athletes try to find more stimulating substitutes among behaviors such as voyeurism and exhibitionism since both offer real life depictions of pornography scenarios. A collegiate hockey player observed that similar to drug and alcohol addictions, excessive exposure to instant sexual gratification can create addictions and/or compulsions that pushed certain athletes to strive for greater extremes because in time "normal" sex becomes routine and unsatisfying. While voyeurism and exhibitionism may be one way athletes satisfy their deeper craving for thrills in the moment, such practices provide only a temporary solution for a deep-seated problem that will resurface again until it is addressed.[24]

Interestingly, the participant observing the athlete in the previous scenario found he did not try to force himself into the encounter, and he was fairly respectful of the woman's limited sexual boundaries. Although every male at the party observed this event at some point that evening and four people ended up in the same bed the next morning, not every situation ends in a seemingly harmless fashion. This is particularly true when athletes attempt to include observers in a sexual encounter without the female's awareness or consent.

WHEN OBSERVERS PARTICIPATE WITHOUT CONSENT

Previous participants noted collegiate and professional athletes from every sport commonly observed teammates' sexual experiences with the intention to participate; however, these practices were not without problems as various athletes revealed. For example, an NBA player admitted that although hiding out to observe a woman without her consent may be "prankster kind of stuff like in high school or college," it can have serious consequences for a "high profile athlete" with much to lose in terms of his professional career and finances. What may appear as innocent fun to some athletes can be perceived as a threatening assault to a woman – particularly when observing athletes' attempt to join a sexual encounter without a female's consent. Two minor leaguers from baseball and basketball elaborated on their awareness and/or observations of these types of circumstances during their careers:

> Some of the girls just went with the flow, some of the girls – I can only remember two or three times...the girl freaked out and went crazy, some of the girls it took them a little bit to get going on it, but they did it anyways, but only...three of them really freaked out...yea, about three or four of them really blew a head gasket there...well they, she jumped out and that was the end of that...

> ...she never knew it, and she went into the room with a guy expecting I guess to sleep with one guy...then there's another guy in the room once they get into their activity and then they sort of switch up, and then she ends up sleeping with another guy that she doesn't even know, and then both guys I think ended up sleeping with her at the same time and I think that that's almost borderline criminal because she's not consenting, and...because there's two guys as opposed to just one, and she might not be able to say, "No" for fear...because she's at a disadvantage...

It is interesting to note that the first participant kept increasing the number of women who "went crazy" as he continued discussing his observation of female reactions to collegiate teammates who attempted to join another player's sexual encounter without a female's permission. The second participant recalled two instances in both his collegiate and professional career where players took "advantage" of a woman who was unaware that the athlete having sex with her had switched with another teammate, and now both were naked and wanted a threesome with her. This put the woman in a very awkward position that created even greater pressure to accommodate the athletes' agenda because she already had sex with both athletes, although unknowingly with the second. And, it is likely that females who were intoxicated from alcohol or drugs would be most vulnerable to succumbing to this type of sexual coercion and assault.

A wrestler recalled having two teammates who were "always about" trying to join the other's sexual encounter whenever one of them picked up a woman. Such events occurred "quite a few times" and produced three different female reactions: Some "didn't care," some "just leave," and "a couple of times it freaked them out." It should come as no surprise to athletes when a woman "freaked out" because it is obvious she realized and then stopped one or more athletes from having nonconsensual sex with her, which essentially amounts to rape. While the previous minor league baseball player subsequently revealed, "We never had anybody blow the whistle or any of that type of stuff," this was in contrast to another wrestler who recalled, "there were a couple of times it escalated to some legal trouble." This occurred because even though certain women allowed athletes to have sex with them in this manner, others realized such practices were illegal and could result an array of consequences for these men. Furthermore, this participant noted that while certain teammates watched an athlete's sexual encounter for the "entertainment factor," others tried "to jump in" as often as once "maybe out of every two occurrences." This is very frequent and risky behavior to attempt at all – much less this often – considering it is unlawful and could result in life changing ramifications.

Previous narratives noted women "freaking out" because they realized another athlete attempted to sexually engage without consent; however, not every female was aware that an observing athlete entered her sexual experience. Such events could also involve multiple athletes according to various participants. For example, the previous minor league baseball player revealed that "out of the 25 times I saw it, maybe five or six" events involved "three" to "six" collegiate teammates who changed partners while having sex with an intoxicated female who was unaware of these partner switches. In addition, a collegiate football player elaborated on his firsthand awareness of one such event that occurred during his collegiate career in the 2000s.

> ...I never had any experiences with it but...I lived with three football players...[and] it was like two or three in the morning one time and I'm upstairs sleeping and I hear him come in and they're downstairs in our living room being rowdy and I can hear some girls down there

and so I'm like, "Whatever, they'll be gone soon" and stayed asleep, but after awhile I could hear people running up and down the stairs so I'm like, "What the fuck is going on?" So I go downstairs and I'm like and I see the one kid on our team...and he's standing at the top of the stairs to the basement like buck naked jacking off (masturbating) and I'm like, "[XXX] what the hell are you doing in my house?" and he's like, "Oh dude, dude we got this girl downstairs," and he's like, "[this teammate's] with her now but, but I'm going to be next, I'm going to be next," and I'm like, "What, what?" I was like, "Whatever dude." I like went upstairs and went back to sleep, but the next morning I got up and I was talking to...my roommate and I was like, "What the fuck did you guys do last night?" He's like, "Oh dude we had that cheerleader downstairs, listen to this, listen to this." He's like, "I went down there she's like hammered, she was drunk, I went down there and you know did my thing with her, and then I came up upstairs when I was done and then this other guy [a second teammate] went down there had sex with her and did whatever, whatever with her, then he was done, and that's when I came down and found [a third teammate] at the top of the stairs you know, and then it was his turn next...but the kicker was in the morning, the chick got up and she went, "[XXX], you're a stud, you got off three times last night," and I was like, "Oh my god, she didn't even know she got ran through by fucking three different guys," I was like, "Oh my god that is just crazy." She thought it was [the same guy] every time of the three times and that's a crazy story to me...I mean you'd hear stuff like that after every frickin weekend it seemed like.

Both of the previous participants provided strong evidence that intoxication makes women very vulnerable to experiencing a host of physical, mental, and emotional dangers via sexual assault. This was particularly highlighted in the previous narrative when the woman surprisingly never realized that she had been sexually assaulted by several athletes in succession the previous night. As a result, there was no upset the following day because the woman was totally unaware of what had transpired, and the athletes avoided an array of team and legal consequences. This participant also believed this event resulted from the woman's stupidity for being so drunk that she was unaware different males had sex with her in combination with the athletes' desire to engage in a "huge" status-producing experience that provided them with bragging rights and "a good story." Today, sexual intercourse with an intoxicated woman always makes the encounter nonconsensual, and any additional athletes who sexually engage with or without permission under such circumstances essentially participate in group sexual assault and/or rape.[25]

Alcohol intoxication is not always a factor when athletes changed partners without the woman's awareness. For example, an NBA player with recent experience revealed that although collegiate teammates engaged in about "four" voyeuristic events per season during his career, "there were two situations where a guy switched up, you know the lights were out and...she of course had no knowledge that the other guys were in there, and they would switch up and take turns." This participant was subsequently asked if the female ever discovered that another athlete observing her encounter also had sex with her, and he responded, "One time she did...she was surprised at first and then she continued." This participant further noted there were no consequences that ever resulted once the woman realized that another athlete had sex with her following her initial encounter. A wrestler with recent experience described a similar event that included the same female reaction. Because these women reacted positively to these situations by continuing in the sexual encounter, this gives athletes both implicit and explicit messages that their behavior is acceptable. Consequently, these athletes are likely to continue their actions because they were positively reinforced with sex and participation in a successful bonding event that created no problems or consequences for them.

In contrast, not all women accommodated athletes' voyeurism and switching sexual partners without her awareness and consent in a positive, fun-loving manner. For example, a minor league basketball player recalled a voyeuristic event that turned into nonconsensual participation for one of his professional teammates who did, in fact, get caught by the woman. This participant noted, "She was mad, [and] I think she tried to press charges on that guy" because she knew it was nonconsensual sex. While this participant was unsure of the legal ramifications that followed this assault, a different minor league basketball player recalled that one of his professional teammates participated in a similar event involving nonconsensual sex during high school and received "some form of conviction" that involved "community service." Such practices may appear as harmless fun and entertainment to certain athletes in the moment; however, there is nothing humorous about team and legal consequences linked to voyeuristic practices that result in sexual assault and/or rape charges. Another minor league basketball player suggested a solution for addressing these behaviors at the collegiate level:

> I think that it would benefit colleges to have a course similar to what the rookie symposium for NFL and NBA players does and actually have a program that teaches guys what type of issues they're going to have to deal with and women being one of those issues and how to treat them because like I said there's a fine line between making a mistake and being lucky you know when you're hidden in a closest watching your roommate have sex with a girl, you know all it takes is a noise in the

closet for them to stop and the girl get curious and find out that there's a guy in the closet and the next thing you know, you have a lawsuit or a court case on your hands so I think they should definitely educate the player – whether or not they can have an impact on it that would remain to be seen.

It is apparent that women are vulnerable to such practices because of their intoxication, being in a darkened room, and the fact that most do not expect a group of athletes to victimize them in this manner. Tremendous access to women in combination with constant privileges unfortunately encourage some athletes to believe they are entitled to do whatever they please; this includes victimizing women for the purpose of entertainment and sexual gratification. Higher frequencies of voyeuristic practices make it essential for female victims to hold perpetrators accountable for their actions by alerting team officials and pressing charges whenever possible because negative consequences are likely to cause most athletes to think twice about their behaviors in the future. This is in contrast to certain women who allowed athletes to have nonconsensual sex with them even after they discovered a male partner had switched with another athlete. In the end, it is likely that certain athletes will continue to engage in unacceptable and often illegal practices that become normalized with various athlete cultures until they are educated and/or held accountable.

ATHLETES' CORNER: POINTS TO PONDER

1. Voyeurism is a common phenomenon within certain athlete cultures that can involve both elaborate staging and demeaning practices. Targeting vulnerable women with voyeuristic rituals for the sake of entertainment, sex, and/or showmanship is often looked upon as humorous activities. However, it is no joke when collegiate and professional athletes have experienced criminal convictions as well as expulsions from teams and colleges because of such practices. Be aware that sexual assault occurs whenever observers attempt to join a sexual encounter without a female's awareness or consent – or whenever sex involves an intoxicated woman. Think carefully before engaging in any behavior that has life-changing consequences; then, refuse to participate or give attention to any group bonding activity that uses or degrades others.

2. Despite the high prevalence of pornography within certain athlete cultures, some athletes choose to record nudity and their sexual activities with and without their female partner's consent. Both consensual as well as nonconsensual recordings have resulted in personal harm and an array of negative consequences that can impact oneself, family, relationships, and career years after the fact; this is particularly true for those involved in nonconsensual recordings. Do not wait for yourself or someone you know to be victimized before taking a stand against making and/or viewing nonconsensual sexual recordings because such practices have no place in respectable athlete cultures. Striving for excellence on and off the field includes avoiding association with any practices that sexually demean, use, or entertain at another's expense.

3. Like voyeurism, exhibitionism is also common among certain athletes and females who perhaps have allowed themselves to be influenced by society's liberal messages that constantly encourage casual sex and nudity and flaunting this to others. This has caused various athletes and women to sink to new levels of poor behavior by using nudity and/or sexual practices of all kinds to entertain audiences; the same applies to observing others engaged in such behaviors. Always avoid any sexual behavior that can humiliate yourself, your family, and your team. Then, take this inner strength and leadership a step further by voicing your objection to negative behaviors whenever you encounter them. Doing this will allow weaker athletes, who have followed poor leaders against their better judgment, to observe positive leadership that uplifts rather than demeans others and/or oneself.

Chapter 10
Athlete Sexual Assault

The prevalence of different types of sexual deviancy is undeniable based on the findings revealed in the previous chapters. Although such practices are not always illegal, they promote negative attitudes and activities which, in time, can lead to more harmful sexual behaviors. For instance, participants' insistence that sexual pressure was unnecessary because so many females were "easy" proved false because athletes' frequent use of "game," manipulation, and coercion was often used to promote sexual encounters with reluctant women. This contradiction between athletes' perceptions and the reality of their sexual behaviors with women raises a host of questions concerning other clandestine activities that may be occurring – although often denied – within various athlete cultures. The potential for sexual aggression became evident when numerous participants observed collegiate and professional athletes becoming belligerent to the point that intervention was needed in order to stop the escalation of verbal and potential physical aggression directed against a woman who publicly rejected an athlete's sexual advances. The fact that teammate and/or coaches' intervention was frequent, and more importantly, necessary, is alarming because one can only imagine the possible outcomes that could occur in private intimate encounters with women who similarly reject an athlete's sexual advances, but with one distinct difference – no one is there to intervene. If some athletes' public reaction to rejection is any indication of their potential to use sexual aggression to promote their sexual agendas behind closed doors, it would be logical to conclude that athlete sexual assault may be more common than many people, including athletes, realize.

NEGATIVE VIEWS OF WOMEN
FUELING SEXUAL AGGRESSION

Negative views of women emerged as a reoccurring theme within many athlete cultures. This was highlighted when over 75% of the participants observed athletes, which could include themselves, holding harmful attitudes toward women during their careers. This is problematic because various researchers have consistently linked rape with adversarial sexual beliefs, rape myths, lack of empathy for victims, anger and hostility toward women, and a higher acceptance of interpersonal violence.[1] Numerous participants including a minor league baseball player recalled an "absolute non-respect factor" among teammates who "made fun of girls" they thought were "filthy" and "dirty." A collegiate hockey player further elaborated, "[They're] whores, bitches, sluts, idiots, you know dumb, dumb people...especially the women that have made a name for themselves on the team are always brought up." A wrestler discussed his own behaviors by saying, "I'd treat them good...but I was an asshole a lot of times, you know say mean shit, 'Lady you're getting fat,'...or I said, 'What are you talking to that broad for, she's a pig,' and all the guys did that, you know we were a pretty shallow group." Peer influences fueled certain athletes' negative attitudes and treatment of women because such behaviors are often used to impress teammates and show off their perceptions of manliness. Some participants attributed and/or rationalized negative attitudes and treatment of women to Title IX issues, break-ups, infidelity, or rejection while others noted negative family experiences including a lack of positive male role models, child or sibling abuse, and witnessing domestic violence against their mother. Over 10% of participants thought family influences and upbringing related to athlete sexual aggression including a wrestler who said, "I think it's a learned behavior from your parents." Researchers supported such notions by noting an unusually high number of sexual offenders were physically and sexually abused as children.[2] Other researchers noted a strong relationship between abusive males, who witnessed parental violence (father against mother) as a child or adolescent, and participation in sexual aggression toward their wives.[3] However, such experiences do not destine a person to be violent because most people, who witnessed or experienced violence in their family of origin, do not participate in violence later on during their intimate relationships.[4]

As some participants previously implied, athletes' level of respect – or lack thereof – was often tied to females' sexual behaviors as numerous participants including a minor league basketball player revealed, "It didn't really help the image if...there's 16 girls on campus that on any given night will, you know, be doing sexual things that you wouldn't even be able to discuss." A collegiate basketball player further elaborated by saying, "Other than your girlfriend, they were for the most part sexual objects...you didn't really pay them a lot of mind or attention other than when you wanted sex with them." One collegiate hockey player explained, "They're ours to do what we please and whatever we want, consensually, cause...we are who we are, we'll do what we want... there's an element of respect to it, [but] you're not going to hear it...they're like winning a game, they're a prize." At the same time, professional athletes attitudes toward women could be just as demeaning as collegiate athletes since women were often viewed as "an amusement," "a piece of meat," "a cunt," people to "use and abuse," or "tales of conquest" that were used "to get off" on rather than a potential partner. Numerous participants observed these attitudes flourished during their professional careers including a football minor leaguer who found a "how am I gonna get in their pants type of mentality" was common among athletes.

Negative attitudes toward females thrived within various athlete cultures although they were not universal. Approximately one third of the participants saw positive attitudes along with negative ones including a collegiate baseball player who noted athletes' attitudes were "as varied as the guys." One minor league hockey player observed, "I think that there is two schools: There's the school that really respects women and then there's the kind that don't. I mean there doesn't appear to be the gray line, I don't see the gray line." A collegiate football player supported these notions by saying, "In general guys do talk very degrading about women...they refer to them as bitches and whores or sluts or whatever, but a lot of the other guys are very respectful towards women." Other participants revealed that athletes' diverse attitudes related to the role a woman played within a particular team. For example, a wrestler explained that while female groupies were often degraded, girlfriends were placed "on a higher level" and defended to the point that "if another guy talks bad about another guy's girlfriend, you'd better be ducking, [because] they stand up for their girlfriends." While numerous participants believed attitudes toward "party girls" differed greatly from female partners, a collegiate hockey player revealed that this impacted their treatment of certain women, "We give respect to girls who deserve it and a lot of girls don't...the ones that don't, you treat them like shit." A minor league hockey player elaborated on these notions:

> ...I think that the wives and the girlfriends get their respect...the spectator is another, and then the hockey whore is another, and I don't think they have any respect for them whatsoever – I think they are there to serve their purpose and they're pieces of shit and if they want to be treated that way, I treat them that way, but don't talk bad about my mother or sister or somebody else's wife or girlfriend just because she's not yours or somebody you don't know – that's being a dirtball...my wife or girlfriend – she's human, she's a lady – she [a female groupie] might be too, but you abused her and...they don't give a shit about [those] people, they really look down upon [them] – those are the ones that show up week after week at the party...then there are wives and girlfriends...you know treated like gold, so I think they're split into three groups.

Negative attitudes toward promiscuous women appeared to represent a common mindset among many athletes that could potentially translate into negative treatment because certain athletes have no problem using such women for sex even though they do not like or respect them at all. Although this participant found athletes treating their significant partners well in comparison to promiscuous women, this is not to say that all athletes treated their female partners with respect and dignity as one wrestler revealed:

> I don't know of any [sexual assaults], but [with] some of the guys, when I'm talking about this stuff...you can't say that I recorded it, but it

wouldn't surprise me in a second, not in a second…[because] they're so fucking aggressive man [with] the disrespect they have for women and the way they treated women, including their own partners at the time.

While this participant's observation of certain collegiate teammates' behavior made him believe that sexual assault was a very real possibility, it will become apparent that many collegiate and professional athletes' attitudes and treatment of women are in need of major improvement within a variety of athlete cultures.

WHEN "GAME" CARRIES INTO ATHLETES' SEXUAL BEHAVIOR

Previous narratives indicate that collegiate and professional athletes' use of "game" has a darker side that could involve abusive interaction, sexually inappropriate and/or intimidating innuendoes, and even blatant hostility whenever certain athletes experienced rejection. While these illustrations occurred in public settings for athletes to observe and/or intervene, "game" sometimes involved darker tactics that carried into their sexual behaviors with women behind closed doors. Nearly 13% of participants revealed their own use sexual pressure with women including a collegiate baseball player who said, "Just verbal threats [like] maybe I…wouldn't stick around, you'd go onto the next one…and that's a pretty common underlying threat…because there's so many women that are you know eager to be with an athlete." A collegiate football player recalled such tactics could become abusive, "Probably the harshest stuff I've ever heard is, 'You know what, you don't want to do it (have sex) now, you don't want to do whatever, leave, go, I've got other bitches' or…'Don't call me anymore if you don't want to do that.'" It is apparent that some athletes refer to women they are "seeing" in a very derogatory fashion since these females are viewed as "bitches" who take care of their sexual needs. Similar practices also occurred during intimate encounters as a wrestler admitted, "I was watching a movie and it was with this girl, and we started fooling around and then she stopped, so I told her, 'I thought we were going to have sex, I could watch movies with anybody…and if not, you can get out of my fuckin room [laughs] – she left, she was upset." While this wrestler found his behavior humorous, engaging in sexual coercion has caused regret among certain participants particularly when they had children and realized their young daughters could be victimized in the same way. Despite this, a minor league baseball player noted his use of sexual ultimatums were successful about 25% of the time during his professional career. Furthermore, this participant believed athletes' unbridled egos were responsible for promoting unhealthy attitudes such as woman "should be pleased that I'm talking to her," provide sex or be discarded, and "if she's not going to accept the terms of the relationship from my point of view, than the hell with her." With coercive practices flourishing among certain collegiate and professional athletes who have little or no remorse for their attitudes and treatment of women, it is easy to understand how women can feel powerless in such situations. Furthermore, females can easily feel outrage and learn not to trust once they have been manipulated for sex in this fashion. Such attitudes coupled with coercive practices can take athletes to new personal lows that have their own unique set of consequences that a collegiate hockey player and a minor league basketball player revealed:

> You have to tell them they're pretty, lying to them about [it], they always ask you how many girls you've been with. The answer is always seven. You want to make it...believable, but nothing too high where they think it's bad you know – so seven is a good answer. [Of] course they always say one. You know they're full of shit too. Tell them you care about them, I told one girl I loved her. That was one of the lowest points in my life I think [laughs] saying that to a girl, but she actually made me say it. She told me she loved me while we were having sex, and I looked at her like, "What the hell are you talking about it?" Then she made me stop until I said it. So I went, "I love you." She just kept saying it and making me say it. That was one of the most screwed up things I've ever done, but you do what you've got to do I guess [laughs].

> Well you know basically when you got "game," I mean you have what they called "a silver tongue"...I wouldn't say it was right, but I was cunning and would say anything. I remember one time I told a girl that I was sterile and she says, "I want to have sex, but I don't want to have a baby," so I told her I was sterile and I wasn't, and we ended up having sex and I went, "Oh my God what did I do? What if she's pregnant?" but you know having game meant that you could meet a young lady and, you know, if not that night the next night you could get her up to your room or convince her that you guys were going to be an item – whether you were or not – you told them that [but] hey, like the whole contest was you know to get laid.

It is interesting to note that even though both participants experienced negative emotional reactions from using coercive behaviors, this did not change their subsequent behavior which perhaps had become imbedded within their personality and identity.

The second scenario could have easily produced life-changing consequences from an unwanted pregnancy because this participant recalled women dropping out of college when they became pregnant by an athlete. At the same time, numerous athletes experienced paternity lawsuits that resulted from their casual sexual encounters with women, and often these situations were filled with conflict and difficulties for the athletes, the unwed mothers, and the children who are often left without paternal involvement in their lives.[5] Such events have even escalated into tragedy. This was highlighted when former Carolina Panthers wide receiver, Rae Carruth, hired an assassin to kill the woman who was carrying his child because he wanted to avoid the financial repercussions when she refused to have an abortion.[6] In 2001, Carruth was found guilty of conspiring to murder 24-year old Cherica Adams and was sentenced to just under 19 years in prison; Carruth was later ordered to pay the Adams estate $5.8 million in a civil suit.[7]

Sexually coercive practices were not limited to collegiate athletes as a minor league baseball player admitted, "I mean you're going to talk, you're going to try to coerce, you're going to use your lines...work your 'game' however, whatever kind of 'game' you've got, to try to get whatever you want." Similarly, an NFL player recalled his own use of manipulation:

I would have to answer yes, where I'm laying in bed with some girl and she took it to step four but wouldn't go to step five. Yeah, I would say that I probably did try to talk her into taking that next step...[when] a girl has gone to the brink and maybe had second thoughts and you're trying to coax her into it.

Professionals from every sport noted athletes, including themselves, using manipulation and/or coercion to engage in casual sex. One minor league hockey player explained that such practices could turn into "not a physical struggle or anything like that, [but] more of a verbal struggle to get them to do something." This is not to say that athletes do not use physical pressure to have casual sex as certain participants, including a collegiate hockey player and a wrestler, revealed:

I've certainly pressured. You always put the pressure on...you have to sometimes. They'll say, "No, no, no" and that 16th time they finally say, "No" – they just give in. I never physically forced anything on a girl. Never really had to in college...it was pretty easy, [so]...usually they don't say, "No" anyway – [but] the few times they did, usually I was just drunk enough...to sleep it off, just pass out, and forget about it...

There's a lot of situations where the girl might kind of want to, but [is] second guessing herself and...a lot of times it takes a little pressure to get what you're seeking...[like] in a movie sometimes where a girl says, "I'm not sure if I want to," and the guy is like, "Come on, there's nothing wrong, it will be okay," and they talk about it for 10 or 20 minutes and the girl ends up giving in...

A minor league football player supported these notions by admitting that "game" involved "continuously staying on top of them" verbally until "they just break down" a female. As athletes learn to persist and play through adversity in sports, some use their competitive skills in their sexual behaviors so that a woman's "no" is virtually meaningless and simply viewed as another challenge to overcome. Unfortunately, women who do not remove themselves from such situations and give in to sexual pressure inadvertently teach athletes that persistence will be rewarded with sex.

The second participant noted influential role models appearing on television and in movies can teach negative behaviors that can include inappropriate and coercive sexual scripts which some individuals adopt without considering the consequences. One study highlighted these dangers by revealing that mainstream, non-pornographic movies that portray women reacting positively to sexual aggression increased men's acceptance of violence against women and rape myths.[8] Pushing one's sexual agenda on an unwilling partner is a poor decision many have regretted, and this is further promoted when athletes have supportive beliefs about sexual pressure and force as the previous collegiate hockey player discussed:

> Well, forcing it is an interesting word because...I mean first of all, at bars, it's tough to talk to them, and they don't want to go home with you – but sometimes they do – and then of course, they never want to fool around at first...so it's one big force right from the beginning that you're kind of just working on...you see a guy with a girl and you're like, "His hard helmet is on and his hammer is out, he's doing work" – basically, the whole thing, most of the time, is working, working, trying to get a girl to bed with you, and it's not that hard in college actually...

Such beliefs that combine with aggressive behavior become problematic and dangerous whenever certain collegiate and professional athletes buy into the myth that sexual pressure and/or force are needed to accomplish their sexual goals. One two-sport athlete observed this potential among his collegiate wrestling and football teammates by saying, "I know that guys were aggressive towards females when it came to trying to pick them up...[because] your confidence level was so high...in season you felt on top of the world and you feel like you could do anything and be with anybody." Approximately 10% of participants thought athletes' desire for power, control, and dominance motivated their sexual assaults. This was supported by another wrestler who revealed, "They want to try to prove they can control somebody and be

307

dominant" while a minor league football player added, "It's having a sense of power over somebody...a feeling of power." A collegiate hockey coach and a collegiate hockey player further elaborated on what they believed was the source of sexual aggression:

> Dominance, this ego, you know we're teaching them all the time to put the nail in the coffin, you know stick a fork into them – strive to be the best – be dominant – be in charge – take...[control] etc. etc. etc. – and then all of a sudden we think they're going to just turn that off – then you get in a room where you have to deal with people, you know, so many of them are so high strung...

> ...players in contact sports have to be tough or they aren't going to be on the team, and that's what the coach wants and the public [wants] if you're in a big-time sport...a team or a coach or a fan, you know, fans demand you to be tough, they demand you to do those things, and you have to do that if you want to succeed, so that becomes ingrained in what you do everyday and it's going to carry over into off-ice violence because you consider yourself tough and you want to be that person all the time – and you can't just turn it off...

Sports participation teaches athletes the importance of power, control, and dominance and like the previous athletes, various participants also noted some players were not able to "turn it off" by keeping aggression out of their personal lives; this included sexual behaviors with women. Approximately 10% of participants identified sports socialization and athletes' competitive nature as influences that motivated their sexual assaults. This included a wrestler who supported these ideas by saying, "I think it's just [being] that high strung constantly, you know working out, the war, the battle, you know in the room type of thing." It is interesting to note that power and control issues worked together with sports socialization influences in explaining some athletes' motives for sexual assault. However, certain influences alone may not be predominant factors in all cases. Because there are different kinds of athlete sexual assault, multidimensional influences converge to provide a more complete explanation for athlete sexual aggression. This was not surprising given the fact that previous studies of interpersonal violence identified biological, psychological, and social factors were all important in predicting violence.[9]

Various participants discussed their observation and/or use of sexual force including another collegiate hockey player who revealed, "That's a broad definition...I'd have to say yes, but I don't think it was anything criminal...I've seen guys really push the envelope." A wrestler admitted to his own use of such practices by saying, "Did I? We tried to...[and] might have crossed the line a little bit. Fortunately you wake up and you understand 'no' does mean 'no.' [Laughs] I took it to the limit you know what I'm saying...[laughs] 'I'm gonna call the cops' is basically what she would say [laughs]...'Okay, see ya.'" Similarly, a minor league basketball player elaborated on his awareness as well as questionable sexual practices with women:

> I think that again talking basketball, we like to think of ourselves more as smooth talkers and don't have to use our physical-ness...so we don't like to see ourselves that way so...[with] basketball players it's... more directed toward our words to get our way as opposed to using our bodies you know cause the stories I know about basketball players and any incidences that could be described as rape, I would almost say that none of them involved physically assaulting the woman, but you give me enough time to talk to you, we're gonna end up there [having sex]. And you're going to go, "How the heck did this happen?" which to many imply is the same thing as physically raping a woman – that's why some of the questions that you asked I am like I'm not sure to this day...I've got a couple borderlines in my life where looking at it now, you know I pushed the envelope there...

Each of the previous participants noted athletes, including themselves, towing a fine line between sexual pressure and force that may have even crossed the line to sexual assault during a sexual encounter with a reluctant woman. Other participants recalled their awareness of teammates using sexual force with women including another wrestler who admitted that this could occur as often as twice a season during this career and result in legal charges. One minor league football player recalled similar practices during his career by saying, "Every team I've been on, there's been a few guys...that are, you know, gonna be very forceful on women." While such practices were more common during this participant's professional career compared to his collegiate career, he also admitted, "I know it happened in college." It is apparent that there are some collegiate and professional athletes who use pressure as well as force to have sex with reluctant or unwilling women for a variety of reasons, and this occurs in spite of the seemingly constant supply of sexually available females that many athletes report.

EXAMINING ATHLETE SEXUAL ASSAULT

The actual prevalence of rape and sexual assault in the United States is unknown because most victims do not report the crime; however, the Rape, Abuse, and Incest National Network estimated in 2008 that someone is sexually assaulted every two minutes in the U.S.[10] A recent national survey conducted by the National Institutes of Justice (NIJ) revealed that 20-25% of women

309

experienced an attempted or completed rape during their time in college.[11] Women between the ages of 15 and 24 are most likely to be the victim of a sexual assault with often the victim, perpetrator, or both under the influence of drugs or alcohol.[12]

Sexual assault is a legal term that is used by the criminal justice system to describe different types of forced sexual contact such as petting, oral-genital sex, anal sex, and sexual intercourse, while rape is usually defined as penile-vaginal penetration performed against a woman's will through the use or threat of force.[13] The broader definition for sexual assault enables prosecution for engaging in different types of sexual aggression such as forced oral sex, anal intercourse, or for penetrating someone with objects other than a penis through the use of force, argument, pressure, positions of authority, or drugs and alcohol.[14] In cases involving substance abuse, even if a female voluntarily becomes intoxicated to the point that she is unable to give consent to sexual intercourse with a male who "forces his affections on her," he is guilty of a sex crime that could imprison him.[15]

Research involving athlete sexual assault has produced mixed findings. While some studies have found weak associations or no significant relationship at all, other studies revealed that athletes were overrepresented in sexual assault reports when compared to control groups.[16] For example, Dr. Scot Boeringer studied 477 male undergraduates, which included athletes, at a large southeastern university and discovered that 60% of the athletes reported at least one instance of using verbal coercion to obtain sexual favors, 28% reported using alcohol and drugs to obtain sexual favors, and 15% reported using physical force.[17] Although athletes did not differ significantly from non-athletes in their use of coercive/aggressive sexual behavior, athletes differed significantly from nonathletes in their readiness to engage in sexual force with women in a no-penalty situation.[18] Another group of researchers found that although the population of male athletes at a large Midwestern university was less than 2% of the male student population, 21% of the reported sexual assaults, 18% of the attempted sexual assaults, 14% of the cases involving sexual abuse of women, and 11% of the incidents involving battery, intimidation, and illegal restraint were committed by members of sports teams or sports clubs on campus.[19]

In another study, Dr. Todd Crosset and his colleagues reviewed records from police and judicial affairs offices at 20 Division I universities (five of which were perennial sports powers) and found that although male athletes accounted for 3% of the total male student population, they accounted for 19% of sexual assaults and 35% of physical battering reports on the college campuses.[20] Male football and basketball players comprising 30% of the student-athletes were responsible for 67% of the reported sexual assaults.[21] Reports of sexual aggression among college athletes are not surprising according to Sports Sociologist Dr. Tim Curry because his study of locker room talk revealed that intercollegiate male athletes' conversations often focused on sex, aggression, and sexist attitudes towards women.[22] Since women are often viewed as depersonalized objects that exist for men's pleasure, it can almost be expected that athletes will engage in sexual aggression when so much of their conversations focused on aggression, sex, and women.[23]

I first became aware of sexual behaviors that appeared to cross the line into sexual assault during my collegiate career when I overheard a teammate discussing a sexual encounter with a woman who had apparently passed out while he was with her. While the details were sparse, I had the impression that this player had some type of sexual contact with her. During my professional career, I spoke with a female friend who told me she believed that an athlete had raped her when she passed out at a party; a subsequent medical examination confirmed her rape.

In this study, approximately 50% of participants representing every sport were able to discuss their awareness, observation, and/or participation in athlete sexual assault allegations and/or incidences that occurred within their own collegiate and/or professional teams during playing and/or coaching careers spanning the 1960s through 2010. This included two minor leaguers from football and basketball and a wrestler who discussed their awareness in this way:

...when I was at [XXX University] and I was a fifth year senior, a younger kid [teammate] had brought a girl home from a bar, she was intoxicated but she knew what was going on, and all she wanted to do was have oral sex, well...she was doing what she was doing and he said, "Ok you know, I can't finish the job [by experiencing orgasm] that way, I got to finish it the other way" [through sexual intercourse] – as soon as that happened, rape, rape charge, he got kicked out of school he has a felony on his record for rape – now we all know the girl and we know her as the girl who likes to do that [oral sex]...but he couldn't relate to that and nobody...nobody chose to talk about it – that's the travesty seriously, and it bothered me cause as I said I was in that situation to a certain extent, I just was afraid that "no" meant "no" period, no matter how excited you get – if she said, "Stop" you stopped you know, but again...when you take men to a certain level, you're teasing them if you don't finish, don't tell a man you're going to cook for him, you cook the food, you serve it on a plate, and then you throw the plate on the floor. What's the point? And I think what happens in college is that these girls take it to a point, then they say, "We got to stop," and I don't care if he's an athlete or not, he's sitting there going, "Now what?"

...the law's a lot more stricter today...in those days you know it was a dead line between rape and not rape and I think if you got a woman in your room...guys got pretty aggressive and could do anything that they wanted to and it'd be her word against his, and I think today people are called on the carpet a lot more for that than in the past...once you got her in your room she was just yours, and I didn't do that per se, but you know I did see a lot of guys kind of strong arm women but... it generally happened more with the football players, I don't know that the basketball players were a smoother lot, but I think we were, but the football players always seemed like the kind of guys that were always getting into those kinds of behaviors, they tried to have a few drinks with a girl and try to invite her back to the room and if she said, "No" they didn't honor that they just kept going with that, they could hold her down and do what they wish and...girls kind of knew that once you go up there, you were asking for trouble...I didn't hang around those guys too much, but I have seen it happen, generally like it was in the football clientele more than anything else, you know these guys were 200 and 300 pound linemen and girls just wasn't knocking down their doors to get to them, so they had to almost resort to every means necessary to get what they wanted, so it was generally those type of people...[and] the two guys I told you that got kicked out of school, they were basically like that, I mean they were kind of like pigs you know...they tried to talk a girl into their room and...if she got in there, then it was being a fly getting in a spider web you know – they tried to have sex with her, but I think women kind of knew that, girls knew, some of them did, that if you went up to this person's room then anything could happen...there might have been freshmen and some of the new girls that didn't [know], but you grew up fast if that happened to you...

Ah yeah, there's definitely been athletes up here who have raped and friends of mine who have been kicked out of school for, you know, forcibly pressuring a female to have sex with them and you know, like, eventually ended up raping the female...there's a couple of them who were football players, there were two who were wrestlers, who you know eventually were kicked out of school, but they went to another school and graduated. I would say mainly football and wrestling, maybe a couple in lacrosse...yeah, definitely [experienced legal consequences]... if they were caught and the female pressed charges, then yeah, they were dealt with criminally...yea, there's still a case pending from a couple years ago...two guys were accused actually, but one got off because he had prior relations with the female and the other guy is doing jail time right now...it was more of a, more what we talked about earlier where the one was hooking up with a [female]...and then the other one came along, the other male came along while the male and female were hooking up...[so] yea, he ended up getting involved and then...it turned into sex and later, later on it turned out that the female said she was raped.

The first participant believed that because sexual expectations and behaviors were so different among lower socioeconomic African Americans, like himself, and upper-class Caucasian women at some universities, certain athletes could be at greater risk for participating in sexual assault or rape. He found that many white suburban women readily engaged in oral sex to the exclusion of sexual intercourse while lower socioeconomic African American women engaged in sexual intercourse, but rarely oral sex. Consequently, this participant felt such cultural differences in combination with heightened sexual drives and poor impulse control could prompt certain African American athletes to pressure and/or force Caucasian women to have sexual intercourse when they were not able to reach orgasm through oral sex alone. Regardless of cultural differences involving sexual behaviors, athletes are still responsible for controlling their sexual drives and behaviors. Athletes, who cannot handle a woman's "no" when it pertains to certain sexual behaviors, would be better off leaving the encounter rather than risk forcing sex and being charged with rape like the previous narrative revealed.

Unlike the second participant who discussed events that occurred over 40 years earlier, the third participant noted heightened consequences during the mid to late 2000s were undoubtedly the result of increased sexual assault awareness and legal accountability which enabled more women to feel supported when they revealed their victimization. While lacrosse players were not interviewed for this study, various participants including this wrestler noted their involvement in sexual deviancy and/or aggression. The second participant elaborated on the manner in which certain athletes, including his collegiate basketball teammates, would attempt to entrap women for sex:

Well I mean first off they'd be really nice to them cause the whole object is to get them to your room, so basically you know it could start at a bar, it could start anywhere, you know but they'd be nice to them – like I said I never wanted to be involved in anything like that because they just seemed like trouble to me so – but I just knew some of my friends that that's what they did, so they promised them anything, say anything to them to get them into their room, and then once in the room it's their word against theirs and what happens...[this happened] all the time, I mean that was something that you come back to the next practice or game or whatever the next...and guys talk, guys tell each other everything so that happened quite a bit, even if you didn't think it was not right, you listened to it a lot of times, I could say that I did, people talk about their experience and what they did and I'd go, "Wow, you know I wouldn't do it," but at the same time, some people did.

When asked if any teammates or other athletes were ever brought up on charges for a sexual assault, this participant replied, "Never, I think that back in those days it just didn't happen, I mean...a girl would be discouraged if she came forward more or less – it was her word against his and the whole school knew it, everybody knew it, so a lot of times I'd probably say that women kept quiet." Because this was an era before sexual assault awareness was promoted through campus education, women were not encouraged to disclose a sexual assault and if they did, they were not supported. Furthermore, it appeared that shame and peer pressure worked together to keep women from revealing sexual assaults they might have experienced during this time. As a result, athletes often avoided consequences for their sexual assaults and escaping accountability usually means that one can expect to see more of the same behavior. These notions were supported by anthropologist Dr. Peggy Reeves Sanday who compared the incidence of rape in 95 societies and found those with a high tolerance for male aggression, dominance, and sex segregation also had higher frequencies of individual and gang rape; "rape-prone" cultures also lacked societal constraints or had socially encouraging arrangements which permitted sexual aggression.[24] Participants representing various sports in this study noted coaches and university administrators taking steps to insure that athlete sexual assaults were kept quiet in order to avoid negative publicity particularly when women dropped or did not pursue legal charges. Some collegiate coaches avoided confronting their players' sexual deviancy and/or aggression perhaps because they did not want to risk losing a star athlete, their position, or tarnish their team, university, and program. Remaining ignorant to such issues is another way for coaches to truthfully say they did not know the extent of their players' sexual behaviors. Unfortunately, it appears that various aspects of our society, including the athlete culture, meets the criteria of a rape culture because failing to punish such crimes is, in fact, permitting them to continue. However, there are signs of progress according to a wrestler who observed, "Nowadays, 'No means no,' back when we were going to school, 'No meant no,' but...the implications weren't as strong, the fines and the laws were a lot less stringent than they are now." This participant noted striking changes in the enforcement of sexual assault laws during his collegiate career in the 1990s through his collegiate coaching career in the late 2000s. Over 25% of the participants noted their awareness of collegiate and/or professional athletes, which could include themselves, experiencing some type of legal, team, and/ or university consequence as a result of sexual assault and/or rape allegations during their careers. While some athletes have avoided deterring punishment, it remains to be seen whether coaches, managers, owners, administrators, and even legal authorities are willing to confront athlete sexual assault and hand out appropriate consequences that will ultimately end it.[25] A wrestler revealed his involvement in what appeared to be a potential rape in progress that he failed to confront at the time: *bystander effect*

> Now I've come across it maybe...one time...I was a grad assistant and I was in the room with a another wrestler and...we just won our [XXX] title and he invited a female [in] and I was sleeping and I remember waking up to this girl saying, "You know I don't want to, I don't want to, you know I don't want to" and of course he's saying, "Come on, come on, come on" and...I mean I didn't do anything or say anything, I just kind of got up and ended up sleeping in another wrestler's closet... you know and to this day, I was wondering why I didn't intervene in that or say something in that...that kind of bothered me for a long time you know, but...when I woke up I mean he was you know on top of her you know and they both were unclothed...maybe she thought that they were just going to be kissing around or whatever but...when I heard her saying you know, "No, no"...and she was still kissing him, and I got up at that moment and I was just like, "Man you know, dude you know," [and] he's like, "Ah, it'll be alright" I'm like, "Man, you need to don't bring somebody in the room like this you know," and he's like, "Ah, she's alright, she's alright." I'm like, "I'll talk about it tomorrow, I'm gone" you know and I left so I don't know if you know at that moment if she was afraid to leave or if she didn't want to leave or I don't know, but she didn't leave you know so...[next day] I just told him you know basically, I didn't ask him what happened, I just told him, "Hey you know listen, if we're in a room together...I don't condone that type of behavior, you know, if somebody's saying "No" you need to respect that...and he's like, "Oh...she said, 'No' for a little bit and that was basically it." I said, "Well, you know I really don't want to talk about it you know" so...we didn't talk about it anymore, of course me and the guy after that never hung out or talked after that anyway so.

While this participant regretted that he did not do more to intervene at the time, he was unsure what to do because the woman's nudity and continuing participation in intimacy while saying "no" confused him. It is apparent that this woman desired sexual intimacy with this wrestler, but not to the point of sexual intercourse. Furthermore, this participant's status as a graduate assistant coach as opposed to a regular assistant or head coach perhaps made him hesitant to confront this wrestler's behavior at the time. Although this incident bothered this participant enough to sever ties with this athlete, avoidance is not an acceptable solution particularly for authority figures. A better alternative to doing nothing and leaving the room would have been to just ask the female if she felt safe or wanted to leave since this would have given the woman the support she may have needed to perhaps exit a potentially frightening and/or dangerous situation.

CONSENSUAL OR FORCED SEX?

Previous narratives leave little doubt that certain athletes were nearing or in some cases had crossed the line to sexual assault or rape even though most incidences went unreported. However, not all incidences were as obvious because some contained ambiguous circumstances – at least from the athlete's perspective – and particularly when alcohol was involved. Approximately 7% of participants described personal incidences that appeared to cross the line into sexual assault or rape, and some were even accused by a woman of rape. One minor league hockey player happened to comment on what he believed was the precarious nature of certain sexual encounters, "I've never observed anything that was nonconsensual, yet...one word could make it nonconsensual." This participant was well aware that the two-letter word "no" differentiated consensual sex from sexual assault. At the same time, his observations supported the findings that certain events, including group sexual encounters, were indeed precarious situations that could include one or more females who were under the influence of alcohol as well as additional athletes who attempted to join the group sexual experience they were observing. While such circumstances could easily blur the line between consent and no consent, ambiguous sexual encounters were not limited to group sex. Certain athletes, including the previous minor league hockey player and a collegiate basketball player, discussed individual experiences which raised questions as to whether these encounters were consensual or forced:

> ...one time in college...[it] wasn't really that date rape thing, it was both, both [of us were] absolutely liquored up, no idea really what happened, neither of us really know what happened [the] next morning. Somehow, I vaguely remember her saying, "No." We had been together all night [as] we'd hooked up at a college party. We were both hammered, and...I think she said, "No," but...I know we fucked. The next morning, we both woke up, neither one of us really knew what happened, and that would probably be the closest thing I could think of to something happening. And I think, she said, "No" because I think she had the hots for me, and she didn't want it to happen that way, and it just did. So, in that whole, big circle of forcing...that's the closest I could say I ever came to anything like that...

> Yea...there were a couple of times – including myself – where it could have been a potential, what was considered a rape situation, alcohol

was involved, the girl was willing then not willing, and then it was like crying afterwards of so and so took advantage of me...it usually involved a new girl, alcohol, kissing, heavy petting, and into intercourse of some type, where it could be like a Koby Bryant situation where yes it was consensual, or no it was not consensual, you know we started, but I wanted to stop, and he kept going forward...[it happened] just once for me, nothing happened from that because she was the one that initiated it, but it scared me because...my roommate told me the next day, "Well so and so's sister came back crying and said...you took advantage of her" and other than me being freaked out, nothing ever happened [legally] after that...[but] it could be that, you know, the alcohol loosened up the behavior and then the behavior started to become active, and then there was regret of wait, really I don't want to go through with this behavior for you know a multitude of reasons and now, you know, I want this to stop or I wish that would have stopped, or maybe I did say to stop it and he kept going.

The first participant's repeated statement of not really knowing "what happened" appeared to rationalize his participation in nonconsensual sex. This is not surprising because researchers who conducted a national study found that 88% of college men who reported an assault that met the legal definition of rape were unwavering in their belief that their behavior was definitely not rape; this does not mean all rapists are liars, but rather it implies that some men interpret their sexual behaviors as consensual – even when it involves the use of coercion and physical force.[26] While no charges were filed against this participant, he was asked if he experienced any type of ramifications from this incident:

No, I mean we hooked up a couple of more times, you know, but it never developed into a relationship. It was more, one of them drunken things, that then occurred a couple more times...I mean, willfully occurred after that, but whatever happened that first night prevented anything from – [a] relationship type thing – from developing I think.

This athlete's declaration that subsequent sexual encounters "willfully occurred" perhaps relieved some of his guilt for earlier behavior that appeared to highlight the true nature of his first nonconsensual encounter with this woman. Additional sexual encounters also may have enabled the female to overlook the events of their first night together and rethink the rape in a less traumatic manner so she would not have to deal with it. One study revealed most sexual assaults in college occurred between males and females who had known each other for almost a year while another study reported that 42% of victims had sex with their perpetrator at a later time.[27] Such findings contradict the belief that sexual assault occurs among strangers. The fact that only 27% of women whose experiences met the legal definition of rape label themselves as rape victims also suggests that denial may be operating in many of these cases.[28]

The second participant, like other athletes, discussed an incident during his collegiate career where he was accused, without being legally charged, of raping a woman he was sexually intimate with. Alcohol intoxication was again involved in the situation, and accusations stemmed from a younger and perhaps more naïve woman, who was impaired by alcohol and perhaps had become more sexually active than she wanted to be. Or, it could be that the athlete had indeed taken advantage and raped this woman as she had claimed. Because certain incidences occurred before female intoxication was deemed a significant factor in determining consensual from nonconsensual sex, the athletes often did not believe they had engaged in rape. Consequently, these incidences were not viewed as the consequence-producing crimes that they are in the present day. Such beliefs were not surprising because the one consistent finding about both acquaintance and stranger rapists is that many men define their behaviors in such a way that they actually believe that the victims of their assaults wanted to have sex.[29] Nevertheless, this participant, like others, noted the fear of experiencing firsthand the possibility of sustaining rape charges from having sex with an intoxicated woman. Furthermore, this participant revealed that he was not the only member of his team to be accused of rape:

> ...there's six or seven of us like that at least admitted [we] had been through that and again the common thread there was alcohol...usually [it happened] just once and that would scare them too and...cause we didn't have to really work hard for sex – so why have to be like that? And, nobody had like a power trip with them that they, you know, were turned on by having a woman say, "No" I mean not to my knowledge.

The above participant discovered that it only took one scare for about half of his collegiate team to change their behaviors because he did not believe his teammates, who had easy access to high female availability and sex, had issues with rejection, power, and control. However, athletes with such issues would not be readily known unless someone happened to be in the room observing an athlete while his sexual advances were being rejected. Although it will never be known for sure whether or not certain accusations involved a legitimate rape, such narratives raise definite questions. Moreover, athletes need to know that engaging in sexual intercourse with an intoxicated woman can be considered sexual assault and/or rape today.[30]

Approximately 15% of participants noted a connection between substance abuse and sexual assault or rape including a minor league baseball player who said, "I think 90%...probably 99% of the time I think it's alcohol or drug related, and the fact that...I think you're willing to do more things and pressure girls and...I know alcohol stimulates your sexual drive a bit." A minor league hockey player elaborated in this way:

> In college you go to these parties and there's nobody who's sober by the end of the night. Nobody. And when you're hammered, anything goes by the end of the night. Maybe the person [is someone] you're not attracted to at all when you're sober, but when you have 15 drinks in you, it doesn't matter at all. You're willing to do anything. I think that a lot of that [sexual aggression], if alcohol wouldn't have been involved... they would have just dropped it [trying to have sex with an unwilling woman], but with the alcohol...not in all cases.

Columbia University's Center for Addiction and Substance Abuse supported such notions when it reported alcohol involvement in 95% of violent campus crimes, while the Office of Substance Abuse and Prevention similarly revealed that alcohol, more than any other drug, has been linked with a high prevalence of aggression and violence.[31] Therefore, it was no surprise to find arrested athletes often cited drinking as the predominant activity preceding their troublesome behaviors.[32] Alcohol intoxication has been linked to both individual as well as group sexual assaults, and it is often used to rationalize sexual behavior and impair females in order to obtain sex.[33] In addition, alcohol increases aggression, impairs communication and perceived intentions, reduces inhibitions, and interferes with a woman's ability to resist sexual advances and/or attack.[34] While it cannot be argued that alcohol causes sexual assault, unwanted sexual experiences are often a product of student lifestyles that include alcohol consumption.[35]

Sexual Assault By Way of Converging Influences

Alcohol abuse is an undeniable influence often associated with rape and sexual assault; however, this does not mean that alcohol is always involved.[36] Furthermore, such events are not limited to the collegiate level because they occurred among professional athletes from every sport including an NFL player who discussed his own use of sexual pressure and/or force in this way:

> Well it started where you get a girl back to the place, you know, you guys got your clothes off, and then she's like, "No I don't want to have sex, I'm on my period or whatever" then you know you might try to force a girl, you know or whatever, and borderline rape type of stuff, yea I've done that, I've done that maybe 5 or 10 times in my life, but I mean that's the extent of it though where, you know, you get to the point,

get to the pinnacle, both buck naked and then you [hear] like, "No I ain't giving you none tonight, I want you to wait two or three weeks or whatever, I just want you to see what my body looked like, I just wanted to lay next to you naked," and you be like, "That's some bullshit," you know I'm some 30 years old, whatever age I am, I'm not trying to lay next to you buck naked and not hit that you know what I mean, so I mean that's borderline rape.

It is apparent that some athletes' unbridled sexual advances occur without the use of alcohol, and subsequent questioning revealed that no charges were ever filed against this athlete. Interestingly, this participant attempted to explain his behavior in this way:

What causes the physical pressure?...just greed, lust, desire, you know just wanting to have his own way, I mean we pampered individuals, you know what I mean we always have things go our way and you know I mean me, myself, you know at one point in time I was a sex addict, you know I was a sex maniac, I mean I just wanted to have sex so you know at every opportunity... [never] turn it down and say, "No," you know...I just wanted to have sex, [and] I really, really didn't care who she was, what her name was, or whatever, I mean she had to be attractive and good looking, but I mean I'd say, so, it's just greed, lust.

The above participant attributed his own use of sexual pressure and/or force to athlete privilege and his own sexual addiction. About 2% of participants also identified sexual addiction as an important influence promoting sexual assault. While any kind of addiction is problematic, certain sexual addictions may be particularly dangerous when they involve a partner, who may not be willing to satisfy an addict's needs and obsessions. As a result, such individuals may be at-risk for engaging in sexual aggression when they cannot get what they need because their addiction takes control in order to satisfy their fixation as this participant revealed.

Athlete privilege in conjunction with an absence of deterrence also appeared as major influences motivating sexual assault according to nearly 20% of the participants. Playing sports afforded numerous benefits that included "bending the rules" academically to keep athletes eligible, and this was only the tip of the iceberg. A wrestler revealed receiving more than 10 "illicit handshakes" in airports and after collegiate tournaments that would provide him with anywhere from "a couple $100 bills rolled up" to "$1500." Collegiate and professional athletes from all eras noted receiving an array of "services," "free drinks," and "comp meals" from business owners because they were both "pampered" and "worshipped" during their career. Casual sexual encounters with women were among these privileges. Phrases such as "own the world," "heightened self perceptions," "God complex," "cockiness of being a professional athlete," "you're the king," and an "overall sense of being untouchable" described certain athletes' perceptions of themselves that resulted from their sports participation. Such preferential treatment becomes problematic when it is ongoing and causes athletes to believe they deserve to be catered to – particularly in the area of sexuality as a collegiate basketball coach discussed:

> You know...rarely do guys, at least really good players anyway...get said "no" to, I mean even my players, I mean if somebody says "no" to them it's rare, I had one kid tell me that I'm the first white guy that ever told him "no" – and so when somebody says, "No" whether it's a sexual advance or it's something in terms of a guy, you know, getting mad at another guy, the word "no" has a strange meaning to athletes sometimes and I think that that's a big, big thing with girls, you know girls saying "no" – "Well, you can't say 'no' to me I'm so and so," and I think that's a big deal to guys because not very many people are telling them "no"...that's the truth...and my job as coach slash, I don't know if it's slash father, but coach slash whatever is to put parameters on things and tell them "no," and this is the way the world will work, but sometimes they don't like that, well it's the same thing with girls and when girls say "no" to a guy, they have a hard time dealing with that two letter word.

Because no one is putting parameters on certain athletes' behavior, this participant felt this could lead to sexual force and aggression whenever a woman told an athlete to stop his sexual advances. Moreover, these insights were supported through the previous NFL player's account of his sexual pressure/force with females. Furthermore, women who make themselves somewhat sexually available to an unfamiliar athlete become particularly vulnerable to assault because the use of token resistance in order to avoid appearing promiscuous increases the likelihood of sexual victimization.[37] This may occur because an unfamiliar woman on a date and particularly someone who has just been picked up at a party or bar may not be respected in the first place, and much less so when they are willing to comply with some, but not all of an athlete's sexual agenda. Sexual frustration and subsequent anger from rejection can lead to force/aggression whenever athletes believe a woman should accommodate all of their sexual requests. In addition, many collegiate and professional athletes have avoided consequences for harmful behaviors including sexual aggression, and this absence of deterrence suggests that some athletes may be more willing to engage in criminal acts because they have observed other athletes avoiding consequences for similar behaviors.[38]

Speculation surrounding athlete privilege was put to the test when researchers examined arrest and conviction rates for collegiate and professional athletes accused of felony sexual assaults against women and compared these with national crime data to determine whether elite athletes were receiving preferential treatment by the criminal justice system.[39] From the 217 complaints in the study relating to athletes who were initially reported to police for felonious sex crimes between 1986 and 1995, 79% of the athletes were arrested while only 24% were successfully prosecuted by law enforcement officials.[40] In contrast, national data for rape convictions in 1990 revealed that although 32% of these reports resulted in arrests, 54% of nonathletes from the national sample were convicted.[41] Athletes were not treated with more leniency because they were more likely to be arrested for sex charges than men in the national sample; however, athletes managed to avoid convictions much more readily than nonathletes perhaps because athletes have the resources to hire the best defense attorneys available.[42] While this has enabled certain athletes to escape accountability, most would agree that legal proceedings are both emotionally and financially costly regardless of the outcome.

SEXUAL ASSAULTS ON YOUNGER FEMALES

Females between the ages of 15 and 24 are most likely to be the victim of a sexual assault, and so it was no surprise to discover collegiate or professional athletes' sexual assaults also targeted younger females.[43] State law determines whether sexual interaction between an adult and a child is considered child molestation (usually involving children under 12), statutory rape (involving youth 12-17), or a consensual act which can involve individuals between the ages of 16 and 18 although it can be as low as 14 or 15 in certain states.[44]

I encountered numerous high school females actively trying to become sexually involved with teammates during my professional hockey career. As the team captain, I tried at times to discourage underage females as well as my teammates from these liaisons although I was often unsuccessful. Because sexual encounters with underage females carry much harsher legal ramifications today compared to when and where I competed professionally, athletes must think before they sexually act because they have much to lose as the following narratives reveal. Participants were not asked specifically about sexual involvement with younger females; however, approximately 5% of participants revealed their awareness of athletes being charged with statutory rape, child molestation, or gang raping a teenage female. Two wrestlers and a major league baseball player discussed their awareness of such sex crimes in this way:

My freshman year, there was a football player who was a dorm man on the lower level. He was accused of raping a 16-year-old who apparently had run away from her home and was staying with him. I don't know if he met her at a party or whatever, but I guess when she finally decided to go home, she accused him of rape, [he was a] 19-year-old college student and I believe the girl was 15 or 16. I guessed he housed her for a week or something...I don't know if he was convicted or not, but he was accused and had to go through court many times, I believe. I'm not sure what the result was...[but] yeah, he was kicked off the football team...I don't know if he was kicked out, but he left school.

I had a guy that I coached come up on sexual charges, child molestation charges, about I want to say probably about four or five years after he graduated...[and] he ended up getting sentenced to prison. He was a counselor at a group home for children and, you know, I remember when I was going back to town I saw him...with the children and I was like, "Man, what a great job this guy's doing you know," and come to find out I got a call from another ex-wrestler who I coached and was telling me about the situation, and what happened and I was like, "Geez, I would never have suspected this kid, he was always so nice, making good grades, always volunteering in the community," and to have something like that happen, just totally like shocked me...I know he was sentenced to prison, I didn't follow it too much after that.

One guy I played with in the...major leagues ended up, actually I think convicted [and] served some type of a sentence, you know, he was in a town and ended up having sex with a 15-year-old and I'm positive the girl lied about her age and he just you know went through what he did – not realizing that the girl was that young, but he ended up in trouble for it...[still] he went out and had a decent career...I think that most people realize that he was lied to and, you know, I don't remember the whole details, but...we'd go to cities and fans would heckle him about it, but it really didn't bother him that much.

An NFL football player in this study also revealed that as 21 and 22-year-old rookies, he and his teammate met a 16-year-old girl and her 16 to 17-year-old female friend when they happened to sneak past the hotel security and make it up to their floor. Although it is not known for certain whether this encounter resulted in sexual activity, it is likely. Like the previous narrative, this event raised similar concerns because it involved perhaps one and possibly two underage females. Because some younger females are willing to lie and manipulate in order to meet with athletes often for the purpose of having sex, athletes must take precaution because this could result in harsh legal ramifications as some have discovered. At the same time, athletes as well as coaches who act as sexual predators targeting children or teenagers often find themselves experiencing long-term prison sentences as we have seen.

Not all sexual assaults on younger females involved individual athletes because some incidences involved multiple perpetrators as a major league baseball player with recent experience and two minor leaguers from baseball and basketball revealed in this way:

> This guy I played with in college...he was with another [pro] team... [and] these two guys got this underage girl drunk in spring training, next thing you know she's passed out in the bed and they both of them had their way with her and she came to and yea just left. And I'm like, "Did they get in trouble?" And...they're like, "No, she just left" and they haven't heard from her since. So nothing happened, I knew one of the guys that did it and I mean he was kind of a high profile guy and nothing, nothing came of it so yea he didn't get in trouble...[at the] minor league [level].

> I do remember an incident...about four or five [affiliated] minor leaguers that were all from the Dominican Republic that were 18 or 19 years old in the United States for maybe the first or second time and they'd actually gang raped a...[high school] girl...I don't want to necessarily say gang rape, it wasn't like they held her against her will, but they all had sex with her at the same time over a two or three hour period and they were all brought up on charges...

> Oh yeah in the [minor leagues for basketball], there was a guy who was charged with the standing in the room unbeknownst [to] the female... and they would come out and participate unbeknownst...until she found out and then he was arrested. This happened when this guy was in high school before I started playing with him, before his pro career... apparently as the story goes they came out of a closet or something and started participating and switched and the person [the girl] wasn't supposed to know and then found out. I don't know how you can even conjure up such a situation but that is apparently what occurred...[they were] definitely charged and I think definitely had to serve community service time, so yeah some form of conviction. I'm not exactly sure what it finally was but [he] was penalized by the courts.

Unlike the group sexual assault in the first narrative, the second participant was aware of a group sexual assault during his professional career that resulted in three of the five players being convicted of sexual battery and sentenced to two years in prison while a fourth player's charges were dropped after he testified in the case against the fifth player who was subsequently acquitted.[45] Although the players insisted the female consented to group sex, Assistant State Attorney Steve Levin found the men targeted the girl because she was naïve and scared.[46] In addition, the third participant described a voyeuristic event in which his teammate observed a friend's sexual encounter in order to participate in nonconsensual sexual intercourse with the girl, who pressed charges after discovering this. Athletes must carefully examine their sexual conduct and discipline their behavior because sexual involvement with an underage female often results in legal consequences.

SEXUAL ASSAULTS ON SEVERELY INTOXICATED FEMALES

Nonconsensual sex does not only include coercion, pressure, or force to engage in sexual behaviors against a female's will because it can also involve sexual activities with a woman who is so severely intoxicated and/or passed out from drugs or alcohol that she is unaware of her involvement. In these instances, athletes cross the line into sexual assault and rape whenever intimacy involves a semi- or unconscious female who does not have the ability consent or resist someone's advances once a sexual encounter begins.[47] Numerous participants from all sports noted athletes leaving with a woman despite her highly intoxicated condition including a minor league baseball player who revealed, "Passed out no, basically, physically in a state that they shouldn't [be so] that a 'yes' from a girl in that state shouldn't ever be thought of as a true 'yes?' yea, I mean guys having sex with girls that were way too drunk to know anybody... that was [in] college for sure." This participant was aware of his teammates' involvement in "two or three" of these incidences while other participants, including a collegiate football player, noted situations where teammates implied they had sex with highly intoxicated women who were in all likelihood passed-out during the sexual encounter because they could hardly stand and were not able to walk home. Such practices were highlighted by a wrestler who recalled, "I know someone, a teammate, basically he had the girl draped over his shoulder and walked out the door with her, but where he was headed with her I'm not sure...I don't know the final result, but...yea, her motor skills weren't good."

While the previous disclosures raised definite concerns regarding females' ability to give sexual consent, approximately 30% of the participants representing every sport and level of competition from high school through the major leagues described their awareness of athlete sexual assaults on passed-out women, which means this was not an uncommon event. Sexual assaults on passed-out females involving high school athletes representing several different sports accounted for 10% of these incidences while the remaining cases involved collegiate or professional athletes. An NFL player recalled two such incidences during his collegiate career that produced investigations, legal "discussion," arbitrators, and intervention but no formal charges against any teammates. Similarly, a minor league basketball player revealed that certain collegiate teammates were seldom if ever charged with attempted or completed sexual assaults on passed-out women because such practices were kept quiet at his private, religious-affiliated university. Furthermore, the females who were victimized often had deviant sexual histories which they did not want revealed publicly. Therefore, it is easy to understand how sexual assaults and rapes continue to flourish when institutions, teams, and the women themselves have no desire to disclose or confront sexual misconduct. Interestingly, a collegiate hockey player highlighted these practices in this way:

> Oh yeah, you know when I was at [XXX University] – [some players] just feeling that they've been kind of like let down like, "Don't pass out on me…you know I spent the night with you and you can't handle your liquor so you're just going to" – sort of just…talking about it in the locker room, you know, "I pulled the girl's [pants off] – banged her up the butt and took off."

This participant, as an assistant coach, overheard one of his collegiate players discussing his own sexual assault on a passed-out woman, and yet he did not mention confronting this athlete's behavior. He did, however, attribute this type of assault to athletes' "sense of entitlement" because "these guys think that they're invincible, that they had some God-given right that they get to be forgiven for whatever they decide to do." However, coaches, like universities, that fail to address negative behaviors such as sexual assault are essentially giving permission for these behaviors to continue. Interestingly, another collegiate hockey player along with a minor league hockey player elaborated on their firsthand observations and/or experiences with these practices:

> I've come across that once. I did see it and guys were talking about it the next day. [It was a] situation was where the girl is passed [out] and he just kept going further and further. I don't think he had sex with her, but he was fondling her while she was passed out. He was scared the next day. He probably knew he went too far. That was the one instance that I've been part of that I seen [it]…but as far as the other things it's just been second hand stories. But you do hear things like that, unfortunately…the one guy was in the room by himself and the next day he was scared. And at the other end, a couple of guys would laugh about it the next day. And there were a couple of other guys who were like, "That's serious stuff.

Stay away from that girl. That's serious. That's not good. That's serious charges, accusations if that stuff comes out."

Again, I think most were college and no, actually go back to high school a little bit, [but] more so college....stories, you know a dozen maybe, you know actual like being [there], whether I was involved personally with a girl that was fairly close [to] something [like that], a couple times... knowledge of guys, walking in on [that], just knowing, half dozen times, I don't know something like that...[it's] just late night you're wanting to get a piece of ass, and it's going fine, and you're both drinking, and you get back to wherever you're both going to...and you're half out of it [drunk], she's half out of it, yet whether you really know you're saying, "Yes" or saying, "No," or whether you were a little bit more [drunk], or whether she was a little bit more [out of it]. At that point you just want to get your dick wet, and you get your dick wet.

The previous participants were among the 10% who actually witnessed a sexual assault, and although the above incidences involved individual assaults, group assaults on a highly intoxicated or passed out female were even more common. Different reactions to the assault the first participant observed such as laughter can be interpreted as a defense mechanism for feeling uncomfortable, or it can also imply a high level of apathy for women in these situations.

Sexual assaults on passed out women also occurred at the professional level as a major league baseball player revealed by saying, "Yea, I heard about it but I was never around it – [at] all levels" which included college, minor, and the major leagues. Similarly, an NHL player discussed the prevalence of such incidences by saying, "Yea, I think there's probably been a bunch of times that that's happened...[and] I would probably say it was one [player rather than a group assault] – [in the] majors." Another minor league hockey player elaborated on the extent of such practices during his professional career:

Oh yeah...it goes back to the alcohol factor, I mean the girl drinks too much, [and] that would be a case of forcing something on somebody that maybe doesn't want it...so yeah....probably about 10 times during my whole career did I hear something like that. I don't think any guy wants to admit that...I think that's where your sex addict comes in and a guy like that is oversexed...no normal person would do that – no normal thinking person would.

This participant attributed his awareness of approximately 10 sexual assaults on passed-out women to professional athletes' intoxication in combination with their sexual addiction because he believed these practices were outside the realm of normal behavior.

Sometimes athletes were the victims of such practices as a wrestler recalled a female's sexual assault on teammate by saying, "I remember one night at a party and this guy was in the back of the car and they had a T-top, and this girl was groping on this guy while he was passed out." Another wrestler recalled a teammate aggressively removing a woman from his room after realizing she was raping him while he was incoherent from alcohol intoxication. Still another wrestler discovered his teammates encouraged a woman to disrobe and have her way with him when he was passed out. Although he awoke naked and confused, he considered this event more of a prank than an assault. In general, women's sexual assaults on men are uncommon although previous disclosures prove that athletes are not immune to being sexually assaulted when they are incapacitated.[48] Still, most participants found female-generated sexual assaults to be laughable events; however, there is nothing humorous when a group of athletes sexually assault a highly intoxicated and/or passed-out woman.

GROUP SEXUAL ASSAULTS ON HIGHLY INTOXICATED WOMEN

Sexual assaults and rapes targeting highly intoxicated and/or passed out females often involved groups of athletes during collegiate and/or professional careers spanning the early 1960s through 2010. As previously noted, approximately 30% of the participants were aware of sexual assaults on passed out females, 25% had awareness of group sexual assaults, and 10% witnessed a sexual assault that often involved multiple athletes and a highly intoxicated or passed out woman. Various participants, including an NBA and an NFL player, recalled their observations of group sexual assaults on highly intoxicated and/or passed-out females during their collegiate careers:

> College...[whew] I was just in a certain situation and there was numerous athletes at this party and a bunch of excessive drinking and you know one particular female there she was nice and nice looking and everybody always wanted her and whatever, she did pass out, and she wasn't necessarily passed out, but she wasn't coherent and guys basically they – I didn't see it – but they were going in and out of the room like running a train on her...I'd say it had to be at least four or five and there was probably more than that, but there was certain guys that went in and just came right back out like they're not going to have any part of that – as a matter of fact, certain guys you know after they came out of the room, they left...it was probably three or four [different

sports]...basketball, football obviously, baseball, and track – and there were some female sports people there too [laughs].

...I even seen a girl get raped, you know, she was literally passed-out and you know football players was just running in there, just running in you know so...they wasn't a part of the original group, you know set, so...like guys just tag teaming, shutting the door, and coming on in, "You can go now, you can go." I would say maybe like six or seven outsiders that wasn't even involved in the original, you know, throw down [group sex]...maybe she had sex with only like two or three guys and then you know as she passed out, then you know like I said, you get on the cell phone and start calling and people just randomly come by yea, I seen that...maybe like four original guys and like 6-8 extra guys... additional guys after she passed out...I actually saw them raping the girl, one girl, and it was probably like 12 guys.

Participants in this study mentioned no more than several occasions where group sexual encounters involved athletes from different sports, and usually this occurred in dormitories where college athletes lived together. Therefore, the first participant's observations of an off campus group sexual assault on an incoherent female that involved "at least four or five" athletes from "basketball, football obviously, baseball, and track" as well as "some female sports people there too" highlighted the only incident of its kind. The circumstances of this assault further suggested that the male and female athletes from different sports shared a high level of camaraderie since everyone was aware that athletes were sexually assaulting and/or raping a very intoxicated woman and yet no one bothered to stop it. It is not known whether the female athletes acted as bystanders, observers, or actual participants during this group assault although their presence implied silent consent and a desire to maintain friendship and acceptance with the offending athletes. Furthermore, this was one of two incidences where track and field athletes, who were not interviewed for this study, were mentioned for their involvement in a group sexual assault on a passed out woman.

In the second narrative, as many as four collegiate football players were originally involved in what appeared to be consensual group sex with the woman; however, it is likely that her intoxication levels during the initial group sexual experience made the encounter nonconsensual as well since she passed-out soon afterward. Although this participant was present during this incident, he made no attempt to stop the assault or assist the woman like certain athletes have revealed. It is evident that it takes a very strong individual to confront teammates simply because teammate bonds and the fear of exclusion often supersede any concern for a casual female sexual partner who happened to pass-out and become victimized.

Such events were not uncommon or even a new phenomenon according to a minor league basketball player who observed "lesser" collegiate teammates and football players without "game" luring more vulnerable women with alcohol in order to promote group sex and/or group sexual assault at a rate of "once every couple of months." Once inebriated, women were coerced or even forced to have sex with a "train" of athletes in succession. Again, the presence of alcohol as a salient factor contributing to incidences of group sex as well as individual and group sexual assaults cannot be ignored. Although many people do not consider alcohol a date rape drug, it is the most frequently used substance to promote drug-induced assaults.[49] Alcohol has been linked to one to two thirds of all sexual assaults, and various researchers reported a high prevalence of substance abuse related to group rapes as well.[50] However, alcohol is not the only drug that was used to entrap females as this participant revealed:

> ...LSD that was used a lot to get girls so...[in] different situations...they'd slip it into the drink...and give it to the girl, and she's yours after that – the biggest problem was probably how long it last on her and when she comes to her senses what's going to happen [as] then that was the scary part – like I said I never participated in that because I valued my scholarship and staying in school...not to say that I was an angel, but that's just something I would never do or did...there were some known guys around the dorm that I think was LSD users, that's what they did, I kind of didn't hang out with them too much, [but] they were friends of mine, so I'd say once a month or something like that [it happened].

Because this player competed when hallucinogenic drugs were common throughout college campuses in the late 1960s/early 1970s, LSD was used as a date rape drug in his generation in the same way that drugs such as flunitrazepam (Rophypnal or "roofies"), gamma hydroxybutyrate (GHB or "liquid ecstasy"), ketemine hydrochloride ("Special K"), and ecstacy are used today.[51] However, because these incidences occurred over 40 years ago when sexual assault awareness and acquaintance rape were not familiar terminology, males often sustained no consequences while female victims suffered silently with little support and few options.

Although there were no consequences linked with the previous group rapes, a wrestler revealed his awareness of a group sexual assault and/or rape on an unconscious female that resulted in police involvement:

Oh yea, I mean a couple of occasions and then once as a grad assistant where guys did it with a girl who was out cold, so I've seen that you know maybe three or four times throughout my time as a wrestler or as a coach...just excessive drinking usually at a party you know where there's some isolated room, she passes out, guys know it, they go in, and you know I know the one time [it] happened upstairs in a house and I went up and I actually saw the girl out cold, and I mean as a grad assistant I knew that was trouble and you know I just know guys had been with her, and then kind of when she came to, that was one of those incidences that led to some legal actions.

This athlete continued discussing the legal repercussions from police investigations in this way:

Just a lot of stress, but nothing was ever proven, nobody was ever convicted because I left the next year and was called, you know, by the police on a few occasions, but so much time had elapsed and so much alcohol was involved and, you know, her not having a clear conscience you know, and I think a lot of wrestlers are hesitant to say, "Yea, I saw so and so do that," you know I certainly didn't say that, but nothing ever came of it, but it was certainly investigated.

Approximately 10% of the participants noted camaraderie motivated participation in group sex while 6% identified peer pressure along with a group's mindset as the underlying motives fueling athlete sexual assault. This is noteworthy because in some cases, there can be a fine line between group sex and group sexual assault since some group assaults begin as consensual encounters. Both events also involve high-level male bonding as a minor league hockey player revealed, "The guy's dick [is] this far away from your face...you have to be comfortable with that guy, real comfortable, you don't have to touch him or anything, but the guy is right there...he might be hitting you on the head...if that's not camaraderie with buddies, I don't know what it is." Another wrestler added, "You know it's a bonding experience because they still talk about [it], so I don't think it's so much that I had sex, it's I had sex with this girl and six of my best friends." Such notions were further highlighted when the participant in the previous narrative as a graduate assistant coach revealed that he and the athletes he coached withheld information during police investigations that attempted to identify the group of perhaps "four" wrestlers who had sexually assaulted an unconscious female. Limited testimony, excessive alcohol, and elapsed time prevented any wrestlers from experiencing legal consequences; however, it is apparent that strong team bonding was perhaps the true underlying reason that the wrestlers along with their coach prevented police from gathering incriminating information to make a strong case. Anytime athletes prioritize team camaraderie over rational thinking and ethical behaviors, this will enable crimes of all types to go unchallenged. Psychologist Bernice Sandler supported such notions by revealing that group members often do anything to please each other because they are raping for each other, and therefore, the women are virtually insignificant.[52] Not to participate is to invite substantial pressure, suspicions of one's loyalty, and sexual preference which can lead to social rejection from the group.[53]

Interestingly, this participant discussed the combination of influences that he observed and believed motivated this particular group sexual assault. "Just the lack of common sense, alcohol...the, 'I got to get off right now,' you know I mean literally just, you know the loss of common sense for a moment, or the desire to be with a woman so bad they want to sleep with somebody who was passed-out." Because perpetrators are not trying to exercise power and control over an unconscious woman, this suggests that sexual gratification in combination with other influences may be an important factor that is overlooked these kinds of athlete assaults. Indeed, it appears that some athletes are looking for easy sexual gratification with passed-out women in an effort to satisfy their heightened sexual drive. One minor league basketball player elaborated on the manner in which sports competition impacted sexual drive:

> Well I think that competition is interesting, I think when you're competing you're exerting a large amount of energy, you know from adrenaline to everything, you still have the same sexual appetites like any normal human being would, [but] I just think that they become maybe more intense...because the stress level (physically) – even unbeknownst to you I think as the athlete – it does increase your drive and your desire simply because when you're competing...you've been doing [it] for years, your levels increase, and I think that increases across the board, and it increases from you ability to want to be successful to your...sexual drive, your sexual intentions, or whatever, so I think that yea, being a professional...I just think that it intensifies it.

Because elite-level athletes are among the most physically fit individuals as a result of their constant training, this participant believed heightened sexual drives were a normal, expected outcome within the athlete population. Scientific research has acknowledged that testosterone increases result from physical activity and particularly when this involves a competitive challenge or physically demanding sport.[54] Approximately 15% of the participants believed that increased sexual libido resulting from competition in conjunction with poor impulse control offered an explanation for sexual aggression because some athletes may experience difficulties managing their sexual drive. A major league baseball player supported these notions in this way:

Not [just] testosterone but the sexual chemicals in your body when they get to a certain point, I think some people can control them when they get up that high, and some people cannot and some people choose not to control it, so...they just get so worked up that they don't know where the line is, [and] they cross over the line easy into you know physical pressure.

Dr. Eugene Kanin's research described date rapists as hypersexual and very sexually frustrated because although they are sexually active, they are not as active as they want to be.[55] Not surprisingly, date rapists were also more likely to be involved in a "gang bang," which is a slang term for group sex and/or group sexual assault, when compared to a male control group.[56] Participants' belief that sexual drive and poor impulse control were responsible for fueling athlete sexual assault was even more likely when substance abuse was added to the equation. This was highlighted when researchers noted a relationship between alcohol abuse and group sexual assault since alcohol impairs individual judgment and control enabling men to rationalize peer group behavior as acceptable practices.[57] In the end, these narratives provide ample evidence that certain athletes have been satisfying their sexual urges at the expense of incapacitated women since the 1960s, and these practices continue today.

GROUP SEXUAL ASSAULTS THAT MAKE USE OF PENETRATING OBJECTS

In his book, *Our Guys: The Glen Ridge Rape and the Secret Life of the Perfect Suburb*, author Bernard Lefkowitz detailed the extent of certain athletes' darker group sexual practices.[58] In this case, three high school football players were eventually convicted and served jail time for sexually assaulting a mentally challenged female classmate using a broomstick and a small baseball bat as penetrating devices while other athletes watched the assault.[59] Although this case highlighted high school athletes' darker sexual behavior, similar assaults were discovered among collegiate and professional athletes in this study. For example, a collegiate basketball player noted his awareness of two football players at his university who were required to perform community service, but no jail time, after they violated an intoxicated woman with "hair brushes and cokes bottles." In addition, a wrestler and a minor league hockey player elaborated on their awareness as well as participation in similar events in this way:

...when I was on the wrestling team...yea, well I think she was basically passed out from drinking and some people were doing you know as far as I know, they took some different objects and inserted them and took some pictures of them and she was quite upset with it. Prior to that she had had a lot of experiences with several of those people already, but

333

she didn't appreciate what had happened at all…maybe…two or three [guys]…I think she threatened them…I think that was the motive for threatening them so that she got them [the pictures] back.

…one night I pick up one out of there, brought her over, five, six guys, and I just sat back and watched, you know, "Hell, go for it boys." I mean she's all fucked up on dope and shit, you know, keep the boys happy…I was at the bar, I just brought her from the bar. I still to this day don't know her name. You know, brought her up there, fucked her with a tennis racket for a little bit you know, and the boys jumped on her you know. I think it was one right after another, or a couple guys watching you know…

The second participant highlighted the fact that larger group sexual encounters and/or assaults are all about male bonding and entertainment – at the female's expense. It appeared that this woman's name was as insignificant as her identity and despite this athlete's belief that this female was a willing sexual partner, her highly intoxicated state raised definite concerns about her ability to consent to such an experience. Furthermore, this participant revealed other events that provided additional entertainment during his minor league career and involved "different toys you use to do them" including "Pepsi…or Seven Up bottles." It is not known whether this athlete used penetrating devices in his individual sexual encounters although it is unlikely because there would be no male audience to consider – or entertain. Psychologist Chris O'Sullivan's research revealed that the purpose of group/gang rape often was to humiliate the woman in a public setting during the assault since this enabled the males to bond and demonstrate their shared dominance in full view of one another.[60] The previous player-narratives shared striking similarities to this description, and certain circumstances leave little doubt that what some athletes considered group sex or a harmless prank, in reality, was their participation in a group sexual assault. While it is apparent that certain athletes need to examine their conscience to explain their participation in these darker practices, women must avoid becoming intoxicated to the point that they put themselves at risk for being victimized.

OBSERVING GROUP SEXUAL ASSAULT ON A SOBER FEMALE

Previous narratives highlighted different kinds of group sexual assaults on highly intoxicated and/or passed out females; however, not all assaults included intoxicated women as an NFL player observed during his collegiate career:

I've seen a couple of times where it was more malicious where I was privy to watch and it got a little out of control where she didn't want to be penetrated doubly and they did so anyway against her wishes...it was very aggressive, it was something that she did not want to have happen, it happened anyway, she bled anally, and there was face slapping, hair pulling, and punching as well...[whew] it was three guys in the room [engaging with the woman] and probably a good 10 that watched.

Because this situation included "face slapping, hair pulling, and punching" in addition to anal penetration that was forced against the female's wishes, there is little doubt that what began as a group sexual encounter evolved into a group sexual assault which produced an array of injuries. This participant was asked to discuss his reaction to this scenario, which he did in this way:

The first time and the only time that that actually happened, I actually confronted the individuals and they just said that they knew what they were doing and I said, "Okay fine, I'm not going to be a part of it" and that was it for me I was done...and [I] just wanted to express my dissatisfaction and if that's what they wanted me to do, then I wasn't even going to be a party to watch, so that was it.

While it was admirable that this participant challenged his teammates' abuse by himself, he did not assist the woman in leaving this assault when he did. Again, it is very difficult for some athletes to challenge and confront their teammates particularly during a group sexual encounter and/or assault because it can mean being permanently ostracized from their primary reference group. Gail Abarbanel, Director of the Rape Treatment Center at Santa Monica-UCLA Hospital in California, noted in a 1991 article that there had never been a single case at their center where one man tried to stop a group rape, and this included those like the previous participant, who experienced a degree of guilt while observing an assault, but did not stop or report their peers.[61] A follow-up conversation 20 years later in May 2011 verified the same held true to this day.[62] This participant's leaving the situation as opposed to trying to stop the assault probably kept him in good standing with his peers, but perhaps not with his own conscience. Although this participant was uncertain whether legal charges were filed, the coach suspended the player initiating the assault for several games and subsequently released him from the team the following season. Still, it is apparent that this perpetrator along with his teammates experienced minimal consequences because they avoided legal prosecution. At the same time, women must know that prosecutors are hesitant to take on cases involving consensual group sex that turn into a group sexual assault because a female's credibility and sexual history are closely examined during legal procedures involving rape.[63]

STOPPING SEXUAL ASSAULT AND RAPE

Not all athletes choose to do nothing when confronted with a potential sexual assault because some participants discussed instances where they were proactive as well as protective of certain females that they knew were in dangerous situations. Approximately 10% of the participants intervened in some way in an effort to try to prevent and/or stop an incident that appeared to be nearing or crossing the line into sexual assault or rape. For example, a MLB player with recent experience recalled stopping an intoxicated minor league teammate who was "trying to get this girl…kind of grabbing a hold… trying to get her in the room, and I'm like, 'Hey man she's not going for this, you know this isn't good' and so you know a long story made short…he finally, finally like didn't exactly agree, but he kind of gave up and she left." A minor league hockey player revealed confronting a married and intoxicated teammate on a road trip during his professional career by saying, "Listen, no means no" when the player began "groping and grabbing" a woman in their hotel room after she had rejected his sexual advances. While this participant thought the woman was very naïve to think that being in an athlete's hotel room late night would only result in conversation, he also acknowledged a woman's right to say "no" and have this respected. In addition, a minor league baseball player and an NHL player elaborated on their personal intervention during more extreme experiences in this way:

> …one of my teammates on the team, we were on spring break after we were all seniors and we walked in the room, we were in [XXX], and he had a girl like by her neck and she was up over the balcony and we had to wrestle him…he was a guy that we thought, I thought was certainly on steroids…I didn't hang around those type of guys that did that type of stuff…[but] yea, he had her bent over around the balcony like that… we were all out doing our own thing and we just walked into the room, and that was happening so we fricken, we grabbed him right away, we threw him in the room, threw him in the bed, and just beat the shit out of him…that was at night…[and] he didn't even know what was going on, I mean he was either on steroids and drugged out of his mind or just flat out drugged out of his mind…he laid there for awhile and I mean he pretty much passed out after that…she did not [report him]…he got up the next morning, he had a black eye, a couple of bruises here and there, we took care of him [with a beating], and she just ran out of the room, we never saw her the rest of the trip…[but] he was trying to pressure her into something…[and] it was the one time I've ever seen any guy like force girls to try and do some stuff [sexually] or hit girls or any of that type of shit.

Only once that I can say that I was aware of [it], and it was a guy obviously that had issues because he was kind of involved in all these different [sexually deviant] things...when you're in the minor leagues you generally live with a group of guys, and it was a guy that I lived with...and so this guy...he wasn't a regular player due to a lack of skill, but he wasn't a regular player due to you know mental toughness or focus or commitment...[and] I woke up to hear a female at my place saying she didn't want to and "no" – you know more or less like a whimper or a cry, not a full out you know bawling or anything like that, but I heard that and went and intervened on it and you know I had a physical altercation with the teammate and then just sent the girl out of my place out of my house...[basically] I called the player's name and he wouldn't come out of his room, so I finally went in there and grabbed the guy and threw him out of the room and then he tried to go back, you know he was inebriated, so it ended up being a physical confrontation and I think that kind of sobered that person up and it gave me time to you know help the other [female] person get out of there before something everyone would regret you know happening...that was in [AAA minor league]...

It is interesting to note that in each of the above scenarios, participants described teammates who were highly intoxicated on drugs or alcohol to the point that the perpetrators in half of the previous scenarios remembered little, if anything, following their assaults on women. Experiencing an alcohol and/or drug induced blackout is dangerous because regardless of whether or not an athlete remembers his assault, he is still responsible for his actions. In addition, the second participant noted the woman placed herself in a very compromising position by staying overnight with a very intoxicated athlete that perhaps she knew very little about. Although athletes are solely responsible for their assaults on females, women also need to take responsibility for their actions by making intelligent choices regarding their sexual partners and the conditions in which they put themselves. This is important because often the victim, rapist, or both are under the influence of drugs or alcohol; and women who use alcohol in excess and get drunk more often are more likely to be victims of sexual aggression.[64]

The second participant subsequently revealed that his teammate was quickly ostracized by his closest supporters, including this participant, which contradicts the belief that all athletes who sexually assault women share unwavering team bonding. This offending athlete also suffered the consequence of being sent to a lower minor league soon after this incident even though his assault was not reported to team or legal officials. This participant attributed his teammate's attempted rape to his lack of social skills, and nearly 20% of participants identified social retardation/sexual rejection as influences that could motivate certain athletes to commit sexual assault or rape. As previously noted, athlete privilege means that many do not hear the word "no" often enough to realize its true meaning, and this can cause hostility against the woman. Moreover, this athlete perpetrator's constant involvement in sexually deviant behaviors included his use of more assertive/aggressive "game" in an effort to entice women wherever he went. Additionally, his participation in male bonding experiences such as larger group sexual encounters also suggested that this offender had become part of an erotic peer group that used and sexually objectified women. Researchers discovered a relationship between male peer support groups that sexually objectified women and the occurrence of sexual assault.[65] Essentially peer groups influence sexual deviancy and/or aggression by reinforcing others for adopting attitudes and behaviors their group subscribes to or by pressuring members to conform to group norms.[66] These factors in combination with substance abuse provide a probable explanation for this attempted rape.

STOPPING SEXUAL ASSAULTS TARGETING INTOXICATED FEMALES

Research findings in conjunction with the previous narratives provide ample evidence that intoxication makes women susceptible to sexual aggression. This fact prompted certain participants to take action before a sexual assault or rape could occur. For example, a wrestler noted, "When you get to college, you hear so much about date rape and consent and all that stuff, so usually if a girl's passed out, these guys on my team do what we can to actually help her out and get her out of that situation cause a passed out female is a very vulnerable person to a lot of people." While this participant's team in the mid to late 2000s was educated to protect intoxicated women who were vulnerable to rape, other participants including a current minor league basketball player detailed specific experiences. "[A] girl passed out at a party and he [a college teammate] was talking about having sex with her, he didn't...because we talked about him so bad saying, 'That's wrong,' so he ended up not doing anything – but he thought about it." A minor league baseball player with recent experience revealed, "[In] pro, it was just one of my roommates and...she was just passed out and you know he was trying to have sex with her and he didn't know what to do...I told him it probably wouldn't be the right thing to do and it didn't happen." Other participants including a current minor league football player and two wrestlers elaborated on their efforts to stop sexual assaults and rapes on intoxicated females:

> ...we actually almost had to fight one of our teammates because of that. Yea...it was a little party at one of my teammate's house, this

was once again at junior college...and we're just getting wasted with alcohol drinking it, so it's a couple of girls that are there wasted, kissing everybody, and one girl kind of passes out, and one teammate's on the couch slowly trying to take her pants off and like the lights are kind of off and kind of dim, so it's not like it's fully bright and in the open, and he's trying to mess around with her, and one of my other teammates saw him and he's like, "You don't need to do nothing like that," and he was like, "Bullshit, she'll never know." So it took like two or three of us to actually go over and convince him, he was a bigger guy too, to convince him that's not the route he needs to go, and so we finally convinced him and long story short...he left her alone and she was just sitting there passed out, but she could have easily been taken advantaged of just like that.

When I was a freshman in college I remember...the seniors had a Halloween party and a girl passed out and I just remember thinking... "You can't take advantage of this girl," and so you know I kind of sat with her and tried to help her out and get her back on her feet and because like I said that's kind of the way my parents raised me to be is that's not right in any situation to take advantage of somebody who's passed out, and I did it one other time in college with a girl who ran track you know, and I took care of her and I kind of hung out with her, she was puking and would pass out and puke and pass out, and we were at a party and I mean I've always felt like personally it's not worth it to take that chance and so I tried to err more on the side of, "We'll take care of them than not," so those were two personal cases where you know I tried to take care of somebody instead of taking advantage of them – and all the time of course there were people trying to take advantage of them...and in the second case, like I said she ran track and I wrestled and we became pretty good friends after that and I think we dated for awhile just because she understood that I was – even though I was a wrestler – I'm more than just a crude individual.

...the most notable one I remember, we were at a party and this girl was drunk and they were carrying her up the stairs and...two wrestlers dated this girl at different times, and the one guy for whatever reason was bitter behind it and didn't care too much for her, and I thought she was a nice girl, and it was going on with about five of the guys and the girls were like telling me that like, "You got to go up there and you got to stop it," so I went up there and said, "What are you guys doing?" and the girl was so drunk she was waking up and she was going, "No, no, no, no, no, no more, no more, no more" and I'm like, "Guys, knock it off, just knock it off" I said, "You're just going to get in trouble," now nothing came out of it because she didn't say anything, but you know it angered some people, you know there was a lot of people at the party by the way and I was by far not the only one, but I was the only one I guess brave enough to try to stop it...they stopped because I had the whole party come up like after about five minutes, five minutes into it the whole party got up and they got her dressed and they got her out of there... [but] you know guys would be laying on the bed touching her breasts and then another guy would be having sex with her you know and...I'm talking about it now and I was sickened, I'm sick about it...it was a bad situation.

While each of the previous participants described their involvement in protecting an overly intoxicated woman, the second participant noted his actions contested the stereotypical belief that all wrestlers were crude, heartless individuals. Such notions were further challenged when the third participant described a disturbing, yet one-of-a-kind experience in which he stopped his teammates' group sexual assault and rape of a severely intoxicated woman. Without question, this wrestler displayed tremendous strength of character that many athletes lack when it requires confronting teammates' negative behaviors because this can lead to breaking close bonds and being ostracized from their primary peer group. By having everyone at the party come up to this room five minutes after he entered, this ensured that the incident ended while enabling this wrestler to draw on emotional support from numerous individuals who were non-athletes. In spite of the outcome, this participant was still "sickened" by this incident years after the fact because he had to stop his teammates from raping a woman he knew. Because this incident was never reported, these wrestlers suffered no legal consequences which could have seriously impacted each of them as well as their collegiate program. Moreover, it takes a very strong individual to go out of their way to protect a female from being sexually victimized, and therefore, women must be very cognizant of the dangers they can face from being severely intoxicated and/or passed-out. Both women and offenders in the previous scenarios were fortunate to have one or more athletes intervene on their behalf since this prevented potential sexual assaults, ended individual and group rapes, and protected everyone involved from experiencing a host of negative consequences. In the end, the athlete world and society in general need to see more of these heroic actions because unfortunately, such events highlight the exception rather than the rule.

WHAT CAN COACHES DO?

Athletes, like the previous participants, are certainly encouraged to confront teammates' nefarious behaviors whenever possible because sexual assault intervention is indeed a courageous and noteworthy feat on multiple levels.

At the same time, coaches also have responsibility because they can strongly impact their players' behaviors by taking a stance, using their power to model appropriate behaviors, and by addressing sexual behaviors periodically. Ignoring negative practices, including athlete sexual deviancy and/or aggression, is unacceptable, and this was evident when various coaches revealed that they had the opportunity to address athlete sexual assault – sometimes while it was in progress – and yet chose to say or do nothing. Such actions imply silent consent which compounds the problem by temporarily sweeping it under the carpet until it resurfaces again. Failing to address incidents involving sexual aggression enables them to continue because without consequences, they remain unchallenged.

The time that it takes to briefly address sexual aggression is insignificant compared to the potential it has to reduce negative treatment and female abuse as well as potential sexual assaults that would unquestionably impact a team, the athlete-perpetrators, and female victims. One collegiate hockey coach reminded his players to always use "the newspaper test" before considering any questionable behavior because visualizing how they would feel when they appeared on the front page headlines while experiencing an array of consequences helped to reduce deviant behavior. Moreover, a collegiate basketball coach would post newspaper clippings in the locker room which depicted various athletes' involvement in criminal activities along with their accompanying consequences. Another collegiate coach had his players use "the five-second decision," which involved taking time to think and consider the consequences of a behavior – before engaging in it, while a major league hockey coach reminded his players that if they had to think about whether to engage in a certain behavior, this was a sure sign to avoid the behavior and leave the situation. Such practices involve minimal time and effort and serve to constantly reinforce the idea that engaging in negative behaviors can take athletes and their team down. This was highlighted when a minor league basketball player revealed that he lost his athletic scholarship when the university dropped their basketball program following an investigation of one of the player's involvement in an alleged sexual assault that simultaneously uncovered various NCAA infractions. While the accused athlete experienced no jail time and minimal consequences by falling to a slightly lower position in the NBA draft, numerous collegiate athletes were negatively impacted by losing their scholarships and having to transfer to other universities since the rippling effects of this incident ended their program. Such repercussions serve to emphasize one collegiate football player's recollection of a simple statement from his coach that tremendously impacted him even after his playing career was over:

> ...the coaching staff does not involve themselves with that [sexual assault prevention] but...they'll bring in like specialists in the area to deal

with that stuff and the coaches will always introduce them and they'll tell them how important it is to listen to them, but they'll never speak on the subject themselves...the thing is [the head coach] did always say one thing that always stuck with me; he said, "Always remember, that when you lay your hands on a girl, you're laying your hands on someone else's child," and he said, "Just imagine if that were your child, would you want someone to lay their hands on them like that – like you did?" and that always kind of struck me and I think that probably hit a lot more guys more deeply than any of the seminars they set up for us – like put your hands on somebody, you're putting your hands on somebody else's child, and then you'd be like ..."Would you like someone to put their hands on your child like that?" "No like, hell no," but that's the only thing like from a coach [because] the coaches are always so preoccupied with the X's and O's...

This participant revealed that although most coaches were too preoccupied with teaching game strategies to address negative treatment of females, he was struck by his head coach's simple statement which made more impact on him, and perhaps other athletes, than the speakers who discussed these issues with his team. Essentially, this coach asked his players to look at the human side of women because they were someone's daughters as opposed to sexual objects to use and abuse. Athletes and coaches have families and children of their own and such messages can produce a rippling effect that can one day impact their own daughter, sister, female relative, partner, or friend. While visualizing a close female's victimization is never desirable, the prevalence of sexual aggression makes these behaviors a probable occurrence. Therefore, a coach's presence in combination with his brief yet powerful message could be the difference between athletes taking a moment to consider their sexual behaviors and treatment of women versus those who do not. Such messages from well-respected coaches can only assist in making their male athletes better boyfriends, husbands, fathers, and family men because they may begin to view women, their own behaviors, and relationships in a different manner. Raising awareness, which occurs through changing athletes' mindsets little by little, is always worth the time because if one woman is saved from being sexually victimized and one athlete chooses a different course of sexual behavior with a sexually reluctant female, it will have been well worth the effort. In the end, the more that influential role models address the problem of sexual deviancy and aggression, the better off all of society will be including women and athletes from diverse sports and cultures.

ATHLETES' CORNER: POINTS TO PONDER

1. Sexually deviant and aggressive behaviors are a prevalent within various athlete cultures, and these practices appear to thrive whenever they are not confronted. Athlete sexual assaults – whether reported or not – are the result of an array of firmly established negative attitudes and behaviors toward women that have been reinforced by peer groups and allowed to flourish over time. It is time athletes use their power to end sexual deviancy and aggression by being the solution rather than the problem. This occurs only when athletes take individual responsibility for the way they treat women.

2. There is no single cause or motive for athlete sexual assault and/or rape because a variety of influences, often including alcohol abuse, converge to promote its occurrence. However, certain factors carry more impact during specific types of sexual assaults and particularly those that involve individual versus group assaults or assaults targeting a highly intoxicated and/or passed-out woman versus someone who is coherent. Refuse to allow others and/or the media to influence your thinking or behavior particularly when it involves sexual behavior with women. Accept the physical intimacy you are offered, or leave a situation if it is not to your liking. Know that using sexual pressure or force to satisfy your personal agenda is creating disastrous circumstances for everyone involved.

3. Leaders with true strength find the courage to challenge and confront harmful attitudes and behaviors the moment they are encountered. This occurs whether or not negative practices originate at the hands of strangers or bonded teammates. Numerous athletes and potential female victims alike owe their gratitude and continued well-being to those rare athletes who acted fearlessly on their behalf to prevent and/or stop sexual assaults and/or rapes in progress. The athlete world needs more heroes who are willing to step up and police their own. Think about what actions you will take when real leadership is called upon because doing nothing is a poor choice that often comes with regret.

Demographic Profile of Total Sample (n=135)

Age at the Time of Interview	35 Mean 35 Median 31, 35 Mode (Both Appeared 9 Times) 20 – 58 Range Approximately one third of participants were in their 20s. Just over one third of participants were in their 30s. Approximately one third of participants were in their 40s. Approximately 4% of participants were in their 50s.
Race	101 Caucasian 29 African American 5 Hispanic
Country of Origin	121 United States 12 Canada 2 Europe
Highest Level of Education	4 Doctorate Degree 17 Master's Degree 81 Bachelor's Degree 27 Some College 6 High School/GED
Playing Experience	84 Professional Experience (Minor and/or Major Leagues) 32 Major League Experience 75 Minor League Experience U.S./Overseas 5 Olympic Team 8 National Team (non-Olympic) 123 Collegiate Experience 23 Junior Experience (Ice Hockey Related)
Coaching Experience	42 Junior/Collegiate/Minor/Major League Experience 3 Major Leagues 16 Minor Leagues 27 Collegiate 4 Juniors (Ice Hockey Related)

Playing/Coaching Eras	Over two thirds competed and/or coached in college and/or pro sports during 2000-2010; 1990-1999. 50% competed and/or coached in college and/or pro sports during 1980-1989. 20% competed and/or coached in college and/or pro sports during 1970-1979. Approximately 3% competed and/or coached in college and/or pro sports during 1960-1969. *Participants' collegiate and/or pro playing and/or coaching careers in multiple decades account for percentages totaling over 100%.
Career at the Time of the Interview	17 Education 9 Human Service Occupation 33 Business 5 Construction/Industry 13 Sports Related Career (Includes: General Manager/ Director of Player Personnel for Pro Sports Teams, Pro Scouts, TV/Radio Sports Analyst, Personal Trainer) 20 Current Collegiate/Professional Athlete 31 Current Collegiate/Professional Coach 5 Non-athlete College Student/Graduate Student 2 Retired

Basketball Sample Summary Information (n=27)

- 8 Participants were ages 22-29; 11 participants were ages 30-36; 7 participants were ages 40-45, and 1 participant was in his 50s.
- 52% of the participants were African American and 48% were Caucasian.
- 23 Participants with minor and/or major league experience have approximately 155 years of combined professional experience.
- 21 Participants with minor professional experience in North America and/or Overseas have approximately 90 years of combined minor league experience.
- 7 Participants with NBA experience have approximately 65 years of combined major league experience.
- Sample includes: 1 National Team Member (Non-Olympic); 1 International Medalist; Players involved in 3 NBA playoff finals produced no NBA Championships.
- 100% of the participants played collegiate basketball; over 95% competed at Division I institutions.
- 7 Participants with coaching experience at the collegiate and/or minor professional level have over 30 years of combined coaching experience; 100% of the collegiate coaches coached at Division I institutions.

Baseball Sample Summary Information (n=27)

- 6 Participants were ages 25-29; 10 participants were ages 31-38; 9 participants were ages 40-49, and 2 participants were in their 50s.
- 93% of the participants were Caucasian and 7% were African American.
- 23 Participants with minor and/or major league experience have approximately 155 years of combined professional experience.
- 23 Participants with minor professional experience in North America and/or Overseas have over 90 years of combined minor league experience.
- 8 Participants with major league experience have over 60 years of combined major league experience.
- Sample includes: 1 Olympic Team Member; 1 National Team Member (Non-Olympic), 1 International Medalist; Players involved in 4 World Series produced 3 MLB Championships.
- 96% of the participants played collegiate baseball; 85% competed at Division I institutions
- 10 Participants with collegiate and/or minor professional coaching experience have over 70 years of combined coaching experience; over 60% of the collegiate coaches coached Division I.

Wrestling Sample Summary Information (n=27)

- 10 Participants were ages 22-29; 7 participants were ages 31-38; 9 participants were ages 41-49, and 1 participant was in his 50s.

- 81% of the participants were Caucasian, 15% were Hispanic, and 3% were African American.
- 100% of the participants wrestled and/or trained in college; approximately 90% competed at the Division I level.
- Sample includes: 2 NCAA Champions, 12 All Americans, 3 Olympic Team Members, 4 National Team Members (Non-Olympic); 4 International Medalists.
- 10 Participants with coaching experience at the collegiate level have approximately 80 years of combined coaching experience; 80% of the collegiate coaches coached at Division I institutions.

Football Sample Summary Information (n=27)
- 7 Participants were ages 23-29; 12 participants were ages 30-39; 7 were participants ages 40-48, and 1 participant was in his 50s.
- 56% of the participants were Caucasian and 44% were African American.
- 19 Participants with minor and/or major league experience have approximately 120 years of combined professional experience.
- 12 Participants with minor professional experience in the North America and/or Overseas have over 55 years of combined minor league experience.
- 9 Participants with NFL experience have approximately 65 years of combined major league experience.
- Sample includes: Participants with 2 Pro Bowl appearances, 2 Super Bowl Championships; 1 Two-Sport Professional Athlete.
- 100% of the participants played collegiate football; over 80% of competed at the Division I level.
- 3 Participants with coaching experience at the collegiate and/or minor professional level have approximately 10 years of combined coaching experience; 50% of the collegiate coaches coached at Division I institutions.

Hockey Sample Summary Information (n=27)
- 10 Participants were ages 20-29; 9 participants were ages 31-39; 7 participants were ages 40-49, and 1 participant was in his 50s.
- 100% of the participants were Caucasian.
- 19 Participants with minor and/or major league experience have approximately 160 years of combined professional experience.
- 19 Participants with minor professional playing experience in North America and/or Overseas have approximately 90 years of combined minor league experience.
- 8 Participants with NHL experience have over 70 years of combined major league experience.
- Sample Includes: 1 Olympic Team Member; 3 National Team Members (Non-Olympic); 1 NHL Hall of Fame Inductee; Players involved in 8 Stanley Cup Finals produced 7 Championships.

- Approximately 60% of the participants played collegiate hockey; approximately 40% of this group played at the Division I level.
- 23 Participants have junior hockey experience.
- 12 Participants with coaching experience at the junior, collegiate and/or minor/major professional level have over 60 years of combined coaching experience; one third of the collegiate coaches coached at the Division I level.

Extra Participants Sample Summary Information (n=7)
- 3 Participants were ages 23-28; 1 participant was in his 30s; 2 participants were ages 40-42 and 1 participant was in his 50s.
- 100% of the participants were Caucasian.
- 1 Participant played Division I collegiate football.
- 6 Participants with minor professional hockey experience in North America and/or Overseas have approximately 35 years of combined minor league experience.
- 3 Participants played collegiate hockey; two thirds of this group played at the Division I level
- 6 Participants have junior hockey experience.
- 3 Participants with coaching experience at the junior, collegiate and/ or professional level have approximately 10 years of combined coaching experience; 1 collegiate coach coached at the Division I level.

References

Notes to Introduction

1   Benedict, J. (1997). *Public heroes private felons: Athletes and crimes against women.* Boston: Northeastern University Press.
    Benedict, J. (1998). *Athletes and acquaintance rape.* Thousand Oaks, California: Sage.
    Benedict, J. (2004). *Out of bounds: Inside the NBA's culture of rape, violence, and crime.* New York: HarperCollins.
    Benedict, J., & Yaeger, D. (1998). *Pros and cons: The criminals who play in the NFL.* New York: Warner Books, Inc.
    Pappas, N. T. (2002). *On the ice and off the rink: A qualitative study of hockey players' aggression.* Unpublished doctoral dissertation, The Ohio State University – Columbus.
    Pappas, N. T., McKenry, P. C., & Catlett, B. S. (2009). On the rink and off the ice: Athlete violence and aggression in hockey and interpersonal relationships. In M. S. Kimmel & M. A. Messner (Eds.) *Men's lives (8th ed).* (pp. 535-550). Boston: Allyn and Bacon.
    Robinson, L. (1998). *Crossing the line: Violence and sexual assault in Canada's national sport.* Toronto: McClelland & Stewart Inc.
2   Benedict, (1997); Benedict, (1998); Benedict, (2004); Benedict & Yaeger, (1998); Robinson, (1998).
    Lefkowitz, B. (1997). *Our guys: The Glen Ridge rape and the secret life of the perfect suburb.* New York: Random House.
3   Pappas, (2002).
4   Strong, B., Yarber, W. L., Sayad, B. W., & DeVault, C. (2008). *Human sexuality: Diversity in contemporary America* (6th ed.). Boston: McGraw-Hill.
5   *Roget's II: The new thesaurus, expanded edition.* (1988). Boston, MA: Houghton Mifflin.
6   Pappas, N. T., McKenry, P. C., & Catlett, B. S. (2004). On the rink and off the ice: Athlete violence and aggression in hockey and interpersonal relationships. *Men and Masculinities, 6*(3), 291-312.
7   Pappas, (2002).
8   Bandura, A. (1973). *Aggression: A social learning analysis.* Englewood Cliffs, N.J.: Prentice Hall.
    Bandura, A. (1979). The social learning perspective: Psychological mechanisms of aggression. In H. Toch, (Ed.), *Psychology of crime and criminal justice.* New York: Holt, Rinehart, & Winston.
9   Lore, R. K., & Schultz, L. A. (1993). Control of human aggression. *American Psychologist, 48,* 16-26.

Miller, J. L., & Knudsen, D. D (1999). Family abuse and violence. In M. Sussman, S. K. Steinmetz, & G. W. Petersen, (Eds.), *Handbook of marriage and the family* (pp. 705-742). New York: Plenum Press.

O'Leary, D. K. (1988). Physical aggression between spouses: A social learning theory perspective. In V. B. Van Hasselt, R. L. Morrsion, A. L. Bellack, & M. Hersen (Eds.), *Handbook of family violence.* New York: Plenum Press.

The National Research Council. (1996). *Understanding violence against women.* Washington, D.C.: National Academy Press.

10 Arias, I. (1984). *A social learning theory explication of the intergenerational transmission of physical aggression in intimate heterosexual relationships.* Unpublished doctoral dissertation. State University of New York – Stony Brook.

Barnett, I. W., Miller-Perrin, C., & Perrin, R. D. (1997). *Family violence across the lifespan.* Thousand Oaks, CA: Sage Publications.

O'Leary, (1988); The National Research Council, (1996).

11 Patterson, G. R., Reid, J. B., & Dishion, T. J. (1992). *Antisocial boys.* Eugene, OR: Castalia Publishing Company.

12 Lore & Schultz, (1993); Miller & Knudsen, (1999); O'Leary, (1988); The National Research Council, (1996).

13 Benedict, (1997); Benedict, (1998); Benedict, (2004).

Messner, M. A. (1992). *Power at play: Sports and the problem of masculinity* Boston: Beacon Press.

14 Curry, T. J. (1998). Beyond the locker room: Campus bars and college athletes. *Sociology of Sport Journal, 15,* 205-215.

Lefkowitz, (1997).

Muir, K. B., & Seitz, T. (2004) Machismo, misogyny, and homophobia in a male athletic subculture: A participant-observation study of deviant rituals in collegiate rugby. *Deviant Behavior, 25,* 303-327.

15 Curry, (1998).

16 Curry, (1998); Lefkowitz, (1997).

Messner, M, A., & Sabo, D. F. (1994). *Sex, violence and power in sports: Rethinking masculinity.* Freedom, CA: The Crossing Press.

17 Curry, (1998); Lefkowitz, (1997); Messner & Sabo, (1994).

Notes to Chapter 1

1 Curry, T. J. (1991). Fraternal bonding in the locker room: A profeminist analysis of talk about competition and women. *Sociology of Sport Journal, 8,* 119-135.

Pappas, (2002).

2 Curry, (1998); Lefkowitz, (1997); Muir & Seitz, (2004).

3   Muir & Seitz, (2004).
4   Flood, M. (2008). Men, sex, and homosociality: How bonds between men shape their sexual relations with women. *Men and Masculinities, 10*(3), 339-359.
    Muir & Seitz, (2004); Strong et al., (2008).
5   Muir & Seitz, (2004).
6   *Nebraska wrestlers dismissed after posing nude.* (2008, August 12). Retrieved May 10, 2009, from http://sports.espn.go.com/ncaa/news/story?id=3532146
7   Indecent Exposure (nd). *In glossary of terms - criminal law lawyer source.* Retrieved June 23, 2009, from http://www.criminal-law-lawyer-source.com/terms.html
8   Crooks, R., & Baur, K. (2008). *Our sexuality (10th ed.).* Belmont, CA: Wadsworth.
9   Crooks & Baur, (2008).
10 American Psychiatric Association. (2000). *Diagnostic and statistical manual of mental disorder* (4th ed., text revision). Washington, DC.
    Berah, E. F., & Meyers, R. G. (1983). The offense records of a sample of convicted exhibitionists. *Bulletin of the Academy of Psychiatry and Law, 11,* 365-369.
    Marshall, W., Eccles, A., & Barbaree, H. (1991). The treatment of exhibitionists: A focus on sexual deviancy versus cognitive and relationship features. *Behavior Research and Therapy, 29,* 129-135.
    Mohr, J. W., Turner, R. E., & Jerry, M. B. (1964). *Pedophilia and exhibitionism.* Toronto: University of Toronto Press.
11 Murphy, W. (1997). Exhibitionism: Psychopathology and theory. In D. R. Laws & W. O'Donohue (Eds.), *Sexual deviance: Theory, assessment, and treatment* (pp. 22-39). New York: Guilford Press.
    Strong et al., (2008).
12 Person, E. S., Terestman, N., Myers, W. A., Goldberg, E. L., & Salvadori, C. (1989). Gender differences in sexual behaviors and fantasies in a college population. *Journal of Sex and Marital Therapy, 15,* 187-198.
    Templeman, T. L., & Stinnett, R. D. (1991). Patterns of sexual arousal and history in a "normal" sample of young men. *Archives of Sexual Behavior, 20*(2), 137-150.
13 Nash, B., & Zullo, A. (1986). *The baseball hall of shame 2.* New York: Simon and Shuster.
14 Murphy, (1997).
15 Karpman, B. (1957). *The sexual offender and his offenses.* Washington, D.C.: Julian Press.
16 Lang, R. A., Langevin, R., Checkley, K. L., & Pugh, G. (1987). Genital exhibitionism: Courtship disorder or narcissism? *Canadian Journal of Behavioral Science, 19*(2), 216-232.

17 Lang et al., (1987).
18 Rentzel, L. (1972). *When all the laughter died in sorrow.* New York: Saturday Review Press.
19 Mohr et al., (1964).
20 Rentzel, (1972).
21 Rentzel, (1972).
22 Rentzel, (1972).
23 Rentzel, (1972).
24 Kennedy, K. (1999, September 13). Ciccarelli hangs it up, Dino was a dinosaur. *Sports Illustrated, 91*(10). Retrieved March 14, 2009, from http://vault.sportsillustrated.cnn.com/vault/article/magazine/MAG1017004/index.html
25 Doyel, G. (2006, July 17). *Bengals have character, all right – a lot of it bad.* Retrieved March 14, 2009, from http://www.cbssports.com/print/nfl/story/9557948
   Klein, G., & Farmer, S. (2006, June 22). Rucker is charged with battery. *The Los Angeles Times.* Retrieved March 15, 2009, from http://articles.latimes.com/2006/jun/22/sports/sp-newswire22
26 Doyel, (2006); Klein & Farmer, (2006).
27 Crooks & Baur, (2008).
28 Kinsey, A., Pomeroy, W. B., & Martin, C. E. (1948). *Sexual behavior in the human male.* Philadelphia: W. B. Saunders.
   Kinsey, A., Pomeroy, W. B., Martin, C. E., & Gebhard, P. H. (1953). *Sexual behavior in the human female.* Philadelphia: W. B. Saunders.
29 Strong et al., (2008).
30 Lefkowitz, (1997).
31 Wahl, G., & Wertheim, L. J. (2003, December 22). Special report: A rite gone terribly wrong. *Sports Illustrated, 99* (24), 68-76.
32 Curtis, J., & Ennis, R. (1988). Negative consequences of leaving sport? Comparative findings for former elite-level hockey players. **Sociology of Sport Journal, *5***(3), 87-106.
33 Kwee, A., W., Dominguez, A., W., & Ferrell, D. (2007). Sexual addiction and Christian college men: Conceptual, assessment, and treatment challenges. *Journal of Psychology and Christianity, 26*(1), 3-13.
34 Carnes, P. (1991). *Don't call it love: Recovery from sexual addiction.* New York: Bantam.
35 Kwee, et al., (2007).
36 Bogle, K. A. (2008). *Hooking up: Sex, dating, and relationships on campus.* New York: New York University Press.
37 Pinkerton, S. D., Bogart, L. M., Cecil, H., & Abramson, P. R. (2002). Factors associated with masturbation in a college sample. *Journal of Psychology and Human Sexuality, 14*(2-3), 103-121.

38 Schwartz, M. D., & Dekeserdy, W. S. (1997). *Sexual assault on the college campus: The role of male peer support.* Thousand Oaks, CA: Sage.

39 Boykin, K. (2005). *Beyond the down low: Sex, lies, and denial in black America.* Berkeley, CA: Carroll & Graf.

Edozien, F. (2003, July 8). Fighting AIDS face to face. *The Advocate*, 46-49.

King, J. L. (2004). *On the down low: A journey into the lives of "straight" black men who sleep with men.* New York: Broadway Books.

40 Laumann, E., Gagnon, J., Michael, R. T., & Michaels, S. (1994). *The social organization of sexuality: Sexual practices in the United States.* Chicago: University of Chicago Press.

41 Crooks & Baur, (2008); Messner, (1992).

42 Messner, (1992).

43 Crooks & Baur, (2008); Kinsey et al., (1948); Kinsey et al., (1953).

44 Garner, B., & Smith, R. W. (1977). Are there really any gay male athletes? An empirical survey. *Journal of Sex Research, 13,* 22-34.

45 Southhall, R., Anderson, E., Coleman, F., & Nagel, M. (2006). *Attitudes regarding sexual orientation among university athletes.* Paper presentation at the North American Society for the Sociology of Sport. Vancouver, British Columbia, Canada.

46 Amaechi, John. (2007). *Man in the middle.* New York: Random House.

Anderson, E., & McCormack, M. (2010). Comparing the black and gay make athlete: Patterns in American oppression. *The Journal of Men's Studies, 18*(2), 145-158.

Kopay, D., & Young, P. D. (1977). *The David Kopay story.* New York: Arbor House.

The brief history of gay athletes. (1998, December, 18). ESPN.com. Retrieved April 2, 2009, from http://www.lifesitenews.com/news/archive/ldn/2005/dec/05121603

47 Ellis, B. J., & Symons, D. (1990). Sex differences in sexual fantasy: An evolutionary psychological approach. *Journal of Sex Research, 27,* 527-56.

Leitenberg, H., & Henning, K. (1995). Sexual fantasy. *Psychological Bulletin, 117,* 469-496.

48 Cardamakis, E., Vinakos, G., Lambou, T., & Papathanasiou, Z. (1993). Comments by the "information by phone" department of the Sex Medical Institute on the telephone calls related to sexuality and contraception. *European Journal of Obstetrics, Gynecology, and Reproductive Biology, 52,* 125-129.

Coleman, E. (2002). Masturbation as a means of achieving sexual health. *Journal of Psychology and Human Sexuality, 14,* 5-16.

Kitamura, K. (1990). Communicating with adolescents. Telephone counseling and adolescent health clinic services of the Japan family planning association. *Integration, 25,* 40-41.

353

49 Goodman, A. (1993). Diagnosis and treatment of sexual addiction. *Journal of Sex and Marital Therapy, 19*(3), 225-251.
Kwee et al., (2007).

50 Goodman, (1993); Kwee et al., (2007).

51 Goodman, A. (1992). Sexual addiction: Designation and treatment. *Journal of Sex and Marital Therapy, 18*(4), 303-314.
Kwee, Alex, W., & Hoover, D. C. (2008). Theologically-informed education about masturbation: A male sexual health perspective. *Journal of Psychology and Theology, 36*(4), 258-269.

52 Crooks & Baur, (2008).

53 Crooks & Baur, (2008).

54 Crooks & Baur, (2008).

55 Rentzel, (1972).

56 Pearlman, J. (2008). *Boys will be boys: The glory days and party nights of the Dallas cowboys dynasty.* New York: HarperCollins.

57 Pearlman, (2008).

58 Caron, S. L., Halteman, W. A., & Stacy, C. (1997). Athletes and rape: Is there a connection? *Perceptual and Motor Skills, 85,* 1379-1393.

59 Montpetit, J. (2005, October 18). *McGill cancels football season after investigation confirms hazing.* Retrieved October 25, 2005, from http://news.yahoo.com/s/cpress/ftbl_mcgill_hazing
Wahl & Wertheim, (2003).

60 Strong et al., (2008).

61 Money, J. (1986). *Lovemaps: Clinical concepts of sexual/erotic health and pathology, paraphilia, and gender transposition in childhood, adolescence, and maturity.* New York: Irvington.

62 King, B. M. (2002). *Human sexuality today* (4th ed.). Upper Saddle River, NJ: Prentice Hall.

63 King, (2002).

64 Janus, S. S., & Janus, C. L. (1993). *The Janus report on sexual behavior.* New York: Wiley.

65 Pearlman, (2008).

66 Pearlman, (2008).

Notes to Chapter 2

1 Strong et al., (2008).
Rye, B. J., & Meaney, G. J. (2007). The pursuit of sexual pleasure. *Sexuality and Culture, 11*(1), 28-51.

2 Lee, M. (2009, July 15). *Porn: Business of pleasure.* CNBC Television Production.

Rich, F. (2001, May 20). Naked capitalists. *New York Times Magazine,* pp. 50-56, 80, 82, 92.

Schultz, G. (2005, December, 16). *Large increase in porn DVD sales indicates growing pornography addiction.* Lifesitenews.com. Retrieved May 8, 2008, from http://www.lifesitenews.com/news/archive/ldn/2005/dec/05121603

3 Laumann, et al., (1994).

4 Padgett, V. R., Brislutz, J. A., & Neal, J. (1989). Pornography, erotica, and attitudes toward women: The effects of repeated exposure. *Journal of Sex Research, 26,* 470-491.

5 Paul, P. (2005). *Pornified: How pornography is transforming our lives, our relationships, and our families.* New York: Times Books.

Schwartz, J. (2004, March 29). Leisure pursuits of today's young men. *The New York Times.* Retrieved January 14, 2009, from http://www.nytimes.com/2004/03/29/technology/29guy.html

6 Paul, (2005); Schwartz, (2004).

7 Cooper, A. (1998). Sexuality and the Internet: Surfing into the new millennium. *CyberPsychology and Behavior, 1,* 181-187.

Cooper, A., Scherer, C. R., Boies, S. C., & Gordon, B. L. (1999). Sexuality on the Internet: From sexual exploration to pathological expression. *Professional Psychology: Research and Practice, 30,* 154-164.

Padgett et al., (1989).

8 Laumann et al., (1994).

9 Stack, S., Wasserman, I., & Kern, R. (2004). Adult social bonds and use of Internet pornography. *Social Science Quarterly, 85*(1), 75-88.

Quinn, J. F., & Forsyth, C. J. (2005). Describing sexual behavior in the era of the Internet: A typology for empirical research. *Deviant Behavior, 26,* 191-207.

10 Websense, Inc. (2004, April 4). *Websense research shows online pornography site continue strong growth.* Retrieved January 20, 2009, from http://www2.prnewswire.com/cgibin/stories.pl?ACCT=104&STORY=/www/story/04-05-2004/0002140810&EDATE=

Stack et al., (2004).

11 Benedict, (1997); Benedict, (1998); Benedict, (2004); Benedict & Yaeger, (1998).

Snyder, E. E. (1994). Interpretations and explanations of deviance among college athletes: A case study. *Sociology of Sport Journal, 11.* 231-248.

12 Osanka, F. M., & Johann, S. L. (1989). *Sourcebook on pornography.* Lexington, MA: Lexington Books.

Paul, (2005).

13 Paul, (2005) p. 82, 106.

14 McKenzie-Mohr, D., & Zanna, M.P. (1990). Treating women as sexual objects: Look to the (gender schematic) male who has viewed pornography. *Personality and Social Psychology Bulletin, 16,* 296-308.

Oddone-Paolucci, E., Genuis, M., & Violato, C. (2000). A meta-analysis of the published research on the effects of pornography. In C. Violato, E. Oddone-Paolucci, & M. Genuis (Eds.), *Changing family and child development* (pp. 48-59). Aldershot, England: Ashgate.

15 Paul, (2005).

16 Paul, (2005) p. 80, 92, 133.

17 Zillmann, D., & Bryant, J. (1988). Pornography's impact on sexual satisfaction. *Journal of Applied Social Psychology, 18,* 438-453.

18 Paul, (2005) p. 91.

19 Zillmann, D., & Bryant, J. (1988). Effects of prolonged consumption of pornography on family values. *Journal of Family Issues, 9,* 518-544.

Zillmann, D. (1989). Effects of prolonged consumption of pornography. In D.Zillmann & J. Bryant (Eds.) *Pornography: Research advances and policy considerations* (pp. 127-157). N.J.: Lawrence Erlbaum.

20 Paul, (2005) p. 15, 147.

21 Paul, (2005).

22 Paul, (2005) p. 246.

23 Crooks & Baur, (2008).

Hart, A. D. (1994). *The sexual man: Masculinity without guilt.* Dallas, TX: Word Publishing.

Sanday, P. R. (2007). *Fraternity gang rape: Sex, brotherhood, and privilege on campus* (2nd ed.). New York: New York University Press.

24 Crooks & Baur (2008); Hart, (1994); Sanday, (2007).

25 Hart, (1994); Paul, (2005).

26 Hart, (1994); Paul, (2005).

27 Paul, (2005) p. 87.

28 Paul, (2005); Sanday, (2007).

29 Bandura, (1973); Bandura, (1979).

30 Castleman, M. (2004). *Great sex: A man's guide to the secret principles of total-body sex.* Emmaus, PA: Rodale Books.

Castleman, M. (2005, May). *XXX harmful: How pornography misleads men about women's sexuality and their own and contributes to sex problems.* Paper presented at the What's New and What Works: Pioneering Solutions for Today's Sexual Issues (AASECT 37th Annual Conference), Portland, OR.

Cook, I. (2006). Western heterosexual masculinity, anxiety, and web porn. *The Journal of Men's Studies, 14,* 47-64.

Crooks & Baur, (2008).

Malamuth, N. M. (1978, September). *Erotica, aggression, and perceived appropriateness.* Paper presented at the meeting of the American Psychological Association, Toronto, Canada.

Malamuth, N. M. (1999). Pornography. In L. Kurtz (Ed.) *Encyclopedia for violence, peace, and conflict, volume 3* (pp. 77-89). New York: Academic Press.

Malamuth, N. M., & Billings, V. (1985). The Functions and effects of pornography: Sexual communication versus the feminist models in light of research findings. In J. Bryant & D. Zillmann (Eds.), *Perspective on media effects* (pp. 83-108). Hillsdale, N.J: Erlbaum.

Strong et al., (2008).

31 Malamuth, N. M. (1987). Do sexually violent media indirectly contribute to antisocial behavior? In M. R. Walsh (Ed.) *The psychology of women: Ongoing debates* (pp. 441-459). New Haven, CT: Yale University Press.

32 Carnes, (1991).

Rediger, G. L. (1990). *Ministry and sexuality: Cases, counseling and care.* Minneapolis, MN: Fortress Press.

Schaumburg, H. W. (1992). *False intimacy: Understanding the struggle of sexual addiction.* Colorado Springs, CO: NavPress Publishing Group.

33 Denizet-Lewis, B. (2009). *America anonymous: Eight addicts in search of a life.* New York: Simon and Schuster.

Topkin, M. (2005, July 24). *Boggs: No doubt, at least not now, among baseball's elite.* Retrieved January 26, 2008, from http://www.sptimes. com/2005/07/24/Sports/Boggs_No_doubt_at_l.shtml

34 Carnes, (1991).

Goodman, A. (1997). Sexual addiction. In J. H. Lowinson, P. Ruiz, R. B. Millman, & J. G. Langrod (Eds.), *Substance abuse: A comprehensive textbook* (pp. 340-354). Philadelphia: Williams and Wilkins.

Rediger, (1990); Schaumburg, (1992).

35 Carnes, (1991); Goodman, (1997); Rediger, (1990); Schaumburg, (1992).

36 Kafka, M. P. (1997). Hypersexual desire in males: An operational definition and clinical implications for males with paraphilias and paraphilia-related disorders. *Archives of Sexual Behavior, 26*(5), 505-526.

37 Kafka, (1997).

38 Kafka, (1997).

39 American Psychiatric Association, 2000; Kwee et al., (2007).

40 Bancroft, J., & Vukadinovic, Z. (2004). Sexual addiction, sexual compulsivity, sexual impulsivity, or what? Toward a theoretical model. *The Journal of Sex Research, 41*(3), 225-235.

41 Carnes, (1991); Rediger, (1990).

42 Carnes, (1991).

Coleman, E., Miner, M., Ohlerking, F., & Raymond, N. (2001). Compulsive sexual behavior inventory: A preliminary study of reliability and validity. *Journal of Sex and Marital Therapy, 27*(4), 325-332.

43 George, R. L. (1990). *Counseling the chemically dependent: Theory and practice.* Boston: Allyn and Bacon.

Schaumburg, (1992).

44 Earle, R. H., & Crow, G. M. (1990). Sexual addiction: Understanding and treating the phenomenon. *Contemporary Family Therapy, 12*(2), 89-104.

Hart, (1994).

Schneider, J. P., & Schneider, B. (1991). *Sex, lies, and forgiveness: Healing from sexual addiction.* Center City, MN: Hazelden.

45 Grace, K. M. (2000). Sex-floggers. *Newsmagazine, 27*(16), 43.

46 Cooper et al., (1999).

47 Paul, (2005) p. 153, 156.

48 Cooper et al., (1999).

The Harris Poll. (2008, November 17). *Four out of five adults now use the Internet.* Retrieved August 4, 2009, from http://www.harrisinteractive. com/harris_poll/index.asp?PID=973

49 Schneider, J. P., & Weiss, R. (2001). *Cybersex exposed: Simple fantasy or obsession?* Center City, MN: Hazelden.

50 Carnes, (1991); Paul, (2005); Rediger, (1990); Schaumburg, (1992).

51 Earle & Crow, (1990).

52 Curry (1991); Curry, (1998); Lefkowitz (1997); Schwartz, & Dekeserdy, (1997).

53 Slade, J. W. (2000). *Pornography in America: A reference handbook.* Santa Barbara, CA: ABC-CLIO, Inc.

54 Slade, (2000).

55 Hite, S. (1985). *The Hite report on male sexuality.* New York: Ballantine Books.

56 Robinson, (1998).

57 Robinson, (1998).

58 Griffin, S. (1981). *Pornography and silence: Culture's revenge against nature.* New York: Harper and Row.

Mawhinny, V. T. (1998). Behavioral sexual maladaption contagion in America: An applied theoretical analysis. *Behavior and Social Issues, 8,* 159-193.

59 Lefkowitz, (1997); Sanday, (2007).

60 Kelly, K. D., & Dekeserdy, W. S. (1994). Women's fear of crime and abuse in college and university dating relationships. *Violence and Victims, 9,* 17-30.

Lefkowitz, (1997).

Sanday, P. R. (1996). *A woman scorned: Acquaintance rape on trial.* New York: Doubleday.

Sanday, (2007).

61 Koss, M. P., & Dinero, T. E. (1989). Predictors of sexual aggression among a national sample of male college students. In R. A. Prentky & V. Quinsey (Eds.), Human sexual aggression: Current perspectives. *Annals of the New York Academy of Sciences, 528,* 133-146.

Lefkowitz, (1997); Sanday, (1996) Sanday, (2007); Schwartz and Dekeseredy, (1997).

62 Kanin, E. J. (1984). Date rape: Unofficial criminals and victims. *Victimology, 9,* 95-108.

Kanin, E. J. (1985). Date rapists: Differential sexual socialization and relative deprivation. *Archives of Sexual Behavior, 14,* 219-231.

63 Crooks & Baur, (2008).

64 Crooks & Baur, (2008).

Stock, W. (1985, September). *The effect of pornography on women.* Paper Presented at A Hearing of the Attorney General's Commission on Pornography, Houston, TX.

65 Barron, N., & Kimmel, M. (2000). Sexual violence in three pornographic media: Towards a sociological explanation. *Journal of Sex Research, 37,* 1-8.

Lebegue, B. (1991). Paraphilias in U.S. pornography titles: "Pornography made me do it" (Ted Bundy). *Bulletin of the American Academy of Psychiatry and the Law, 19,* 343-48.

Scott, J. E., & Cuvelier, S. J. (1993). Violence and sexual violence in pornography: Is it really increasing? *Archives of Sexual Behavior, 22,* 357-371.

Strong et al., (2008).

66 Barron & Kimmel, (2000).

Scott & Cuvelier, (1993).

67 Fisher, W. A., & Grenier, G. (1994). Violent pornography, antiwoman thoughts, and antiwoman acts: In search of reliable effects. *Journal of Sex Research, 31,* 23-38.

68 Allen, M., D'Alessio, D., & Brezgel, K. (1995). A meta-analysis summarizing the effects of pornography: II. Aggression after exposure. *Human Communication Research, 22,* 258-283.

Malamuth, N. M., Addison, T., & Koss, M. (2000). Pornography and sexual aggression: Are there reliable effects and can we understand them? *Annual Review of Sex Research, 11,* 26-94.

Oddone-Paolucci et al., (2000).

Simmons, C. A., Lehmann, P., & Collier-Tenison, S. (2008). Linking male use of the sex industry to controlling behaviors in violent relationships: An exploratory analysis. *Violence against Women, 14*(4), 406-417.

69 Donnerstein, E., Linz, D., & Penrod, S. (1987). *The question of pornography: Research findings and policy implications.* New York: Free Press.

Linz, D. (1989). Exposure to sexually explicit materials and attitudes toward rape: A comparison of study results. *Journal of Sex Research, 26,* 50-84.

Malamuth, N. M., & Donnerstein, E. (Eds.). (1984). *Pornography and sexual aggression.* New York: Academic Press.

70 Malamuth et al., (2000).

71 Gladwell, M. (2000). *The tipping point: How little things can make a big difference.* London, England: Little, Brown.

Granovetter, M., & Soong, R. (1983). Threshold models of diffusion and collective behavior. *Journal of Mathematical Sociology, 9,* 165-179.

72 Huesmann, L. R., & Malamuth, N, M. (1986). Media violence and antisocial behavior: An overview. *Journal of Social Issues, 42*(30), 1-6.

Steinfield, J. (1972). *Statement in hearings before subcommittee on communications of committee of commerce* (United States Senate, Serial #92-52, pp. 25-27). Washington, D.C.: U.S. Government Printing Office.

73 Olivia, N. v. National Broadcasting Co., Inc. (1978). *California Reporter, 141,* 511-515.
Malamuth, N. M. (1989). Sexually violent media, thought patterns, and antisocial behavior. In G. Comstock (Ed.), *Public Communication and Behavior, vol. 2* (pp. 150-204). New York: Academic Press.

74 Malamuth, (1989).

75 Malamuth, (1987); Malamuth, (1989).

76 Parrot, A. (1988). *Coping with date rape and acquaintance rape.* New York: Rosen Publishing Group.

77 Brooks, D. L. (1997). Rape on soaps: The legal angle. In M. A. Fineman & M. T. McCluskey (Eds.), *Feminism, media, and the law* (pp. 104-119). New York: Oxford University Press.

78 Brooks, (1997).

79 Burt, M. (1991). Rape myths and acquaintance rape. In A. Parrot & L. Bechhofer (Eds.), *Acquaintance rape: The hidden crime* (pp. 26-40). New York: John Wiley.

80 Crooks & Baur, (2008).

81 King, (2002); Slade, (2000).

82 Brockman, J. (2006, April 5). Child sex as Internet fare, through the eyes of a victim. *The New York Times,* p. A20.
Quinn & Forsyth, (2005).

83 Canadian archer facing child porn charges. (2009, February 12). *CBC Sports.* Retrieved March 4, 2009, from http://www.cbc.ca/sports/amateur/story/2009/02/12/burnes-archer-charged.html
Crawford, T. (2009, February 6). 31 arrested in child porn sweep: Ont. police. *Canwest News Service.* Retrieved March 4, 2009, from http://www.montreal gazette.com/news/arrested+child+porn+sweep+police/1 256653/story.html

84 Canadian archer facing child porn charges. (2009, February 12); Crawford, (2009).

85 Brown freshman dismissed in light of child porn charges. (2008, February 21). *College Hockey News Staff Report.* Retrieved March 16, 2009, from http://www.collegehockeynews.com/news/2008/02/21_brownfreshman.php
Morrow, S. (2008, August 18). Harding sentenced in video porn case. *Times Colonist.* Retrieved March 16, 2009, from http://www.canada.com/victoriatimescolonist/news/story.html?id=f9e4809a-0993-4075-806a-9539d5e23716
Roehrkasse, A. (2008, March 14). Brown U. officials knew freshman hockey player faced child porn charges. *Brown Daily Herald* (Brown University). Retrieved March 16, 2009, from http://www.unogateway.com/home/index.cfm?event=displayArticlePrinterFriendly&uStory-id=obc4cb44-4216-bc92-f7

Vancouver Island hockey star sentenced on voyeurism charges. (2008, June 11) *CBC News*. Retrieved March 16, 2009, from http://wwww.cbc.ca.canada/british-columbia/story/2008/06/06/bc-zolnierczyk-pornography-charges.html

86 Morrow, (2008), Roehrkasse, (2008); Brown freshman dismissed in light of childporn charges, (2008, February 21).

87 Morrow, (2008), Roehrkasse, (2008); Brown freshman dismissed in light of childporn charges, (2008, February 21).

88 Morrow, (2008); Roehrkasse, (2008); Brown freshman dismissed in light of childporn charges, (2008, February 21).

89 Morrow, (2008); Roehrkasse, (2008); Brown freshman dismissed in light of childporn charges, (2008, February 21).

90 Morrow, (2008); Roehrkasse, (2008); Brown freshman dismissed in light of childporn charges, (2008, February 21); Vancouver Island hockey star sentenced on voyeurism charges, (2008, June 11).

91 Morrow, (2008); Roehrkasse, (2008); Brown freshman dismissed in light of childporn charges, (2008, February 21); Vancouver Island hockey star sentenced on voyeurism charges, (2008, June 11).

92 Former swimming coach sentenced for child porn. (2008, October 18). The Times (Northwest Indiana), p. A2.

93 Former swimming coach sentenced for child porn. (2008, October 18)

94 Former swimming coach sentenced for child porn. (2008, October 18)

95 Marshall, W. L. (1988). The use of sexually explicit stimuli by rapists, child molesters, and nonoffenders. *The Journal of Sex Research, 25,* 267-288.

96 Carter, D. L., Prentky, R. A., Knight, R. A., Vandeveer, P. L., & Boucher, R. J. (1987). Use of pornography in the criminal and developmental histories of sexual offenders. *Journal of Interpersonal Violence, 2,* 196-211.

97 Bourke, M. L., & Hernandez, A. E. (2009). The 'Butner Study' redux: A report of the incidence of hands-on child victimization by child pornography. *Journal of Family Violence, 24*(3), 183-191.

98 Bourke & Hernandez, (2009).

99 Bourke & Hernandez, (2009).

100 Bourke & Hernandez, (2009).

101 Dolan, B. (2006, May 12). Candiano gets 82 months in prison. *The Times* (Northwest Indiana), p. A9.

102 Dolan, (2006).

103 Carlson, J. (2007, July 8). Web identities haunt ex-coach. *The Times* (Northwest Indiana), pp. A1, A9.
Carlson, J. (2008, January 12). Ex-Andrean coach gets 10 years. *The Times* (Northwest Indiana), pp. A3, A4.
Chase, M., & Carlson, J. (2006, August 22). NWI men among 24 in sex bust. *The Times* (Northwest Indiana), pp. A1, A7.

104 Carlson, (2007); Carlson (2008); Chase & Carlson, (2006).

105 Mora, C. (2008, November 13) Joseph Okoh found guilty. *NBC 29.com.* Retrieved June 10, 2009, from http://nbc29.com/Global/story.asp?S=9346623

Times Staff and Wire Report (2008, January 29). The sports world in brief. *The Times* (Northwest Indiana), p. B2.

106 Nack, W., & Yaeger, D. (2008, September 13). Special report: Every parent's nightmare. *Sports Illustrated, 91*(10). Retrieved November 18, 2009, from http://vault.sportsillustrated.cnn.com/vault/article/magazine/MAG1127274/index.html

Robinson, (1998).

107 The Sheldon Kennedy/Graham James case; Sexual abuse in Canadian junior hockey. (2004, January 8). *Silent Edge.* Retrieved July 7, 2009, from http://www.silent-edge.org/kennedy.html

Robinson, (1998).

108 Kennedy, S., & Grainger, J. (2006). *Why I didn't say anything: The Sheldon Kennedy story.* Toronto: Insomniac Press.

109 Sanserino, M. (2011, November 7). Penn State campus subdued as scandal details air. *Pittsburgh Post-Gazette.* Retrieved November 7, 2011, from http://www.post-gazette.com/pg/11311/1188147-143-0.stm?cmpid=newspanel3

Notes to Chapter 3

1 Jones, L. (1967). *Striptease.* New York: Simon and Schuster.

Radziwill, A. (1998). *Strippers: The naked stages,* HBO America undercover series New York: HBO.

2 Fairbank, K. (2003, February 22). *Dancing for dollars.* Dallas Morning News, pp. 2F, 3F.

Sherman, W. (2007, July 8). The naked truth about strip clubs. *NY Daily News.* Retrieved June 8, 2009, from http://www.nydailynews.com/news/2007/07/08/2007-07-08_the_naked_truth_about_ strip_clubs_html

3 Sagal, P. (2007). *The book of vice: Very naughty things (and how to do them well).* New York: HarperCollins.

Sherman, (2007).

4 Thompson, W. E., Harred, J. L., & Burks, B. E. (2003). Managing the stigma of topless dancing: A decade later. *Deviant Behavior, 24,* 551-570.

5 Pearlman, (2008).

6 McCarthy, M. (2007, November 13). Strip clubs, athletes can be risky mix. *USA Today.* Retrieved April 8, 2008, from www.usatoday.com/sports/2007-11-12- clubs-athletes-cover_N.htm?csp=34

7   Schmidt, M. S. (2006, October 27). Colleges; Coach resigns over trip to strip club. *The New York Times*. Retrieved May 6, 2009, from http://query.nytimes. com/gst/ fullpage.html?res=9D03E4DE153FF934A1573C19609C8B63

8   McCarthy, (2007).

9   Sagal, (2007); Thompson et al., (2003).

10 McCarthy, (2007).

11 McCarthy, (2007); Pearlman, (2008).

12 Berti, N. (2004). *A face in the crowd: My life as an NFL wife*. Bloomington, IN: Xlibris.
    McCarthy, (2007).

13 McCarthy, (2007).

14 Pearlman, (2008).

15 Benedict, (1997); Pearlman, (2008).

16 Benedict, (1997).

17 Pearlman, (2008).

18 Benedict, (1997); Pearlman, (2008)
    Yaeger, D. (2007). *It's not about the truth: The untold story of the Duke lacrosse case and the lives it shattered*. New York: Simon and Schuster.

19 Chandy, J. M., Blum, R. W., & Resnick, M. D. (1996). Gender-specific outcomes for sexually abused adolescents. *Child Abuse and Neglect, 20*(12), 1219-1231.
    Dilorio, C., Hartwell, T., & Hanson, N. (2002). Childhood sexual abuse and risk behaviors among men at high risk for HIV infection. *American Journal of Public Health, 92*, 214-219.
    Gorey, K., & Leslie, D. (1997). The prevalence of childhood sexual abuse: Integrative review adjustment for potential response and measurement biases. *Child Abuse and Neglect, 21*, 391-398.
    Stander, V., Olson, C., & Merrill, L. (2002). Self-definition as a survivor of childhood sexual abuse among navy recruits. *Journal of Consulting and Clinical Psychology, 70*, 369-377.

20 Merrill, L. L., Thomsen, C. J., Gold, S. R., & Milner, J. S. (2001). Childhood abuse and premilitary sexual assault in male navy recruits. *Journal of Consulting and Clinical Psychology, 69*, 252-261.

21 Finkelhor, D. (1994). Current information on the scope and nature of child sexual abuse. *The Future of Children, 4*, 31-53.
    Putnam, F. W. (2003). Ten-year research update review: Child sexual abuse. *Journal of the American Academy of Child and Adolescent Psychiatry, 42*, 269-278.
    Sedlack, A. J., & Broadhurst, D. D. (1996). *Executive summary of the third national incidence study of child abuse and neglect*. National Center on Child Abuse and Neglect, National Committee to Prevent Child Abuse. Washington, DC.

22 Pearlman, (2008).

23 Yaeger, (2007).
24 Yaeger, (2007).
25 Yaeger, (2007).
26 Doria, J. (2008, May 28). *Former District Attorney Mike Nifong no longer immune from lacrosse players' lawsuit after stay order lifted.* Retrieved May 16, 2009, from http://www.allheadlinenews.com/articles/7011090157#i xzz0Gjk5ULR4&B
   Yaeger, (2007).
27 Benedict, (1997).
28 Benedict, (1997); Benedict, (1998); Benedict, (2004).
   Benedict, J., & Klein, A. (1997). Arrest and conviction rates for athletes accused of sexual assault. *Sociology of Sport Journal, 14,* 86-94.
   Benedict & Yaeger, (1998).
29 Slade, (2000).
30 Thompson et al., (2003) p. 561.
31 Thompson et al., (2003) p. 564.
32 Martin, P. (2008, March 27). Sports as usual: Sex, scandal, and March madness. *Yale Daily News.* Retrieved June 7, 2009, from http://www.yaledailynews.com/articles/printarticle/24058
33 Rushin, S. (2001, August 6). Golden moments: Testimony in the Gold Club trial offers images of our heroes that are, regrettably, hard to forget. *SI Vault, 95*(5). Retrieved June 9, 2009, from http://vault.sportsillustrated.cnn.com/vault/article/magazine/MAG1023095/index.htm
34 Cabell, B. (2001, July 24). NBA star Ewing testifies at strip club trial. *CNN. com.* Retrieved May 11, 2008, from http://archives.cnn.com/2001/LAW/07/23/gold.club.trial/index.html
   Rushin, (2001).
35 Yaeger, (2007).
36 Yaeger, (2007).
37 King, (2002).
38 Janus & Janus, (1993); King, (2002); Kinsey et al., (1948); Laumann et al., (1994).
   Rodman. D., & Keown, T. (1996). *Bad as I wanna be.* New York: Bantam Doubleday Dell Publishing Group.
39 King, (2002).
   Potterat, J. J., Woodhouse, D. E., Muth, J. B., & Muth, S. Q. (1990). Estimating the prevalence and career longevity of prostitute women. **Journal of Sex Research, 27,** 233-243.
40 Janus & Janus, (1993).
   Joseph, C. (1995). Scarlet wounding: Issues of child prostitution. *Journal of Psychohistory, 23,* 2-17.
41 Pearlman, (2008).
42 Pearlman, (2008).

43 Meggyesy, D. (1971). *Out of their league.* New York: Coronet Communications.
44 Meggyesy, (1971).
45 Lewandowski, D. (1981, January 8). York suspends seven players for training violations. *The BG News* (Bowling Green State University), p.10.
46 Lewandowski, (1981).
47 Freund, M., Lee, N., & Leonard, T. (1991). Sexual behavior of clients with street prostitutes in Camden, N.J. *Journal of Sex Research, 28,* 579-591.
48 Sawyer, S., Metz, M. E., Hinds, J. D., & Brucker, R. A. (2001-2002). Attitudes toward prostitution among males: A consumers' report. *Current Psychology, 20,* 363-376.
49 Taylor, L., & Serby, S. (2003). *LT: Over the edge.* New York: HarperCollins.
50 Taylor & Serby, (2003).
51 Farley, M. (2004). *Prostitution, trafficking, and traumatic stress.* New York: Haworth Maltreatment and Trauma Press.
52 Farley, (2004).
53 Chelala, C. (2000, November 28). The unrelenting scourge of child prostitution. *San Francisco Chronicle,* p. A27.
   Willis, B. M., & Levy, B. S. (2002). Child prostitution: Global health burden, research needs, and interventions. *The Lancet, 359,* 1417-1421.
54 Strong et al., (2008).

Notes to Chapter 4

1 Bogle, (2008).
2 Bogle, (2008).
   Glenn, N., & Marquardt, E . (2001). *Hooking up, hanging out, and looking for Mr Right: College women on dating and mating today.* An Institute for American Values Report to the Independent Women's Forum.
3 Bogle, (2008).
4 Canseco, J. (2005). *Juiced: Wild times, rampant 'roids, smash hits, and how baseball got big.* New York: HarperCollins.
   Esposito, P., & Golenbock, P. (2003). *Thunder and lightning: A no – b.s. hockey memoir.* Chicago: Triumph Books.
   Johnson, E., & Novak, W. (1992). *My Life.* New York: Ballantine Books.
   Rodman & Keown, (1996); Taylor & Serby, (2003).
5 Canseco, (2005); Rodman & Keown, (1996).
6 Berti, (2004); Bogle, (2008).
7 Berti, (2004), p. 86.
8 DeKeseredy, W. S., & Kelly, K. (1995). Sexual abuse in Canadian University and college dating relationships: The contribution of male peer support. *Journal of Family Violence, 10,* 41-53.
   Schwartz & DeKeseredy, (1997).

9   Kanin, (1984).
10 Christopher, F. S., & Frandsen, M. M. (1990). Strategies of influence in sex and dating. *Journal of Social and Personal Relationships, 7,* 89-105.
Sanday, (2007).
11 Bogle, (2008).
Cooper, M. L. (2002). Alcohol use and risky sexual behavior among college students and youth: Evaluating the evidence. *Journal of Studies on Alcohol, 63,* 101-117.
Peralta, R. (2001). *Getting trashed in college: Doing alcohol, doing gender, doing violence.* Unpublished Dissertation, University of Delaware – Newark.
Williams, K. M. (1998). *Learning limits: College woman, drugs, and relationships.* Westport, CT: Bergin & Garvey.
12 Faurie, C., Pontier, D., & Raymond, M. (2004). Student athletes claim to have more sexual partners than other students. *Evolution and Human Behavior, 25*(1), 1-8.
13 Koss, M. P. (1989). Hidden rape: Sexual aggression and victimization in a national sample of students in higher education. In M. A. Pirog-Good & J. E. Stets (Eds.), *Violence in dating relationships: Emerging social issues* (pp. 145-168). New York: Praeger.
Koss, M. P., Gidycz, C., & Wisniewski, N. (1987). The scope of rape: Incidence and prevalence of sexual aggression in a national sample of higher education students. *Journal of Consulting and Clinical Psychology, 55,* 162-170.
14 Benedict, (1997); Benedict, (1998).
Melnick, M. (1992). Male athletes and sexual assault. Journal of Physical Education, *Recreation, and Dance, 63*(5), 32-35.
15 Brown, J. (1989). *Out of bounds.* New York: Kensington.
16 Brown, (1989), p. 183, 184, 190.
17 Messner, M. A. (1994). Women in men's locker room? In M. A. Messner & D. F. Sabo, (Eds.), *Sex, violence and power in sports: Rethinking masculinity* (pp. 42-52). Freedom, CA.: The Crossing Press.
18 Strong et al., (2008).
19 Cates, J. R., Herndon, N.L., Schulz, S. L., & Darroch, J. E. (2004). *Our voices, our lives, our futures: Youth and sexually transmitted diseases.* Chapel Hill: School of Journalism and Mass Communication, University of North Carolina at Chapel Hill.
National Center for Health Statistics. (2004). *Health, United States, 2004, with chartbook on trends in the health of Americans.* Hyattsville, MD: Author.
20 Strong et al., (2008).
21 Hopson, J. L., Donatelle, R. J., & Littrell, T. R. (2009). *Get fit, stay well.* New York: Benjamin Cummings.
22 Johnson & Novak, (1992).

23 Johnson & Novak, (1992).
24 Rodman & Keown, (1996).
25 Rodman & Keown, (1996).
26 Times Staff and Wire Report. (2006, April 25). The sports world in brief: Vick suit settled. *The Times* (Northwest Indiana), p. B2.
27 Times Staff and Wire Report, (2006, April 25).
28 Strong et al., (2008).
29 Hite, (1985).
   Hite, S. (1993). *Women as revolutionary agents of change: The Hite reports and beyond.* Madison, WI: University of Madison Press.
30 Johnson & Novak, (1992).
31 Benedict, (2004).
32 Benedict, (2004).
33 Yaeger, (2007).
34 Strong et al., (2008).
35 Benedict, (1997); Benedict, (1998); Benedict, (2004); Robinson, (1998); Yaeger, (2007).
36 Benedict, (1997); Benedict, (1998); Benedict, (2004).
   Parrot, A., & Bechhofer, L. (1991). *Acquaintance rape: The hidden crime.* New York: John Wiley.
   Robinson, (1998).
   Russell, D. (1984). *Sexual exploitation: Rape, child sexual abuse and workplace harassment.* Beverly Hills, CA: Sage.
   Warshaw, R. (1994). *I never called it rape: The Ms. report on recognizing, fighting, and surviving date and acquaintance rape.* New York: HarperCollins.
37 Benedict, (1997); Benedict, (1998).
   Estrich, S. (1987). *Real rape.* Cambridge, MA: Harvard University Press.
38 Benedict, (1997); Benedict, (1998); Benedict, (2004); Robinson, (1998).
39 Benedict, (1997); Benedict, (1998); Robinson, (1998).
40 Estrich, (1987).
41 Koss (1989); Koss & Wisniewski, (1987).
42 Matoesian, G. (1993). *Reproducing rape: Domination through talk in the courtroom.* Chicago: The University of Chicago Press.
43 DeKeseredy & Kelly, (1995); Kanin, (1984); Kanin, (1985).

Notes to Chapter 5

1   Canseco, (2005), p. 95, 96.
2   O'Toole, S. (2006). *Wedded to the game: The real lives of NFL women.* Lincoln, NE: University of Nebraska Press, p. 21.
3   White, E. (2002). *Fast girls: Teenage tribes and the myth of the slut.* New York: Berkley Books.

4 Rodman & Keown, (1996), p.149.
5 Rodman & Keown, (1996); O'Toole, (2006).
6 Canseco, (2005), p. 273.
7 Berti, 2004.
8 Johnson & Novak, p. 258, (1992).
9 Johnson & Novak, p. 258, (1992).
10 Esposito & Golenbock, (2003).
11 Esposito & Golenbock, (2003), p. 66.
12 Swift, E. M. (1991, November 18). Dangerous games. *Sports Illustrated, 75*(22), 40-43.
13 Classen, C. A., Palesh, O. G., & Aggarwal, R. (2005). Sexual revictimization: A review of the empirical literature. *Trauma, Violence, and Abuse, 6*(2), 103-129.
14 Classen et al., (2005).
15 Classen et al., (2005).

Notes to Chapter 6

1 Pitino says scandal is taxing family, rips media for opening wounds. (2009, August 27). *Chicago Tribune*, p. 75.
   Tresniowski, A. (2009, December 14). Tiger in the rough. *People, 72*(24), 83-89.
   Tresniowski, A., Bartolomeo, J., & McNeil, E. F. (2009, December 21). Inside Elin's nightmare. *People, 72*(25), 73-77.
2 Canseco, (2005); Esposito & Golenbock, (2003); Johnson & Novak, (1992); Taylor & Serby, (2003).
3 Laumann et al.,(1994).
4 Ortiz, S. M. (1997). Traveling with the ball club: A code of conduct for wives only. *Symbolic Interaction, 20*(3), 225-249.
   Ortiz, S. M. (2004). Traveling with the Ball Club: A code of conduct for wives only. In J. Z. Spade & C. G. Valentine (Eds.), *The kaleidoscope of gender: Prisms, patterns, and possibilities* (pp. 481-486). Belmont, CA: Wadsworth.
5 Canseco, (2005), p.91.
6 Ortiz, (1997); (2004).
7. Ortiz, (1997); (2004).
8 Ortiz, (1997); (2004).
9 Ortiz, (1997); (2004).
10 Ortiz, (1997); (2004).
11 Ortiz, (1997); (2004).
12 Ortiz, (1997); (2004).
13 Ortiz, (1997); (2004).

14 Ortiz, (1997); (2004).
15 Canseco, (2005).
16 Canseco, (2005), p. 95.
17 Canseco, (2005).
18 Tresniowski, A., & McNeil, E. (2010, March 8). Was it enough? *People, 73*(9)
   p. 66-68.
   Tresniowski, A. (2009, December 14); Tresniowski, et al., (2009, December 21).
19 Laumann et al., (1994).
   O'Sullivan, L. F., Hoffman, S., Harrison, A., & Dolezal, C. (2006).
   Men, multiple sexual partners, and young adults' sexual relationships:
   Understanding the role of gender in the study of risk. *Journal of Urban
   Health: Bulletin of the New York Academy of Medicine, 83*(4), 695-708.
   Wiederman, M. W. (1997). Extramarital sex: Prevalence and correlates in a
   national survey. *Journal of Sex Research, 34,* 167-174.
20 O'Sullivan et al., (2006).
21 Adimora, A. A., Schoenbach, V. J., & Doherty, I. A. (2007). Concurrent
   sexual partnerships among men in the United States. *American Journal
   of Public Health, 97,* 2230-2237. Retrieved July 22, 2009, from doi:
   10.2105/AJPH.2006.099069
22 Wahl, G., & Wertheim, L. J. (1998, May 4). Paternity ward. *Sports Illustrated,
   88*(18), 62-70.
23 Wahl & Wertheim, (1998).
24 Wahl & Wertheim, (1998).
25 Wahl & Wertheim, (1998).
26 Wahl & Wertheim, (1998).
27 Wahl & Wertheim, (1998).
28 Johnson & Novak, (1992).
29 Johnson & Novak, (1992).
30 Kitson, G. C., & Holmes, W. M. (1992). *Portrait of divorce: Adjustment to
   marital breakdown.* New York: The Guilford Press.
31 Heyman, J. D. (2002, April 29/May 6). Did a starlet become a batterer? *US
   Weekly, 376/377,* 58-60.
32 Heyman, (2002).
33 *Wife of Colt's Harper says stabbing was accidental.* (2006, January 16).
   Retrieved May 14, 2009, from http://sports.espn.go.com/nfl/playoffs05/
   news/story?id=2293484
   Court date set for criminal recklessness charge. (2006, January 17). Retrieved
   May 15, 2009, from http://sports.espn.go.com/nfl/playoffs05/news/
   sory?id=2295555
34 Wife of Colt's Harper says stabbing was accidental. (2006, January 16);
   Court date set for criminal recklessness charge. (2006, January 17).
35 Archer, J. (2000). Sex differences in aggression between heterosexual
   partners: A meta-analytic review. *Psychological Bulletin, 126,* 651-680.

Cook, P. W. (1997). *Abused men: The hidden side of domestic violence.* Westport, CT: Greenwood Publishing Group.

Gelles, R. J., & Straus, M. A. (1988). *Intimate violence: The causes and consequences of abuse in the American family.* New York: Simon and Schuster.

Straus, M. A. (1997). Physical assaults by women partners: A major social problem. In M. R. Walsh (Ed.), *Women, men, and gender: Ongoing debates* (pp.210-221). New Haven CT: Princeton University Press.

36 Archer, (2000).

37 Stets, J. E., & Straus, M. A. (1989). The marriage license as a hitting license: A comparison of assaults in dating, cohabiting, and married couples. In M. A. Pirog-Good and J. E. Stets (Eds.), *Violence in dating relationships: Emerging social issues* (pp. 33-52). New York: Praeger.

38 Ford, B. (2001). *Violent relationships: Battering and abuse among adults.* Farmington Hills, MI: Gale Group, Inc.

Gelles & Straus, (1988).

Notes to Chapter 7

1 Coakley, J. (2010). *Sport in society: Issues and controversies.* (10th ed.). Boston: McGraw-Hill.

2 The body counters. (1993, April 12). *People Weekly, 39*(14), p. 34-37.

3 The body counters. (1993, April 12)

4 The body counters. (1993, April 12)

5 The body counters. (1993, April 12)

6 The body counters. (1993, April 12).

7 The body counters. (1993, April 12)

8 Messner & Sabo, (1994).

9 The body counters. (1993, April 12)

Pipher, M. (1994). *Reviving Ophelia: Saving the selves of adolescent girls.* New York: Ballantine Books.

10 Benedict, (1997); Benedict, (1998); Benedict, (2004); Benedict & Yaeger, (1998).

Crosset, Todd. W., Ptacek, J., McDonald, M. A., & Benedict, J. R. (1996). Male student-athletes and violence against women. *Violence Against Women, 2*(2), 163-179.

Crosset, T. W., Benedict, J. R., & McDonald, M. A. (2009). Male student-athletes reported for sexual assault: A survey of campus police departments and judicial affairs offices. In D. Stanley Eitzen (Ed.), *Sport in contemporary society: An anthology* (8th Ed.) (pp. 171-183). Boulder, CO: Paradigm.

Nixon, H. L. (1997). Gender, sport, and aggressive behavior outside of sport. *Journal of Sport and Social Issues, 21*(4), 379-391.

Robinson, (1998).
11 Sanday, (2007).
12 Borges, R. (1992, January 26). Trouble follows Tyson. *The Boston Globe,* p. 53.
13 Canseco, (2005) p. 93.
Coad, D. (2008). *The metrosexual: Gender, sexuality, and sport.* Albany, New York: SUNY Press. p. 168.
14 Swift, (1991).
15 Johnson & Novak, (1992).
McKay, J. (1993). "Marked men" and "wanton women": The politics of naming sexual "deviance" in sport. *Journal of Men's Studies, 2*(10), 69-87.
16 Swift, (1991).
17 Chamberlain, W. (1994). *A view from above.* New York: Random House Value Publishing.
Swift, (1991).
18 Swift, (1991).
19 Bogle, (2008).
20 Laumann et al., (1994).
21 National Center for Health Statistics. (2005). *Sexual behavior and selected health measures: Men and women 15–44 years of age, United States, (2002).* Retrieved May 1, 2009, from http://www.cdc.gov/nchs/products/pubs/pubd/ad/361-370/ad362.htm
22 American College Health Association. (2006). *American College Health Association national college health assessment: Reference group executive summary,* Spring 2006. Baltimore, MD: Author.
23 American College Health Association, (2006).
24 Cooper, (2002).
Dermen, K. H., Cooper, L., & Agocha, V. B. (1998). Sex-related expectancies as moderators between alcohol use and risky sex in adolescents. *Journal of Studies on Alcohol, 59,* 71-77.
25 Ferguson, D. (2010, February 20). Woods issues public apology. *The Times* (Northwest Indiana), p. B-8.
Tresniowski & McNeil, (2010, March 8).
26 Borges, (1992).
27 Borges, (1992).
28 Benedict, (1997); Benedict, (1998).
29 Benedict, (1997); Benedict, (1998).
30 Benedict, (1998); Wahl & Wertheim, (1998).
31 Benedict, (1997); Johnson & Novak, (1992).
32 Benedict, (1997); Johnson & Novak, (1992).

Notes to Chapter 8

1 Sex-for-athletes, grade-fixing schemes reported at SMU. (1987, March 24). *Democrat and Chronicle* (Rochester, NY), p. 4D.

2 Anderson, K., & Dohrmann, G. (2004, February 23). Out of control? *Sports Illustrated, 100*(8), 64-69.

Dohrmann, G. (2004, 7 June). All-star survivor reunion: After a scandal, Gary Barnett returns to Colorado; not everyone is pleased. *Sports Illustrated, 100*(23), 22.

Kimmel, M. (2008). *Guyland: The perilous world where boys become men.* New York: HarperCollins.

3 Wechsler, H., & Wuethrich, B. (2002). *Dying to drink: Confronting binge drinking on college campuses.* Emmaus, PA: Rodale.

4 Curry, (1998).

Frintner, M. P., & Rubinson, L. (1993). Acquaintance rape: The influence of alcohol, fraternity, and sports team membership. *Journal of Sex Education and Therapy, 19*(4), 272- 284.

Office for Substance Abuse and Prevention. (1991). *Alcohol practices, policies, and potentials of American colleges and universities.* U.S. Department of Human Services. Washington, DC.

5 Kay, J. (2010, April 4). Police: Notre Dame recruit 'drunk' on fatal fall. *The Times* (Northwest Indiana), p. B2.

6 Anderson & Dohrmann, (2004).

7 Anderson & Dohrmann, (2004).

8 Anderson & Dohrmann, (2004).

9 Anderson & Dohrmann, (2004).

10 Anderson & Dohrmann, (2004).

11 Anderson & Dohrmann, (2004).

12 Anderson & Dohrmann, (2004).

13 Anderson & Dohrmann, (2004); Dohrmann, (2004).

14 Anderson & Dohrmann, (2004).

15 Bogle, (2008).

16 Insel, P. M., & Roth, W. T. (2002). *Core concepts in health* (9th ed). New York: McGraw-Hill.

Yarber, W. L., Sayad, B. W., & Strong, B. (2010). *Human Sexuality: Diversity in contemporary America* (7th ed.). Boston: McGraw-Hill.

17 Ex-SU recruit indicted on sex charges. (1991, February 16). *Democrat and Chronicle* (Rochester, NY), p. 1A.

18 Anderson & Dohrmann, (2004); Dohrmann, (2004).

19 Anderson & Dohrmann, (2004).

20 Kimmel, (2008).

21 Kimmel, (2008).

22 Anderson & Dohrmann, (2004).

23 Anderson & Dohrmann, (2004); Kimmel, (2008).
24 Kimmel, (2008).

Notes to Chapter 9

1   Crooks & Baur, (2008); Hart, (1994); Sanday, (2007).
2   American Psychiatric Asociation, (2000); Crooks & Baur, (2008); Yarber et al., (2010).
3   Yarber et al., (2010).
4   Yarber et al., (2010).
5   Lauman et al., (1994).
6   Lauman et al., (1994).
7   Lefkowitz, (1997).
8   Canseco, (2005); Esposito & Golenbock, (2003); Rodman & Keown, (1996); Taylor & Serby, (2003).
9   Curry, (1998).
10 Curry, (1998).
11 Curry, (1998).
12 Curry, (1998).
13 Curry, (1998).
14 Aisner, A. (2008, April, 3). Former wolverine Larry Harrison wants probation lifted to revive career in arena football league. *Ann Arbor News*. Retrieved May 13, 2009, from http://blog.mlive.com/annarbornews/print.html
   Burke, C. (2004, December 8). Football player charged as flasher. The *Michigan Daily News*. Retrieved from May 13, 2009, http://www.michigandaily.com/content/football-player-charged-Flasher
   Philp, D. (2006, February 9). Former 'M' football player pleads no contest to charge of indecent exposure. *The Michigan Daily News*. Retrieved May 13, 2009, from http://www.michigan daily.com/content/former-m-football-player-pleads-no-contest-charge-indecent-exposure
15 Aisner, (2008); Philp, (2006).
16 Aisner, (2008); Philp, (2006).
17 Robinson, (1998).
18 Crooks & Baur, (2008).
   Sullivan, M. S. (2004, July 23). Law may curb cell phone camera use. *PC World Communications*. Retrieved August 6, 2009, from http://pcworld.com/article/117035/law_may_curb_cell_phone_camera_use.html
19 Benedict, (1997).
20 Benedict, (1997).
21 Two students arrested, expelled in connection with video of rape. (1999, November 16). *The Ohio State Lantern*, p.22.

Heidelberg College athletes plead innocent to videotaped rape charges. (1999, November 30). *The Ohio State Lantern,* p.19.

22 Two students arrested, expelled in connection with video of rape, (1999, November 16);

Heidelberg College athletes plead innocent to videotaped rape charges, (1999, November 30).

23 Two students arrested, expelled in connection with video of rape, (1999, November 16);

Heidelberg College athletes plead innocent to videotaped rape charges, (1999, November 30).

Heidelberg College: Sexual assault videotaping. *Campus Watch, Fall/Winter 2001.* Retrieved May 2, 2009, from http://www.securityoncampus.org/ newsletter/v07i2.pdf

Seneca County Common Pleas Court. *Case # 01 CR 0067. Case # 99 CR 0305.* Retrieved May 4, 2009, from www.senecaco.org

24 Hart, (1994); Paul, (2005).

25 Sanday, (2007).

Notes to Chapter 10

1 Burt, (1991).

Check, J. V. P., & Malamuth, N. M. (1983). Sex role stereotyping and reactions to depiction's of stranger verses acquaintance rape. *Journal of Personality and Social Psychology, 45,* 344-356.

Koss & Dinero, (1989).

Koss, M. P., & Gaines, J. A. (1993). The prediction of sexual aggression by alcohol use, athletic participation, and fraternity affiliation. *Journal of Interpersonal Violence, 8,* 94-108.

Lisak, D., & Roth, S. (1990). Motives and psychodynamics of self-reported, unincarcerated rapists. *American Journal of Orthopsychiatry, 60,* 268-280.

Muehlenhard, C. L., & Linton, M. A. (1987). Date rape and sexual aggression in dating situations: Incidence and risk factors. *Journal of Counseling Psychology, 34*(2), 186-196.

Rice, M. E., Chaplin, T. C., Harris, G. T., & Coutts, J. (1994). Empathy for the victim and sexual arousal among rapists and nonrapists. *Journal of Interpersonal Violence, 9,* 435-449.

Rosenthal, E. H., Heesacker, M., & Neimeyer, G. J. (1995). Changing the rape-supportive attitudes of traditional and nontraditional male and female college students. *Journal of Counseling Psychology, 42,* 171-177.

2 Dhawan, S., & Marshall, W. L. (1996). Sexual abuse histories of sexual offenders. *Sexual Abuse: A Journal of Research and Treatment, 8,* 7-15.

3   Hotaling, G. T., & Sugarman, D. B. (1986). An analysis of risk markers in husband to wife violence: The current state of knowledge. *Violence and Victims, 1*, 101-124.
    Sugarman, D., & Hotaling, G. (1989). Violent men in intimate relationships: An analysis of risk markers. *Journal of Applied Social Psychology, 19*, 1034-1048.

4   Hotaling & Sugarman, (1986); Sugarman & Hotaling, (1989).

5   Wahl & Wertheim, (1998).

6   Carruth transferred to another prison. (2001, Janurary 31). *The New York Times.* Retrieved July 23, 2009, from http://www.nytimes.com/2001/01/31/sports/plus-court-news-carruth-transferred-to-another-prison.html
    Gunman sentenced in Carruth case. (2001, April 6). *The New York Times.* Retrieved July 23, 2009, from http://www.nytimes.com/2001/04/06/sports/plus-court-news-gunman-sentenced-in-carruth-case.html

7   Carruth transferred to another prison, (2001, Janurary 31); Gunman sentenced in Carruth case, (2001, April 6).

8   Malamuth, N. M. & Check, J. V. (1981). The effects of mass media exposure on acceptance of violence against women: A field experiment. *Journal of Research in Personality, 15*, 436-446.

9   McKenry, P. C., Julian, T. W., & Gavazzi, S. M. (1995). Toward a biopsychosocial model of domestic violence. *Journal of Marriage and the Family, 57*, 307-320.

10 Rape, Abuse, and Incest National Network. (2008). How often does sexual assault occur? Retrieved June 3, 2009, from http://www.rainn.org/get-information/statsitics/ frequency-of-sexual-assault
    Yarber et al., (2010).

11 Fisher, B., Cullen, F., & Turner, G. (2000). *The sexual victimization of college women.* National Institutes of Justice, Bureau of Justice Statistics. Washington, DC.

12 Abbey, A. (1991). Acquaintance rape and alcohol consumption on college campuses: How are they linked? *Journal of American College Health, 39*, 165-169.
    Abbey, A., Clinton-Sherrod, A. M., McAuslan, P., Zawacki, T., & Buck, P. O. (2003). The relationship between the quantity of alcohol consumed and the severity of sexual assaults committed by college men. *Journal of Interpersonal Violence, 18*(7), 813-833.
    Abbey, A., Ross, L. T., McDuffie, D., & McAuslan, P. (1996). Alcohol and dating risk factors for sexual assault among college women. *Psychology of Women Quarterly, 20*, 147-169.
    Fischer, G. J. (1995). Effects of drinking by the victim or offender on verdicts in a simulated trial of an acquaintance rape. *Psychological Reports, 77*, 579-586.
    Pike, D. (1997, November 6). Is 'date rape' a myth? *FW Weekly*, pp. 8-11.

13 Strong et al., (2008).
14 Strong et al., (2008).
15 Schwartz & DeKeseredy, (1997) p. 104.
16 Boeringer, S. D. (1996). Influences of fraternity membership, athletics, and male living arrangements on sexual aggression. *Violence Against Women, 2,* 135-147.
Caron et al., (1997).
Crosset, Todd. W., Benedict, J. R., & McDonald, M. A. (1995). Male student-athletes reported for sexual assault: A survey of campus police departments and judicial affairs offices. *Journal of Sport and Social Issues, 19*(2), 126-140.
Crosset et al., (2009); Crosset et al., (1996); Frintner & Rubinson, (1993); Koss & Gaines, (1993).
17 Boeringer, (1996).
18 Boeringer, (1996).
19 Frintner & Rubinson, (1993).
20 Crosset et al., (1995); Crosset et al., (2009); Crosset et al., (1996).
21 Crosset et al., (1995); Crosset et al., (2009); Crosset et al., (1996).
22 Curry, (1991).
23 Curry, (1991).
24 Sanday, P. (1981). The socio-cultural context of rape: A cross-cultural study. *Journal of Social Issues, 37*(4), 5-27.
Sanday, (2007).
25 Benedict, (1997); Benedict, (1998); Benedict, (2004); Benedict & Yaeger, (1998); Lefkowitz, (1997).
26 Koss, (1989); Koss et al., (1987); Matoesian, (1993).
27 Koss, (1989); Muehlenhard & Linton, (1987).
28 Koss, (1989).
29 Scully, D. (1990). *Understanding sexual violence: A study of convicted rapists.* Boston; Unwin Hyman.
30 Sanday, (2007); Schwartz & DeKeseredy, (1997).
31 Little, R. (1994). Campus drinking: Who, why, and how much. *U.S. News and World Report, 116*(24), 14-17.
Office Abuse and Prevention, (1991).
32 Special report: Crime and sports. (1995, December 27). *Los Angeles Times,* pp. A1, A12, C3-C10.
33 Abbey, (1991).
Ehrhart, J. K., & Sandler, B. (1985). *Campus gang rape: Party games.* Unpublished manuscript, Association of American Colleges, Project on the Status and Education of Women, Washington, D.C.
Koss & Dinero, (1989); Muehlenhard & Linton, (1987).

Neimark, J. (2006). Out of bounds: The truth about athletes and rape. In D. Stanley Eitzen (Ed.), *Sport in contemporary society: An anthology* (7th ed.) (pp. 180-187). Boulder, CO: Paradigm.

O'Sullivan, C. S. (1991). Acquaintance gang rape on campus. In A. Parrot & L. Bechhofer (Eds.), *Acquaintance rape: The hidden crime.* New York: Wiley.

Sanday, (2007).

34 Abbey, (1991).

35 Ward, S. K., Chapman, K., Cohn, E., White, S., & Williams, K. (1991). Acquaintance rape and the college scene. *Family Relations, 40,* 65-71.

36 Abbey, (1991); Benedict, (1997); Benedict, (1998); Benedict, (2004); Lefkowitz, (1997); Robinson, (1998).

37 Krahe, B., Scheinberger-Olwig, R., & Kolpin, S. (2000). Ambiguous communication of sexual intentions as a risk marker of sexual aggression. *Sex Roles, 42,* 313-337.

Shotland, R. L., & Hunter, B. A. (1995). Women's "token resistance" and compliant sexual behaviors are related to uncertain sexual intentions and rape. *Personality and Social Psychology Bulletin, 21,* 226-236.

38 Benedict, (1997); Benedict, (1998); Benedict, (2004); Robinson, (1998).

39 Benedict & Klein, (1997).

40 Benedict & Klein, (1997).

41 Benedict & Klein, (1997).

42 Benedict, (1997); Benedict & Klein, (1997).

43 Pike, (1997).

44 Crooks & Baur, (2008).

Findholt, N., & Robrecht, L. (2002). Legal and ethical considerations in research with sexually active adolescents: The requirement to report statutory rape. *Perspectives on Sexual and Reproductive Health, 34,* 259-264.

45 Nobles, C. (1999, July 16). Mets minor leaguer acquitted. *The New York Times Archives.* Retrieved May 18, 2009, from http://www.nytimes.com/1999/07/16/sports/baseball-met-minor-leaguer-acquitted.html

46 Baseball: Round up – Mets: Rape convictions for three prospects. (1998, October 17). *The New York Times,* p. D-7.

47 Sanday, (2007); Schwartz & DeKeseredy, (1997).

48 Yarber et al., (2010).

49 Rape, Abuse, and Incest National Network, (2008); Yarber et al., (2010).

50 Abbey, (1991); Abbey et al., (2003); Abbey et al., (1996); Ehrhart & Sandler, (1985); Frintner & Rubinson, (1993); Koss, (1989); Neimark, (2006); O'Sullivan, (1991); Sanday, (2007).

51 Rape, Abuse, and Incest National Network, (2008); Yarber et al., (2010).

52 Toufexis, A. (1990, August 6). Sex and the sporting life. *Time,* p. 77.

53 Melnick, (1992).

54 Archer, J. (2006) Testosterone and human aggression: An evaluation of the challenge hypothesis. *Neuroscience & Biobehavioral Reviews, 30*(3), 319-345.
Giammanco, M., Tabacchi, G., Giammanco, S., Di Majo, D., & La Guardia, M. (2005). Testosterone and aggressiveness. *Medical Science Monitor, 11*(4), RA 136-145.

55 Kanin, (1984); Kanin, (1985).

56 Kanin, (1984); Kanin, (1985).

57 Ehrhart & Sandler, (1985); Neimark, (2006); O'Sullivan, (1991); Sanday, (2007).
Ullman, S. E. (1999). A comparison of gang and individual rape incidents. *Violence and Victims, 14*(2), 123-133.

58 Lefkowitz, (1997).

59 Berry, B., & Smith, E. (2000). Race, sport, and crime: The misrepresentation of African Americans in team sports and crime. *Sociology of Sport Journal, 17*, 171-197.
Lefkowitz, (1997).

60 O'Sullivan, (1991).

61 Neimark, J. (1991, May). Out of bounds: The truth about athletes and rape. *Mademoiselle,* pp.196-199, 244-246.

62 G. Abarbanel, personal communication. (May 25, 2011).

63 Benedict, (1997).

64 Abbey, (1991); Abbey et al., (2003); Abbey et al., (1996); Koss, (1989); Muelhenhard & Linton, (1987).
Ullman, S. E., Karabatsos, G., & Koss, M. P. (1999). Alcohol and sexual assault in a national sample of women. *Journal of Interpersonal Violence, 14*, 603-625.

65 Kanin, (1984); Kanin, (1985); Sanday, (2007); Schwartz & Dekeserdy, (1997).

66 Kanin, (1984); Kanin, (1985); Koss & Dinero, (1989); Sanday, (2007).

Acknowledgments

There are many people who helped bring *The Dark Side of Sports* to print, and I am very grateful to these individuals because this book would not have been written without their efforts.

The first person I want to thank is my special partner/friend Lori Hathaway, a high school English/Drama teacher par excellence. Lori's contribution was unmatched because her five-year involvement from the earliest stages of this book included countless hours of editing and re-editing even though she often had a full plate of school work and/or master's degree classes to contend with. Lori provided additional assistance in whatever was needed, when it was needed, and her relentless work helped shape this book in remarkable ways. Thank you so much Lori for ALL your help, support, and unwavering belief in the importance of this project. In short, I know this book's success is unquestionably related to Lori's input and all her over and above efforts.

I also want to give my special thanks to Dr. Matt Wagenheim for all his time and editing assistance during a crucial stage of this project when I was condensing the manuscript. Matt provided a fresh vision with excellent editing from an academic perspective which was very helpful in shaping this book. A big thank you again Matt for ALL your help.

I am grateful to Meyer & Meyer Sport Publishers for believing in this book. I particularly want to thank Hans Jurgen Meyer, Thomas Stengel, and the series editors Dr. Karin Volkwein-Caplan, Dr. Jasmin Tahmaseb McConatha, and Dr. Keith Gilbert for all their assistance. My special thanks to Dr. Volkwein-Caplan for her vision and work addressing this subject matter.

I would like to give special thanks to my academic mentors whose influence over the years helped me write this book. This includes the late Dr. Patrick McKenry, Dr. Tom Davis, Dr. Tim Curry, Dr. Stephen Gavazzi, Dr. Jerelyn Schultz, Dr. Albert Davis, and Dr. Christine Price.

I would also like to acknowledge special friends who influenced my athletic career and/or supported me and this project over the years. My special thanks to John and Chris Tortorella, Joe Battista, Jon Shellington, Mark DiVincenzo, Dr. Kevin Bush, Suzanne Klatt, Dr. Cathy Grover, Dr. Sara Bradley-Hering, Irene Bowman, Scott Jolly, Don Coppinger, the Devaney, Sipe, Dexter, Montebell, McQuillan, Hornack, Krutz, Mowitz, Rose, Brueckman, Califano, and Marcin families, Larry Rocha, Ricky Schiermer, Lennart Sundberg, Moose Lallo, Toby

O'Brien, Craig McCarthy, Father David Klein, Randy Ehrsam, Eddie Swiss, Whitey Stapleton, Pete Iussig, and Sam Samardzija. Others who assisted/ supported this project include Chris Whittemore, John Bacon, Jackie Bowe, Heather Landis-Flower, Christina Hermsdorfer, Renee Long, Claire Cook, Lori Campbell, Billy Jo Cano, Tricia Ziegler, Caitlin Allen, Dr. Julie Serovich, Dr. Susan Hastings-Bishop, Dr. Todd Stanislav, Kwabena Sekyeie, Emily Mitchell, James Gregorio, and Tim Haist.

I am also grateful to numerous individuals who assisted with referrals for this study and would like to acknowledge the efforts of: Bill Kelly, Bob Spence, Renaldo Thomas, Toby O'Brien, Joe and Jan Battista, Lynn Sipe, Gary and Lisa Montebell, Dave Pishkur, Donna Bombassaro, Kendra Clark, James Dye, Nate Althouse, John Davis, Mike Lee, Shana Clary, Bill Masullo, Mike and Heidi Gilliam, Mike and Steve Krutz, Rich Renn, Cathy Grover, Tom Davis, Molly McQuillan, Randy Glynn, Lowell Leefers, Scott Bream, Julie Elsass, Mark Rasmussen, Glen Cawood, Ted Seroma, Josh Mandel, Andy Slaggert, Marty Hutsell, Larry Tharp, Michelle Williams, Dan Monthley, Mary Ann Nowak, Lori Hathaway, Jaime, Dick, and Mark Huyge, Vincent Terry Smith, John Crawford, and Latasha Crenshaw.

This study and book would not have happened if it were not for the many athletes who gave their time to speak with me about these sensitive issues. Many of these individuals also referred other teammates and/or athletes to the study. Although these athletes' efforts remain anonymous, I am forever grateful for their help in bringing this work to completion.

Finally, I want to thank my family for all their love and support over the years which enabled me to focus on writing this book without interruption. My mom was particularly helpful by taking care of numerous domestic necessities while my dad's landscaping and handyman work allowed me to remain focused on my work. My sister Val and her husband Randy were always good people to talk with while my older sister Kim provided a fine rest stop for my frequent northern travels. My brother-in-law Jaime was another great person to converse with and his chapter by chapter examination was especially helpful in keeping my book readable and understandable. My dad's partner Elaine, brother Chris and wife Melissa, nephews Mark and his fiancé Rachael and Matt provided additional support periodically as well.

In the end, it is evident that this book is the result of many individual's time and effort that occurred both in direct and indirect ways. While I am thankful for all these people's efforts, I also grateful for all the divine assistance and inspiration that I am convinced guided and supported this work from the beginning.

About the Author

Nick Pappas, Ph.D., PC., NCC, brings an impressive background with more than 25 years of diverse work experiences that highlight a rare combination of practical, athletic, and academic excellence. Dr. Pappas completed his doctorate degree in Human Development and Family Science with a minor in Sociology of Sport from The Ohio State University. His doctoral dissertation, *On the Ice and Off the Rink: A Qualitative Study of Hockey Players' Aggression*, highlighted out-of-sport athlete aggression against males and females through interviews with 23 collegiate and/or minor professional athletes. This work served as the foundation for *The Dark Side of Sports* because the information Dr. Pappas discovered and withheld from his dissertation included sexually deviant, but not necessarily aggressive behavior.

Dr. Pappas worked as an assistant coach for the Johnstown Chiefs of the East Coast Hockey League, which was the AA minor professional affiliate for the NHL's Calgary Flames. He also coached the OSU Women's Club Hockey Team during his doctoral program. While earning a master's degree at Ohio University in the areas of school, college, and mental health counseling, he served as an assistant coach for the OU Men's Ice Hockey Team, helping the Bobcats to win back-to-back League, Playoff, and National Championships. Dr. Pappas coached for 25 consecutive years as an instructor at youth hockey camps, including Penn State University.

As a minor professional hockey player for five seasons, Dr. Pappas played on championship teams in his first three seasons and was his team's captain during his third season. He played his final two seasons of professional hockey in Europe – first in Sweden and then in Denmark as a player-coach. As a collegiate athlete, Nick played a season as a "walk-on" at Division I Bowling Green State University before transferring to Penn State University. At PSU, where he earned a bachelor's degree in elementary education, he was part of a National Championship team and was named the team's Most Valuable Player. Overall, Nick has been a part of six championship teams in his hockey career – two as a collegiate coach, three as a minor professional athlete, and one as a collegiate athlete. Dr. Pappas was inducted into the Penn State Hockey Hall of Fame and the Andrean High School Sports Hall of Fame in 2004.

As a University Adjunct Professor, Dr. Pappas has taught undergraduate and graduate-level classes including sociology of sport, counseling, sport marketing, health and wellness, fitness, and strength training at several state universities. His academic publications and presentations have addressed athlete aggression, counseling, and family issues. Dr. Pappas' study titled, *Athlete Aggression on the Rink and off the Ice: Athlete Violence and Aggression in Hockey and Interpersonal Relationships* continues to draw significant attention from academic scholars and students alike.

In addition, Dr. Pappas worked as an adult and adolescent drug and alcohol counselor, a teenage group home counselor, a school counselor, and he is a licensed Professional Counselor (PC) and a National Certified Counselor (NCC). He has taught at the elementary, middle, and high school levels.

Dr. Pappas provides presentations on athlete-related topics and issues including out-of-sport athlete deviancy and aggression in order to promote personal and team excellence for athletes at all levels. His work with individual athletes as a personal / athletic life coach uses a holistic approach to impact multiple aspects of the self. He resides in Big Rapids, Michigan and can be contacted through his website (www.drnickpappas.com).

Index